Australia's Competitiveness

Australia's Competitiveness

From Lucky Country to Competitive Country

MICHAEL J. ENRIGHT

RICHARD PETTY

WILEY |

Other Wiley Editorial Offices
John Wiley & Sons, 111 River Street, Hoboken, NJ 07030, USA
John Wiley & Sons, The Atrium, Southern Gate, Chichester, West Sussex, P019 8SQ, United Kingdom
John Wiley & Sons (Canada) Ltd., 5353 Dundas Street West, Suite 400, Toronto, Ontario, M9B 6HB,
    Canada
John Wiley & Sons Australia Ltd., 42 McDougall Street, Milton, Queensland 4064, Australia
Wiley-VCH, Boschstrasse 12, D-69469 Weinheim, Germany

ISBN 978-1-118-49736-4 (Paperback)
ISBN 978-1-118-68119-0 (Cloth)
ISBN 978-1-118-49737-1 (ePDF)
ISBN 978-1-118-49738-8 (Mobi)
ISBN 978-1-118-49739-5 (ePub)

Typeset in 10/12 pt. Garamond-Light by MPS Limited, Chennai, India
Printed in Singapore by Markono Print Media Pte Ltd.

10 9 8 7 6 5 4 3 2 1

Contents

Foreword

Australia's economy has performed very well on most measures over the last few decades when compared to the vast majority of Organisation for Economic Co-operation and Development (OECD) nations. This has been particularly true in recent years as demand for Australia's resources has generated wealth that has helped shield Australia from the worst of the Global Financial Crisis. However, Australia's economic future appears less assured and less certain. While some sectors, like mining, have boomed, others have struggled with higher costs, an appreciating currency, and tougher international competition in tighter world markets. Productivity growth has slowed and economic imbalances have resulted in a multi-speed economy. While impressive when compared to other OECD nations, Australia's growth rates have trailed behind rapidly growing economies in Asia.

The imbalances and growing uncertainty as to how long the resources boom will continue have fuelled debate over what should be done to make Australia more competitive. However, this debate is often unfocussed and has resulted in no real answers as to the best way forward. It has lacked support from sufficiently detailed analysis and has been politically charged in an unhelpful way. The result appears to be an environment where good suggestions for change and reform to policies are not implemented, and where business often views government as the source of both problems and answers, rather than focusing on what business itself can do to push the economy forward.

CPA Australia believes that a better understanding of Australia's international competitiveness is vital to addressing the nation's present and future challenges in ways that can enhance Australia's productivity and prosperity. Without such an understanding, policies are unlikely to focus on what is important and strategies are unlikely to leverage Australia's advantages and mitigate its disadvantages sufficiently to ensure business success at home and abroad.

CPA Australia's growing concern about Australia's international competitiveness, both now and in the future, and the lack of sufficient political and public discourse on this all-important subject, have led us to collaborate with one of the world's leading experts on competitiveness in a year-long investigation of Australia's economy that has resulted in this book. CPA Australia, as a leading professional body with wide membership across the private and public sectors, views the competitiveness project and this book as important parts of its programme of thought leadership and engagement in the debates that are of critical interest to its members and Australian society as a whole.

The investigation assessed how the world sees Australia, but also how we in Australia see ourselves. A key element of the research was a survey of business decision-makers both inside and outside Australia on Australia's competitiveness. With more than 6,000 responses, we understand that this is the largest ever survey of Australia's competitiveness. These responses allow for an analysis of the competitiveness of a wide range of Australian industries spanning the whole economy. In contrast, 68 Australian respondents largely shaped Australia's ratings in the World Economic Forum's 2012 Global Competitiveness Report.

The present book is particularly important in light of the globalisation that allows businesses to place each activity in the best location, the rise of information and communication technologies that allow businesses to penetrate remote markets, and the emergence of what many call the Asian Century. For Australia to succeed going forward, it will need to leverage global trends, look beyond its traditional benchmarks, integrate more closely with the rest of the Asia-Pacific region, learn to compete against new competitors, and improve its productivity by improving its competitiveness. This book provides insights into how this can be done.

Australia is presently in a position of relative strength in many dimensions. While this should make it easier for Australia to take positive action, it also makes it easier to fall victim to complacency. The reality is that Australia cannot rely on its luck indefinitely. It must go from being the "lucky country" to being the "competitive country." We need a vision for Australia and a long-term reform agenda to achieve that vision. In this book, Michael Enright and Richard Petty have made an important contribution to outlining such a vision and agenda. Their message to those of us who live in Australia is clear. Our future prosperity is in our hands; it is time for action.

CPA Australia has more than 144,000 members in 127 countries. Most have significant business, professional, or personal ties to Australia, and a strong interest in the nation's continued prosperity. Many are leaders in their respective fields, with influence in their organisations, industries, and communities. We hope that they and others find this book helpful as they strive to make Australia a more productive, competitive, and attractive place to live and work.

JOHN CAHILL
CPA Australia President

ALEX MALLEY FCPA
CPA Australia CEO

Introduction

When the Australian historian Donald Horne first coined the phrase "lucky country" to describe Australia in 1964, it was meant to be ironic and pejorative, as part of the description, "Australia is a lucky country, run by second-rate people who share its luck."[1] According to Horne, Australia at the time benefitted from resource wealth and from a system of governance that it had inherited from its colonial past, but had not yet moved beyond its inheritance to chart a creative, dynamic future of its own making. If we fast forward to today, Australia has made enormous progress. In terms of standards of living, Australia has left its formal colonial masters and many other OECD nations far behind. Australia has become much more open to the rest of the world, and Australian society has been transformed. Australia still exports resources, but it also exports higher education and other knowledge-intensive goods and services. Even so, there are concerns that Australia has not used its resources as productively as it should, and that talented Australians continue to emigrate to try their luck elsewhere in alarming numbers. There is also a nagging concern that Horne's assessment still has more truth to it today than many Australians would like to be the case.

At the same time, the Global Financial Crisis, the rise of Asian economies, modern information and communication technologies, the globalisation of production systems, and increasing demand by society for equity and sustainability have made markets tighter, competition tougher, and managing and operating economies and businesses more difficult than ever before. In this world, it is becoming clearer and clearer that it is not possible to borrow or inherit a high standard of living indefinitely. Instead, such standards of living must be earned by improving competitiveness. This is why competitiveness, the ability of a nation or region to succeed in international markets, to achieve high levels of productivity, to create an attractive business environment, and ultimately to provide a high standard of living to its residents, is a pre-eminent issue in many if not most nations. Extensive work undertaken over the last two decades has shown that competitiveness is systemic, involving the interaction of drivers that act at a global or supranational level, national level, cluster (group of interlinked industries) level, industry level, and firm level. Recently, this work has given us new methods and tools to understand and assess competitiveness, as well as ways to chart a course to improve competitiveness in industries and nations.

This book is the result of a year-long investigation of Australia's competitiveness sponsored by CPA Australia and carried out by Professor Michael Enright in conjunction with CPA Australia. The project set out to understand Australia's underlying competitive advantages and disadvantages and to make suggestions that would push the economic debate in Australia forward. Professor Enright was one of the founders of the modern school of competitiveness analysis while at the Harvard Business School in the 1980s and 1990s, and has been based in Asia since 1996. The present project has therefore benefitted from 25 years of experience undertaking major competitiveness studies in more than 20 nations, and has used tools and methodologies that have been refined over more than two decades. Some of these methods and tools are published here for the first time.

The **Introduction** sets the scene for the book by describing the year-long research project on Australia's competitiveness carried out by Professor Michael Enright and CPA Australia.

While Australia's overall economic performance has been strong, not all sectors of the economy or society have benefitted to the same extent. There is also a concern that the resource boom of recent years has masked the impact of poor productivity performance. There is also a view that while several trends in the global economy may work to Australia's benefit, this will only be the case if Australia recognises and acts on its potential to a greater extent than has been the case to date.

Chapter 1 indicates that the starting point for the analysis of any economy should be an understanding of its past and present performance. It is the present and past performance that needs to be explained by the analysis and that provides the baseline that allows us to understand what Australia does well and not so well, and what Australia needs to do to improve. Australia has generally outperformed other OECD nations over the last decade while maintaining a prudent fiscal and monetary stance, a position that provides for greater flexibility than most OECD nations when it comes to dealing with volatility in the global economy. However, there are issues concerning Australia's reportedly poor productivity performance and the impact of the run-up in resource exports in recent years. The chapter also provides background on the forces and trends that are shaping the global economy and provides a context for Australia's economic future. The upshot is that while Australia's economy has performed well over the last several years, there are concerns and debates about its economic future that are best addressed through a detailed understanding of Australia's competitiveness.

Competitiveness has emerged as a pre-eminent issue in many major economies around the world. **Chapter 2** reports assessments of Australia from international sources that focus on international competitiveness and related matters, such as ease of doing business, economic freedom, prices and costs, the knowledge economy, human development, quality of life, transparency, and corporate governance. The major sources are identified, their main findings with respect to Australia summarised, and implications for Australia that come out of the sources provided. Results from all the sources are used to build a detailed picture of Australia's advantages and disadvantages and to identify issues that require further analysis and action. Throughout, Australia is compared with two sets of countries, a comparison group of mostly OECD countries (the United States, Canada, Denmark, Finland, Ireland, Israel, Netherlands, New Zealand, Norway, Sweden, and Switzerland) along with three Latin American countries that are competitors to Australia in some sectors (Argentina, Brazil, and Chile), and a group of Asia-Pacific economies (China, Hong Kong, India, Indonesia, Japan, Korea, Malaysia, New Zealand, the Philippines, Singapore, Taiwan, Thailand, and Vietnam). The idea is to capture how Australia stacks up against similar economies and against economies that are increasingly important as markets and competitors.

The sources that assess economies as a whole that are described in Chapter 2 are helpful, but the reality is that nations, regions, and companies compete in specific industries versus specific competitors to serve specific customers. Aggregate measures cannot tell us what drives a nation's competitiveness in individual industries. **Chapter 3** introduces a framework to assess competitiveness in specific industries across the economy and the results of a detailed survey on Australian competitiveness based on this framework. The chapter uses results from individual Australian industries: the iron ore, wine, automotive, and higher education industries, to show the shortcomings of the aggregate assessments of competitiveness and the value of the present approach. The chapter also shows how the approach introduced here can be used to develop specific strategies to improve the competitiveness of individual industries and of economies.

Chapter 4 uses the methods and survey introduced in Chapter 3 to examine the drivers of competitiveness across the entire Australian economy. Survey responses from hundreds of individual industries were aggregated up to 32 sectors that cover the entire economy. The results show clear differences in importance and in Australia's performance in firm-level drivers, industry-level drivers, cluster-level drivers, national-level drivers, and supranational-level drivers of competitiveness. They show the importance of institutions, financial systems, economic conditions, infrastructure, workforce, tax systems, and regulatory systems to competitiveness in Australia's industries. They also show Australia's strength in institutions, society, macro-economy, and financial systems, as well as concerns about taxation, regulation, some work-force-related drivers, and infrastructure. In addition, from a methodological standpoint, the results show how the methods employed can generate a comprehensive picture of the competitiveness of the nation's economy and can allow analysts and governments to home in on the drivers that are important to the key industries in an economy, in order to identify which advantages can be leveraged and which disadvantages need to be overcome.

The first four chapters show that there are a number of key issues that cut across Australia's economy that must be understood, and dealt with, in order to improve Australia's competitiveness. **Chapter 5** focuses on an assessment of Australia's workforce, infrastructure, and natural resources. The prosperity of any economy depends on the effectiveness and productivity of its workforce. As a nation with a small population in a huge land mass, and one that is distant from many of the world's traditional economic centres, Australia has distinctive infrastructure challenges that it has yet to master. While Australia might be the lucky country when it comes to natural resources, luck will only get Australia so far, particularly if resource abundance is not managed properly. Australia has high levels of education participation, and achievement, but there are mismatches between the education and training base in the country and the needs of business, and counterproductive workplace relations sometimes prevent Australia from fully realising its advantages.

Chapter 6 outlines some of the main features of Australia's economic policy, regulation, and tax policy, as they influence Australia's competitiveness. Economic policy—in particular fiscal policy, monetary policy, competition policy, exchange rate policy, industrial support policy, trade policy, and investment policy—influence the position of Australian companies, industries, and the economy as a whole. Australia generally gets high marks on economic policy, but there are fears that politics might eventually get in the way of good policy. Regulation on entry, product standards, safety standards, the workplace, the environment, and numerous other areas provide the rules within which businesses can operate. Australia's regulatory system is rated highly by international standards, but a cumbersome, redundant, and sometimes conflicting regulatory regime leaves many frustrated. A nation's tax system influences its competitiveness through the number and type of taxes, tax rates, tax thresholds, compliance costs, and the way in which taxes are collected. While Australia's tax system appears to have advantages versus several OECD nations, the efficiency of the system has been questioned, and emerging competitors in Asia are seen as having more favourable systems. The tax system also appears to provide incentives for some talented Australians to emigrate to other destinations.

Chapter 7 looks at the opportunities and challenges for Australia associated with the emergence of the knowledge economy, the rise of the economies of the Asia-Pacific region, and the growing importance of cities as engines of economic development and competitiveness. While the knowledge economy—in which value is generated through the intellectual property that is embedded in high-value goods and services—has the potential of freeing Australian companies from the tyranny of distance, the reality is that relatively few Australian companies seem to be able to sell knowledge-intensive products and services globally. The rise of the Asia-Pacific region would appear to be a huge advantage for Australia, but there is a question of whether Australia and Australian companies have the knowledge, connections, and drive to penetrate these markets in the face of cultural differences and tough competition from both inside and outside the region. Cities are becoming increasingly important as engines of development and competitiveness, as they generate new knowledge, connect countries to the rest of the world, and leverage national advantages into international markets. However, Australia's cities are too spread out, do not function in a particularly efficient fashion, and are less plugged into regional and global information, financial, and managerial flows than they need to be for Australia to maximise its competitiveness.

Australia's future is not pre-ordained, but instead will be influenced by both external forces and internal strategies. **Chapter 8** maps out several scenarios for Australia's future depending on how it manages the opportunities and challenges associated with globalisation, increased use of ICT, the rise of the Asia-Pacific, increased emphasis on sustainability, potential resource constraints, the increase in importance of quality of life in influencing competitiveness, and a range of other trends. The chapter identifies four pairs of scenarios, half positive, half negative, depending on the outcomes of the interaction of external forces and internal strategies. Australia's resource position could allow it to move From Lucky Country to Competitive Country or could create a limited One-Legged Stool economy. Globalisation and the flat world, in Thomas J. Friedman's phrase, could result in Australia as *Flattenor* in the Flat World or Australia as *Flattenee* in the Flat World. The rise of the Asia-Pacific region could result in Australia Riding Tigers, Dragons, and Elephants or being Eaten by Tigers, Burned by Dragons, and Trampled by Elephants. Trends in globalisation, information and communication technology (ICT), the knowledge economy, sustainability, and quality of life issues could result in a situation in which The World Turns toward Australia or one in which The World Turns away from Australia. Perhaps the most interesting feature of the scenarios, positive and negative, is that they are all plausible, and the choices that Australia makes will go a long way toward determining which outcomes occur.

Chapter 9 outlines the implications that come out the earlier chapters. There are global implications involving the challenges created by the Global Financial Crisis, the emergence of new competitors, the increasing ability of companies to place individual corporate activities in different locations, and increasing interconnections around the world that are combining to make the competitiveness of nations and regions more important than ever before. There are numerous implications that are specific to Australia. Australia's recent economic performance gives the nation the opportunity to act from a position of strength, but raises the potential for complacency. The rise of Asia-Pacific economies will provide Australia a unique opportunity, but only if Australia and Australian companies can outcompete others to serve regional markets and take advantages of regional resources. Modern ICT can allow Australian businesses to penetrate world markets like never before, or could allow foreign businesses to penetrate Australia like never before, or both. The increasing importance of sustainability, resource constraints, and quality of life in driving competitiveness can provide additional advantages for Australia provided the country can leverage these drivers appropriately.

There are many implications for specific drivers of competitiveness. Chapter 9 highlights many of Australia's significant advantages and disadvantages and makes suggestions as to how to leverage the advantages and minimise or overcome the disadvantages in order to improve the country's competitiveness. It shows that Australia has been a lucky country in many ways, but that Australians have made a good deal of that luck themselves. The challenge is how to move from being the *lucky country* to being the *competitive country*. What is daunting, but exciting, is that while Australia is certainly subject to global forces, global markets, and global competition, its economic fate is to a great extent in its own hands.

We hope that policy makers, business people, and business/economic analysts in Australia find the tools, conclusions, and suggestions in this book useful as they move forward the competitiveness agenda in Australia. We also hope that policy makers, business people, and business/economic analysts elsewhere learn from the Australian experience as well as from the approaches to competitiveness suggested in this volume.

Note

1. Donald Horne, *The Lucky Country: Australia in the Sixties* (Melbourne: Penguin Books, 1964).

Acknowledgments

First and foremost, we wish to thank CPA Australia for sponsoring the project upon which this book is based. In particular, we wish to thank CEO Alex Malley, President and Chairman John Cahill, and Past-President and Chairman Low Weng Keong for their unwavering support through a long and challenging project. We would also like to thank Paul Drum and Gavan Ord of CPA Australia, who managed the process and provided valuable insights throughout, and we thank the rest of the CPA Australia team as well. We would also like to thank Nick Melchior, Emilie Herman, Stefan Skeen, and the team at John Wiley & Sons for their input and for shepherding this book through the publication process. We would also like to thank the dozens of senior academics, business leaders, and government officials who gave generously of their time to meet with us or attend project workshops, and the thousands of survey participants whose responses provided a unique source of information and insights.

About the Authors

Michael J. Enright is the Sun Hung Kai Properties Professor at the School of Business of the University of Hong Kong; Director of Asia-Pacific Competitiveness Programs at the Hong Kong Institute of Economics and Business Strategy; Director of Enright, Scott & Associates Ltd. (Hong Kong) and Enright, Scott & Associates (Singapore) Pte. Ltd. economic and business strategy consultancy; an Independent Non-Executive Director of Johnson Electric Holdings Ltd.; a Director of the Harvard Business School Alumni Association of Hong Kong; and Founder and present Advisory Board Member of The Competitiveness Institute, a global professional body with members in more than 100 countries.

Professor Enright's research and consulting focus on issues of international and regional competitiveness, national and regional economic development, international strategies of multinational companies, and strategy in the face of volatility and uncertainty. He has worked with governments, multilateral organisations, and leading companies on six continents and has appeared as a keynote speaker and executive educator in 38 countries. Enright's work has been featured in *Asia Inc.*, *Asian Business*, the *Economist*, the *Financial Times*, *Fortune*, the *Wall Street Journal*, the *Asian Wall Street Journal*, the *Washington Post*, *Newsweek*, *BusinessWeek*, the *South China Morning Post*, the *Straits Times*, *Business Times*, *Time*, *WorldLink*, and numerous national newspapers and other publications all over the world.

In addition to numerous monographs, Professor Enright has co-authored or edited the following books: with Edith E. Scott and Richard Petty, *The Greater Pearl River Delta*, 6th ed. (Hong Kong: Invest Hong Kong, 2010); with W. John Hoffmann, *China into the Future: Making Sense of the World's Most Dynamic Economy* (New York and Singapore: John Wiley & Sons, 2008); with Edith Scott and Chang Ka-Mun, *Regional Powerhouse: The Greater Pearl River Delta and the Rise of China* (New York and Singapore: John Wiley & Sons, 2005); with Edith Scott and David Dodwell, *The Hong Kong Advantage* (Hong Kong: Oxford University Press, 1997); with Antonio Francés and Edith Scott Saavedra, *Venezuela: The Challenge of Competitiveness* (New York: St. Martin's Press, 1996); with Rolf Weder, *Studies in Swiss Competitive Advantage* (Bern: Peter Lang, 1995); with Graham Crocombe and Michael Porter, *Upgrading New Zealand's Competitive Advantage* (Auckland: Oxford University Press, 1991); and with Silvio Borner, Michael Porter, and Rolf Weder, *Internationale Wettbewerbsvorteile: Ein strategisches Konzept für die Schweiz* (Frankfurt: Campus/NZZ, 1991).

Professor Enright received his AB (with honors) in Chemistry in 1980, his MBA (with distinction) in 1986, and his PhD (Dean's Doctoral Fellow) in Business Economics in 1991, all from Harvard University. Before moving to Asia in 1996, Professor Enright was a Professor at the Harvard Business School from 1990 to 1996.

Richard Petty is Professor (Accounting and Finance) and Executive Director International at the Macquarie Graduate School of Management. He is Chairman of The Australian Chamber of Commerce Hong Kong & Macau, a past President and Chairman of CPA Australia, and a director of several other companies. Richard is Deputy Chairman of the Australasian Reporting Awards and is Chairman of the Judging Panel for Hong Kong's Best Annual Reporting Awards. Professor Petty was Chairman of CPA Australia (Shanghai) Limited from 2007–2012.

Professor Petty commenced his professional career as an analyst and then worked at Ernst & Young before founding and also co-founding several successful companies. Richard has more than 20 years of consulting experience and has advised a broad range of multinational firms and several governments on financial and strategic issues, competitive issues, governance issues, and on doing business in Asia, particularly in China.

Professor Petty was appointed as a Senior Foreign Consultant to the State Economic Trade Commission in Shanghai and Tianjin, China, from 1999–2001. He also was formerly Senior Research Fellow to the Securities Industry Research Centre of Asia-Pacific.

Professor Petty has been a faculty member at the University of New South Wales and the University of Hong Kong and adjunct faculty at the University of Sydney and at the Australian Graduate School of Management. He has been awarded both as a researcher and as an editor of academic works, and he has won awards as an educator in Hong Kong and in Australia.

Professor Petty is on the management board of the *Australian Accounting Review*, the editorial board of the *Journal of Intellectual Capital*, and the editorial advisory board of the *Accounting, Auditing and Accountability Journal.*

Professor Petty has published extensively across various fields including on governance issues, nonfinancial reporting, valuation, China's economy, and the management and measurement of intangible assets in journals including the *Australian Accounting Review*, the *Journal of Management Accounting Research*, the *Journal of Intellectual Capital*, the *Journal of Law and Financial Management*, the *Accounting, Auditing and Accountability Journal*, and others. He co-authored a research monograph for The Institute of Chartered Accountants of Scotland on *Intellectual Capital Reporting* (2007) with James Guthrie and Federica Ricceri and *The Greater Pearl River Delta*, 6th ed., with Michael J. Enright, Edith E. Scott, and Enright, Scott & Associates (2010).

Professor Petty is frequently invited to speak on topics relating to the global economy, China's economy, corporate governance, and other topics. He has been interviewed and profiled by channels including *CNBC, Bloomberg, Wall Street Journal Asia*, the *Australian Financial Review*, the *Sydney Morning Herald, Business Review Weekly, CFO Magazine*, the *Australian*, the *South China Morning Post, Business Spectator, Channel News Asia*, the *Standard*, and others.

Professor Petty graduated with first class honours in Accounting from the University of Western Sydney (1993) and was awarded the university medal. He holds a Master's degree (with honours) in Commerce from the University of New South Wales (1997), and a PhD from the Macquarie Graduate School of Management (2004). Richard is a Fellow and Life Member of CPA Australia and a Fellow of the Australian Institute of Company Directors.

CHAPTER 1

Australia's Economic Performance

The starting point for the analysis of any economy should be an understanding of its past and present performance. The performance is what needs to be explained by more detailed analysis. This in turn provides the baseline from which we can try to build a picture of what Australia does well, and not so well, and assess what Australia needs to do to improve performance in the future.

Aggregate Performance

Australia's economy has been one of the best performing in the OECD since 1990. Nominal GDP went from just over AUD 400 billion in 1990 to just under AUD 1,400 billion in 2011 (Figure 1.1). This was around 1.6 percent of global GDP. Australia's annual GDP growth has been positive every year since 1991. Australia experienced real annual GDP growth on the order of 3 to 4 percent per year until the onset of the Global Financial Crisis in 2008, when growth dipped down to roughly 2 percent per year (Figure 1.2), which was still better than most other OECD nations. Australia stayed in positive territory, in part as the result of a stimulus package, which at AUD 42 billion was one of the world's largest in proportional terms.[1]

Australia's nominal per capita GDP went from nearly AUD 24,000 per person per annum in 1990 to AUD 62,337 per person per annum in 2011 (Figure 1.3). In US dollar terms, Australia's 2011 per capita GDP of USD 67,554 comfortably outstripped the USD 48,043 figure of the United States. It has also been well ahead of the OECD average (Figure 1.4). At the same time, Australia's Gini coefficient in the late 2000s of 0.336 was only slightly above the OECD average of 0.316, indicating income inequality slightly greater than the OECD average.

Australia has seen its workforce participation rate increase from around 63 percent in the late 1990s to over 65 percent since 2007. Australia's unemployment rate spiked at over 12 percent in the early 1990s before falling below 5 percent before the Global Financial Crisis. Although the unemployment rate approached 6 percent in 2009–2010, it was back down near 5 percent by 2011 (Figure 1.5). Australia has high workforce participation and relatively low unemployment.

Perhaps the most interesting comparison of Australia with other countries is in GDP per person of employment age (taken as 15 to 64 years of age) in current US dollars shown in Table 1.1. This measure is, in our view, a better measure of an economy's strength than GDP per capita or GDP per employed person, because the

TABLE 1.1 GDP Per Person 15–64 Years Old, Current US Dollars

	Australia	Canada	Denmark	Finland	Ireland	Netherlands	New Zealand	Norway	Sweden	Switzerland	United States
2002	44,557	44,065	61,234	51,704	68,117	52,724	30,814	81,455	55,629	72,079	73,062
2003	56,072	50,774	75,178	63,158	85,341	64,390	40,841	95,928	69,607	83,321	76,181
2004	67,262	57,458	85,562	72,938	97,347	72,529	48,795	110,205	79,790	92,672	80,501
2005	73,282	65,162	90,205	74,926	100,863	75,320	53,212	127,927	79,566	94,493	84,771
2006	76,813	72,596	94,832	78,610	108,090	79,261	50,406	141,244	84,948	98,215	88,884
2007	90,408	79,321	107,646	92,263	123,263	89,884	60,850	159,564	97,068	107,875	92,667
2008	94,336	82,545	117,910	100,872	124,751	98,616	58,680	178,601	101,054	123,628	93,647
2009	89,187	73,217	106,722	90,314	107,159	89,674	52,411	147,809	84,415	119,202	91,745
2010	111,753	85,779	108,212	89,315	99,398	89,524	63,110	164,510	95,367	128,714	95,541
2011	130,701	93,625	115,041	99,424	103,386	95,831	70,912	189,704	110,563	154,019	98,696

Sources: International Labour Organization, *Economically Active Population, Estimates and Projections*, 6th ed., October 2011; World Bank, *World Development Indicators*, September 2012.

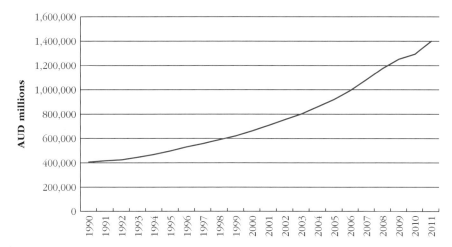

FIGURE 1.1 **Australia Nominal GDP, 1990–2011**
Source: Australian Bureau of Statistics, *Australian National Accounts*, June 2012.

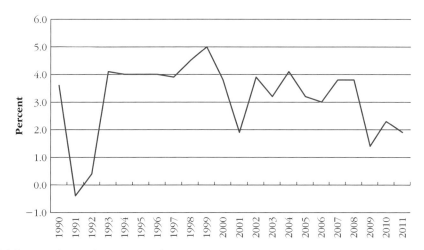

FIGURE 1.2 **Australia Real GDP Growth Rate, 1990–2011**
Source: Australian Bureau of Statistics, *Australian National Accounts*, June 2012.

former counts a very young or very old population against the country, and the latter in essence penalises the country for employing marginal workers. GDP per person of employable age indicates the output the economy can generate given the potentially productive population. On this measure, Australia was nearly 40 percent below the United States in 2002 and more than 30 percent above the United States in 2011. Figure 1.6 shows that over the 1990 to 2011 period, Australia actually outperformed all of the other countries in the figure in growth in this measure.

Despite the notoriety of Australia's primary sector, its proportion of GDP has remained remarkably constant over the last 20 years, at 9.5 percent of GDP in 1990 and 9.7 percent in 2011.[2] Of course, there are multiplier effects of the primary sector

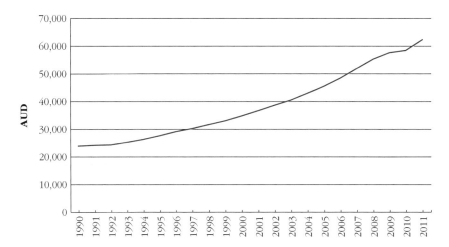

FIGURE 1.3 **Australia Nominal per Capita GDP, 1990–2011**
Source: Australian Bureau of Statistics, *Australian National Accounts,* June 2012.

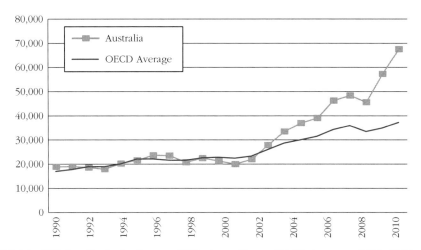

FIGURE 1.4 **GDP Per Capita in Current USD, Australia vs. OECD Average, 1990–2011**
Source: OECD, *StatExtracts,* April 2012.

that are not captured in the simple ratio. The main shifts in the composition of Australia's GDP over the last 20 years have been in manufacturing (22.1 percent of GDP in 1990 and 18.0 percent in 2011); the service sector (51.5 percent in 1990 and 57.7 percent in 2011); and the sum of use of residential housing, taxes net of subsidies, and statistical discrepancies (16.9 percent of GDP in 1990 and 14.7 percent in 2011).

Australia's trade has grown substantially over the last two decades (Figure 1.7). Exports were around 19.8 percent of GDP in 2010, indicating that Australia is more trade dependent than the United States (exports equal to 12.6 percent of GDP in 2010), but much less so than Canada (29.4 percent) and several small European economies which in some cases have exports equal to 50 percent of GDP or more. Australia moved from a fixed to floating exchange rate in 1983. The low for the Australian dollar was 47.75 US cents in April 2001, and the high was 110 US cents in

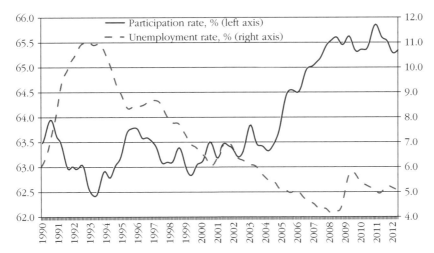

FIGURE 1.5 **Australia Workforce Participation Rate vs. Unemployment Rate, 1990 to May 2012**
Source: Australian Bureau of Statistics, *Labour Force, Australia*, May 2012.

July 2011 (Figure 1.8), indicating a substantial strengthening of the currency. By October 2012, the Australian dollar was still above 100 US cents.

Measured as a percentage of GDP, Australia has a significantly lower level of public debt compared to most OECD nations, and a debt level even lower than fiscally conservative Switzerland and Hong Kong (see Table 1.2). Australia's debt level had been even lower before the stimulus package put in place to combat the Global Financial Crisis. The Australian Government's 2012–2013 budget called for a return to surplus in that year.[3]

Table 1.3 compares Australia's economic performance with a selection of comparator countries. With respect to the OECD comparators, Australia's GDP growth for the period 1990–2011 was higher than most, GDP per capita for 2011 was near the middle, and exports as a percentage of GDP were lower than most, indicating less trade dependence than most of the OECD countries. Measuring productivity as GDP per hour worked for 2011, only Canada, Israel, and New Zealand performed worse than Australia, although taking the compound annual growth rate (CAGR) for this measure for the period 1990–2011, Australia's performance was middling.

Table 1.4 compares Australia's performance with other Asia-Pacific economies. Comparing Australia against Asia-Pacific economies, Australia's GDP growth for the period 1990–2010 was higher than Japan and New Zealand, but lower than all other countries. Australia's 2010 GDP per capita was significantly higher than all other nations in the table, and only Japan was less trade dependent.

According to the IMF, Australia's projected real GDP growth to 2017 is much lower than that of China, Developing Asia, and Emerging and Developing Economies for each year, and is projected to be lower than the world overall each year. Australia is projected to outperform advanced economies, major advanced economies, and the European Union each year to 2017, and to outperform or equal the performance of the United States (Table 1.5).

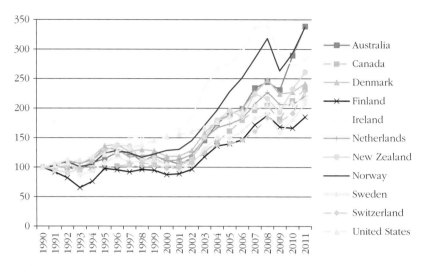

FIGURE 1.6 **GDP Per Person 15–64 Years Old, Current USD, 1990 = 100**
Sources: International Labour Organization, *Economically Active Population, Estimates and Projections*, 6th ed., October 2011; World Bank, *World Development Indicators*, September 2012.

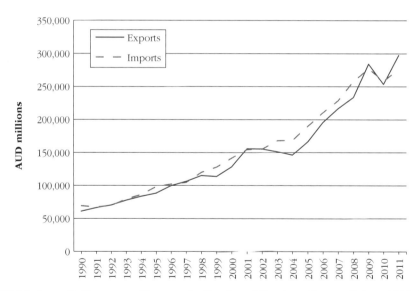

FIGURE 1.7 **Australia Exports and Imports in Goods and Services, Current Prices, 1990–2011**
Source: Australian Bureau of Statistics, *Australian National Accounts*, June 2012.

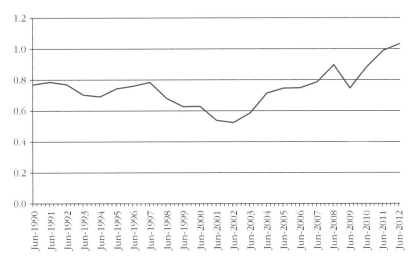

FIGURE 1.8 **Exchange Rate, USD per AUD, June 1990 to June 2012**
Source: Australian Bureau of Statistics, *Balance of Payments and International Investment Position*, June 2012.

TABLE 1.2   **Public Debt as a Percent of GDP, Selected Nations 2011**

Japan	229.8	United Kingdom	82.5
Greece	160.8	Germany	81.5
Italy	120.1	Spain	68.5
Portugal	106.8	Netherlands	66.2
Ireland	105.0	Switzerland	48.7
United States	102.9	New Zealand	37.0
Iceland	99.2	Hong Kong	33.9
France	86.2	China	25.8
Canada	84.5	Australia	22.9

Source: International Monetary Fund, *World Economic Outlook Database*, April 2012.

Australia's interest rates have been fairly high compared to those of many other OECD nations. Figure 1.9 shows Australia's interest rates against selected OECD countries and the Euro Area for the period 1997 to 2011. Australia cut interest rates 50 basis points in May 2012 and a further 25 basis points in June 2012 with additional cuts being projected by many economists.[4] The cash rate of 3.5 percent in the latter portion of 2012 was the lowest since 2009.

Australia's consumer price index (CPI) shows the country's headline inflation. Australia's CPI has been relatively high compared to many other OECD countries during the period 2001 to 2011 as shown in Table 1.6.

TABLE 1.3   Major Indicators Compared with Selected OECD Economies

Country	GDP, 2011 (USD million)	GDP CAGR, 1990–2011 (%)	GDP per Capita, 2011 (USD)	Exports as a % of GDP, 2010 (%)	Productivity— GDP per Hour Worked, 2011 (USD)	Productivity CAGR, 1990–2011 (%)
Australia	1,522,421	3.3	56,395	19.8	48.4	1.6
Canada	1,736,868	2.4	46,236	29.4	46.6	1.3
Denmark	332,757	1.5	59,752	50.3	53.4	1.3
Finland	266,309	2.0	49,432	40.4	48.4	2.2
Ireland	217,470	4.4	46,160	101.1	66.0	3.4
Israel	243,128	4.5	28,529	37.0	36.7	0.8
Netherlands	837,007	2.2	50,148	78.0	60.8	1.2
New Zealand	161,353	2.6	32,436	28.7	34.6	1.0
Norway	485,404	2.5	98,002	41.1	74.9	1.6
Sweden	537,838	2.2	56,962	50.0	51.8	2.0
Switzerland	636,059	1.4	81,061	53.6	50.3	0.6
United States	15,011,000	2.5	46,588	12.6	60.6	1.8

Note:
GDP per capita for Australia, Canada, Ireland, Israel, New Zealand, and United States are 2010 data.

Sources: OECD, *StatExtracts*, April 2012; World Bank, *World Development Indicators*, September 2012.

TABLE 1.4   Major Indicators Compared with Asia-Pacific Economies

Country	GDP, 2010 (USD million)	GDP CAGR, 1990–2010 (%)	GDP per Capita, 2010 (USD)	Exports as a % of GDP, 2010
Australia	1,131,623	3.2	56,395	19.8
China	5,926,612	10.5	4,428	29.6
Hong Kong	224,458	4.0	31,757	223.0
India	1,727,111	6.6	1,410	21.5
Indonesia	706,558	4.7	2,946	24.6
Japan	5,458,837	0.9	42,831	15.2
Korea	1,014,483	5.1	20,757	52.4
Malaysia	237,797	5.9	8,373	97.3
New Zealand	142,197	2.7	32,436	28.7
Philippines	199,589	3.8	2,140	34.8
Singapore	208,765	6.4	41,120	211.1
Thailand	318,522	4.4	4,608	71.3
Vietnam	106,427	7.4	1,224	77.5

Sources: OECD, *StatExtracts*, April 2012; World Bank, *World Development Indicators*, September 2012.

TABLE 1.5   World Economic Outlook on Real GDP Growth, 2012–2017, Percent

Economies	2012	2013	2014	2015	2016	2017
World	3.5	4.1	4.4	4.5	4.6	4.7
Advanced Economies	1.4	2.0	2.4	2.6	2.7	2.7
Major Advanced Economies	1.5	1.9	2.3	2.5	2.6	2.5
Emerging and Developing Economies	5.7	6.0	6.2	6.3	6.3	6.3
Developing Asia	7.3	7.9	7.9	7.9	7.9	7.9
European Union	0.0	1.3	1.9	2.0	2.1	2.1
United States	2.1	2.4	2.9	3.3	3.5	3.3
Japan	2.0	1.7	1.5	1.3	1.1	1.1
China	8.2	8.8	8.7	8.7	8.6	8.5
Australia	3.0	3.5	3.5	3.5	3.5	3.5

Notes:

1. Advanced economies include the United States, the Euro Area, Japan, the United Kingdom, Canada, Korea, Australia, Taiwan, Sweden, Hong Kong, Switzerland, Singapore, Czech Republic, Norway, Israel, Denmark, New Zealand, and Iceland.

2. Major advanced economies refer to Group of Seven (G7) countries, including the United States, Japan, Germany, France, Italy, the United Kingdom, and Canada.

3. Emerging and developing economies include Central and Eastern Europe, the Commonwealth of Independent States, developing Asia, Latin America and the Caribbean, the Middle East and North Africa, and Sub-Saharan Africa.

Source: International Monetary Fund, *World Economic Outlook Database*, April 2012.

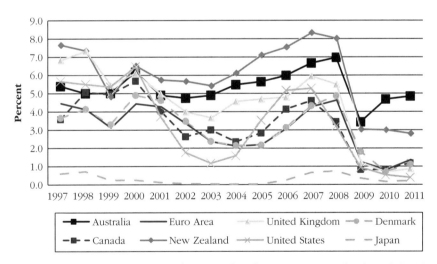

FIGURE 1.9 **Short-Term Interest Rates for Australia, the Euro Area, and Selected OECD Countries, 1997–2011**

Notes:

1. Three-month money market rates.

2. No individual interest rates for the Eurozone members since the formation of the Eurozone in 1999.

Source: OECD, *StatExtracts*, April 2012.

TABLE 1.6   Consumer Price Inflation for Australia and Selected OECD Countries, 2001–2011

Economies	Australia	Canada	Denmark	Finland	France	Germany	Japan	New Zealand	United Kingdom	United States
2001	4.4	2.5	2.4	2.6	1.6	2.0	−0.8	2.5	1.2	2.8
2002	3.0	2.3	2.4	1.6	1.9	1.4	−0.9	2.7	1.3	1.6
2003	2.8	2.8	2.1	0.9	2.1	1.0	−0.2	1.5	1.4	2.3
2004	2.3	1.9	1.2	0.2	2.1	1.7	0.0	2.6	1.3	2.7
2005	2.7	2.2	1.8	0.9	1.7	1.6	−0.3	3.2	2.0	3.4
2006	3.5	2.0	1.9	1.6	1.7	1.6	0.2	3.2	2.3	3.2
2007	2.3	2.1	1.7	2.5	1.5	2.3	0.1	2.6	2.3	2.9
2008	4.4	2.4	3.4	4.1	2.8	2.6	1.4	3.9	3.6	3.8
2009	1.8	0.3	1.3	0.0	0.1	0.3	−1.3	1.9	2.2	−0.4
2010	2.8	1.8	2.3	1.2	1.5	1.1	−0.7	2.9	3.3	1.6
2011	3.4	2.9	2.8	3.4	2.1	2.3	−0.3	4.0	4.5	3.2

Note:

2011 data are taken from OECD as data from the World Bank were not available. Data for 2001–2010 are taken from the World Bank.

Sources: World Bank, *World Development Indicators*, September 2012; OECD, *StatExtracts*, April 2012.

Productivity

A nation's economic performance is heavily influenced by its productivity performance. In Australia, there is widespread agreement that following a period in the 1990s during which there were significant improvements, productivity growth has slowed (Figure 1.10).

When comparing Australia's productivity position versus other countries, charts like that in Figure 1.11 show Australia's productivity growth being far lower from 2001 to 2010 than it was from 1991 to 2000 and being near the middle of the countries shown from 2001 to 2010. Charts like Figure 1.12, which compare unit labour costs in manufacturing, are used as evidence that Australia is losing competitiveness in manufacturing, at least since around 2004.[5]

The Reserve Bank of Australia (RBA) has used data from the Australian Bureau of Statistics to assess labour productivity growth and multifactor productivity growth across sectors of the Australian economy. Labour productivity measures output per labour hour worked, while multifactor productivity measures output for a given amount of labour and capital inputs combined. Labour productivity growth is mostly higher than multifactor productivity growth because it includes the labour productivity that is generated by capital deepening. Taking the periods 1993/1994 to 2003/2004 and 2003/2004 to 2010/2011, the RBA has shown that multifactor productivity

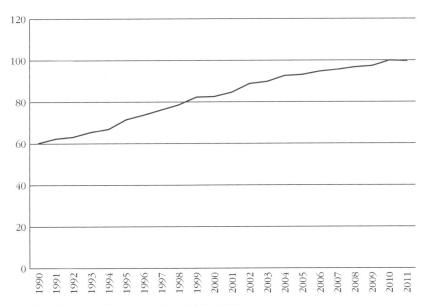

FIGURE 1.10 **Labour Productivity Index, 1990–2011**
Notes:
1. Due to data availability, the labour productivity index for 1990–1993 does not include Rental, Hiring, and Real Estate Services; Professional, Scientific, and Technical Services; Administrative and Support Services; and Other Services.
2. Reference year for indexes is 2009–2010 = 100.0.
Source: Australian Bureau of Statistics, *Experimental Estimates of Industry Multifactor Productivity*, 2010–2011, December 2011.

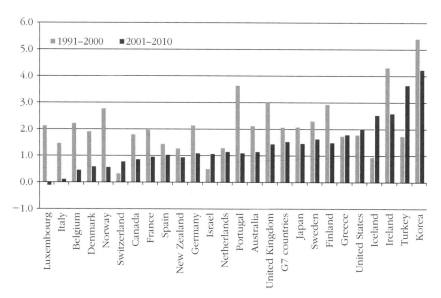

FIGURE 1.11 **International Labour Productivity, Average Annual Growth in Period**
Note:
Labour productivity is defined here as real GDP per hour worked.
Source: OECD, *StatExtracts*, April 2012.

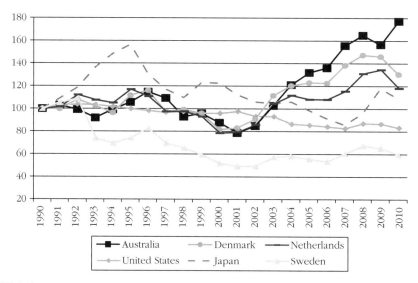

FIGURE 1.12 **Unit Labour Costs in Manufacturing, US Dollar Basis, 1990–2010**
Notes:
1. Unit labour costs are defined as the costs of labour input required to produce one unit of output, and are computed as compensation in nominal terms divided by real output. Indexes: 1990 = 100.
2. The data relate to all employed persons (employees and self-employed workers).
3. For Australia and Sweden, compensation is adjusted for employment taxes and government subsidies to estimate the actual cost to employers.
Source: Bureau of Labor Statistics, US Department of Labor, *International Comparisons of Manufacturing Productivity and Unit Labor Cost Trends*, October 2011.

growth in the latter period in Australia was lower than in the former period in 15 out of 16 major sectors, with only the Administrative and Support industry exhibiting marginally positive growth. The Mining and Utilities industries showed the biggest declines; followed by Wholesale Trade and Other Services sectors; the Accommodation and Food Services; Manufacturing; Rental, Hiring, and Real Estate; Transport, Postal, and Warehousing; and Professional, Scientific, and Technical sectors.

The RBA analysis (see Table 1.7) shows that for the market (essentially nongovernmental) sector as a whole, labour productivity growth was positive for both periods, but in the 2003/2004 to 2010/2011 period labour productivity growth was slower than the growth in capital stock, indicating negative multifactor productivity growth. Excluding mining and utilities, both labour productivity growth and multifactor productivity growth were positive in both periods, though lower in the second than the first. The mining and utilities sectors both exhibited negative labour productivity growth from 2003/2004 to 2010/2011, with capital deepening and multifactor productivity growth both negative. This indicates that more capital and more labour were needed for a unit of output toward the end of the period than the beginning in both sectors.

TABLE 1.7   Decomposition of Trend Productivity Growth, Annual Average Percentage Change

	1993/1994 to 2003/2004 [a]	2003/2004 to 2010/2011 [b]	Change [b] − [a]
Selected Market Sector Industries			
Labour productivity of which:	3.1	1.4	−1.7
Capital deepening	1.3	1.8	0.5
Multifactor productivity	1.8	−0.4	−2.2
Excluding Mining and Utilities			
Labour productivity of which:	3.1	1.7	−1.4
Capital deepening	1.3	1.3	0.0
Multifactor productivity	1.9	0.4	−1.5
Mining			
Labour productivity of which:	3.6	−6.3	−9.9
Capital deepening	2.9	−0.6	−3.5
Multifactor productivity	0.6	−5.7	−6.3
Utilities			
Labour productivity of which:	1.8	−5.5	−7.3
Capital deepening	2.0	−0.8	−2.8
Multifactor productivity	−0.2	−4.7	−4.5

Notes:
1. Market sector excluding Rental, Hiring, and Real Estate Services; Professional, Scientific, and Technical Services; Administrative and Support Services, and Other Services due to difficulties with measuring capital services for these industries.
2. Contributions to labour productivity growth may not sum to totals due to rounding.
Sources: Australian Bureau of Statistics; Reserve Bank of Australia; Author Analysis.

The fall in measured productivity in the Mining sector is consistent with increasing commodity prices making it profitable to develop more marginal and costly resource deposits, resulting in additional capital and labour investments. In the Utilities sector, it is suggested that that structural changes and significant investment in new large-scale desalination plants that have been built as part of the solution for the droughts that vex Australia have been a drag on productivity in that sector. In both cases, investments take a long time to come to fruition, meaning that increased capital investment and labour deployment in the short term is not matched by increases in output, thus detracting from productivity measures in the short term.[6] Thus in both cases, estimated productivity declines can be completely consistent with rational investments that benefit Australia as a whole, but register as having a negative impact on productivity. Given this situation, we have to take the reports of productivity declines in these sectors with some circumspection.

Explaining Australia's productivity situation is complicated by the fact that it is hard to identify statistically the causes for the slowdown, there is measurement error in the estimates of productivity growth that are used, and productivity is the result of many interacting factors that make it very difficult to disaggregate the impact of the various effects. According to the RBA, there are several theories as to why productivity growth has slowed for the economy as a whole.[7] One is that gains from incorporating modern information and communication technology (ICT) that were made in the earlier period have not been matched subsequently, indicating that some of the benefit might have been one-off rather than continuous. Another is that the quality of the workforce did not improve as much (as measured by an increasing percentage of the workforce with qualifications or other measures) in the second period as the first. Another is that Australia introduced major reforms in the 1980s and 1990s, including an opening up of the financial markets, labour reforms, tariff reductions, privatisation, a national competition policy, and tax reform, and that the benefits from these reforms were already obtained in the earlier period.

Others have suggested that instead of productivity-enhancing reforms, in recent years Australia has seen productivity-destroying regulation and taxation.[8] The Productivity Commission has come up with a long list of suggested reforms, including improvements to regulations and to the setting of regulations, removing impediments to the efficient allocation of resources, creating better incentives for firms to perform while working to enhance their flexibility and capabilities, making further commitment to an open and competitive economy, and making investments in human and physical capital to improve productivity.[9] There is clear frustration within the business community at the lack of productivity-promoting reform, which has been mirrored by the Treasury Secretary saying that a lack of reforms is worsening the productivity situation, and the Governor of the Reserve Bank calling on the Australian Government to implement productivity-enhancing reforms.[10]

There is also a complacency hypothesis[11] that suggests that Australia's improved terms of trade have led to gross national income increasing faster than productivity, that this has kept wages high, corporate profits up, and unemployment down, and that there has therefore not been an imperative to improve productivity. Complacency seems to have developed a political culture that is focused on finding narrow political advantage rather than on improving the productivity of the economy,[12] leading to calls for Australian politics to be rehabilitated and for proper leadership to emerge to serve the national interest.[13] Complacency is dangerous because most observers agree that

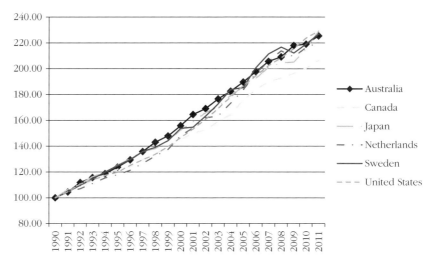

FIGURE 1.13 **Output per Hour Worked, Current USD, 1990 = 100**
Source: OECD, *StatExtracts*, April 2012.

Australia's terms of trade are likely to weaken in coming years. As this happens, real income growth will slow unless productivity growth picks up.

The question that arises is if Australia's overall economic performance has been good, how is that consistent with faltering productivity performance? The apparent answer is that the effects of lower productivity growth have been masked by the resources boom, which has had a positive impact on Australia's terms of trade, put upward pressure on the exchange rate, and caused national income to grow faster than productivity. In fact, an analysis of data from the Australian Bureau of Statistics for the period 1992 to 2012 reveals that real gross national income per hour worked in Australia grew at roughly the same rate from 2003 to 2012 as it did from 1992 to 2002. In addition, comparing Australia's growth in GDP per hour worked in current US dollars to that of other countries indicates that Australia has been an excellent performer by this measure (see Figure 1.13).

The effect of this situation on the manufacturing sector has been an increase in costs, which, because of international competition, cannot be passed on as higher prices. Lack of increased productivity in the resources sector has been offset, or even caused, by rising demand and prices. Lack of increased productivity growth in the nontradable sectors has resulted in higher prices for nontradables in Australia.[14]

In considering productivity growth in the future it is worth noting that in the event that there is a continuation of the slowdown in the resources sector, which started in 2012, then capital and labour will shift to other sectors, at least in part. Investment decisions are not static, and if commodity prices fall, the economy will adjust, albeit with costs associated with the adjustment. The fear is that the adjustment might come too late for some sectors and companies that could be lost in the meanwhile, and that a failure to raise productivity will make Australia worse off than it would have been otherwise.

We should note that while productivity concerns in Australia are valid, the way productivity growth is typically measured has to be related to the specifics of the Australian context. International productivity growth measures usually fix prices and exchange rates to a base year. The idea is that productivity growth should be growth in volume for a particular set of inputs independent of price changes and exchange rate changes. That is fine for modest changes in prices and exchange rates, but not for large changes. When resource prices double, or increase by a factor of seven, which iron ore prices did from 2004 to 2011, or the Australian dollar nearly doubles in value versus the US dollar, which it did from 2002 to 2011, and companies then make completely rational investments to expand output in some industries and contract it in others, then the productivity measures are less meaningful than they would otherwise be, particularly when combined with the known difficulties of estimating productivity. We know of no managers in 2012 making investments based on the assumption that the inputs or outputs of their firms are priced at year 2000 or year 2005 prices and exchange rates, though that is what the productivity comparisons tend to do.

In addition, there is the question of what to do about the productivity issue. It is a nonstarter to tell companies to avoid making profitable resource investments because they don't show up as improvements in productivity or based on the possibility that terms of trade may shift. On the other hand, when it comes to government or the nation, the responsible course is to prepare for an uncertain future by working to improve productivity. One way to avoid complacency is to push ahead on the reform agenda to improve efficiencies throughout the economy. Another is to invest in education, training, infrastructure, enhanced workforce participation, and in building linkages with foreign markets. Another is to provide some limited support to industries that can become winners in the future, by providing information on technologies, markets, and best practices, or by support for research and development. The trouble with such support is that such investments must be funded. While the resources sector is an apparent source of revenue, there are limits to the tax revenue that can reasonably be raised from this sector, particularly if programs are to be sustainable in the face of volatile resource prices. In any case, working to improve the economy's productivity is always a good idea, particularly when it might be politically difficult or inopportune to do so.

Global Trends

Australia will also need to understand, mitigate, and leverage trends in the global economy if it is going to chart a prosperous path into the future. Among the trends in the global economy that will influence Australia going forward are the aftermath or potential repetition of the Global Financial Crisis (GFC), the rise of Asia-Pacific economies, the improved connectivity possible through modern information and communication technology, the globalisation of companies and industries, and the development of the so-called *Flat World*.

The GFC and Its Aftermath

The Global Financial Crisis and its lingering aftermath will affect world markets for at least a decade. The crisis, which started with US financial institutions with large exposures to the US real estate market when it collapsed, showed numerous structural weaknesses in national and international financial systems. Policies to foster home ownership in the US in particular brought new customers and new types of loans into the market. Implicit or explicit guarantees through agencies like Fannie Mae and Freddie Mac encouraged financial institutions to make loans to customers who would not have been considered good credit risks previously. The packaging and securitisation of mortgages created securities that received ratings from ratings agencies that were much higher in retrospect than they should have been. The development of numerous synthetic securities and derivatives based on these and other instruments drove rapid growth in the financial sector, but created entire classes of assets that few people really understood.

When the housing market in the United States started turning down, the illusion of diversification of risks became apparent. While many mortgages might have been packaged into securities in an attempt to diversify risk, this strategy came undone when the entire asset class starting going down together. The illusion of diversification became even more apparent when it became clear that numerous financial institutions had insured their securities with a single insurer, AIG. The collapse of Bear Stearns and then Lehman Brothers precipitated a global crisis as the financial system became frozen, counterparty risk became unknowable and therefore unacceptable, and companies and individuals throughout the major economies could not get financing. Only massive intervention by governments and central banks prevented much of the world's financial system, and with it much of the world's economy, from collapsing.

The ripple effects seen during the GFC showed the extent to which the global economic system is connected in sometimes unexpected ways, how risk could be dramatically mispriced, how regulatory systems were inadequate to deal with modern financial engineering, how ratings agencies could not possibly assess some of the securities they rated, how boards of directors could not adequately oversee managers, how the interests of bankers could diverge dramatically from everyone else, and how there is no international architecture to protect the global economy from similar crises.

The GFC left several legacies. Perhaps the most important is a legacy of wealth and job destruction that has affected the savings and employment prospects for millions around the world. Another is a massive amount of government debt that was run up in the attempt to stave off catastrophe. Another is massive deleveraging on the part of banks and other financial institutions that is making finance generally less available for many companies and individuals in many parts of the world. Another is a more conservative approach toward investing and financing on the part of "real economy" companies. Another is consumer caution in the face of economic and financial uncertainty. Overall, it is likely that the effects will be felt for a decade or more.

The run-up in government debt in many countries around the world has created a crisis of its own. While Greece's problems preceded the GFC, the crisis created the perfect storm of global and domestic downturn, financial instability, and difficult financial conditions that has made its debt unsustainable. The spectre of the potential impact on European banks and other Eurozone countries has resulted in massive bailout packages orchestrated by the main European Union countries, the European Central Bank, and the IMF to try to stave off a disorderly default. However, even if Greece manages to avoid such a default, and even if it manages to get its fiscal house in order, this will require wrenching austerity in the midst of its worst recession in decades. Even that will not fix another underlying problem, which is that the adoption of the euro has prevented less productive Eurozone economies from devaluating against the German and French currencies in order to stay competitive. Without the ability to devalue and without the ability to increase productivity faster than more advanced Eurozone countries, Greece and some of the other European countries, like Portugal, Spain, and Italy, may face difficult times well into the future.

In the United States, several rounds of stimulus, bailouts, and quantitative easing have run up massive debts and have devalued the US dollar substantially. This combination is likely to leave the US unable to upgrade its infrastructure and business support systems, and unable to change what has become an uncompetitive tax system for companies. Japan is in an even worse situation, with government debt already significantly higher than GDP, political paralysis, and a domestic economy that appears impervious to reform and positive change.

Uncertain government finances, shaky banking systems, deleveraging, and uncertain financial markets will continue to have a strong impact on employment, aggregate demand, trade, and investment. As indicated above, uncertainty and shakiness will probably be a feature of the global economy for a decade or more. In such a situation, in which governments are printing money and many countries appear to be trying to export their way out of their problems, the international competitive environment is likely to be tougher than ever, even for countries that have avoided the worst excesses.

The Rise of Asia-Pacific Economies

One of the bright spots in the global economy in recent years has been emerging markets, particularly emerging markets in Asia. The rise of Asia-Pacific economies, most notably China and India, but Indonesia and other economies as well, has been one of the most important stories in the world economy for the last few decades. The rise of these economies is rebalancing the global economy toward the Asia-Pacific region. These markets represent substantial new opportunities for companies from the rest of the world, but particularly from the rest of the Asia-Pacific region where proximity and familiarity should allow for easier market development.

The Asian Development Bank (ADB) estimates that Asia as a whole will increase its share of global GDP from 26 percent in 2010 to 40 percent in 2030 and 52 percent in 2050, which would be similar to its share of global population. During that period, the ADB expects that the urban population of the region will grow from 1.6 billion to 3 billion and that Asian cities will be leading engines of the world economy.[15]

China's economy has grown at an average of roughly 10 percent per year in real terms since the onset of the country's economic reform program in 1979–1980. Even in the recent Global Economic Crisis, the slowest rate at which China's economy grew during the period was 8.5 percent. For the 12th Five Year Program period, the Chinese Government has forecast that real GDP growth will average 7.5 percent. By 2010, China was the world's second-largest economy, its leading exporter, its third-leading importer, its leader in terms of international reserves, the leader in terms of inward greenfield foreign direct investment, and the leading producer and market in a wide range of industries crossing most industrial sectors. While the Chinese Government's attempts to rein in inflation and property prices have slowed the economy's growth, there are still several positive dynamics, including rapid urbanisation, improved infrastructure, increasing affluence and purchasing power, the development of national and regional markets, improvements in the financial sector, and the spread of development into the interior of the country. The IMF claims that China is on a path to become the world's leading economy according to purchasing power parity exchange rates (PPP) by 2016, and the World Bank claims that China will have the world's largest economy at market exchange rates by 2030.

India has the world's tenth-largest GDP at market exchange rates and the third-largest in terms of purchasing power parity exchange rates. While India's development has not been nearly as spectacular as China's (the two economies were similar in size in 1980; today China's economy is three-and-a-half times the size of India's), India's recent development has also been impressive. India began its economic reform process in 1991. By 2010, in real terms, its GDP was 3.5 times the 1991 level, while per capita GDP was 2.6 times the 1991 level, and exports were 10 times the 1991 level.[16]

The rise of the Asian economies has several implications for companies and governments around the world. Asia has already become the location of choice for production in many manufacturing industries and for service provision in a range of service industries. Asia's position as a manufacturing and service location is only going to improve. In addition, Asian nations are becoming far more attractive as markets for goods and services across the board. Already Asian nations are not only the leading consumers for a wider range of industrial goods, and low-priced consumer goods, they are also the most important customers for high-end luxury consumer goods as well. Asian nations will also increasingly be the sources of new companies that will compete first domestically and then in international markets. Japanese and Korean firms are already major international players. They are being joined by Indian and Chinese companies as well. In some cases, Asian companies will be able to generate huge cash flows at home and then use those cash flows to fund international expansion.

Another feature of the emerging Asian markets is that competitive positions in many of the markets are not as well-entrenched as they are in the traditional OECD markets. In established markets, it can be difficult or impossible to gain market share against entrenched competitors. In the emerging markets of Asia, competitive positions are less fixed, and customers are often less loyal. The result is that there is more scope for companies to improve their positions than in the better established markets.

Companies and countries that can penetrate emerging Asian markets will be well-situated going forward. This is clearly a key issue for Australia. Historically, the world's large markets have been geographically far away and in some senses culturally similar to Australia. Going forward, many of the large markets will be geographically closer, but culturally far more different, to Australia than the traditional markets. Thus while there will be opportunities, there will also be the challenges associated with understanding and serving markets that are unfamiliar to many Australian companies.

Modern Information and Communication Technology

The Internet and modern communications technologies, which offer low cost communication, the availability of virtually infinite information, and unprecedented interactivity, are reshaping the way business is done around the world. The information and communications industries themselves have seen the biggest impact, though the impact is also felt throughout the financial, professional service, manufacturing, and even agricultural sectors. Although much of the focus of attention on the impact of the technologies has been on the United States and Europe, arguably the impact of the technologies could be even more dramatic in smaller peripheral economies that have the potential to plug into the rest of the world to an unprece-dented extent.

When most people think of the new technologies, they think of Internet com-panies, like Amazon, or Facebook, and that certainly has been part of the story. However, a more significant part of the story is the ways that individuals, organisa-tions, companies, and governments are using the modern technologies to create or deliver new products and services, reach their customers and constituents, and organise and co-ordinate their businesses and activities. The ability to obtain real-time operating information on all of a company's operations and activities has changed how companies manage. Staying ahead of customer complaints before they go viral has become crucial. Technologies that allow companies to manage over vaster dis-tances allow them to slice up their activities into smaller and smaller slices, place each slice in its optimal location, and tie it all together with modern management systems. On the one hand, the new technologies allow a corporate centre to have greater knowledge and to exert more direct influence on local operations than before. On the other hand, they also allow for more distributed management and decision making across organisations. Thus, both centralising and decentralising tendencies can be supported.

The new technologies also have had other effects on economies. Business cen-tres, such as Hong Kong and Singapore, have used the new technologies to super-charge existing business relationships and to enhance their positions as business hubs. Relatively remote locations, such as Australia and New Zealand, have become better plugged into the rest of the region. Australia, with its relatively advanced software industry and its diverse population, has benefited by attracting regional software, data processing, and call centre activities. The *death of distance* also has fostered the development of call centres, data input, and computer software in lesser-developed economies like India and the Philippines with pockets of modern infrastructure and skills.

There are clear implications that are emerging from the revolution in information and communication technology. Nations and regions clearly need the right hardware, but they also need the right software, including policy regimes that support the development of new ways of using technologies. A variety of skills is needed to ensure maximum benefit from the Internet and modern communications technolo-gies. While many nations are focusing on expanding education and training in soft-ware engineering and related disciplines, fewer seem to have grasped the fact that the new developments actually create far greater demand for writers, editors, graphic artists, and other content creators than for software engineers.

The Internet and modern communications technologies have had a dramatic impact on economies around the world. By limiting the tyranny of distance, they are bringing different economies closer together, facilitating management and co-ordination, and allowing new nations and regions to join the global economy. By allowing for new levels of interactivity, they are supercharging existing business relationships and enabling the formation of new relationships. They have facilitated economic booms and busts as well as the emergence of political movements that have toppled some governments and put fear into others. The key for nations interested in improving their competitiveness is the extent to which the nation, its residents, and its companies can leverage the modern technologies to understand, serve, and compete in wider and wider international markets.

The Rise of the Knowledge-Innovation Economy

Much has been written about the rise of the knowledge-innovation economy. Over time, the story goes, the main source of wealth has shifted from assets such as land, natural resources, and unskilled labour; to manufactured tangible assets, such as plant and equipment; to created intangible assets, such as knowledge and innovation capacity. Today, advanced economies are dominated by people who work with their heads rather than their hands. This is reflected in the dominance of the service sector in advanced economies, the fact that the market capitalisation of companies that produce intangibles, such as Microsoft and Oracle, has soared past that of traditional manufacturing leaders, such as General Motors and Ford, and the proliferation of knowledge and innovation programs in leading companies, universities, and other organisations.

Knowledge and innovation have been important in every stage of economic development. The difference today is the sheer percentage of wealth that is linked to intangible assets. No nation or region today can hope to become truly prosperous unless it develops a knowledge-innovation economy. This fact has enormous implications, and poses enormous challenges, for many economies around the world.

Hardly a day goes by without news of dozens of seminars, articles, and books about the *knowledge-innovation economy*, but the true nature of the knowledge-innovation economy is ill-defined and little understood. Many analysts equate the term with participation in a limited number of "high-technology" industries, or to specific activities like R&D. In reality, the knowledge-innovation economy is determined more by the activities it performs than on the specific industries in which it competes, and even more by the way the activities are carried out. The question should not be "Does an economy compete in knowledge-innovation-intensive industries?" but "Does it perform knowledge-innovation-intensive activities, and does it do so in creative ways?" Knowledge and innovation can be competitive weapons in all industries, and while R&D activities may be knowledge-intensive and innovative, they are not the only knowledge-intensive activities that firms perform. Nor are they the most important. Our work with scores of major companies over the last two decades has convinced us that the most knowledge- and innovation-intensive activities of firms are strategy setting, international co-ordination, and market development, not R&D.

The types of knowledge and innovation that generate wealth in today's economy are those that result in products and services that create value for customers and are difficult to imitate or substitute. Knowledge that becomes widespread because it cannot be protected or is not continually upgraded eventually becomes less valuable. Thus, developing a knowledge-innovation economy means developing the ability to create and use new knowledge and innovations on an ongoing basis. The rise of economies that can perform manufacturing and assembly activities has both forced and allowed the more advanced economies to focus on knowledge creation and innovation. In the process, the returns to those who perform the development, design, branding, and marketing have increased dramatically.

The upshot is that the advanced economies have seen a shift from manual work to knowledge and innovation work, from manufacturing as a major source of growing wealth to manufacturing as a commodity, from an emphasis on hard infrastructure alone to an emphasis on soft infrastructure as well, from competition on costs to competition on development and branding, from a focus on tangible assets to a focus on intangible assets. The key question then is "How does any particular economy stack up in the new knowledge-innovation economy?" There is no single accepted metric that defines the knowledge- or innovation-intensity of an economy. Numbers of patents, the presence of global companies, measures of educational achievement, and the portion of knowledge workers in an economy are all, at best, partial measures. If we believe that wealth is generated by knowledge, then, with the exception of countries with overwhelming resource endowments, presumably the most knowledge-intensive economies will be the wealthiest economies.

There are some clear implications of the rise of the knowledge economy for the nations and regions around the world. One is that education and training are key to the knowledge-innovation economy. A second is that companies and economies should seek to *"learn from the world,"*[17] since no economy, however large, can come up with all the good ideas it needs. A third is that knowledge creation and innovation are socially complex, often requiring proximity to advanced sources of information, customer demand, and complementary knowledge that is difficult to codify and communicate. This is one reason that such a high proportion of commercially useful knowledge is generated in specific geographic clusters and why specific management, knowledge, and creative centres, such as New York, London, Los Angeles, Tokyo, and Silicon Valley, are becoming more important in the global economy.

A fourth implication is that countries need to promote free flows of information while safeguarding intellectual property. Knowledge is created, and innovation achieved, by extending or combining existing sources of knowledge and by having the right incentives to do so. A fifth implication is that there are many types of knowledge and sources of knowledge, and that different types and sources may be appropriate at different stages of an economy's development. A sixth implication is that knowledge can be generated and applied in any industry. A seventh implication is that governments have critical roles in fostering the development of a knowledge-innovation economy, but that governments can rarely do so by themselves. It is hard to foster the creativity necessary to succeed in the knowledge-innovation economy when government calls all the shots.

The nations that succeed in the knowledge-innovation economy will become leaders in absorbing, using, and creating complex knowledge to power innovation on an ongoing basis. Those that cannot will eventually fall behind.

Globalisation and the Flat World

The globalisation of companies and industries has been facilitated by reduced barriers to trade and investment, improved transportation and logistics, the emergence of new countries as markets and production locations, international financial flows, and enhanced communication and information systems. Reduced trade and investment barriers have allowed companies to set up operations around the world. Improved transportation and logistics, including investments in ports and airports, containerisation, the advent of IT-based logistics management systems, and the development of specialised transport and logistics firms have improved the ability of companies to create and manage global supply chains. The emergence of new countries as markets and as production locations has been fostered by more internationally oriented development policies, the spread of production know-how, investments in education and infrastructure, and the availability of international finance.

These have opened up new market opportunities for firms and have raised competitive pressures. As a result, companies not only seek out new markets, they also seek out new locations to perform various corporate activities and tie them all together with modern information and management systems. Companies are globalising much earlier in their development and at a much smaller scale than before. In fact, the emergence of "born global" and "mini-multinational" companies has become an active area of research and analysis. The "born global" company may start with an idea for a new product, immediately set up or outsource its production in China, IT development and business processes in India, call centres in the Philippines, and so on, without ever intending to employ more than a handful of people in the home country.

This globalisation means that countries do not have to be able to host all of the activities necessary in an industry in order to succeed; they just have to be able to host sufficient activities to employ their workforces in good jobs. This is tremendously good news to developing countries. They do not have to be able to perform every activity in a business in order to succeed. They do not have to generate all the finance necessary to fund the relevant investments. They do not have to generate all the technologies necessary to compete. All this can be sourced globally, or brought in by foreign firms if the local skill set and conditions are otherwise favourable.

It is also good news to small and relatively peripheral economies, as globalisation has reduced their traditional disadvantages. The emergence of the Internet and global logistics companies has allowed small companies from remote locations to penetrate international markets like never before. The Internet can be the marketing tool. International logistics companies can take care of distribution. Production can be outsourced or placed offshore, which means companies from small and peripheral countries do not have to achieve large-scale production at home before selling overseas. Call centres and service centres can be readily set up abroad. For a country with a small population distant from major markets, the developments could be transformational.

Globalisation has given rise to what Thomas Friedman has called the *flat world*.[18] The flat world is a concept in which the rise of emerging market economies, modern information and communication technologies, and the globalisation of companies and industries results in factor price equalisation that prevents companies and people from earning high incomes just because they are located in a particular place. In essence, these features have allowed much more direct competition among companies and workers with a given skill level than ever before. In the past, the tendency was for one to be far better off being moderately skilled or educated but living in an advanced country, than being high skilled and living in a relatively backward country. The barriers between national systems tended to lock people into those systems, and limited their potential economic outcomes. Today, the flat world concept posits, this is no longer the case. This notion helps explain why relatively unskilled workers in developed economies have seen their wages under pressure and why companies have chosen to move so many activities to developing countries.

Our own view is that the world is not flat per se. Rather, it is more like an inverted "T." While the human resources, factories, offices, and locations that are used to carry out projects and business activities may compete against each other in a flat world, the people, companies, and locations that can generate the ideas that create new products and services live in anything but a flat world. These people, companies, and locations can now use modern technologies to access global markets to an unprecedented extent. They can also use globalisation to harness productive resources anywhere in the world to an unprecedented extent. The result is larger potential markets, lower potential costs, and greater potential efficiencies than ever before, leading to unprecedented profit potential.

In this new world, those that can generate the ideas that can capture global markets, and harness global productive resources to carry out their strategies, will have unprecedented opportunity. In this new world, the key is who is going to be the *flattenor* (i.e., the one with the ideas that reaps the benefits) and who is going to be the *flattenee* (i.e., the one without the ideas forced to compete against increasingly capable and cost-effective competitors from all over the world). The key to being the flattenor is knowledge of global markets, global tastes, technological possibilities, and emerging trends, while at the same time having knowledge of global sources of production and support, and the ability to create and manage a system that brings these all together.

The key for economically advanced nations and regions in this new world is to ensure that their residents and companies are plugged into global markets, can generate new ideas for products and services, understand the trends in key markets, have access to sources of technology or knowledge anywhere in the world, are knowledgeable about offshore as well as onshore productive capabilities, and have the skills to create and manage international networks to leverage these ideas.

Looking Ahead

The picture of Australia that emerges is one of an economy that has outstripped most other OECD economies in terms of growth for the last two decades, has provided a per capita income above the OECD average, and has experienced income inequality only slightly higher than the OECD average. Overall, Australia's performance looks good, but there are issues and challenges, some that are sector specific and some that span the entire economy. Perhaps the biggest is whether a resource-induced increase in prices and value of the Australian dollar has masked poor productivity and what can be done about apparently deteriorating productivity performance. Other issues and challenges involve Australia's ability to anticipate and react to the global trends we have identified.

To better understand the issues and the trends, we need to get behind the aggregate data to figure out what is driving economic performance and productivity, and how Australia is situated to meet the challenges arising from trends in the global economy. In other words, we have to delve into Australia's underlying sources of advantage and disadvantage, i.e., its competitiveness. This is what we do in the next several chapters. Chapter 2 will focus on international assessments of Australia's overall competitiveness and the forces that are believed to influence that competitiveness. Chapters 3 and 4 focus on the results of a large-scale survey of Australia's industry-level competitiveness carried out for this project. Chapters 5, 6, and 7 take more detailed looks at particular issues that cut across Australia's economy. Chapter 8 sets forth a series of positive and negative scenarios for Australia's economic future. Chapter 9 provides a series of conclusions and implications for actions that can be taken by government at various levels, companies, other organisations, and individuals to improve Australia's competitiveness and thereby improve its economic performance. The goal is to build on the vast quantity of excellent work that has already been done on Australia's economy and to add new information and insights in order to help move the economic debate in Australia forward.

Notes

1. "Australian Government Announces Second Fiscal Stimulus Package, RBA Cuts Interest Rate To Record Low," *International Business Times*, 4 February 2009.
2. Australian Bureau of Statistics.
3. Alan Oster and Robert Henderson, *Australian Federal Budget 2012–2013*, National Australia Bank, 9 May 2012 at financialmarkets.nab.com.au.
4. "Australia Cuts Interest Rates in a Bid to Boost Growth," *BBC News Business*, 5 June 2012.
5. The OECD, US Bureau of Labour Statistics, and Statistics Canada all define unit labour cost as nominal labour cost divided by real GDP and use this measure to link the rise in unit labour cost to productivity growth and wage inflation. The indicator is frequently used to analyse industry competitiveness, particularly for the manufacturing industry, and inflation pressure caused by wages (Bank of England, *Inflation Report*, May 2012). The OECD also has an indicator called Annual Labour Income Share (sometimes referred to as Real Unit Labour Cost), which is calculated using nominal labour cost divided by nominal GDP; this measure is not frequently used however. It has been argued that Nominal Unit Labour Cost (NULC) is a better proxy for competitiveness than real ULC as NULC captures both cost and price competitiveness (see www.voxeu.org).
6. Patrick D'Arcy and Linus Gustafsson, *Australia's Productivity Performance and Real Incomes*, RBA Bulletin, Economic Analysis Department, Reserve Bank of Australia, June Quarter 2012; and "Productivity Critical: RBA," *Australian Financial Review*, 22 June 2012. Note also an added benefit of the desalination plants is that they have provided environmental benefits and should help the next time Australia suffers long-term drought, though such benefits are not captured when one looks at present productivity measures.
7. Patrick D'Arcy and Linus Gustafsson, *Australia's Productivity Performance and Real Incomes*, RBA Bulletin, Economic Analysis Department, Reserve Bank of Australia, June Quarter 2012.
8. Saul Eslake and Marcus Walsh, *Australia's Productivity Challenge*, Grattan Institute, February 2011 and Ross Garnaut, "Climate Change, China Booms and Australia's Governance Struggle in a Changing World" (2010 Hamer Oration, The University of Melbourne and Hamer Family Fund), 5 August 2010.
9. Australian Productivity Commission, *Australia's Productivity Performance, Submission to the House of Representatives Standing Committee on Economics*, September 2009.
10. "Productivity Critical: RBA," *Australian Financial Review*, 22 June 2012.
11. Most notably by Professor Ross Garnaut.
12. "To Become Wealthier We Need to Become More Productive," *The Australian*, 16 September 2010.
13. Ross Garnaut, "Climate Change, China Booms and Australia's Governance Struggle in a Changing World" (2010 Hamer Oration, The University of Melbourne and Hamer Family Fund), 5 August 2010.

14. Patrick D'Arcy and Linus Gustafsson, *Australia's Productivity Performance and Real Incomes*, RBA Bulletin, Economic Analysis Department, Reserve Bank of Australia, June Quarter 2012.

15. Asian Development Bank, *Asia 2050: Realizing the Asian Century*, 2001.

16. The World Bank, *World Development Indicators*, 2012.

17. This phrase comes from Yves L. Doz, José Santos, and Peter Williamson, *From Global to Metanational: How Companies Win in the Knowledge Economy* (Boston: Harvard Business School Press, 2001).

18. This phrase comes from Thomas L. Friedman, *The World Is Flat: A Brief History of the Twenty-first Century* (New York: Farrar, Straus and Giroux, 2005).

CHAPTER 2

International Assessments of Australia's Competitiveness

In the last chapter, we focused on Australia's economic performance. In this chapter, we will start focusing on what underpins this performance. In particular, we will focus on issues of economic and business competitiveness. We define competitiveness for firms as the ability of the nation's firms to succeed in international competition against leading international competitors for firms in the traded sector and as the ability to be as efficient and effective as leading firms from around the world in the relevant industry for firms in the non-traded sector. We define competitiveness for industries as the ability of the industries in a country to compete successfully against competing industries from other countries (for industries in the traded sector) and the ability of the industries in a nation to be as efficient and effective as those in internationally leading nations for those industries (for industries in the non-traded sector). We define competitiveness at the national level as the nation's ability to foster an environment that allows for the development of a sufficient number of competitive firms and industries to allow the nation to prosper and generate a high standard of living.

Competitiveness has emerged as a pre-eminent issue in many major economies around the world. The ability of a nation or region to succeed in international markets, to achieve high levels of productivity, to create an attractive business environment, and to provide a high standard of living has long been a focus of analysis and policy. Work on competitiveness over the last two decades has shown the importance of a systemic approach that encompasses overall economic conditions, government policies, links between industries, industrial economics, and the effectiveness of firms in competing in international markets.

In the present chapter, we report information related to Australia's competitiveness from several international sources, draw conclusions on what this information means for Australia, and identify areas for further analysis and action. The chapter aims to show how the rest of the world, or at least how international sources of rankings and ratings related to competitiveness, view Australia, and what the views mean for the country.

The proliferation of works on competitiveness and comparisons of economies around the world means that some selection is required. For purposes of this chapter, we have compiled information from sources that focus on international competitiveness, ease of doing business, economic freedom, prices and costs, the knowledge economy, human development, quality of life, corruption, and corporate governance.

In each area, we identify the main sources, summarise the main findings with respect to Australia, and provide implications for Australia that come out of the individual sources. We then pull together the picture of Australia that emerges when we combine information from the different sources.[1]

We will compare Australia with two sets of countries, a comparison group of mostly OECD countries (the United States, Canada, Denmark, Finland, Ireland, Israel, the Netherlands, New Zealand, Norway, Sweden, and Switzerland) along with three Latin American countries that are competitors to Australia in some sectors (Argentina, Brazil, and Chile), and a group of Asia-Pacific economies (China, Hong Kong, India, Indonesia, Japan, Korea, Malaysia, New Zealand, the Philippines, Singapore, Taiwan, Thailand, and Vietnam). The idea is to capture how Australia stacks up against similar economies and against economies that are providing increasing market opportunities and competition for Australia.

As the underlying project on which this book is based has had a duration of over a year, the analysis is of the sources available at the time of access. This means the 2011 version of most of the source material. We note that there is relatively little movement from one year to the next in the underlying variables used by these sources and that the analysis of a nation's position according to these sources tends to be stable over time. Thus, the overall analysis of this chapter is unlikely to change much from one year to the next.

Overall Competitiveness

The World Economic Forum (WEF), the International Institute for Management Development (IMD), and the Chinese Academy of Social Sciences (CASS) produce indices of overall competitiveness. Each of the sources has explicit or implicit models of competitiveness that influence the features that are incorporated and their respective weighting into summary indices. Each provides ratings and rankings in an overall index, a variety of sub-indices, and numerous individual features believed to influence competitiveness. In terms of definitions, we note that the WEF defines competitiveness as "the set of institutions, policies, and factors that determine the level of productivity of a country."[2] IMD states its "World Competitiveness Yearbook analyses and ranks the ability of nations to create and maintain an environment that sustains the competitiveness of enterprises."[3] CASS compiles information on various aspects of economic performance and combines this information into an index.[4]

Australia ranked 20th (out of 142 economies) in the WEF's 2011 Competitiveness Index. Australia was ranked behind 8 of 14 comparison countries and ahead of 9 of 13 Asia-Pacific economies (see Tables 2.1 and 2.2). Among the WEF sub-indices, Australia ranked 6th in Financial Market Development, 10th in Health and Primary Education, 11th in Higher Education and Training, 24th in Infrastructure, 26th in Macroeconomic Environment, and 29th in Business Sophistication. In more detailed features, Australia ranked in the top 10 globally in Soundness of Banks, Legal Rights, Regulation of Securities Exchanges, Life Expectancy, Quality of Primary Education, and Secondary Education Enrolment. Australia performed less well in Quality of Overall Infrastructure (37th), Quality of Roads (34th), Quality of Port Infrastructure (40th), Quality of Electricity Supply (33rd), Mobile Telephone Subscriptions per 100 Population (69th), Government Budget Balance (86th), Gross National Savings (43rd),

TABLE 2.1 WEF Global Competitiveness Index and Sub-indices, Australia and Comparison Nations, 2011

Economies	2011 Global Competitiveness Index		Basic Requirements										Efficiency Enhancers														Innovation and Sophistication Factors					
			Overall		Institutions		Infrastructure		Macroeconomic Environment		Health and Primary Education		Overall		Higher Education and Training		Goods Market Efficiency		Labour Market Efficiency		Financial Market Development		Technological Readiness		Market Size		Overall		Business Sophistication		Innovation	
	Value	Rank	Value	Rank	Value	Rank	Value	Rank	Value	Rank	Value	Rank	Value	Rank	Value	Rank	Value	Rank	Value	Rank	Value	Rank	Value	Rank	Value	Rank	Value	Rank	Value	Rank	Value	Rank
Switzerland	5.74	1	6.18	3	5.78	6	6.15	5	6.28	7	6.53	8	5.53	2	5.80	3	5.24	5	5.95	1	5.35	7	6.30	1	4.51	39	5.79	1	5.82	3	5.77	1
Sweden	5.61	3	6.06	4	6.06	2	5.74	13	6.08	13	6.35	18	5.33	7	5.81	2	5.21	7	4.82	25	5.24	11	6.29	2	4.59	31	5.79	2	5.83	2	5.76	2
Finland	5.47	4	6.02	5	5.98	5	5.62	19	5.71	20	6.76	1	5.19	10	6.09	1	4.89	21	4.94	15	5.34	9	5.75	12	4.15	54	5.56	4	5.40	9	5.72	3
United States	5.43	5	5.21	36	4.64	39	5.68	16	4.49	90	6.05	42	5.49	3	5.57	13	4.80	24	5.57	4	4.87	22	5.23	20	6.92	1	5.46	6	5.35	10	5.57	5
Netherlands	5.41	7	5.88	7	5.61	10	6.02	7	5.34	36	6.54	7	5.29	8	5.66	8	5.17	9	4.84	23	5.01	17	6.13	5	5.10	18	5.30	9	5.58	5	5.03	12
Denmark	5.40	8	5.86	8	5.94	5	5.89	10	5.39	31	6.24	28	5.27	9	5.75	6	5.06	16	5.39	6	5.20	13	6.20	4	4.21	53	5.31	8	5.53	6	5.10	10
Canada	5.33	12	5.77	13	5.57	11	5.88	11	5.06	49	6.58	6	5.36	6	5.59	12	5.12	12	5.43	5	5.20	13	5.40	16	5.44	14	5.36	6	4.91	24	5.07	11
Norway	5.18	16	5.85	9	5.74	7	4.95	35	6.45	4	6.28	21	5.15	14	5.49	15	4.69	31	4.89	18	5.46	5	6.08	7	4.30	50	4.78	19	5.04	18	4.53	20
Australia	**5.11**	**20**	**5.74**	**14**	**5.39**	**13**	**5.43**	**24**	**5.62**	**26**	**6.51**	**10**	**5.18**	**12**	**5.62**	**11**	**4.84**	**22**	**5.04**	**13**	**5.38**	**6**	**5.11**	**22**	**5.10**	**19**	**4.57**	**26**	**4.67**	**29**	**4.48**	**22**
Israel	5.07	22	5.23	35	4.81	33	4.98	33	5.00	53	6.11	36	4.86	21	5.03	27	4.65	33	4.82	24	5.30	10	5.12	21	4.25	51	5.32	16	5.11	16	5.53	6
New Zealand	4.93	25	5.66	17	5.98	3	4.97	34	5.07	48	6.61	4	4.99	18	5.53	14	5.18	8	5.11	11	5.21	12	5.10	23	3.80	65	4.34	28	4.62	30	4.05	27
Ireland	4.77	29	5.20	37	5.19	23	5.12	29	4.01	118	6.49	12	4.67	28	5.15	22	5.10	13	4.90	17	3.44	115	5.34	17	4.12	56	4.65	23	4.93	22	4.37	23
Chile	4.70	31	5.37	29	5.06	26	4.67	41	6.07	14	5.68	71	4.54	34	4.67	43	4.79	25	4.64	39	4.56	37	4.26	45	4.35	46	3.88	42	4.32	39	3.45	46
Brazil	4.32	53	4.33	83	3.72	77	3.99	64	4.16	115	5.45	87	4.40	41	4.35	57	3.81	113	4.19	83	4.47	43	3.98	54	5.61	10	4.02	35	4.54	31	3.50	44
Argentina	3.99	85	4.33	84	2.93	134	3.70	81	4.88	62	5.80	56	3.85	84	4.48	54	3.23	137	3.52	131	3.26	126	3.71	64	4.88	24	3.43	77	3.78	79	3.08	78

Source: Global Competitiveness Report 2011–2012, World Economic Forum, Switzerland, 2011.

TABLE 2.2 WEF Global Competitiveness Index and Sub-Indices, Australia and Asia-Pacific Economies, 2011

| | 2011 Global Competitiveness Index | | Basic Requirements | | | | | | | | | | Efficiency Enhancers | | | | | | | | | | | | | | Innovation and Sophistication Factors | | | | | |
| | | | Overall | | Institutions | | Infrastructure | | Macroeconomic Environment | | Health and Primary Education | | Overall | | Higher Education and Training | | Goods Market Efficiency | | Labour Market Efficiency | | Financial Market Development | | Technological Readiness | | Market Size | | Overall | | Business Sophistication | | Innovation | |
Economies	Value	Rank	Value	Rank	Value	Rank	Value	Rank	Value	Rank	Value	Rank	Value	Rank	Value	Rank	Value	Rank	Value	Rank	Value	Rank	Value	Rank	Value	Rank	Value	Rank	Value	Rank	Value	Rank
Singapore	5.63	2	6.33	1	6.11	1	6.33	3	6.22	9	6.65	3	5.58	1	5.77	4	5.57	1	5.86	2	5.84	1	5.90	10	4.56	37	5.23	11	5.13	15	5.33	8
Japan	5.40	9	5.40	28	5.18	24	5.69	15	4.20	113	6.52	9	5.19	11	5.27	19	4.98	18	5.04	12	4.64	32	5.06	25	6.12	4	5.75	3	5.91	1	5.59	4
Hong Kong	5.36	11	6.21	2	5.63	9	6.71	1	6.26	8	6.25	27	5.48	4	5.13	24	5.41	3	5.67	3	5.78	2	6.11	6	4.76	28	4.58	25	4.99	19	4.18	25
Taiwan	5.26	13	5.69	15	4.94	31	5.62	20	5.70	22	6.51	11	5.10	16	5.64	10	5.13	11	4.71	33	4.84	24	5.08	24	5.21	16	5.25	10	5.23	13	5.27	9
Australia	**5.11**	**20**	**5.74**	**14**	**5.39**	**13**	**5.43**	**24**	**5.62**	**26**	**6.51**	**10**	**5.18**	**12**	**5.62**	**11**	**4.84**	**22**	**5.04**	**13**	**5.38**	**6**	**5.11**	**22**	**5.10**	**19**	**4.57**	**26**	**4.67**	**29**	**4.48**	**22**
Malaysia	5.08	21	5.45	25	4.94	30	5.22	26	5.50	29	6.14	33	4.88	20	4.76	38	5.06	15	4.87	20	5.53	3	4.29	44	4.75	29	4.65	22	4.99	20	4.32	24
Korea	5.02	24	5.65	19	3.89	65	5.94	9	6.37	6	6.38	15	4.86	22	5.44	17	4.57	37	4.30	76	3.95	80	5.33	18	5.57	11	4.87	18	4.86	25	4.89	14
New Zealand	4.93	25	5.66	17	5.98	3	4.97	34	5.07	48	6.61	4	4.99	18	5.53	14	5.18	8	5.11	11	5.21	12	5.10	23	3.80	65	4.34	28	4.62	30	4.05	27
China	4.90	26	5.33	30	4.32	48	4.63	44	6.22	10	6.16	32	4.70	26	4.34	58	4.42	45	4.68	36	4.42	48	3.57	77	6.77	2	4.15	31	4.37	37	3.92	29
Thailand	4.52	39	4.88	46	3.85	67	4.65	42	5.52	28	5.49	83	4.38	43	4.25	62	4.47	42	4.75	30	4.35	50	3.47	84	5.02	22	3.75	51	4.20	47	3.30	54
Indonesia	4.38	46	4.74	53	3.81	71	3.77	76	5.66	23	5.74	64	4.18	56	4.16	69	4.23	67	4.06	94	4.06	69	3.33	94	5.22	15	3.90	41	4.22	45	3.59	36
India	4.30	56	4.25	91	3.84	69	3.60	89	4.30	105	5.25	101	4.46	37	3.88	87	4.21	70	4.20	81	4.93	21	3.36	93	6.16	3	3.92	40	4.27	43	3.58	38
Vietnam	4.24	65	4.41	76	3.63	87	3.59	90	4.78	65	5.66	73	4.05	66	3.47	103	4.16	75	4.60	46	4.00	73	3.51	79	4.59	33	3.44	75	3.72	87	3.16	66
Philippines	4.08	75	4.17	100	3.22	117	3.09	105	4.99	54	5.38	92	4.03	70	4.13	71	4.05	88	3.92	113	4.02	71	3.47	83	4.57	36	3.45	74	4.11	57	2.79	108

Source: Global Competitiveness Report 2011–2012, World Economic Forum, Switzerland, 2011.

Local Supplier Quantity (46th), State of Cluster Development[5] (37th), Nature of Competitive Advantage (67th), Value Chain Breadth (75th), Control of International Distribution (54th), Extent and Effect of Taxation (88th), Total Tax Rate (99th), Flexibility of Wage Determination (116th), and Hiring and Firing Practices (97th).

In 2011, IMD ranked Australia 9th (out of 59 economies) in terms of overall competitiveness, which was higher than 10 of the 14 comparison countries and 10 of 12 Asia-Pacific economies (see Table 2.3) In the sub-indices, Australia ranked 13th in

TABLE 2.3   IMD World Competitiveness Index and Sub-Indices, Selected Economies, 2011

Economies	2011 Overall Value	Rank	Economic Performance Value	Rank	Government Efficiency Value	Rank	Business Efficiency Value	Rank	Infrastructure Value	Rank
Australia and Comparison Countries										
United States	100.0	1	100.0	1	59.3	19	69.4	10	87.6	1
Sweden	94.1	4	65.3	11	68.9	5	77.2	4	81.2	2
Switzerland	92.6	5	62.2	15	76.2	3	68.6	11	79.6	4
Canada	90.8	7	64.8	12	66.0	9	70.6	8	78.0	5
Australia	**89.3**	**9**	**63.9**	**13**	**67.5**	**7**	**71.1**	**7**	**70.8**	**14**
Denmark	86.4	12	45.3	40	63.4	13	73.4	6	79.9	3
Norway	86.3	13	51.8	26	65.1	11	68.5	12	76.1	8
Netherlands	85.7	14	59.7	19	60.4	18	67.5	13	71.5	12
Finland	84.4	15	46.0	37	63.3	14	66.5	15	78.0	6
Israel	81.6	17	48.3	36	60.8	16	63.5	17	70.2	15
New Zealand	79.8	21	49.3	33	67.5	8	56.3	24	62.4	23
Ireland	77.1	24	50.5	28	49.7	30	63.2	18	61.3	24
Chile	76.8	25	60.2	17	64.9	12	60.1	21	38.4	40
Brazil	61.0	44	50.0	30	29.4	55	52.1	29	29.0	51
Argentina	54.7	54	45.4	39	27.6	57	29.7	51	32.4	45
Australia and Asia-Pacific Economies										
Hong Kong	100.0	1	82.1	4	87.6	1	82.2	1	64.2	21
Singapore	98.6	3	79.8	5	79.8	2	78.7	2	72.2	10
Australia	**89.3**	**9**	**63.9**	**13**	**67.5**	**7**	**71.1**	**7**	**70.8**	**14**
Malaysia	84.1	16	71.4	7	60.6	17	67.0	14	53.7	27
China	81.1	19	83.8	3	47.7	33	56.1	25	53.1	28
New Zealand	79.8	21	49.3	33	67.5	8	56.3	24	62.4	23
Korea	78.5	22	52.4	25	55.6	22	55.7	26	66.6	20
Japan	75.2	26	50.9	27	39.0	50	55.6	27	71.7	11
Thailand	74.9	27	68.1	10	54.8	23	62.3	19	30.7	47
India	70.6	32	59.8	18	50.8	29	59.2	22	29.1	50
Indonesia	64.6	37	49.5	32	53.7	25	49.2	33	22.5	55
Philippines	63.3	41	50.5	29	46.3	37	51.5	31	21.1	57
Vietnam	N/A	N/A	N/A	N/A	N/A	N/A	N/A	N/A	N/A	N/A

Source: International Institute for Management Development, *World Competitiveness Yearbook 2011*, Lausanne, 2011.

Economic Performance, 7th in Government Efficiency, 7th in Business Efficiency, and 14th in Infrastructure. In more detailed features, Australia was in the top 10 in Employment, Business Legislation, Customs, Lack of Protectionism, Capital Markets, State Ownership, Competition Legislation, Ease of Doing Business, Creation of Firms, Justice, Personal Security and Property Rights, Attitudes and Values, Flexibility and Adaptability, Management Practices, and Financial System. Less favourable rankings were received for Relocation Threats of Production (33rd), Relocation Threats of R&D Facilities (44th), Prices (36th), Productivity and Efficiency (25th), and Technological Infrastructure (25th).

Australia was ranked 12th (out of 100 economies) in overall competitiveness by the Chinese Academy of Social Sciences for 2009–2010. It was ahead of 10 of the 14 comparison countries and 8 of 11 Asia-Pacific economies on this measure. In terms of sub-indices, Australia ranked 19th for Technological Innovation, 15th for Industrial Structure, 18th for Economic Efficiency, 15th for Economic Scale, and 72nd for Economic Growth. We note that the absence of results for Hong Kong and Taiwan, two economies that rank ahead of Australia in at least one other competitiveness ranking, might lead to an overstatement of Australia's regional position in the CASS ranking.

Several conclusions emerge from the competitiveness reports. Australia does reasonably well in the aggregate assessments of competitiveness. The sources suggest that Australia gets many of the basic conditions regarding government, openness, and flexibility right. It also has good educational achievement, quality of life, environment, and social conditions. Australia gets high marks in terms of transparency and integrity of public service, openness to local and foreign business, ease of starting businesses, education, and quality of life. However, Australia's infrastructure, sophistication of companies, business systems, clusters of firms and industries, tax system, regulatory burden, labour rules, innovation support, and international outlook do not measure up with the world's best, in some cases by a significant margin. We note that these features might exacerbate the disadvantages resulting from Australia's remoteness from other markets. Limited diversification of the economy, the potential for the relocation of core activities, limited immigration and foreign investment, and a relatively high cost of capital give an outlook perhaps less robust than we might hope given Australia's recent economic performance and strength in basic conditions.

Ease of Doing Business

The ease with which companies can start and carry out business has an important influence on competitiveness and economic development. The leading source on the environment for business is the International Financial Corporation (IFC), the investment arm of the World Bank, which compiles an index of how easy or difficult it is to do business in countries around the world. According to the IFC, the Ease of Doing Business Index was developed with the aim of "investigating the regulations that enhance business activity and those that constrain it."[6]

Australia ranked 15th out of 183 economies in the 2012 IFC Ease of Doing Business Index, ahead of 6 of the 14 comparison countries, and 9 of the 13 Asia-Pacific economies (see Table 2.4). Among the sub-indices, Australia ranked 2nd in Starting a Business, 8th in Getting Credit, 17th in Enforcing Contracts, 17th in Resolving Insolvency, 37th in Getting Electricity, 38th in Registering Property, 42nd in Dealing with Construction Permits, 65th in Protecting Investors, and 53rd in [ease of] Paying Taxes.

TABLE 2.4 IFC Ease of Doing Business Index and Sub-Indices, Selected Economies, 2012

Economies	Overall Ranking	Starting a Business	Dealing with Construction Permits	Getting Electricity	Registering Property	Getting Credit	Protecting Investors	Paying Taxes	Trading Across Borders	Enforcing Contracts	Resolving Insolvency
Australia and Comparison Countries											
New Zealand	3	1	2	31	3	4	1	36	27	10	18
United States	4	13	17	17	16	4	5	72	20	7	15
Denmark	5	31	10	13	11	24	29	14	7	32	9
Norway	6	41	60	12	8	48	24	27	9	4	4
Ireland	10	13	27	90	81	8	5	5	21	62	10
Finland	11	39	45	25	25	40	65	28	6	11	5
Canada	13	3	25	156	41	24	5	8	42	59	3
Sweden	14	46	23	8	19	48	29	50	8	54	19
Australia	**15**	**2**	**42**	**37**	**38**	**8**	**65**	**53**	**30**	**17**	**17**
Switzerland	26	85	46	6	14	24	166	12	41	23	43
Netherlands	31	79	99	67	48	48	111	43	13	28	7
Israel	34	43	137	93	147	8	5	59	10	94	45
Chile	39	27	90	41	53	48	29	45	62	67	110
Argentina	113	146	169	58	139	67	111	144	102	45	85
Brazil	126	120	127	51	114	98	79	150	121	118	136
Australia and Asia-Pacific Economies											
Singapore	1	4	3	5	14	8	2	4	1	12	2
Hong Kong	2	5	1	4	57	4	3	3	2	5	16
New Zealand	3	1	2	31	3	4	1	36	27	10	18
Korea	8	24	26	11	71	8	79	38	4	2	13
Australia	**15**	**2**	**42**	**37**	**38**	**8**	**65**	**53**	**30**	**17**	**17**
Thailand	17	78	14	9	28	67	13	100	17	24	51

(Continued)

TABLE 2.4   Continued

Economies	Overall Ranking	Starting a Business	Dealing with Construction Permits	Getting Electricity	Registering Property	Getting Credit	Protecting Investors	Paying Taxes	Trading Across Borders	Enforcing Contracts	Resolving Insolvency
Malaysia	18	50	113	59	59	1	4	41	29	31	47
Japan	20	107	63	26	58	24	17	120	16	34	1
Taiwan	25	16	87	3	33	67	79	71	23	88	14
China	91	151	179	115	40	67	97	122	60	16	75
Vietnam	98	103	67	135	47	24	166	151	68	30	142
Indonesia	129	155	71	161	99	126	46	131	39	156	146
India	132	166	181	98	97	40	46	147	109	182	128
Philippines	136	158	102	54	117	126	133	136	51	112	163

Source: World Bank and IFC, *Doing Business in 2012: Doing Business in a More Transparent World,* Washington, 2012: www.doingbusiness.org.

The Ease of Doing Business data indicate that Australia has done an outstanding job in making the country a relatively friction-free place to set up a business. However, once a company is set up, Australia compares poorly in many of the features that are required to operate and grow a business, with infrastructure, regulation, and taxation particular causes for concern. Most of the OECD countries in the comparison set (even those we tend to think of as highly regulated) perform better than Australia on these latter drivers, as do four Asia-Pacific economies. Thus, while Australia's overall ease of doing business is rated highly, it is not clear that Australia has any advantage over traditional benchmarks or over leading regional competitors in ease of doing business.

Knowledge and Knowledge Economy

Developing a strong knowledge economy is crucial for advanced economies around the world. To capture the essence of the knowledge economy, the World Bank has developed its Knowledge Economy Index and Knowledge Index. These are based on a framework that focuses on the economic and institutional environmental incentives to use new knowledge in an entrepreneurial fashion; a population sufficiently educated to create, share, and use knowledge; an efficient innovation system that can generate new knowledge and tap into existing sources of knowledge; and the information and communication technology necessary to facilitate the generation, acquisition, and processing of information.[7]

The World Bank provides four indices related to the knowledge economy depending on the features included and on whether some data are on a per capita (weighted) or absolute (unweighted) basis. In 2011, Australia ranked 11th in the Weighted Knowledge Economy Index, 8th in the Weighted Knowledge Index, 10th in the Unweighted Knowledge Economy Index, and 7th in the Unweighted Knowledge Index (the Knowledge Economy Index includes additional variables representing the economic and institutional regime in an economy). Australia ranked ahead of 5 to 8 of the 14 comparison countries, depending on the individual index, and ranked ahead of all of the other Asia-Pacific economies in all four indices. We show results for the Weighted Knowledge Economy Index (where some features are taken on a per capita rather than absolute basis) in Table 2.5.

In the sub-indices, Australia ranked 4th in Education, 22nd in Economic Incentive and Institutional Regime, 18th in ICT (information and communication technology), and 20th in Innovation. In individual features, Australia ranked in the top 10 for Adult Literacy, Secondary Enrolment, Regulatory Quality, and Science and Engineering Journal Articles per Million People, and it ranked in the top 20 in Rule of Law, Internet Users per 1,000, Computers per 1,000, Royalty Payments and Receipts, and Patents Granted by the US Patent Office per Million People. It did less well in Tariff and Non-Tariff Barriers (ranked 41st) and in Telephones per 1,000 population (31st).

Compared with High Income Countries, Australia scored in the top 10 percent in Adult Literacy Rate, Gross Secondary Enrolment Rate, Difficulty of Hiring Index, Rigidity of Hours Index, School Enrolment for Females, Soundness of Banks, Days to Start a Business, Gender Development, ICT Expenditures as Percent of GDP, Employment to Population Ratio, Human Development Index, Life Expectancy at Birth, Reliance on Professional Management, and Firing Costs.

TABLE 2.5 World Bank Weighted Knowledge Economy Index Rank and Sub-Indices, Selected Economies, 2009

		Economic and Institution Regime						Innovation Index						Education Index						ICT Index					
		Tariff & Nontariff Barriers		Regulatory Quality		Rule of Law		Royalty Payments and Receipts		S&E Journal Articles/Mil.		Patents Granted by USPTO/Mil.		Adult Literacy		Secondary Enrolment		Tertiary Enrolment		Telephones per 1,000		Computers per 1,000		Internet Users per 1,000	
Weighted KEI Rank	Economies	Value	Rank	Value	Rank	Value	Rank	Value	Rank	Value	Rank	Value	Rank	Value	Rank	Value	Rank	Value	Rank	Value	Rank	Value	Rank	Value	Rank
Australia and Comparison Countries																									
1	Denmark	9.02	20	10.00	1	9.79	4	N/A	N/A	9.86	3	9.11	14	10.00	1	9.86	3	9.49	8	8.97	16	8.80	18	9.86	3
2	Sweden	9.02	20	9.32	11	9.66	6	9.75	4	9.93	2	9.59	7	10.00	1	8.75	19	9.13	13	9.38	10	9.79	4	9.79	4
3	Finland	9.02	20	9.38	10	9.52	8	9.50	7	9.79	4	9.73	5	10.00	1	9.44	9	9.86	3	8.01	30	8.45	23	9.73	5
4	Netherlands	9.02	20	9.59	7	9.04	15	9.66	5	9.65	6	9.04	15	10.00	1	9.72	5	7.90	30	8.77	19	9.86	3	9.93	2
5	Norway	9.86	3	8.63	21	9.93	2	9.16	11	9.44	9	8.56	22	10.00	1	9.51	8	9.28	11	8.15	28	9.15	13	10.00	1
6	Canada	9.72	5	9.18	13	9.45	9	9.41	8	9.51	8	9.38	10	10.00	1	9.65	6	8.12	27	6.23	56	10.00	1	9.38	10
8	Ireland	9.02	20	9.66	6	9.11	14	10.00	1	8.75	19	8.49	23	10.00	1	9.38	10	8.04	28	8.70	20	8.94	16	8.49	23
9	United States	9.44	10	8.77	19	8.90	17	9.33	9	9.10	14	10.00	1	10.00	1	6.67	49	9.57	7	7.33	40	9.72	5	9.45	9
10	Switzerland	7.34	39	9.04	15	10.00	1	N/A	N/A	10.00	1	9.79	4	10.00	1	6.53	51	6.52	49	9.45	9	9.93	2	9.66	6
11	**Australia**	**7.20**	**41**	**9.45**	**9**	**9.32**	**11**	**8.57**	**18**	**9.38**	**10**	**8.70**	**20**	**10.00**	**1**	**10.00**	**1**	**9.06**	**14**	**7.95**	**31**	**9.01**	**15**	**9.04**	**15**
14	New Zealand	7.13	42	9.52	8	9.73	5	8.32	21	9.24	12	8.42	24	10.00	1	9.93	2	9.42	9	7.47	38	8.73	19	9.18	13
26	Israel	9.09	14	7.95	31	7.67	35	8.82	15	9.72	5	9.66	6	6.30	55	6.32	54	7.97	29	8.70	20	7.61	35	6.30	55
42	Chile	9.02	20	8.77	19	8.49	24	6.55	42	7.22	41	6.78	48	6.10	58	6.18	56	7.17	40	5.82	62	6.41	52	6.58	51
54	Brazil	3.22	98	5.00	74	4.73	79	5.88	50	6.46	52	6.23	56	4.38	83	9.03	15	4.64	75	4.86	76	6.55	50	6.99	45
59	Argentina	2.52	108	1.64	123	4.18	86	6.47	43	7.08	43	7.12	43	6.64	50	4.79	76	8.48	22	6.78	48	5.21	69	5.89	61
Australia and Asia-Pacific Economies																									
11	**Australia**	**7.20**	**41**	**9.45**	**9**	**9.32**	**11**	**8.57**	**18**	**9.38**	**10**	**8.70**	**20**	**10.00**	**1**	**10.00**	**1**	**9.06**	**14**	**7.95**	**31**	**9.01**	**15**	**9.04**	**15**
14	New Zealand	7.13	42	9.52	8	9.73	5	8.32	21	9.24	12	8.42	24	10.00	1	9.93	2	9.42	9	7.47	38	8.73	19	9.18	13
18	Taiwan	7.27	40	7.67	35	7.33	40	N/A	N/A	8.61	21	9.93	2	6.44	53	7.85	32	9.64	6	9.11	14	9.58	7	8.70	20
19	Singapore	9.93	2	9.79	4	9.32	11	9.92	2	9.58	7	9.25	12	5.62	65	2.71	106	7.54	35	9.25	12	9.51	8	8.90	17
20	Japan	6.71	48	8.08	29	8.63	21	9.24	10	8.54	22	9.86	3	10.00	1	8.33	25	7.68	33	6.58	51	8.24	26	9.18	13
23	Hong Kong	10.00	1	9.93	2	8.70	20	8.91	14	N/A	N/A	9.18	13	5.68	64	5.14	71	5.29	66	10.00	1	9.44	9	8.56	22
29	Korea	2.59	107	7.53	37	7.88	32	8.24	22	8.26	26	9.32	11	6.78	48	7.57	36	9.93	2	7.19	42	8.94	16	9.66	6
48	Malaysia	4.83	75	6.64	50	6.85	47	7.31	33	5.14	71	8.01	30	4.73	78	3.13	100	4.78	73	5.62	65	7.32	39	8.49	23
63	Thailand	4.27	85	5.34	69	5.75	63	6.72	40	4.72	77	5.82	62	5.48	67	4.51	80	6.74	46	6.99	45	4.58	78	5.34	69
81	China	3.08	100	4.04	88	4.59	80	4.87	62	5.49	66	5.96	60	5.07	73	3.40	96	4.13	82	4.25	85	4.15	84	4.59	80
89	Philippines	5.03	72	4.73	78	3.36	98	4.54	66	1.81	119	5.07	73	5.21	71	4.31	83	4.57	76	3.70	93	4.58	78	2.53	110
100	Vietnam	1.33	126	3.01	103	4.04	88	N/A	N/A	2.43	110	3.01	103	4.18	86	3.47	95	3.33	93	3.63	94	5.56	64	5.34	69
103	Indonesia	4.55	79	3.90	90	2.53	111	4.71	64	0.83	133	4.04	88	4.52	81	2.78	105	3.48	91	3.08	102	2.54	107	2.53	110
109	India	0.28	140	4.18	86	6.03	59	2.52	90	4.38	82	5.55	66	1.44	126	2.36	111	2.83	100	1.85	120	2.75	104	2.88	105

Source: World Bank, *Knowledge Assessment Methodology website (KAM 2009)*, December 2011.

Compared with High Income Countries, Australia was in the bottom 30 percent in Manufacturing Trade as Percentage of GDP, Trade as Percentage of GDP, Export of Goods and Services as Percent of GDP, Value Chain Presence, Daily Newspapers per 1,000 People, Share of Unemployment with Secondary Education, Employment in Industry, FDI Outflows as Percent of GDP, Science and Engineering Articles with Foreign Co-Authorship, Interest Rate Spread, Mobile Phones per 1,000 People, and Labour Force with Secondary Education.

Australia scores among the upper echelon of countries worldwide in the knowledge indices, although it is lower than other advanced economies in terms of internationalisation of the economy, some employment features, labour force, financial features, regulation, the nature of competitive advantage, development of value chains, brain drain, and telecommunications penetration. One major issue for Australia is that a high proportion of its highly educated talent seems to leave the country to work elsewhere. Australia scores poorly in several features that point to this, but particularly in the area of Brain Drain. Another key issue is the limited extent to which Australia appears to be plugged into the global economy, something that will be increasingly important to the nation's future.

Economic Freedom

The United States–based Heritage Foundation (in conjunction with the *Wall Street Journal*) and the Canada-based Fraser Institute are the two leading sources on the economic freedom of economies around the world. Both organisations see economic freedom as a major determinant of national prosperity. According to the Heritage Foundation, "Economic freedom is necessary for people to prosper. By reducing obstacles, it creates a framework within which people can choose how to use their time, skills, and resources: a framework in which innovation is welcomed and economic growth is enhanced. Simply put, around the world, countries with a higher degree of economic freedom enjoy a higher standard of living."[8] According to the Fraser Institute, "the cornerstones of economic freedom are personal choice rather than collective choice, voluntary exchange co-ordinated by markets rather than allocation via the political process, freedom to enter and compete in markets, and protection of persons and their property from aggression by others."[9]

Australia ranked 3rd out of 184 nations in the 2012 Heritage Foundation Index of Economic Freedom, behind only Hong Kong and Singapore. It was ahead of all of the comparison set countries (again mostly consisting of small and medium-sized OECD countries), and behind only 2 of 13 other Asia-Pacific economies (see Table 2.6). In the sub-indexes, Australia receives a high rank for Financial Freedom (1st), Property Rights (2nd), Freedom from Corruption (8th), Labour Freedom (8th), Monetary Freedom (11th), Business Freedom (13th), and Investment Freedom (4th). It ranked closer to the middle in Trade Freedom (37th), and did not perform well at all in Government Spending (85th) and Fiscal Freedom (160th).

Australia ranked 5th (out of 141 economies) in the Fraser Institute Economic Freedom of the World Index for 2009, behind Hong Kong, Singapore, New Zealand, and Switzerland. It was ahead of 12 of the 14 comparison economies and 10 of the 13 Asia-Pacific economies (see Table 2.7). In the sub-indices, Australia ranked 9th in Regulation of Credit, Labour, and Business; 9th in Access to Sound Money; and 60th

TABLE 2.6 Heritage Foundation Index of Economic Freedom and Sub-indices, Selected Economies, 2012

2012 Rank	Economies	Overall Score	Rule of Law		Limited Government		Regulatory Efficiency			Open Markets		
			Property Rights	Freedom from Corruption	Fiscal Freedom	Government Spending	Business Freedom	Labour Freedom	Monetary Freedom	Trade Freedom	Investment Freedom	Financial Freedom
Australia and Comparison Countries												
3	**Australia**	**83.1**	**90.0**	**87.0**	**63.4**	**67.1**	**91.9**	**90.6**	**84.5**	**86.2**	**80.0**	**90.0**
4	New Zealand	82.1	95.0	93.0	71.6	45.0	99.9	89.9	85.2	86.8	75.0	80.0
5	Switzerland	81.1	90.0	87.0	67.9	65.8	77.9	87.9	84.4	90.0	80.0	80.0
6	Canada	79.9	90.0	89.0	79.2	41.7	96.6	81.8	77.3	87.9	75.0	80.0
7	Chile	78.3	90.0	72.0	77.4	82.1	68.6	75.1	85.6	82.0	80.0	70.0
9	Ireland	76.9	90.0	80.0	73.9	30.4	92.8	78.4	76.7	87.1	90.0	70.0
10	United States	76.3	85.0	71.0	69.8	46.7	91.1	95.8	77.2	86.4	70.0	70.0
11	Denmark	76.2	90.0	93.0	39.8	0.0	99.1	92.1	80.7	87.1	90.0	90.0
15	Netherlands	73.3	90.0	88.0	51.2	20.9	81.9	60.0	83.6	87.1	90.0	80.0
17	Finland	72.3	90.0	92.0	65.4	5.2	94.9	42.4	81.3	87.1	85.0	80.0
21	Sweden	71.7	90.0	92.0	39.1	8.8	94.6	54.6	80.9	87.1	90.0	80.0
40	Norway	68.8	90.0	86.0	52.5	35.3	88.4	46.3	75.1	89.3	65.0	60.0
48	Israel	67.8	70.0	61.0	64.1	41.0	64.4	65.1	79.0	83.6	80.0	70.0
99	Brazil	57.9	50.0	37.0	69.1	54.8	53.7	59.1	75.8	69.7	50.0	60.0
158	Argentina	48.0	20.0	29.0	65.5	56.9	61.0	48.9	60.7	67.6	40.0	30.0
Australia and Asia-Pacific Economies												
1	Hong Kong	89.9	90.0	84.0	93.1	91.0	98.9	86.5	85.8	90.0	90.0	90.0
2	Singapore	87.5	90.0	93.0	91.3	91.3	97.2	92.1	84.8	90.0	75.0	70.0
3	**Australia**	**83.1**	**90.0**	**87.0**	**63.4**	**67.1**	**91.9**	**90.6**	**84.5**	**86.2**	**80.0**	**90.0**
4	New Zealand	82.1	95.0	93.0	71.6	45.0	99.9	89.9	85.2	86.8	75.0	80.0
18	Taiwan	71.9	70.0	58.0	80.4	92.3	88.5	46.6	83.1	85.0	65.0	50.0
22	Japan	71.6	80.0	78.0	67.1	47.0	81.8	81.4	88.9	81.8	60.0	50.0
31	South Korea	69.9	70.0	54.0	72.8	67.2	93.6	49.7	78.9	72.6	70.0	70.0
53	Malaysia	66.4	50.0	44.0	84.5	72.5	78.1	79.3	81.6	78.8	45.0	50.0
60	Thailand	64.9	45.0	35.0	75.1	87.5	72.5	79.0	69.3	75.2	40.0	70.0
107	Philippines	57.1	30.0	24.0	79.1	89.7	54.3	51.7	77.1	75.5	40.0	50.0
115	Indonesia	56.4	30.0	28.0	83.5	91.6	54.6	52.1	75.2	73.9	35.0	40.0
123	India	54.6	50.0	33.0	76.1	74.8	35.5	74.2	62.9	64.1	35.0	40.0
136	Vietnam	51.3	15.0	27.0	76.5	66.5	61.1	67.3	75.1	79.6	15.0	30.0
138	China	51.2	20.0	35.0	70.4	84.1	46.4	55.4	74.2	71.6	25.0	30.0

Source: The Heritage Foundation and the Wall Street Journal, *Index of Economic Freedom 2012*, Washington, 2012.

TABLE 2.7   Fraser Institute Economic Freedom Index and Sub-Indices, Selected Economies, 2009

2009 Rank	Economies	Size of Government	Legal Structure & Security of Property Rights	Access to Sound Money	Freedom to Trade Internationally	Regulations of Credit, Labour, and Business
Australia and Comparison Countries						
3	New Zealand	6.1	8.8	9.7	7.7	8.7
4	Switzerland	7.6	8.4	9.3	6.6	8.1
5	**Australia**	**6.7**	**8.2**	**9.6**	**7.1**	**8.2**
6	Canada	6.1	8.1	9.6	6.9	8.3
7	Chile	7.7	7.2	9.0	7.8	7.2
10	United States	6.5	7.3	9.6	7.0	7.6
11	Finland	5.2	8.7	9.6	7.2	7.4
15	Denmark	4.1	8.5	9.5	7.4	8.1
25	Ireland	4.6	7.8	9.1	8.3	7.0
30	Netherlands	3.4	8.1	9.5	8.1	7.4
35	Norway	4.9	8.8	9.2	6.5	7.1
39	Sweden	3.2	8.4	9.6	7.6	7.3
83	Israel	4.6	6.0	8.8	7.1	6.2
102	Brazil	6.7	5.3	7.9	6.0	5.1
119	Argentina	6.2	4.5	7.0	5.8	6.0
Australia and Asia-Pacific Economies						
1	Hong Kong	9.4	8.2	9.3	9.3	8.8
2	Singapore	8.1	8.3	9.1	9.4	8.5
3	New Zealand	6.1	8.8	9.7	7.7	8.7
5	**Australia**	**6.7**	**8.2**	**9.6**	**7.1**	**8.2**
22	Japan	6.5	7.5	9.8	5.8	7.7
26	Taiwan	6.9	6.7	9.3	7.2	6.7
30	Korea	6.8	6.6	9.5	7.1	6.6
65	Thailand	7.1	5.7	7.1	7.7	6.8
78	Malaysia	5.5	6.5	6.5	7.2	7.6
84	Indonesia	7.6	4.4	7.7	6.7	6.1
88	Vietnam	6.7	5.9	5.9	7.1	6.7
89	Philippines	7.8	4.6	6.8	6.5	6.6
92	China	4.5	6.4	8.0	7.2	6.0
94	India	6.7	5.7	6.6	6.5	6.5

Source: James Gwartney, Robert Lawson, and Joshua Hall, *Economic Freedom of the World: 2011 Annual Report*, Fraser Institute, 2011.

in Size of Government. In individual features, Australia ranked in the top 10 in Ownership of Banks, Private Sector Credit, Interest Rate Controls/Negative Real Interest Rates, Hiring Regulations and Minimum Wage, Hour Regulations, Mandated Cost of Worker Dismissal, Conscription, Starting a Business, Standard Deviation of Inflation, Freedom to Own Foreign Currency Bank Accounts, Judicial Independence, Military Interference in Rule of Law and Politics, and Government Enterprises and Investment. Australia ranked less well in Hiring and Firing Regulations (69th), Centralised Collective Bargaining (98th), Bureaucracy Costs (114th), Money Growth (38th), Inflation (43rd), Government Consumption (95th), Transfers and Subsidies (83rd), and Top Marginal Tax Rate (78th).

Across the two reports, Australia performs well in the quality of its legal and regulatory framework, most government features, and conditions for setting up companies. However, bureaucracy costs are considered very high, government consumption is high, transfers and subsidies are high, trade taxes are relatively high, taxes in general are high, and labour rules are considered very rigid. Thus, the picture on some specific aspects of economic freedom is not as favourable as that of the whole.

City Competitiveness

City competitiveness has been receiving increased attention in recent years due to evidence that dynamic cities are important contributors to national development and prosperity. Two leading sources on city competitiveness are the Loughborough University World Cities Research Group (LUWCRG) and the Chinese Academy of Social Sciences (CASS). The LUWCRG has focused on the role that world cities play as advanced producer service centres, with services that link together cities and countries in an ever-more-globalised economy, and uses these services as a proxy for the high-level influence and interaction that helps define world cities.[10] The Chinese Academy of Social Sciences has built up a city competitiveness index by combining data on several economic performance features into an aggregate index.[11]

In the 2010 Loughborough University Roster of World Cities, which rates cities in terms of their international linkages and importance, Australia's leading city, Sydney, ranked 10th globally as a world city, Melbourne was 31st, Brisbane 87th, and Perth 105th. Several of the cities that ranked ahead of Sydney were in the Asia-Pacific region, including Tokyo, Singapore, Seoul, Hong Kong, Shanghai, and Taipei. This suggests that that Sydney and other Australian cities play a limited role as major Asia-Pacific regional centres.

According to CASS's Urban Competitiveness Index, Sydney ranked 46th (out of 500 cities) in 2009–2010 (see Table 2.8). Melbourne ranked 91st, Brisbane 136th, Canberra 229th, Hobart 238th, and Adelaide 243rd. Only Sydney was remotely close to the leading cities in the world in this index. In the sub-indices, Sydney ranked 10th in GDP, Melbourne 13th, and Brisbane 35th. Sydney ranked 13th in the Multinational Enterprise Index (a measure of the presence of multinational companies) and Melbourne 49th. In GDP Growth, Hobart ranked 281st, Melbourne 283rd, Canberra 338th, Brisbane 352nd, Sydney 414th, and Adelaide 430th. The leading Australian cities performed poorly in Patent Applications, ranking between 237th and 292nd. Eight Asian cities (Tokyo, Singapore, Seoul, Hong Kong, Yokohama, Osaka, Shanghai, and Taipei) were ahead of Sydney in their overall competitiveness. These other cities have become the lead cities

TABLE 2.8   CASS Urban Competitiveness Ranking, Asia-Pacific Cities, 2009–2010

Cities	Economies	Global Urban Competitiveness		GDP		GDP per capita		GDP per square kilometre		GDP Growth		Patent Application		Multinational Enterprise Index	
		Value	Rank	Value	Rank	Value	Rank	Value	Rank	Value	Rank	Value	Rank	Value	Rank
Tokyo	Japan	0.92	3	1.00	1	0.64	69	0.37	19	0.09	472	0.27	41	0.95	2
Singapore	Singapore	0.76	8	0.25	14	0.44	157	0.28	31	0.36	172	0.05	183	0.91	3
Seoul	Korea	0.74	9	0.40	6	0.31	193	0.53	8	0.16	363	0.07	150	0.63	10
Hong Kong	China	0.74	10	0.33	7	0.39	181	0.24	47	0.28	239	0.05	177	0.90	5
Yokohama	Japan	0.68	21	0.20	17	0.44	160	0.36	22	0.15	387	0.41	16	0.10	168
Osaka	Japan	0.68	24	0.32	8	0.50	126	0.14	117	0.07	499	0.31	34	0.32	36
Shanghai	China	0.64	37	0.26	11	0.14	251	0.04	258	0.57	70	0.09	122	0.72	8
Taipei	China	0.63	38	0.11	42	0.33	190	0.21	60	0.11	443	0.18	75	0.52	12
Sydney	**Australia**	**0.62**	**46**	**0.30**	**10**	**0.56**	**97**	**0.15**	**108**	**0.13**	**414**	**0.01**	**281**	**0.50**	**13**
Nagoya	Japan	0.61	49	0.19	19	0.69	45	0.47	10	0.08	490	0.17	79	0.03	373
Beijing	China	0.59	59	0.20	16	0.10	287	0.01	375	0.56	71	0.08	130	0.79	6
Kawasaki	Japan	0.59	61	0.07	67	0.43	163	0.40	15	0.09	473	0.41	15	0.04	336
Sagamihara	Japan	0.58	70	0.04	149	0.45	148	0.35	23	0.16	364	0.32	31	0.04	319
Shenzhen	China	0.58	71	0.15	25	0.14	252	0.06	223	0.74	21	0.15	85	0.15	112
Chiba	Japan	0.56	82	0.05	100	0.47	134	0.16	95	0.09	476	0.37	23	0.10	165
Saitama	Japan	0.56	84	0.06	84	0.42	166	0.23	53	0.11	440	0.39	20	0.04	323
Kyoto	Japan	0.56	86	0.09	49	0.53	113	0.09	171	0.10	450	0.29	40	0.10	151
Melbourne	**Australia**	**0.55**	**91**	**0.25**	**13**	**0.54**	**110**	**0.03**	**307**	**0.23**	**283**	**0.02**	**237**	**0.28**	**49**
Macau	China	0.55	93	0.02	236	0.36	187	0.54	7	0.56	72	0.00	343	0.09	193
Brisbane	**Australia**	**0.51**	**136**	**0.12**	**35**	**0.51**	**121**	**0.07**	**199**	**0.17**	**352**	**0.01**	**260**	**0.17**	**92**
Canberra	**Australia**	**0.44**	**229**	**0.03**	**205**	**0.67**	**53**	**0.03**	**295**	**0.18**	**338**	**0.01**	**292**	**0.09**	**186**
Hobart	**Australia**	**0.43**	**238**	**0.02**	**293**	**0.67**	**52**	**0.03**	**305**	**0.23**	**281**	**0.01**	**244**	**0.06**	**270**
Adelaide	**Australia**	**0.43**	**243**	**0.06**	**80**	**0.44**	**162**	**0.03**	**297**	**0.12**	**430**	**0.01**	**257**	**0.10**	**158**

Source: Peter Karl Kresl and Ni Pengfei, *Global Urban Competitive Report 2009–2010, Innovation: Sustainable Urban Competitiveness*, Chinese Academy of Social Sciences, Beijing, 2010.

in the Asia-Pacific region, relegating Sydney to middling status in the region. Of course if this is true of Sydney, it is even more so for Australia's other cities.

The city competitiveness sources indicated that Australia's cities do not compare favourably with the world's leading cities, or with the leading cities in the Asia-Pacific region. Only Sydney and Melbourne are in the upper tier on some measures. Cities tend to manage flows of goods, services, finance, and people on a local, national, regional, and global basis. If global cities are not just a result of dynamic national economies, but a major contributor, then Australia would appear to be disadvantaged versus many other countries.

City Costs

Costs are clearly linked with competitiveness. Two leading sources of costs in cities around the world are UBS and Mercer Consulting. UBS also estimates domestic purchasing power using prices as well as incomes.

Sydney ranked 7th out of 73 cities in the UBS 2011 Price Index[12] (Excluding Rent) and 7th in the 2011 Price Index (Including Rent), indicating that Sydney has some of the highest prices in the world. Within the Asia-Pacific region, Sydney was the second-most-expensive city after Tokyo. Sydney ranked 2nd in the world and 1st in the Asia-Pacific region in UBS's Domestic Purchasing Power Index using Net Hourly Pay and 5th globally and 1st in the Asia-Pacific using Net Annual Income. The result indicates that while prices in Sydney are high, so are incomes. While this might be good news for Sydney residents, it actually represents a double whammy for companies seeking to locate internationally mobile activities. Not only will their other costs be high, the wages they have to pay will be high as well.

According to Mercer's 2011 Worldwide Cost of Living Index,[13] Sydney ranked as the 14th-most-expensive city in the world in 2011 (out of 214), while Melbourne ranked 21st, Perth 30th, Brisbane 31st, Canberra 34th, and Adelaide 46th, so Australian cities were viewed as somewhat lower in relative costs in the Mercer ranking than the UBS ranking.

The results indicate that both Sydney and Australia in general are less affordable than nearly all other major cities in Asia-Pacific economies. These results should be viewed in light of the relatively poor performance of Australia's cities in city competitiveness. This means that major Australian cities are not likely to be considered for internationally mobile corporate activities that can be put into other cities in Asia. When we note that Singapore and Hong Kong are considered more competitive than Australia (or Australian cities), have even greater economic freedom, are quite user-friendly, and are much closer to rapidly growing Asian markets, one wonders how important any Australian city will be in Asia-Pacific or global activities. In any case, a high-cost, low-competitiveness result for Australia's cities does not bode well for their roles as drivers of Australia's economy.

Human Development and Quality of Living

The principal goal of competitiveness programs and economic development initiatives around the world is to provide a high and rising standard of living for the local population. In this vein, the United Nations Development Program's Human

Development Index and Mercer Consulting's Quality of Living Index try to capture features related to standard of living that go beyond the economic aggregates.

Australia ranked 2nd out of 192 economies in the Human Development Index[14] in 2011 (see Table 2.9). It ranked ahead of 13 of the 14 comparison countries and all 13 other Asia-Pacific countries. In the sub-indices, Australia ranked 4th in Life Expectancy at Birth, 9th in Mean Years of Schooling, 1st in Expected Years of Schooling, and 18th in Gross National Income (GNI) per Capita.

In Mercer's Quality of Living Index[15] Sydney ranked 11th out of 221 cities globally in 2011. Melbourne ranked 18th, Perth 21st, Canberra 26th, Adelaide 30th, and Brisbane 37th. Among Asia-Pacific cities, Sydney ranked only behind Auckland. Melbourne and Perth were behind Wellington, but ahead of Singapore (25th). Canberra, Adelaide, and Brisbane ranked ahead of Tokyo (46th), Osaka (57th), Hong Kong (70th), Seoul (80th), Taipei (85th), Shanghai (95th), Beijing (109th), and Bangkok (121st), among others. According to the Quality of Living Index, the quality of living in Sydney and Melbourne is comparable to that of most of the top Western European and North American cities in the sample.

Australia has performed consistently well in both the United Nations Development Program's Human Development Index and Mercer Consulting's Quality of Living Index over time. This implies that Australia is delivering a quality of life to its population that is superior in some senses to its economic performance. The extent to which this can be turned into an advantage in industries that are driven by mobile professionals, particularly for Asia-Pacific business, and therefore can improve Australia's competitiveness, remains to be seen.

Corruption and Corporate Governance

Economies with otherwise favourable conditions are unlikely to perform well if they are subject to corruption, or poor corporate governance, or both. Transparency International and GMI Ratings provide indices related to corruption and corporate governance respectively.

Transparency International provides a Corruption Perceptions Index covering a wide range of countries. Australia ranked 8th out of 183 countries in the 2011 index.[16] It was behind 6 of the 14 comparison countries and only 2 of the 13 Asia-Pacific economies (see Table 2.10). To the extent that transparency either allows domestic companies to grow and prosper, or makes the country attractive to domestic and foreign investors, Australia should be in a very good position vis-à-vis the rest of the region and the rest of the world.

Australia ranked 6th (out of 38) in the 2010 GMI Ratings Global Corporate Governance Country Ranking,[17] behind the United Kingdom (1st), Canada (2nd), Ireland (3rd), the United States (4th), and New Zealand (5th), but ahead of all other countries in the sample (see Table 2.11). Among the Asia-Pacific economies, Australia ranked behind New Zealand, and ahead of all other countries in the region.

Australia's performance in the Corruption Perceptions Index and the GMI Global Corporate Governance Country Ranking makes it clear that Australia is more transparent and less corrupt, and has better corporate governance than most other places in the world, though not necessarily the OECD countries in the comparison set. In any case, Australia is close enough to the world leaders and far enough ahead of regional competitors that its position in these features should be viewed as an advantage.

TABLE 2.9   UNDP Human Development Index and Sub-Indices, Selected Economies, 2011

Economies	Human Development Index		Life Expectancy at Birth		Mean Years of Schooling		Expected Years of Schooling		Gross National Income (GNI) per capita		Non-Income Human Development Index		GNI per Capita Rank Minus HDI Rank
	Value	Rank	Years	Rank	Years	Rank	Years	Rank	PPP 2005$	Rank	Value	Rank	
Australia and Comparison Countries													
Norway	0.943	1	81.1	11	12.6	1	17.3	6	47,557	7	0.975	3	6
Australia	**0.929**	**2**	**81.9**	**4**	**12.0**	**9**	**18.0**	**1**	**34,431**	**18**	**0.979**	**1**	**16**
Netherlands	0.910	3	80.7	16	11.6	13	16.8	10	36,402	12	0.944	6	9
United States	0.910	4	78.5	35	12.4	3	16.0	20	43,017	10	0.931	14	6
New Zealand	0.908	5	80.7	16	12.5	2	18.0	1	23,737	35	0.978	2	30
Canada	0.908	6	81.0	13	12.1	6	16.0	20	35,166	16	0.944	6	10
Ireland	0.908	7	80.6	18	11.6	13	18.0	1	29,322	26	0.959	4	19
Sweden	0.904	10	81.4	9	11.7	12	15.7	26	35,837	14	0.936	12	4
Switzerland	0.903	11	82.3	3	11.0	23	15.6	29	39,924	11	0.926	15	0
Denmark	0.895	16	78.8	34	11.4	20	16.9	7	34,347	19	0.926	15	3
Israel	0.888	17	81.6	7	11.9	11	15.5	31	25,849	31	0.939	11	14
Finland	0.882	22	80.0	22	10.3	38	16.8	10	32,438	22	0.911	22	0
Chile	0.805	44	79.1	32	9.7	56	14.7	41	13,329	58	0.862	33	14
Argentina	0.797	45	75.9	51	9.3	63	15.8	25	14,527	54	0.843	41	9
Brazil	0.718	84	73.5	82	7.2	112	13.8	58	10,162	77	0.748	92	−7
Australia and Asia-Pacific Economies													
Australia	**0.929**	**2**	**81.9**	**4**	**12.0**	**9**	**18.0**	**1**	**34,431**	**18**	**0.979**	**1**	**16**
New Zealand	0.908	5	80.7	16	12.5	2	18.0	1	23,737	35	0.978	2	30
Japan	0.901	12	83.4	1	11.6	13	15.1	36	32,295	23	0.940	9	11
Hong Kong	0.898	13	82.8	2	10.0	46	15.7	26	44,805	9	0.910	23	−4
Korea	0.897	15	80.6	18	11.6	13	16.9	7	28,230	27	0.945	5	12
Singapore	0.866	26	81.1	11	8.8	74	14.4	48	52,569	4	0.851	40	−22
Malaysia	0.761	61	74.2	70	9.5	59	12.6	92	13,685	56	0.790	66	−5
China	0.687	101	73.5	82	7.5	104	11.6	118	7,476	94	0.725	106	−7
Thailand	0.682	103	74.1	73	6.6	122	12.3	98	7,694	89	0.714	112	−14
Philippines	0.644	112	68.7	122	8.9	71	11.9	110	3,478	123	0.725	106	11
Indonesia	0.617	124	69.4	114	5.8	132	13.2	77	3,716	122	0.674	121	−2
Vietnam	0.593	128	75.2	57	5.5	138	10.4	143	2,805	136	0.662	126	8
India	0.547	134	65.4	136	4.4	152	10.3	145	3,468	124	0.568	139	−10
Taiwan	N/A	N/A	N/A	N/A	N/A	N/A	N/A	N/A	N/A	N/A	N/A	N/A	N/A

Source: 2011 Human Development Report, United Nations Development Programme.

TABLE 2.10   Transparency International Corruption Perceptions Index, Selected Economies, 2008–2011

Economies	2011 Value	2011 Rank	2010 Value	2010 Rank	2009 Value	2009 Rank	2008 Value	2008 Rank
Australia and Comparison Countries								
New Zealand	9.5	1	9.3	1	9.4	1	9.3	1
Denmark	9.4	2	9.3	1	9.3	2	9.3	1
Finland	9.4	2	9.2	4	8.9	6	9.0	5
Sweden	9.3	4	9.2	4	9.2	3	9.3	1
Norway	9.0	6	8.6	10	8.6	11	7.9	14
Netherlands	8.9	7	8.8	7	8.9	6	8.9	7
Australia	**8.8**	**8**	**8.7**	**8**	**8.7**	**8**	**8.7**	**9**
Switzerland	8.8	8	8.7	8	9.0	5	9.0	5
Canada	8.7	10	8.9	6	8.7	8	8.7	9
Ireland	7.5	19	8.0	14	8.0	14	7.7	16
Chile	7.2	22	7.2	21	6.7	25	6.9	23
United States	7.1	24	7.1	22	7.5	19	7.3	18
Israel	5.8	36	6.1	30	6.1	32	6.0	33
Brazil	3.8	73	3.7	69	3.7	75	3.5	80
Argentina	3.0	100	2.9	105	2.9	106	2.9	109
Australia and Asia-Pacific Economies								
New Zealand	9.5	1	9.3	1	9.4	1	9.3	1
Singapore	9.2	5	9.3	1	9.2	3	9.2	4
Australia	**8.8**	**8**	**8.7**	**8**	**8.7**	**8**	**8.7**	**9**
Hong Kong	8.4	12	8.4	13	8.2	12	8.1	12
Japan	8.0	14	7.8	17	7.7	17	7.3	18
Taiwan	6.1	32	5.8	33	5.6	37	5.7	39
Korea	5.4	43	5.4	39	5.5	39	5.6	40
Malaysia	4.3	60	4.4	56	4.5	56	5.1	47
China	3.6	75	3.5	78	3.6	79	3.6	72
Thailand	3.4	80	3.5	78	3.4	84	3.5	80
India	3.1	95	3.3	87	3.4	84	3.4	85
Indonesia	3.0	100	2.8	110	2.8	111	2.6	126
Vietnam	2.9	112	2.7	116	2.7	120	2.7	121
Philippines	2.6	129	2.4	134	2.4	139	2.3	141

TABLE 2.11   GMI Ratings Corporate Governance Ranking, Selected Economies, 2010

Economies	Rank	Number of Companies	Average Overall Rating
Australia and Comparison Countries			
Canada	2	132	7.36
Ireland	3	19	7.21
United States	4	1,761	7.16
New Zealand	5	10	6.70
Australia	**6**	**194**	**6.65**
Netherlands	7	30	6.45
Finland	8	28	6.38
Sweden	10	40	5.88
Switzerland	11	51	5.86
Norway	16	26	4.90
Denmark	18	24	4.79
Brazil	29	67	3.91
Israel	32	17	3.79
Chile	38	15	2.13
Australia and Asia-Pacific Economies			
New Zealand	5	10	6.70
Australia	**6**	**194**	**6.65**
Singapore	17	52	4.82
India	20	56	4.54
Malaysia	23	28	4.21
Thailand	24	15	4.20
Hong Kong	26	72	4.06
Korea	28	88	3.93
Taiwan	31	78	3.84
China	34	91	3.37
Japan	35	392	3.30
Indonesia	36	21	3.14

Notes:
1. Thirty-eight economies were included in this ranking.
2. Argentina, the Philippines, and Vietnam are not included in the ranking.
Source: GovernanceMetrics International, September 27, 2010.

International Perspectives on Australia's Competitiveness

There are many conclusions that can be drawn from the international assessments of Australia's competitiveness. However, we first must note that the different sources summarised in this chapter are not value neutral. In order to generate the aggregate indices the authors of these sources have to make decisions about what to include and exclude and how to weight the different features. The sources examined in this report all have a model of competitiveness, or doing business, or economic freedom, or the knowledge economy in mind. These must be understood if one is to make sense of the aggregate indices.

We also note that, by their nature the various measures and indices cannot take into account idiosyncrasies of individual economies. Thus, economies that are outliers, and Australia is an outlier in many dimensions, must be careful in using the aggregate indices for strategy or policy purposes. Another feature of the various measures and indices is that they tend not to take globalisation or linkages with other economies into account. Small economies linked to larger economies, as in Europe, but also Hong Kong and Singapore, are actually more competitive than the various indices would indicate because they can readily draw upon markets and resources from neighbouring economies. On the other hand, Australia, being relatively distant from most major markets, is in reality overrated in terms of its competitiveness because it is not able to draw upon the markets or resources of neighbouring economies to nearly the same extent.

All of these lead us to conclude that when it comes to understanding the competitiveness of individual economies, in this case Australia, the best approach is to take several sources, break them down to their components, understand what each tells us about Australia, and build a view of Australia's competitiveness from the bottom up. This is the approach we have taken in this chapter.

The Appropriate Benchmarks

In many countries, new competitiveness rankings and ratings are digested, and soon there are calls to action that usually start with an assessment of where the nation is farthest behind the world's leaders followed by calls for public and private investment to close the gaps. We suggest it is more useful to think of comparisons with similar nations or cities, or those just slightly ahead in terms of their development. We also suggest that it is useful to think of comparisons with countries that are direct competitors, potential markets, or both. Comparisons with countries that are slightly ahead can provide insights into a sequenced approach to improve competitiveness, while comparisons with competitors and potential markets can provide insights that help in meeting international competition. This is why in this chapter we compare Australia to a group consisting mostly of OECD nations from which Australia can learn, and a group of other Asia-Pacific economies where differences and complementarities might mean sales opportunities or potential collaboration for Australia.

The comparisons with other OECD and leading Latin American economies show that Australia tends to rank near the middle (IMD) or near the bottom (WEF) of the OECD comparison countries in overall competitiveness, with better than average positions in government policy, financial system, institutions, education, and health, and lower than average positions in innovation, technological capabilities, business sophistication, infrastructure, and resilience of the economy. Australia ranks in the bottom half of the OECD set in ease of doing business, with a high grade for ease of starting a business and getting credit, but with quite poor grades for anything having to do with regulation, taxation, and investor protection. Australia ranks well in measures of the knowledge economy, but behind nearly all of the OECD countries in the comparison set, scoring well in education and literacy; middling in regulatory quality, rule of law, and some measures of innovation; and relatively poorly in barriers to internationalisation, brain drain, and business sophistication. Australia is viewed as a world leader in economic freedom, with open markets and strong rule of law, but with government spending, taxation, and international linkages being disadvantages. Australia is a world leader in quality of life, with the world's highest Non-Income Human Development Index, and significantly lower performance in per capita income. Australia ranks slightly below the average of the OECD comparison countries in freedom from corruption and corporate governance, but is close enough to the leaders that this is not a disadvantage.

The comparison with Asia-Pacific economies is informative. Australia performs better on most measures than most of the economies of the region, and is a standout in ease of doing business, economic freedom, and a number of other features. This should mean that Australia has advantages selling advanced goods and services to the other economies of the region. However, we note that Hong Kong and Singapore rank higher than Australia in many features, as do Japan and Korea, and that several Asian economies rank higher than Australia in business sophistication and innovation. These facts, plus the fact that Australia is not physically or psychically tied as closely to many of the emerging markets of Asia, might mean that it will be more difficult for Australian companies to penetrate the region than we might hope. Whether Australia can use the fact that its economy is more advanced than most Asian economies to sell into those markets becomes a question that needs to be explored, rather than taken as a foregone conclusion.

Basic, Advanced, and New Age Competitiveness Features

Australia does very well in a number of features that have traditionally been viewed as *basic* to competitiveness. These include fairness, lack of corruption, transparency, openness, business flexibility, ease of creating companies, education, and resource endowments. However, Australia ranks further down the list in any measure of market size and in terms of its location with respect to many of the world's leading markets. Then there is a whole set of features in which Australia ranks above most nations, but below the majority of OECD nations, such as infrastructure, tax system, fiscal environment, and regulation. The conclusion one reaches is that Australia does relatively well in the basic competitiveness features, with some distinct caveats.

It is in what we might call more *advanced* competitiveness features that Australia falls short of other OECD nations and some Asia-Pacific economies. These include business sophistication, density of supply chains, co-operation among companies, science-based innovation, international and domestic connectivity, entrepreneurship, managers with international experience, brain drain, and the potential for relocation of a range of companies and activities. We note that these are precisely the features we might expect will separate the world leaders from the fast followers and also-rans in the future. Australia's position in these features places it in the upper tier globally, but towards the bottom of that upper tier. These features should be high priorities for investigation and potentially some shifts in direction on the part of the Australian Government and Australian companies.

Then there are what we might call *new age* competitiveness features like sustainability, quality of life, and the living environment, in which Australia has a very strong position. The question is whether Australia and its companies can leverage advantages in these features into competitive advantages in specific industries and specific markets, or whether shortcomings in other features will prevent it from doing so. Understanding this dynamic will also be crucial to projecting Australia's future competitiveness.

Areas for Analysis and Action

The results highlighted in this chapter suggest a number of areas for further analysis and potential action to improve Australia's competitiveness. These include:

- **Using competitiveness league tables with caution.** We suggest that while the overall league tables are interesting, it is preferable to use the underlying data to identify Australia's advantages and disadvantages and to build up a picture more useful for policy and strategy from multiple sources.
- **Benchmarking against other OECD nations.** Benchmarking against other OECD nations, as Australia tends to do, is important, because it shows what is possible. It also shows the positions of some countries that are key competitors and markets for Australian industries and companies.
- **Benchmarking against other Asia-Pacific economies.** Benchmarking against other Asia-Pacific economies is also important, in part to show Australia and Australians that the assumption that Australia is more advanced economically than the rest of the region is not necessarily true, and in part because the region is growing rapidly and any asymmetries between Australia and the rest of the region represent potential opportunities for market development and for collaboration.
- **Improving infrastructure to world-class standards.** A country distant from major markets with a dispersed population cannot afford to be less than world-class in infrastructure. This includes transportation, communication, utilities, and technological infrastructure. If Australia is not ahead in infrastructure, it is behind. The results reported in this chapter suggest it is far from being ahead.
- **Assessing workforce requirements, capabilities, and relations.** Australia does well in measures of participation in education and some aspects of labour markets, but tends to fall short of the world leaders in management, scientific, and international capabilities, and workforce relations are rated not as favourable as those in many comparison countries. These issues will have to be addressed if Australia is to improve its overall position. So too will the incentives in place for talented individuals and dynamic companies to stay in Australia as opposed to migrating to other locations.
- **Reviewing government expenditures, the tax system, and the regulatory burden.** The results reported in this chapter indicate that the level of government expenditures, level of taxation, complexity of taxation, and the regulatory burden on industry are potential disadvantages for Australia versus several of the other OECD countries and, perhaps more importantly, versus the United States and several other Asia-Pacific economies. This last point is important because the US and Asia-Pacific economies have the potential to draw entrepreneurs and dynamic companies away from Australia. Again given the size of the Australian

market and its relative remoteness, if Australia is not ahead on government expenditures, taxation, and regulation, it is behind.

- **Improving business sophistication and international outlook.** Improving business sophistication in Australia, including developing better strategic management, denser supply chains, and more interactive clusters of related firms and industries, would appear to be essential for Australia to improve its overall competitiveness. Greater sophistication needs to be coupled with a more international outlook if Australia and Australian business are to improve their international positions, particularly in knowledge-intensive manufactures and services. Greater knowledge of and interaction with Asia would appear to be particularly important.

- **Taking advantage of globalisation and advances in information and communication technology (ICT).** Globalisation and developments in ICT have made it easier for companies from remote economies to sell globally. The evidence suggests that Australia and Australian companies on average are not doing so to the extent one would hope.

- **Working to create more vibrant, internationally oriented business cities.** Much of the interaction in the global economy takes place through dynamic cities that act as links between the local environment and the rest of the world. At present, Australia's cities do not appear to be performing the same international or global roles as the leading cities in the Asia-Pacific region. The lack of competitive cities is a shortcoming that needs to be addressed if Australia and Australian industries are to improve their global position.

The sources cited in this chapter would indicate that each of these themes is crucial to Australia's competitiveness. Many of these themes will reappear in subsequent chapters.

Pushing the Envelope

All of the sources summarised in this chapter provide information on aspects of Australia's competitiveness. Taking the sources apart and recombining the information and data they provide has allowed us to identify numerous areas for further analysis and action.

This makes all of the sources extremely useful, but it leaves some gaps when it comes to understanding Australia's competitiveness. The first is that international business competition takes place between firms and within industries. Firms sell goods and services to specific customers in specific markets against specific competitors. While comparisons of competitiveness features at the national level are useful, actual business outcomes are affected by how the features influence competitiveness versus specific competitors in specific industries. In order to extend our understanding of Australia's competitiveness, we need an approach that allows us to identify the relevant competitors to Australian businesses on an industry-by-industry basis and to assess how Australia stacks up against these economies in the features that influence competitiveness in those industries.

This is crucial because we can compare Australia with other OECD countries in various competitiveness features, but if those countries are not Australia's actual competitors, the comparison will be of limited practical use. It is also crucial because the overall position of the nation in a particular feature may differ from its position at the level of the industry and firm. For example, a nation's infrastructure may be only average in aggregate, but if the nation has invested in specialised infrastructure, to transport minerals and metals for example, infrastructure might be an advantage for the related sectors. A nation's innovation system may be only average in aggregate, but if it has invested heavily in innovation for the agribusiness sector, the innovation system might be an advantage in that sector. Average tendencies might not be good indicators of what affects competition and competitiveness on the ground.

A related point is that sources described in this chapter rate nations on a range of features, but nowhere do they assess the importance of those features to competitiveness for the industries and firms that are found in a nation. In any industry, some features will be more important, some less important. The same will be true for the industries that are the main drivers of growth and development in any economy. Without an understanding of which competitiveness features are important in the industries actually present in an economy, policy makers and strategists that might try to base policy on the results in the various sources will be flying blind. This is true of Australia as it is of any other nation.

This discussion suggests that in order to assess Australia's competitiveness in more detail, we need an approach that allows us to identify specific competitor or benchmark nations, evaluate the importance of competitiveness features, and assess how Australia compares with competitors and benchmarks on an industry-by-industry basis. Such an approach is the subject of the next chapter.

Notes

1. The data described were the latest available at the time of access in early 2012.
2. *The Global Competitiveness Report 2011–2012*, World Economic Forum, Switzerland, 2011.
3. IMD, *World Competitiveness Yearbook 2011*, Lausanne, 2011.
4. Chinese Academy of Social Sciences, *Blue Book of National Competitiveness*, Beijing, 2010.
5. Michael J. Enright, "Regional Clusters: What We Know and What We Should Know," in *Innovation Clusters and Interregional Competition*, ed. Johannes Bröcker, Dirk Dohse, and Rüdiger Soltwedel, 99–129 (Berlin: Springer, 2003). Clusters refer to groups of firms in the same or related industries that might benefit from interaction and whose performance is interdependent.
6. The International Finance Corporation, *Doing Business in 2012: Doing Business in a More Transparent World*, Washington, 2012.
7. The World Bank, *KI and KEI Indexes*, Washington, 2012.
8. The Heritage Foundation and the Wall Street Journal, *2012 Index of Economic Freedom*, Washington, 2012.
9. James Gwartney, Robert Lawson, and Joshua Hall, *Economic Freedom of the World: 2011 Annual Report*, Fraser Institute, 2011.
10. Globalization and World Cities Research Network.
11. Peter Karl Kresl and Ni Pengfei, *Global Urban Competitiveness Report 2009–2010*, Chinese Academy of Social Sciences, Beijing, 2010.
12. UBS, *Prices and Earnings 2011*, Zurich, 2011.
13. Mercer, *Worldwide Cost of Living 2011*, New York, 2011.

14. United Nations Development Program, *Human Development Report 2011*, New York, 2011.

15. Mercer, *Quality of Living Report 2011*, New York, 2011.

16. Transparency International, *Global Corruption Report 2011*, Berlin, 2011.

17. GMI Ratings, *Global Corporate Governance Country Ranking 2010*, New York, 2010.

CHAPTER 3

Competitiveness in the Real World

As we noted in Chapter 2, there has been an enormous increase in interest in international competitiveness in over the last two decades. While the sources cited in that chapter provide useful information, they do not allow us to understand the drivers that influence international competition within specific industries to serve specific customers against specific competitors. Nor do the traditional sources allow us to understand the relative importance of different competitiveness drivers in the industries that matter to a nation. Failure to recognise this simple fact means that most nations do not know what signals aggregate competitiveness studies are sending them. As a result, they often focus their efforts on where the gaps appear to be the largest rather than on where the gaps are most important.

What we need is a method to examine the competitiveness of a nation and its industries that allows us to distinguish not just between positive and negative drivers of an economy, but also the important and unimportant drivers. Such a method should allow us to be guided by the insights of business people engaged in real-world competition rather than by the theorising of far-off analysts. Such a method should be based on a model that allows us to prioritise the key drivers for analysis and action. In short, we need a method to address competitiveness in the real world.

A Model of Competitiveness: The Five Level Competitiveness Framework™

The model employed in the present investigation is the Five Level Competitiveness Framework™* (or FLCF™) developed by one of us (Michael Enright) based on more than 25 years working on competitiveness issues in more than 25 countries on 5 continents. It divides the drivers of competitiveness into five levels: the firm level, the micro or industry level, the meso or cluster level, the macro or national level, and the meta or supranational level (see Figure 3.1).

Meta- or supranational-level drivers are those beyond the control of a single country. These drivers include the nature of global markets, the actions of foreign governments, the actions of foreign companies, and the actions of multilateral orga-nisations and agencies (such as the World Trade Organization, the European Union,

---

*The Five Level Competitiveness Framework and FLCF are trademarks of Michael J. Enright and Enright, Scott & Associates.

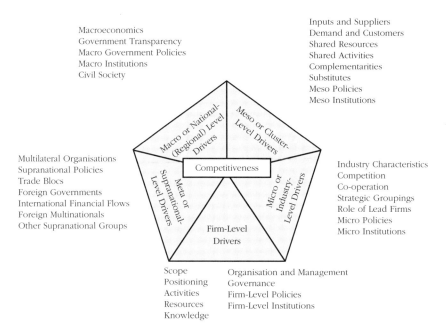

Macroeconomics
Government Transparency
Macro Government Policies
Macro Institutions
Civil Society

Inputs and Suppliers
Demand and Customers
Shared Resources
Shared Activities
Complementarities
Substitutes
Meso Policies
Meso Institutions

Multilateral Organisations
Supranational Policies
Trade Blocs
Foreign Governments
International Financial Flows
Foreign Multinationals
Other Supranational Groups

Industry Characteristics
Competition
Co-operation
Strategic Groupings
Role of Lead Firms
Micro Policies
Micro Institutions

Scope
Positioning
Activities
Resources
Knowledge

Organisation and Management
Governance
Firm-Level Policies
Firm-Level Institutions

FIGURE 3.1 **Drivers of Competitiveness, the Five Level Competitiveness Framework™**
Source. Michael J. Enright.

the World Bank, and others—all of which influence the international business land-scape). The supranational-level drivers set the context within which individual countries operate, and they affect industries from a nation in positive or negative ways.

Macro or national-level drivers operate across an entire nation or region within a nation. They include macroeconomic features, government efficiency, government policy, national-level institutions, and civil society. Macroeconomic features, such as interest rates, exchange rates, inflation rates, and overall macroeconomic conditions, influence the operations of firms and industries within a nation. Government transparency and policy across a range of policy areas influence the business landscape within a country. National-level institutions provide part of the operating environment as well as inputs for companies and industries. Civil society provides the social fabric of a nation. All of these are important to competitiveness.

Meso or cluster-level drivers surround individual industries, providing their business ecosystem. These include inputs involving geographic location (and what that implies for climate, geology, geography, and natural resources), infrastructure (transportation, communication, and IT, for example), financial inputs (financial institutions, availability of finance, and cost of finance), access to business-relevant information, access to input goods and services, access to capital equipment, workforce skills and staff costs, property or land-related costs, and other costs. They include downstream and demand-side drivers, such as the size and sophistication of the local market for an industry's products or services. They include benefits from spill-overs from industries that might share common technologies, capabilities, markets, or distribution systems. They also include specific cluster organisations that seek to foster competitiveness by facilitating interaction and co-operation among firms. Advantages in any of these drivers can often be turned into advantages for industries and firms in the marketplace.

Micro or industry-level drivers operate at the level of groups of firms providing products or services that are alike or nearly alike in form and function. They include competition that can be a spur to improvement, co-operation that allows for pooled resources and shared benefits, and lead firms that open doors and set trends for others.

Finally, a nation will not be competitive if its firms are not capable of meeting and beating international competition in particular industries and industry segments. Firm-level drivers include company strategies (the scope, positioning, activities, resources, and knowledge of the firm), management and organisation, and their capabilities.

While most of the drivers, with the exception of those at the supranational level, are found in other models of competitiveness, the key is how they are organised. Most competitiveness models assume that competitiveness is additive, that one can add up pluses and minuses in a critical mass of determinants to understand competitiveness. The unfortunate fact is that this is not the way that it works in the real world of competition among real firms in real industries to serve real customers.

Decades of experience has taught us that competitiveness is not additive. A nation does not become competitive because it has a critical mass of positive features, or because the features in a competitiveness index add up to a positive result. Advantages at the supranational level, national level, cluster level, and industry level will not lead to success without having firms that can leverage those advantages in the marketplace. Similarly, excellent firms will not succeed if cluster or national conditions are too unfavourable, or if protectionism prevents them from selling in international markets. The very clear conclusion is that when it comes to the real world, no single level can create competitiveness, but any single level can destroy competitiveness.

This is why so many countries that have "done the right things" in terms of government policy, for example, find that they may have hit the wall in terms of improving overall competitiveness and prosperity. To understand this phenomenon, we should start from the meta or supranational level and realise that each level of drivers defines the opportunity set for the next level down. This is represented graphically in Figure 3.2, in which opportunities can be blocked by uncompetitive drivers at any

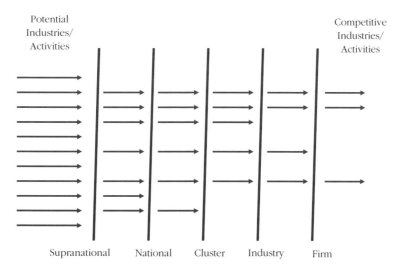

FIGURE 3.2 **The Levels of Competitiveness as Potential Enablers or Disablers**
Source: Michael J. Enright.

single level. The FLCF™ framework is a tool that allows for an efficient assessment of which level or levels are supporting competitiveness and which are blocking competitiveness, and how difficult the task of improving competitiveness can be. If there are advantages in several levels, but disadvantages in one, then competitiveness might be significantly improved by identifying and removing constraints in the troublesome level. If there are problems at several levels, more substantial efforts will generally be required to drill through the obstacles and succeed.[1]

Surveying Competitiveness: The Importance-Performance Competitiveness Analysis™ Approach

After decades of addressing how to best capture industry-level competitiveness, Professor Enright and Enright, Scott & Associates developed a proprietary approach to analysing competitiveness that incorporates the FLCF™ in an *Importance-Performance* setting that allows for a direct measurement of the drivers that influence the industry's competitiveness and the nation's performance in those drivers. The resulting Importance-Performance Competitiveness Analysis™ (or IPCA™)[†] approach employs industry-by-industry survey data to identify the main competitors for a country in a given industry, the most important drivers of competitiveness in the industry, and the performance of the nation relative to the competitors in those drivers. This process allows for a much sharper understanding of an economy's competitiveness and much clearer conclusions with respect to policies and strategies that might enhance competitiveness than previous methods.

IPCA™ tables and charts can be readily created to provide a quick view of the competitiveness situation for a given industry by highlighting the important drivers of competitiveness in the industry and the nation's position relative to competitors or comparators. One of the most important uses of such charts is to identify focal points for government policy and company strategy to improve competitiveness and performance. This can be done by breaking the charts into their four quadrants as shown in Figure 3.3 and understanding what each means for policy and strategy.

The drivers in the High Importance/Strong Performance quadrant are drivers that are important and in which the country has strong advantages. These should be leveraged, enhanced, extended, safeguarded, marketed, and promoted. The drivers in the High Importance/Poor Performance quadrant have disadvantages that are important and that if possible should be fixed, overcome, mitigated, or made less important, perhaps by innovating them out of the game, outsourcing, or through policy or strategy changes. The drivers in the Low Importance/Strong Performance quadrant have advantages that do not contribute much to competitiveness. Nations and their firms can try to make these more important by innovating them into a more prominent position, try to shift the game so that they are called upon to a greater extent, or link the advantages to other drivers to extend them. Drivers in the Low Importance/Poor Performance quadrant should have their status monitored, should be the subject of contingency plans in case they become more important, and

[†]Importance-Performance Competitiveness Analysis and IPCA are trademarks of Michael J. Enright and Enright, Scott & Associates.

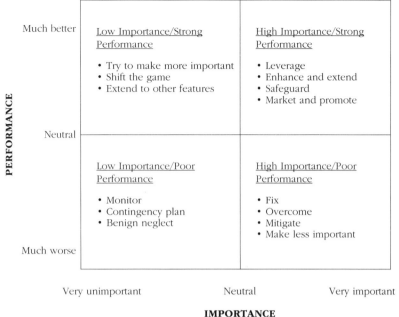

FIGURE 3.3 **Using the IPCA™ Charts for Policy and Strategy**
Source: Michael J. Enright.

otherwise should be treated with benign neglect because addressing other drivers is more important. In our experience, using the IPCA™ framework greatly enhances the ability of nations to understand where they should focus attention and increases the efficiency of policy initiatives to improve competitiveness because it allows one to understand what is important and what is not.

The Australian Competitiveness Survey

The survey used in the present study was based on earlier work by Michael Enright in which managers and business professionals from around the world were surveyed to determine which drivers were most important in determining competitiveness in their respective industries. Over 150 items were included in the initial survey. Based on the responses, some items were combined (as they were conceptually and statistically similar), and others were dropped as being either unimportant or too ambiguous. The resulting set of drivers was built into a second survey instrument that Professor Enright and Enright, Scott & Associates have used in various competitiveness studies around the world.

In the present study, this second survey was augmented based on characteristics of Australia's economy and suggestions by Australian-based managers and professionals. It was piloted with 200 Australian business professionals and modified to improve clarity. The result was a survey that focused on the 76 drivers of competitiveness found in Table 3.1.[2]

The survey asked the respondents to first identify the industry in which they participate according to the Australian and New Zealand Standard Industrial Classification (ANZSIC) 2006 classification. The survey then asked respondents to identify the top three foreign economies that are the most direct competitors to the Australian

TABLE 3.1   Drivers of Competitiveness

Position in the FLCF™	Competitiveness Driver
Firm-Level Drivers	
Strategies, Organisation, Leadership	Level of Technology Employed The Quality of Strategies Used by Firms from the Country
Resources, Knowledge	Knowledge of Regional (Asian) Markets Capabilities of Companies from the Country
Micro or Industry-Level Drivers	
Competition	Tough Local Competition
Co-operation	Co-operation among Local Firms
Lead Firms	Leading Companies that Drive Industry Competitiveness
Associations and Institutions	Industry Associations or Organisations
Micropolicies	Sector Targeting, Government Support Policies Government Incentives for Your Industry
Meso or Cluster-Level Drivers	
Inputs and Supply	Geographic Location Transportation Infrastructure Communication Infrastructure IT and Internet Infrastructure Other Infrastructure Access to Appropriate Staff Skills Access to Local Managerial Skills Access to Multilingual Staff Scientific and Technical Skills Strength of the Local Banking System Access to Debt Finance Cost of Debt Finance Availability of Equity Capital Availability of Venture Capital Access to Business Relevant Information Access to Input Goods and Services Access to Capital Equipment Staff Costs Other Employment Costs Property or Land-Related Costs Other Costs
Customers and Demand	Size of Local Market Demand Sophistication of Local Demand Future Local Market Potential
Related Industries	Support from Related Industries Clustering of Firms in Your Industry

Position in the FLCF™	Competitiveness Driver
Macro or National-Level Drivers	
Macroeconomic Conditions	Overall Local Economic Conditions Macroeconomic Stability Interest Rates Exchange Rates Inflation Rates
Government Transparency	Government Freedom from Corruption Transparency of Government
Government Policy	Overall Government Policy Strength of Government Finances Competition Policy Planning Laws Policies to Encourage Research and Development Environmental Policies Foreign Trade and Tariff Policy Foreign Investment Policy Industrial and Workplace Relations, Labour Laws Science and Technology Policy Tax Regime (Overall) Corporate Tax Rate Personal Income Tax Rate Payroll Taxes Carbon Tax/Emission Trading Scheme Other Taxes and Charges
Institutions	Regulatory and Legal Framework Community Institutions Quality of Education & Training Institutions Quality of Research Institutions and Organisations Social Stability Quality of Life Environmental Consciousness Attitudes of Community toward Business Attitudes of Community toward Entrepreneurship Attitudes of Community toward Innovation Political Stability
Meta or Supranational-Level Drivers	
Regional Markets	Access to the China Market Access to Other Regional (Asia-Pacific) Markets
Foreign Governments	Foreign Government Support for Foreign Companies
Foreign Companies	Presence of International Companies in the Country Strategies of International Companies
Multilateral Agencies	Activities of Multilateral Agencies (e.g., UN, World Bank, International Monetary Fund, World Trade Organization)

Source: Michael J. Enright.

industry if the industry is subject to international competition and the three most appropriate comparator countries for Australia if the industry is not subject to international competition.

The respondents were then asked to rate the importance of the 76 drivers to the competitiveness of their industry globally on a 1 (Unimportant) to 7 (Very important) scale. Then the respondents were asked to rate Australia's position versus the relevant competitors or comparators for the same 76 drivers, on a 1 (Much worse than competitors) to 7 (Much better than competitors) scale. Respondents were then asked about the overall competitiveness of the Australian industry and about their own organisations.

E-mail and survey panels were used to elicit responses across a broad range of the Australian business community. In addition, we also surveyed Australian and non-Australian managers and professionals living abroad about their perspectives on Australia's competitiveness in their industries. A total of 5,947 responses were received. This allowed us to analyse the information down to the four-digit level for many ANZSIC industry classifications. The profile of the organisations represented by survey respondents can be found in Tables 3.2, 3.3, and 3.4, which provide breakdowns of responses by one-digit ANZSIC 2006 industries (Table 3.2), by employment of the organisation of respondents (Table 3.3), and by sales of the organisation of respondents (Table 3.4). In each case, we see a broad range of responses from across the Australian economy.

TABLE 3.2   Survey Reponses by Industry, N = 5,947

Code	1-Digit ANZSIC 2006 Industries	Responses	Percent
A0	Agriculture, Forestry, and Fishing	141	2%
B0	Mining	134	2%
C0	Manufacturing	530	9%
D0	Electricity, Gas, Water, and Waste Services	99	2%
E0	Construction	365	6%
F0	Wholesale Trade	231	4%
G0	Retail Trade	456	8%
H0	Accommodation and Food Services	166	3%
I0	Transport, Postal, and Warehousing	227	4%
J0	Information Media and Telecommunications	359	6%
K0	Financial and Insurance Services	636	11%
L0	Rental, Hiring, and Real Estate Services	104	2%
M0	Professional, Scientific, and Technical Services	641	11%
N0	Administrative and Support Services	209	4%
O0	Public Administration and Safety	168	3%
P0	Education and Training	334	6%
Q0	Health Care and Social Assistance	309	5%
R0	Arts and Recreation Services	117	2%
S0	Other Services	721	12%

Sources: Michael J. Enright and CPA Australia.

TABLE 3.3   Number of Responses by Employment of Company, N = 4,520

Number of Employees in Australia	Number of Responses	Percent
1 to 5	1,256	28%
6 to 9	273	6%
10 to 19	382	8%
20 to 49	395	9%
50 to 99	342	8%
100 to 999	831	18%
1,000 to 4,999	485	11%
5,000 or above	556	12%

Sources: Michael J. Enright and CPA Australia.

TABLE 3.4   Number of Responses by Sales of Company, N = 4,554

Company's Total Worldwide Sales	Number of Responses	Percent
Up to AUD100k	957	21%
AUD100k+ to AUD500k	510	11%
AUD500k+ to AUD1 million	322	7%
AUD1 million+ to AUD5 million	515	11%
AUD5 million+ to AUD10 million	351	8%
AUD10 million+ to AUD50 million	467	10%
AUD50 million+ to AUD100 million	261	6%
AUD100 million+ to AUD500 million	289	6%
AUD500 million+ to AUD1 billion	221	5%
AUD1 billion+ AUD5 billion	249	5%
AUD5 billion+ to AUD10 billion	116	3%
More than AUD10 billion	296	6%

Sources: Michael J. Enright and CPA Australia.

Industry Examples

Before reporting the results of the survey across the entire Australian economy, it is useful to describe the results in a set of specific industries familiar to most Australians. We have selected the iron ore, wine and other alcoholic beverages, motor vehicle, and higher education industries to illustrate what we can learn from the survey and the frameworks on which it is based.

THE INDUSTRIES   We first provide a general description of the four industries and their performance before reporting the survey results.

Iron Ore Mining (B080100)   Australia has the second-largest iron ore reserves in the world.[3] Australia's Economic Demonstrated Resources (EDR) of iron ore is 18.6 gigatonnes (Gt), which is about 11 percent of world EDR. Australia is the largest iron ore producer in the world. Its production was 434.3 million tonnes in 2010, compared to 185.9 million tonnes in 2001. Roughly 99 percent of Australia's EDR is located in Western Australia, with about 89 percent occurring in the Pilbara district. Around 97 percent of Australia's iron ore output comes from Western Australia, with limited amounts coming from Tasmania, South Australia, and New South Wales.

As shown in Table 3.5, Australia's iron ore mining industry had revenues of AUD 51.4 billion in 2010–2011, compared to AUD 7.6 billion in 2002–2003. This figure is expected to reach AUD 69.9 billion in 2016–2017. In 2010–2011, Australia exported AUD 47.3 billion in iron ore, accounting for 92.1 percent of total industry revenue. Australia also imports a small amount of iron ore, mainly from India.[4] With export value equal to around 170 times import value, it is safe to say that the Australian industry is highly competitive in international terms.

In 2010, five markets accounted for virtually all of Australia's iron ore exports: China (68.1 percent), Japan (18.8 percent), Korea (9.6 percent), Taiwan (3.0 percent), and the EU (0.4 percent) (see Table 3.6). We note the preponderance of Asia among Australia's markets. Most of Australia's iron ore is sold under contract to steel manufacturers overseas. Contract prices were historically negotiated with major customers on an annual basis, but since 1 April 2010 the prices have been set quarterly. Average export prices increased nearly seven-fold from 2004 to the end of 2011 (see Figure 3.4), but then fell on the order of 47 percent from February 2011 to the end of September 2012.[5]

The number of enterprises in the iron ore mining industry in Australia has been quite stable, with 19 enterprises each year from 2001–2002 to 2010–2011, and projections this will increase to 21 by 2016–2017. The industry is highly concentrated,

TABLE 3.5   Industry Revenue and Trade in AUD, 2002–2017

	Revenue (AUD million)	Exports (AUD million)	Imports (AUD million)
2002–2003	7,609	7,602	162
2003–2004	8,153	7,265	193
2004–2005	10,621	10,761	192
2005–2006	16,139	16,234	280
2006–2007	19,575	18,648	406
2007–2008	24,787	23,551	357
2008–2009	41,359	37,625	296
2009–2010	37,039	37,929	285
2010–2011	51,384	47,318	496
2011–2012	56,618	52,446	469
2012–2013	53,953	50,329	408
2013–2014	62,382	58,462	442
2014–2015	71,090	66,999	461
2015–2016	64,202	60,796	384
2016–2017	69,886	66,448	389

Note:
Figures for years beginning with 2011–2012 are projections.
Source: IBISWorld, Iron Ore Industry in Australia 2011.

TABLE 3.6   Australia's Iron Ore Exports by Destination, 2001–2010

	China		Taiwan		EU		Japan		Korea		Other	
	kt	%	kt	%	kt	%	kt	%	kt	%	kt	%
2001	38,023	24.3	9,904	6.3	15,867	10.1	66,830	42.6	23,810	15.2	2,284	1.5
2002	44,018	26.5	9,347	5.6	14,450	8.7	70,492	42.5	25,120	15.1	2,443	1.5
2003	59,971	31.9	8,664	4.6	16,051	8.6	75,353	40.1	26,000	13.9	1,669	0.9
2004	80,109	38.2	9,095	4.3	12,563	6.0	80,314	38.3	26,472	12.6	1,276	0.6
2005	117,537	49.1	9,144	3.8	10,914	4.6	76,200	31.8	24,978	10.4	540	0.2
2006	128,568	52.0	9,448	3.8	8,575	3.5	73,834	29.8	26,261	10.6	743	0.3
2007	142,436	53.4	9,997	3.7	6,218	2.3	77,310	29.0	30,503	11.4	421	0.2
2008	183,304	59.2	9,993	3.2	5,886	1.9	76,847	24.8	33,296	10.8	147	0.0
2009	266,779	73.5	8,332	2.3	671	0.2	59,071	16.3	27,869	7.7	199	0.1
2010	273,779	68.1	12,031	3.0	1,748	0.4	75,588	18.8	38,557	9.6	152	0.0

Note:
1 kt = 1,000 tonnes.
Source: Australian Bureau of Agricultural and Resource Economics and Sciences, *Australian Mineral Statistics*, June 2011.

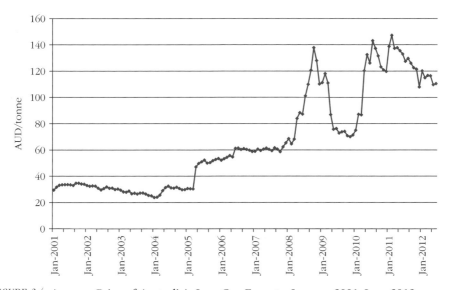

FIGURE 3.4 **Average Price of Australia's Iron Ore Exports, January 2001–June 2012**
Sources: Australian Bureau of Agricultural and Resource Economics and Sciences, *Australian Mineral Statistics*, June 2011; Bureau of Resources and Energy Economics, *Resources and Energy Quarterly*, 2012.

with mines operated by Rio Tinto and BHP Billiton accounting for 78 percent of the revenue of the Australian industry in 2010, Fortescue Metals another 10 percent, and others for 12 percent. In 2010–2011, there were 9,319 persons employed in the industry in Australia, and total wages were AUD 1,581 million. Employment is projected to increase to 13,725 and wages to AUD 2,749 million by 2016–2017.[6]

We note that the iron ore mining industry in Australia has substantial foreign ownership, though the precise amount is a matter of dispute, and as a result there is disagreement over how much of the industry's profits stay in Australia as opposed to being remitted overseas. All analyses appear to indicate that the vast majority of industry profits in recent years have been reinvested in the industry in Australia.[7]

Wine and Other Alcoholic Beverage Manufacturing (C121400)   Wine and Other Alcoholic Beverage Manufacturing refers to units mainly engaged in manufacturing or blending wine, fermented cider or wine vinegar, or alcoholic beverages not elsewhere classified. It does not include beer manufacturing, spirit manufacturing, growing grapes, or just bottling wine and other alcoholic beverages.[8]

Domestic sales of Australia-manufactured wine were 463.9 million litres and AUD 2.33 billion in the year 2010–2011, while exports reached 746.6 million litres valued at AUD 1.99 billion.[9] The United Kingdom was Australia's largest wine export market by volume, while the United States was the largest by value (see Table 3.7). Australia imported 67.0 million litres of wine worth AUD 0.47 billion in the same year. In terms

TABLE 3.7   Australia Exports and Imports of Wine by Countries, 2010–2011

	Exports				Imports			
Country	Quantity (thousand litres)	% of Total	Value (AUD million)	% of Total	Quantity (thousand litres)	% of Total	Value (AUD million)	% of Total
Belgium	17,355	2.3	29.7	1.5	1	0.0	0.02	0.0
Canada	54,524	7.3	205.6	10.3	27	0.0	0.2	0.0
China (excluding Taiwan)	50,305	6.7	177.7	8.9	83	0.1	0.3	0.1
France	1,096	0.1	3.8	0.2	8,620	12.9	146.2	31.0
Germany	19,378	2.6	36.4	1.8	587	0.9	3.2	0.7
India	713	0.1	3.3	0.2	–	–	–	–
Italy	258	0.0	0.7	0.0	6,662	9.9	32.1	6.8
Netherlands	40,683	5.4	67.7	3.4	34	0.1	1.2	0.3
New Zealand	23,987	3.2	73.8	3.7	45,443	67.8	262.4	55.7
Spain	594	0.1	1.5	0.1	1,302	1.9	7.8	1.7
United Kingdom	254,423	34.1	464.6	23.4	67	0.1	1.1	0.2
United States	192,737	25.8	524.2	26.4	142	0.2	1.3	0.3
Others	90,502	12.1	400.2	20.1	4,014	6.0	15.0	3.2
Total	746,555	100.0	1,989.2	100.0	66,982	100.0	470.7	100.0

Note:

Totals may not add up due to rounding.

Source: Australian Bureau of Statistics, Australian Wine and Grape Industry 2010–2011, February 2012.

TABLE 3.8   Number of Australian Wine Producers by State, 2007–2012

Year	NSW/ACT	VIC	QLD	SA	NT	WA	TAS	Total
2007	432	628	109	563	1	332	81	2,146
2008	452	687	107	607	0	356	90	2,299
2009	443	698	106	620	0	361	92	2,320
2010	467	724	111	648	0	372	98	2,420
2011	475	738	111	667	0	382	104	2,477
2012	474	750	107	695	0	394	112	2,532
CAGR 2007–2012 (%)	1.9	3.6	−0.4	4.3	—	3.5	6.7	3.4

Sources: Project analysis; Australian Bureau of Statistics, *Australian Wine and Grape Industry 2010–2011*, February 2012; Winebiz Pty Ltd website.

of both import volume and value, New Zealand was Australia's largest source of imports, accounting for more than two-thirds of import volume and over half of import value. With export value more than four times import value, again it is safe to say that Australia is highly competitive in international terms in this industry.

It was estimated that total employment in the sector as covered in the ANZSIC code was 30,978 in 2010, of which wine manufacturing dominated in employment at 13,526 (43.7 percent), followed by wine growing 9,178 (29.6 percent), wine retail 6,429 (20.8 percent), and wine wholesale 1,845 (6.0 percent).[10] In 2012, there were over 2,500 wine manufacturing companies in Australia.[11] Victoria has had the largest number among Australia's states, followed by South Australia, and New South Wales/ Australian Capital Territory (see Table 3.8).

Of the 20 largest wine companies ranked by Winebiz in litres of wine produced in 2011, 7 had their head office/winery in Victoria, 7 in New South Wales, and 6 in South Australia. In total number of litres of wine produced in 2011, the top 5 companies were Accolade Wines, Treasury Wine Estate, Casella Wines, Premium Wine Brands, and Australian Vintage. Other top 10 producers were Kingston Estate Wines, De Bortoli Wines, Warburn Estate, McWilliam's Wines, and Qualia Wine Services. In sales of branded wine, the top 5 companies were the same as that of wine produced, while other top 10 branded wine sellers were De Bortoli Wines, Warburn Estate, McWilliam's Wines, Littore Family Wines, and The Yalumba Wine Company. In vineyard area, the top 5 companies were Treasury Wine Estate, Australian Vintage, Littore Family Wines, Premium Wine Brands, and Accolade Wines. Other companies in the top 10 for largest vineyards were McWilliam's Wines, Brown Brothers Milawa, Warburn Estate, De Bortoli Wines, and The Yalumba Wine Company.[12]

Motor Vehicle Manufacturing (C231100)   Motor Vehicle Manufacturing refers to units mainly engaged in manufacturing motor vehicles or motor vehicle engines. It does not include converting motor vehicle bodies, manufacturing motor vehicle parts, motor cycles and transport equipment not elsewhere classified, off-highway trucks, forklift trucks, and repairing/maintaining motor vehicles.[13]

The total revenue of the Australian motor vehicle manufacturing industry in 2011– 2012 was estimated at AUD 10.56 billion, with industry value added of AUD 1.84 billion, indicating that the industry largely consists of assembly from imported

TABLE 3.9   Australia's Motor Vehicle Industry, Key Statistics, 2006–2007 to 2011–2012

Year	Revenue (AUD billion)	Industry Value Added (AUD billion)	Motor Vehicle Production
2006–2007	16.62	3.02	333,347
2007–2008	16.83	2.77	345,828
2008–2009	13.67	2.39	252,448
2009–2010	11.11	1.75	248,854
2010–2011	9.71	1.50	219,194
2011–2012	10.56	1.84	240,000

Note:
2011–2012 figures are estimates.
Source: IBISWorld, *Motor Vehicle Manufacturing in Australia*, January 2012.

TABLE 3.10   Australia's Automotive Trade by Export Destination and Import Origin, 2010

	Exports			Imports	
Region	Exports (AUD million)	Share (%)	Region	Imports (AUD million)	Share (%)
Middle East	1,571	43.7	Japan	10,045	34.2
New Zealand	480	13.3	EU25	6,078	20.7
NAFTA	338	9.4	ASEAN	4,731	16.1
ASEAN	212	5.9	NAFTA	3,678	12.5
Korea	191	5.3	Korea	2,589	8.8
EU25	175	4.9	China	937	3.2
China	137	3.8	South Africa	465	1.6
Japan	58	1.6	Taiwan	314	1.1
South Africa	48	1.3	South America	118	0.4
Rest of World	388	10.8	Rest of World	439	1.5
Total	3,598	100.0	Total	29,394	100.0

Sources: Australian Department of Foreign Affairs and Trade; Australian Department of Innovation, Industry, Science and Research, July 2011.

components. Despite growth in both revenue and value added in 2011–2012, both were still far below 2006–2007 levels (see Table 3.9).

Approximately 240,000 motor vehicles were produced in Australia in 2011–2012. In that year, domestic production accounted for only 34.9 percent of the value of local vehicle sales.[14] In 2010, Australia's motor vehicle exports were valued at AUD 3.6 billion and its imports at AUD 29.4 billion.[15] Australia's top motor vehicle export markets were the Middle East, New Zealand, and NAFTA countries, while the top import sources were Japan, the EU25, and ASEAN countries (see Table 3.10). With import values equalling more than 8 times export values, it is pretty safe to say that Australia is uncompetitive to very uncompetitive in the motor vehicle industry.

TABLE 3.11   Financial Performance of Toyota, Holden, and Ford in Australia (automotive manufacturing segment), 2006–2010

Year	Revenue (AUD billion)			Operating Profit (AUD million)		
	Toyota	Holden	Ford	Toyota	Holden	Ford
2006	4.21	5.21	3.45	228.8	(130.0)	(78.9)
2007	5.70	4.21	2.72	205.6	9.8	(86.0)
2008	4.70	4.10	2.06	84.7	(31.2)	(205.4)
2009	3.94	2.88	1.97	81.9	(92.3)	37.7
2010	4.23	2.21	1.74	57.0	78.0	36.0

Note:
Year refers to the beginning of financial year. The financial year for Toyota Motor Corporation Australia Limited ends in March, while those for GM Holden Limited and Ford Motor Company of Australia Limited end in December.
Source: IBISWorld, *Motor Vehicle Manufacturing in Australia*, January 2012.

As of January 2012, employment in Australia's motor vehicle manufacturing industry was estimated at 16,289. There were roughly 71 companies with 100 establishments, down from 82 and 120 respectively in 2006–2007. Victoria accounted for 34.9 percent of establishments, followed by New South Wales (25.5 percent), Queensland (19.8 percent), Western Australia (10.4 percent), South Australia (6.6 percent), Tasmania (1.9 percent), and the Northern Territory (0.9 percent). The leading automotive companies in Australia were Toyota Motor Corporation (45.3 percent market share), GM Holden Limited (23.7 percent), and Ford Motor Company of Australia Limited (18.7 percent). Mitsubishi Motors Australia Limited had been one of the major motor vehicle manufacturers in Australia, but exited from manufacturing in the country in 2008.[16] All three major companies had seen poor or declining performance from 2006 to 2010 (see Table 3.11).

The sector has received significant government assistance in recent years. For example, Toyota was granted AUD 35 million and AUD 15 million by the Federal Government and the Victorian Government respectively in 2010 to support the production of hybrid Camrys in Australia. Holden received AUD 149 million and AUD 30 million grants from the Federal Government and the South Australian Government respectively to support the manufacturing of the Holden Cruze in Australia in 2010. Ford received AUD 42 million from the Federal Government to support part of its AUD 230 million investment to develop the EcoBoost engine for its Falcon model.[17] Total support for the sector was expected to be on the order of AUD 4.5 billion to 5 billion from 2006 to 2015.

Higher Education (P810200)   Higher education is not just a social service in Australia, it is an export industry as well. By 2012, there were 37 public universities, two private universities, two branches of overseas universities, and around 170 non-university providers of higher education (most of which are private enterprises) in Australia.[18] In 2011, 335,273 of the 1,192,657 students studying at higher education institutions in Australia were from overseas.

The Australian Government is the primary funding source for public higher education in the country. Public education funding and policy are administered

TABLE 3.12   Major Indicators of Higher Education Sector in Australia by State

State	*Number of Staff, 2011	Number of All Students, 2010	Number of Overseas Students, 2010	*Revenue (million AUD), 2010
New South Wales	31,633	372,988	78,756	6,293
Victoria	27,549	308,041	110,332	6,160
Queensland	20,854	215,636	55,355	3,807
Western Australia	11,317	126,748	39,621	2,208
South Australia	8,188	82,122	24,304	1,565
Tasmania	2,663	23,452	5,622	476
Northern Territory	927	8,219	575	265
Australian Capital Territory	5,021	32,634	7,983	1,155
Multi-State	1,372	22,817	3,780	230
Total	109,524	1,192,657	335,273	22,158

*Includes public universities only.

Source: Australian Department of Education, Employment and Workforce Relations.

through the Department of Education, Employment and Workplace Relations (DEEWR). Public universities are eligible for a full spectrum of government funding, while other providers have access to limited government funding. In 2010, the revenue of all public universities in Australia was AUD 22,158 million, 60 percent of which was from Government Funding. The remaining 40 percent came from Fees and Charges (23.3 percent); Consultancy and Contracts (4.0 percent); Investment Income (3.7 percent); Upfront Student Contributions (2.4 percent); Royalties, Trademarks, and Licenses (0.4 percent); and Other Income (6.3 percent).

Table 3.12 shows that New South Wales and Victoria have the largest domestic and foreign student numbers (with more than a third of Victoria's students coming from overseas) among Australia's states. Table 3.13 shows that Society and Culture, Management and Commerce, Health, and Education are the most popular fields among domestic students, while Management and Commerce attracts more than 50 percent of the overseas students.

Education services make a significant contribution to Australia's exports, and higher education accounts for around 60 percent of education service exports from Australia. In 2010–2011, Australia's exports of higher education services were AUD 9,402 million, compared to AUD 2,528 million in 2000–2001 (see Table 3.14). The Chinese Mainland accounted for 27.2 percent of overseas students in Australia's higher education sector in 2010, followed by Malaysia (10.0 percent), Singapore (9.9 percent), India (6.4 percent), Hong Kong (6.0 percent), Vietnam (4.7 percent), Indonesia (3.6 percent), the United States (2.3 percent), South Korea (2.2 percent), and Saudi Arabia (1.7 percent).[19] Again we note the preponderance of Asian markets.

TABLE 3.13   Higher Education Students in Australia by Field of Education

Field of Education	All Students (%)	Domestic Students (%)	Overseas Students (%)
Natural and Physical Sciences	7.4	8.5	4.6
Information Technology	4.2	2.8	7.9
Engineering and Related Technologies	7.2	6.8	8.2
Architecture and Building	2.3	2.6	1.6
Agriculture, Environmental, and Related Studies	1.5	1.8	0.9
Health	13.8	16.3	7.2
Education	9.2	11.8	2.5
Management and Commerce	28.5	19.5	51.8
Society and Culture	21.6	27.0	7.6
Creative Arts	7.0	8.0	4.4
Food, Hospitality, and Personal Services	0.1	0.0	0.3
Mixed Field Programs	0.6	0.8	0.2
Non-Award courses	1.8	1.0	3.9
Total	100.0	100.0	100.0

Source: Australian Department of Education, Employment and Workforce Relations.

TABLE 3.14   Higher Education Exports from Australia

Financial Year	Higher Education Fees (AUD million)	Higher Education Related Service Exports (AUD million)	Total Exports of Higher Education (AUD million)	Higher Education Exports As a % of All Education Exports (%)
2000–2001	1,084	1,444	2,528	54%
2001–2002	1,387	1,879	3,266	57%
2002–2003	1,703	2,369	4,072	62%
2003–2004	2,099	2,962	5,061	66%
2004–2005	2,405	3,492	5,898	68%
2005–2006	2,596	3,927	6,524	68%
2006–2007	2,759	4,428	7,187	66%
2007–2008	2,892	5,204	8,096	60%
2008–2009	3,428	6,341	9,770	59%
2009–2010	3,691	6,723	10,414	58%
2010–2011	3,505	5,897	9,402	60%

Note:
Total export of education includes tuition fees and related travel services exports.
Source: Australian Bureau of Statistics.

TABLE 3.15   Top 10 Public Universities by Number of Overseas Students

University	State	Number of Overseas Students in 2010
RMIT University	Victoria	26,568
Monash University	Victoria	22,291
Curtin University of Technology	Western Australia	19,260
University of New South Wales	New South Wales	13,242
Macquarie University	New South Wales	12,944
University of Sydney	New South Wales	12,143
University of South Australia	South Australia	12,072
University of Melbourne	Victoria	11,893
Griffith University	Queensland	11,778
University of Wollongong	New South Wales	10,632

Source: Australian Department of Education, Employment and Workforce Relations.

In 2010, the 37 public universities accounted for 93 percent of higher education students and 91 percent of overseas students in Australia. Table 3.15 lists the top 10 public universities by number of overseas students. Several of these universities have featured prominently in global rankings. The *World University Rankings 2011–2012* by the (London) *Times*[20] ranked four Australian universities in its top 100. These were University of Melbourne (37th), Australian National University (38th), University of Sydney (58th), and University of Queensland (74th). The QS Intelligence Unit's *QS World University Rankings 2011*[21] ranked 8 Australian universities among the top 100; Australian National University (26th), University of Melbourne (31st), University of Sydney (38th), University of Queensland (48th), University of New South Wales (49th), Monash University (60th), University of Western Australia (73rd), and University of Adelaide (92nd).

SURVEY RESULTS FOR THE FOUR INDUSTRIES   This section describes the results of the competitiveness survey for the four industries. We first focus on markets and competitors, then on the Importance-Performance Competitiveness Analysis, and then on charts to organise the information.

Markets and Competitors   The vast majority of respondents in the iron ore, wine, and higher education industries work for Australia-headquartered companies, while the opposite is the case in motor vehicle manufacturing, corresponding to what is widely known about each of the four industries (see Table 3.16). The iron ore industry is the one most focused on international markets (not surprisingly) and the automotive industry most focused on the domestic market (also not surprisingly since much of the industry represents domestically focused branch plants of international companies). Over 90 percent of respondents in each of the four industries report that their industry faces international competition. Respondents from the iron ore industry rate their industry's competitiveness most highly on a 1 to 7 scale (with 1 = the Australian industry having much worse competitiveness than the industry in competitor countries, 7 = the Australian industry having much better competitiveness than the

TABLE 3.16   Respondent Profile and Overall Competitiveness, Four Selected Industries

	Iron Ore Mining (B080100)	Wine and Other Alcoholic Beverage Manufacturing (C121400)	Motor Vehicle Manufacturing (C231100)	Higher Education (P810200)
Australia HQ				
Yes	70%	86%	10%	82%
No	30%	14%	90%	18%
Main Market				
Domestic Market (75 Percent or More)	0%	38%	50%	25%
Both Domestic and International	31%	63%	50%	66%
International Market (75 Percent or More)	69%	0%	0%	9%
Subject to International Competition				
Yes	100%	100%	90%	92%
No	0%	0%	10%	8%
Overall Competitiveness (1 = much worse than competitors, 4 = neutral, 7 = much better than competitors)				
Compared to Main Competitor/ Benchmark Countries	5.50	4.29	3.30	4.48
Compared to at the Beginning of the Global Financial Crisis	5.40	4.43	3.60	4.12

Sources: Michael J. Enright and CPA Australia.

industry in competitor countries, and 4 = neutral or the Australian industry being comparable in competitiveness to the industry in competitor countries). Only respondents from the automotive industry, among the four industries profiled, rated the Australian industry as less competitive than major competitors.

Table 3.17 shows the leading competitor countries for the four Australian industries. The table was built up by assigning a score of 3 to the most-direct competitor indicated by a respondent, 2 for the second-most-direct competitor, and 1 for the third-most-direct competitor and then adding up the scores. The most important competitor countries for these industries are the major global suppliers for the most part. There are few surprises given the discussions of the industries above. Iceland and Finland appear not because they make wine, but because they produce products that fall into the "other alcoholic beverage" category. New Zealand and Taiwan appear as competitors in motor vehicles because the category does include some components. China and India appear as competitors in higher education because their

TABLE 3.17   Leading Competitor Countries, Four Selected Australian Industries

Rank	Iron Ore Mining (B080100)	Wine and Other Alcoholic Beverage Manufacturing (C121400)	Motor Vehicle Manufacturing (C231100)	Higher Education (P810200)
1	Brazil	Chile	Japan	United States
2	China	France	Germany	United Kingdom
3	Canada	United States	United States	China
4	Argentina	New Zealand	Korea	Canada
5	United States	United Kingdom	Thailand	Hong Kong
6	New Zealand	Argentina	China	Singapore
7	India	Italy	Sweden	Germany
8	United Kingdom	Iceland	United Kingdom	India
9	South Africa	Finland	France	New Zealand
10	Chile		New Zealand	Sweden
10	Germany		Taiwan	
10			Switzerland	

Sources: Michael J. Enright and CPA Australia.

domestic institutions compete with Australian institutions for students. In any case, it is clear that the survey has identified the countries known to be the leading competitors of the four Australian industries.

What is also interesting is the fact that the small and medium-sized OECD economies to which Australia is often compared are noticeable largely by their absence. New Zealand appears as a competitor in all four industries; Canada and Sweden in two; and Iceland, Finland, and Switzerland in one each. The relevant benchmarks from a competitiveness standpoint are often larger nations, and as we have already learned, the leading markets are often Asian nations. Thus, while it is informative to compare Australia against small and medium-sized OECD economies, from a competitiveness and market standpoint, in these specific industries, those comparisons are largely irrelevant.

Importance-Performance Competitiveness Analysis™   Table 3.18 reports the response means results for the importance of the competitiveness drivers across the four industries. All but one of the cells have values equal to or above neutral, indicating that all the drivers examined were considered important by the majority of respondents. The only cell that registers as unimportant is the size of the domestic market for the iron ore industry, an industry that exports more than 90 percent of its output. This suggests that all of the drivers listed are important and any policy or strategy approach that relies on less comprehensive information will be incomplete.

As expected, the importance of the drivers differs significantly from each other within industries and for a given driver across industries. The most consistently important drivers across the four industries are Exchange Rates, Knowledge of Asian Markets, Transportation Infrastructure, Access to Appropriate Staff Skills, Staff Costs, Regulatory and Legal Framework, Government Freedom from Corruption, Access to

TABLE 3.18 Importance of Competitiveness Drivers for Four Selected Industries (1 = very unimportant, 4 = neutral, 7 = very important)

Position in the FLCF	Label	Driver	Iron Ore Mining (B080100)	Wine and Other Alcoholic Beverage Manufacturing (C121400)	Motor Vehicle Manufacturing (C231100)	Higher Education (P810200)
Firm	15	Level of Technology Employed	5.20	5.86	**6.10**	5.71
Firm	33	Strategies Used by Firms from the Country	4.29	5.43	**6.20**	5.67
Firm	25	Knowledge of Asian Markets	**6.10**	**6.57**	**6.20**	5.46
Firm	34	Capabilities of Companies from the Country	4.86	5.29	**6.00**	5.47
Industry	31	Tough Local Competition	5.14	**6.00**	5.70	5.14
Industry	32	Co-operation among Local Firms	4.50	4.83	5.40	5.14
Industry	37	Leading Companies that Drive Competitiveness	5.57	4.86	**6.40**	5.40
Industry	38	Industry Associations or Organisations	5.14	4.71	5.70	5.33
Industry	57	Sector Targeting, Government Support Policies	5.70	5.67	**6.10**	5.37
Industry	58	Government Incentives for Your Industry	5.00	5.86	**6.10**	5.55
Cluster	1	Geographic Location	5.64	5.86	5.90	5.43
Cluster	2	Transportation Infrastructure	**6.18**	**6.29**	**6.40**	4.97
Cluster	3	Communication Infrastructure	5.36	5.57	5.70	5.82
Cluster	4	IT and Internet Infrastructure	5.18	5.57	**6.00**	5.81
Cluster	5	Other Infrastructure	5.64	5.00	5.40	5.08
Cluster	6	Access to Appropriate Staff Skills	**6.00**	**6.29**	**6.50**	5.92
Cluster	7	Access to Local Managerial Skills	5.18	**6.00**	**6.30**	5.37
Cluster	28	Access to Multilingual Staff	5.20	5.57	5.80	5.41
Cluster	8	Scientific and Technical Skills	5.00	5.67	**6.40**	5.71
Cluster	9	Strength of the Local Banking System	4.64	5.00	5.70	4.69
Cluster	10	Access to Debt Finance	4.82	5.40	5.60	4.46
Cluster	11	Cost of Debt Finance	5.10	5.71	**6.10**	4.67

(Continued)

TABLE 3.18 Continued

Position in the FLCF	Label	Driver	Iron Ore Mining (B080100)	Wine and Other Alcoholic Beverage Manufacturing (C121400)	Motor Vehicle Manufacturing (C231100)	Higher Education (P810200)
Cluster	12	Availability of Equity Capital	5.50	**6.00**	**6.00**	4.90
Cluster	13	Availability of Venture Capital	4.70	5.17	5.80	4.95
Cluster	14	Access to Business-Relevant Information	5.30	5.14	**6.00**	5.24
Cluster	16	Access to Input Goods and Services	5.20	5.83	**6.10**	5.17
Cluster	17	Access to Capital Equipment	**6.00**	5.25	**6.00**	5.19
Cluster	18	Staff Costs	5.36	**6.50**	**6.60**	5.72
Cluster	19	Other Employment Costs	5.45	5.83	**6.60**	5.60
Cluster	20	Property or Land-Related Costs	4.82	5.40	5.70	5.11
Cluster	21	Other Costs	5.00	5.40	**6.00**	5.25
Cluster	22	Size of Local Market Demand	3.80	5.83	**6.30**	5.52
Cluster	24	Sophistication of Local Demand	4.00	**6.29**	5.90	5.33
Cluster	23	Future Local Market Potential	4.20	**6.29**	**6.10**	5.65
Cluster	29	Support from Related Industries	5.60	5.86	**6.20**	5.26
Cluster	30	Clustering of Firms in Your Industry	4.22	5.17	5.60	4.87
National	39	Overall Local Economic Conditions	5.43	**6.29**	**6.30**	5.67
National	40	Macroeconomic Stability	5.14	**6.00**	**6.10**	5.52
National	41	Interest Rates	5.50	**6.43**	**6.10**	5.34
National	42	Exchange Rates	**6.25**	**6.50**	**6.56**	**6.06**
National	43	Inflation Rates	5.75	**6.14**	**6.00**	5.54
National	47	Government Freedom from Corruption	**6.13**	**6.14**	**6.33**	5.55
National	48	Transparency of Government	5.75	**6.00**	5.80	5.62
National	44	Carbon Tax/Emission Trading Scheme	5.50	5.86	**6.00**	4.32
National	45	Overall Government Policy	5.38	**6.00**	**6.50**	5.69
National	50	Strength of Government Finances	5.75	5.86	5.90	5.50
National	56	Competition Policy	5.30	5.71	**6.30**	5.03
National	60	Planning Laws	5.11	5.00	5.20	4.63

National	62	Policies to Encourage R&D	5.89	5.00	**6.40**	5.77
National	73	Environmental Policies	5.90	5.14	5.70	5.05
National	63	Foreign Trade and Tariff Policy	5.67	5.71	**6.60**	4.97
National	64	Foreign Investment Policy	5.89	4.86	5.89	4.64
National	59	Industrial and Workplace Relations/Labour Laws	5.89	5.71	**6.20**	5.52
National	61	Science and Technology Policy	5.38	5.00	5.70	5.41
National	51	Tax Regime (Overall)	5.20	5.86	5.70	5.25
National	52	Corporate Tax Rate	5.30	**6.00**	**6.10**	5.25
National	53	Personal Income Tax Rate	5.20	5.43	**6.00**	4.62
National	54	Payroll Taxes	4.90	5.57	5.80	5.11
National	55	Other Taxes and Charges	5.70	5.71	5.80	5.25
National	49	Regulatory and Legal Framework	**6.00**	**6.00**	**6.00**	5.17
National	67	Community Institutions	4.67	4.17	5.44	5.73
National	68	Quality of Education & Training Institutions	5.40	5.57	5.90	4.85
National	69	Quality of Research Institutions, Organisations	5.22	5.43	**6.10**	**6.22**
National	70	Social Stability	5.00	**6.00**	5.30	**6.06**
National	71	Quality of Life	5.10	**6.00**	5.60	5.71
National	72	Environmental Consciousness	5.70	5.57	5.70	5.57
National	74	Attitudes of Community toward Business	5.90	5.14	5.70	5.22
National	75	Attitudes of Community toward Entrepreneurship	4.78	4.57	5.50	5.31
National	76	Attitudes of Community toward Innovation	5.00	4.71	**6.10**	5.48
National	46	Political Stability	**6.13**	5.57	**6.00**	5.59
Supranational	65	Foreign Government Support for Their Companies	5.00	4.86	**6.10**	5.65
Supranational	26	Access to the China Market	**6.30**	**6.17**	**6.50**	4.82
Supranational	27	Access to Other Asia-Pacific Markets	5.50	**6.50**	**6.30**	5.54
Supranational	35	International Companies in the Country	5.29	4.29	**6.10**	5.49
Supranational	36	Strategies of International Companies	5.29	4.71	**6.30**	5.19
Supranational	66	Activities of Multilateral Agencies	4.50	4.00	5.56	5.37

Sources: Michael J. Enright and CPA Australia.

the China Market, and Access to Other Asia-Pacific Markets.[22] Infrastructure, workforce skills and costs, government policy, and the importance of Asia to Australia's future are themes we will return to later in this book. The table shows that our method allows us to home in on the details of what is important to competitiveness in individual industries.

Table 3.19 reports mean responses on Australia's performance in the competitiveness drivers on a 1 to 7 scale (with 1 = Australia being much worse than competitor countries, 7 = Australia being much better than competitor countries, and 4 = neutral or Australia being comparable to competitor countries).

The responses indicate that Australia's performance varies between drivers within industries and for a given driver across industries. Australia is rated highly across the four industries in Quality of Life, Social Stability, Environmental Policy, and Environmental Consciousness. Carbon Tax/Emissions Trading Regime, Staff Costs, and Other Employment Costs were viewed as negatives across the industries. Of course there are interesting stories within industries as well. Respondents in the iron ore industry see most drivers as moderate to strong advantages for the Australian industry, with only Size of Local Market, Sophistication of Local Market, Potential of Local Market, Carbon Tax/Emissions Trading Scheme, and Overall Government Policy being viewed as negative. Respondents in the automotive industry indicated that their industry has numerous disadvantages, with Staff Costs and Other Employment Costs being the most problematic. Respondents in the higher education industry indicate that Australia performs better than competitor countries in every competitiveness driver, either indicating that the Australian industry is extremely competitive, a view that its export performance would support, or that participants in Australia's higher education sector (and the authors are academics ourselves) are divorced from reality, or both.

Again, we see that the survey methodology allows us to understand Australia's performance in individual competitiveness drivers versus the relevant competitors on an industry-by-industry basis.

The IPCA™ Charts   There is clearly a great deal of information in Tables 3.18 and 3.19. A useful way of organising the information is to plot the importance and performance ratings on Importance-Performance Competitiveness Analysis™ (IPCA™) charts. Charts for the four industries are found in Figures 3.5, 3.6, 3.7, and 3.8. We have left the charts in their raw form. They can be exploded out for more detailed analysis, or Tables 3.18 and 3.19 can be used to isolate the ratings for each driver.

In Figure 3.5 for the iron ore industry, we see that nearly all drivers are rated as above neutral in importance, and most drivers are advantages for Australia. Access to the China Market (26), Knowledge of Asian Markets (25), and Access to other Asia-Pacific Markets (27) are all seen as highly important, and Australia is seen to have a substantial advantage versus competitors. This makes a great deal of sense, since China is the leading importer of seaborne iron ore, and Japan, Korea, and Taiwan are also major markets; and Australia is better situated from a geographic and logistics standpoint to serve Asian markets than its leading competitor, Brazil. It is also interesting to note that none of the competitiveness sources described in Chapter 2 takes such regional markets into account in their assessments of competitiveness. Clearly this is a major shortcoming that our method can remedy.

The respondents rate Social Stability (70) and Quality of Life (71) as important and Australia's performance much better than competitors. Environmental Consciousness

TABLE 3.19 Performance in Competitiveness Drivers for Four Selected Industries (1 = much worse than competitors/comparators, 4 = neutral, 7 = much better than competitors/comparators)

Position in the FLCF	Label	Driver	Iron Ore Mining (B080100)	Wine and Other Alcoholic Beverage Manufacturing (C121400)	Motor Vehicle Manufacturing (C231100)	Higher Education (P810200)
Firm	15	Level of Technology Employed	**5.13**	**5.43**	4.60	4.84
Firm	33	Strategies Used by Firms from the Country	4.29	**5.00**	4.00	4.50
Firm	25	Knowledge of Asian Markets	**5.18**	**5.71**	*3.80*	4.66
Firm	34	Capabilities of Companies from the Country	4.43	4.57	4.60	4.55
Industry	31	Tough Local Competition	4.29	4.67	4.00	4.76
Industry	32	Co-operation among Local Firms	4.43	4.17	*3.70*	4.48
Industry	37	Leading Companies that Drive Competitiveness	4.71	4.14	4.30	4.42
Industry	38	Industry Associations or Organisations	4.29	4.57	4.40	4.65
Industry	57	Sector Targeting, Government Support Policies	4.22	4.17	*3.30*	4.58
Industry	58	Government Incentives for Your Industry	4.00	4.00	*3.40*	4.54
Cluster	1	Geographic Location	**5.60**	4.43	*3.50*	4.45
Cluster	2	Transportation Infrastructure	**5.10**	4.71	4.60	4.23
Cluster	3	Communication Infrastructure	4.60	4.71	4.30	4.63
Cluster	4	IT and Internet Infrastructure	4.30	4.57	4.30	4.58
Cluster	5	Other Infrastructure	4.70	4.50	4.10	4.62
Cluster	6	Access to Appropriate Staff Skills	**5.30**	**5.29**	4.10	4.81
Cluster	7	Access to Local Managerial Skills	**5.00**	**5.00**	4.30	4.80
Cluster	28	Access to Multilingual Staff	4.64	4.33	*3.80*	4.66
Cluster	8	Scientific and Technical Skills	**5.00**	**5.57**	4.60	4.97
Cluster	9	Strength of the Local Banking System	**5.40**	**5.14**	4.50	**5.18**
Cluster	10	Access to Debt Finance	4.56	**5.17**	4.50	4.79
Cluster	11	Cost of Debt Finance	**5.00**	4.29	*3.30*	4.65
Cluster	12	Availability of Equity Capital	4.50	4.29	*3.60*	4.64
Cluster	13	Availability of Venture Capital	4.50	4.43	*3.60*	4.52

(Continued)

TABLE 3.19 Continued

Position in the FLCF	Label	Driver	Iron Ore Mining (B080100)	Wine and Other Alcoholic Beverage Manufacturing (C121400)	Motor Vehicle Manufacturing (C231100)	Higher Education (P810200)
Cluster	14	Access to Business-Relevant Information	**5.13**	**5.00**	4.70	4.83
Cluster	16	Access to Input Goods and Services	**5.13**	4.40	4.00	4.85
Cluster	17	Access to Capital Equipment	4.56	4.60	4.20	4.70
Cluster	18	Staff Costs	4.00	3.33	2.80	4.44
Cluster	19	Other Employment Costs	4.11	3.83	2.56	4.31
Cluster	20	Property or Land-Related Costs	4.44	3.40	3.22	4.57
Cluster	21	Other Costs	**5.00**	3.20	3.60	4.47
Cluster	22	Size of Local Market Demand	3.55	**5.43**	3.00	4.16
Cluster	24	Sophistication of Local Demand	3.64	**5.14**	4.00	4.42
Cluster	23	Future Local Market Potential	3.73	**5.00**	3.30	4.32
Cluster	29	Support from Related Industries	4.18	**5.14**	3.70	4.35
Cluster	30	Clustering of Firms in Your Industry	4.30	**5.00**	3.90	4.56
National	39	Overall Local Economic Conditions	4.71	**5.43**	4.40	4.97
National	40	Macroeconomic Stability	4.57	**5.17**	4.80	**5.10**
National	41	Interest Rates	4.44	3.57	3.60	4.60
National	42	Exchange Rates	4.11	4.00	3.22	4.28
National	43	Inflation Rates	4.11	3.86	3.70	4.58
National	47	Government Freedom from Corruption	4.44	4.57	**5.20**	**5.20**
National	48	Transparency of Government	4.22	4.43	4.90	**5.20**
National	44	Carbon Tax/Emission-Trading Scheme	2.67	3.43	3.00	4.15
National	45	Overall Government Policy	3.56	3.86	3.50	4.90
National	50	Strength of Government Finances	4.89	**5.00**	4.40	**5.20**
National	56	Competition Policy	4.33	4.29	3.40	4.55
National	60	Planning Laws	4.56	4.00	4.40	4.72
National	62	Policies to Encourage R&D	**5.20**	4.57	4.40	4.53
National	73	Environmental Policies	**5.33**	**5.00**	**5.20**	**5.12**

National	63	Foreign Trade and Tariff Policy	4.70	3.71	3.40	4.43
National	64	Foreign Investment Policy	4.70	3.86	4.00	4.43
National	59	Industrial and Workplace Relations/Labour Laws	3.70	4.57	3.90	4.39
National	61	Science and Technology Policy	**5.33**	4.43	4.60	4.52
National	51	Tax Regime (Overall)	4.00	4.14	4.20	4.42
National	52	Corporate Tax Rate	4.56	4.00	3.89	4.29
National	53	Personal Income Tax Rate	4.00	4.00	3.78	4.30
National	54	Payroll Taxes	4.00	4.14	3.78	4.11
National	55	Other Taxes and Charges	4.22	4.14	3.78	4.19
National	49	Regulatory and Legal Framework	4.67	**5.00**	4.60	**5.12**
National	67	Community Institutions	4.10	4.00	4.40	4.61
National	68	Quality of Education & Training Institutions	4.67	**5.00**	4.80	**5.15**
National	69	Quality of Research Institutions, Organisations	4.88	**5.00**	4.70	**5.10**
National	70	Social Stability	**5.56**	**5.86**	**5.00**	**5.46**
National	71	Quality of Life	**5.78**	**5.71**	**5.44**	**5.67**
National	72	Environmental Consciousness	**5.44**	**5.43**	4.90	**5.23**
National	74	Attitudes of Community toward Business	**5.11**	4.29	4.50	4.90
National	75	Attitudes of Community toward Entrepreneurship	4.67	3.71	4.50	4.76
National	76	Attitudes of Community toward Innovation	4.30	4.43	4.40	4.83
National	46	Political Stability	4.44	4.43	4.50	**5.05**
Supranational	65	Foreign Government Support for Their Companies	4.22	4.14	3.90	4.47
Supranational	26	Access to the China Market	**5.45**	**5.57**	3.20	4.78
Supranational	27	Access to Other Asia-Pacific Markets	4.73	**5.17**	3.40	4.85
Supranational	35	International Companies in the Country	4.86	4.43	4.50	4.26
Supranational	36	Strategies of International Companies	4.86	4.17	3.50	4.43
Supranational	66	Activities of Multilateral Agencies	4.44	4.14	4.30	4.70

Sources: Michael J. Enright and CPA Australia.

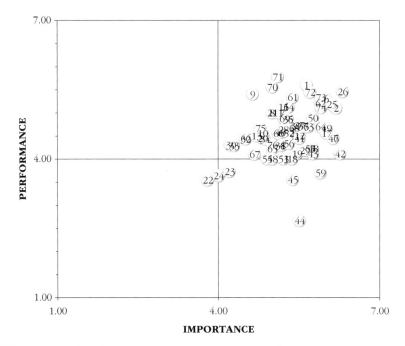

FIGURE 3.5 IPCA™ Chart for Australia's Iron Ore Mining Industry
Sources: Michael J. Enright and CPA Australia.

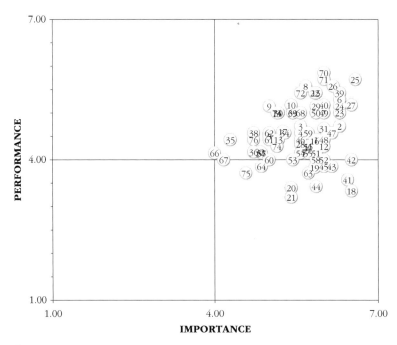

FIGURE 3.6 IPCA™ Chart for Australia's Wine and Other Alcoholic Beverage Manufacturing
Industry
Sources: Michael J. Enright and CPA Australia.

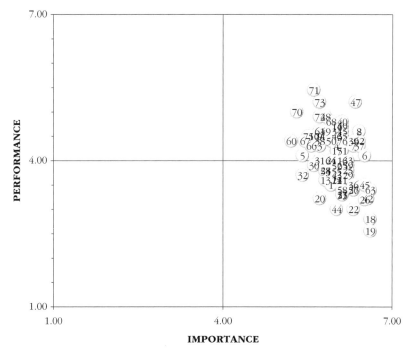

FIGURE 3.7 IPCA™ Chart for Australia's Motor Vehicle Manufacturing Industry
Sources: Michael J. Enright and CPA Australia.

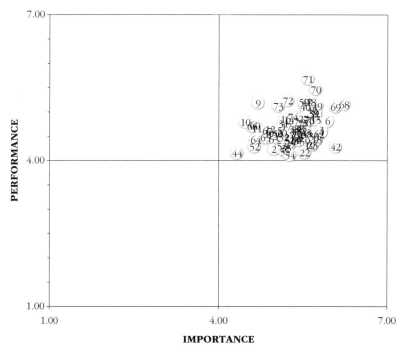

FIGURE 3.8 IPCA™ Chart for Australia's Higher Education Industry
Sources: Michael J. Enright and CPA Australia.

(72), Environmental Policies (73), Policies to Encourage R&D (62), and Staff Skills (6) are also viewed as important and advantageous for Australia.

Respondents see the Carbon Tax[23]/Emission Trading Scheme as important and a strong disadvantage. This is consistent with the views stated by managers of the leading companies in the industry. If Australia has such a tax, and competitors do not, this is a disadvantage. Overall Government Policy (45) is viewed as a negative for the sector, as are Industrial and Workforce Relations/Labour Laws (59). Drivers related to the domestic market (22, 23, 24) are viewed as negative for Australia, but not very important to competitiveness. This is not surprising for an industry that exports over 90 percent of its output. Interestingly, the only negatives that were cited involve drivers that cannot be changed (having to do with the domestic market) and aspects of government policy.

Respondents from the wine industry indicate that all of the drivers are at least neutral in terms of importance, and while Australia is seen as performing better than competitors in most drivers, there are several in which Australia is seen as lagging competitors (see Figure 3.6). Strong points include Knowledge of Asian Markets (25), Access to the China Market (26), Access to Other Asia-Pacific Markets (27), Overall Local Economic Conditions (39), Social Stability (70), Quality of Life (71), and Access to Appropriate Staff Skills (39).

Negatives include Staff Costs (18), Interest Rates (41), Carbon Tax/Emissions Trading Scheme (44), Property or Land-Related Costs (20), and Other Costs (21). Since the responses indicate that this is an industry that is feeling cost pressures, it is somewhat surprising that Australia's performance with respect to Exchange Rates (42) is viewed as neutral.

The IPCA™ chart for the automotive vehicle industry can be found in Figure 3.7. One striking aspect of this chart is that all of the drivers are rated as important, with the lowest rating being 5.2 out of 7 (with 4 being neutral). Foreign Trade and Tariff Policy (63) is viewed as the most important driver, which is interesting given the protection that the Australian industry has received over the years. The strongest drivers for the Australian industry according to respondents are Government Freedom from Corruption (47), Transportation Infrastructure (2), Scientific and Technical Skills (8), Macroeconomic Stability (40), and Policies to Encourage R&D (62).

The weakest points are Staff Costs (18), Other Employment Costs (19), Size of Local Market Demand (22), Access to the China Market (26), and Exchange Rates (42). Clearly costs and the contribution of exchange rates to costs are viewed as important disadvantages. A small local market, and the penetration of imports, makes it difficult for the Australian industry to produce automobiles in a cost-effective manner. As in the iron ore and wine sectors, Access to the China Market is considered important, but since China's automotive industry is still protected, this is viewed as a negative by automotive respondents. Respondents view Sector Targeting, Government Support Policies (57), and Government Incentives for Your Industry (58) as a negative for Australia, which is interesting given that without government support major producers would probably be shutting down Australian facilities.

The IPCA™ chart for the higher education industry can be found in Figure 3.8. What is striking about this chart is that according to respondents all of the competitiveness drivers are important and Australia has advantages versus the competitors in all of them. Not surprisingly, Quality of Education & Training Institutions (68) is viewed as the most important competitiveness driver, and Australia is viewed as having advantages in this driver. The same is true in Quality of Research Institutions, Organisations (69). Other strong advantages are seen in Social Stability (70), Quality of Life (71), Government Freedom from Corruption (47), Transparency of Government (48), Regulatory and Legal Framework (49), and others.

Australia is seen as having only slight advantages in Exchange Rates (42), Size of Local Market Demand (22), and Payroll Taxes (54) compared to competitors.

CONCLUSIONS FROM THE FOUR INDUSTRIES   There are a number of conclusions that we can draw from the survey analysis of the four industries. One is that it is critical to assess competitiveness in the context of specific industries where possible. This is where competition actually takes place, where firms either succeed or fail. Analyses of competitiveness that do not link back to the industries that are critical to an economy are at best partial. The results also show the value of assessing competitiveness versus specific competitors. It is interesting that in the four industries relatively few of the small and medium-sized OECD countries that are usually used as benchmarks in comparisons of Australia's economy are actually competitors to Australia. Since in many cases they are not significant markets for Australia either, one can only conclude that from a competitiveness and market standpoint, they are not as relevant for Australia as they might appear given the usual comparisons.

There are also several conclusions that can be drawn from the IPCA charts and tables. The first is that all of the drivers are viewed as important by respondents from at least one industry, indicating that any view of competitiveness that failed to include these drivers would be incomplete. The second is that the relative importance of the different drivers differs dramatically across industries. This means that aggregate competitiveness analyses that do not get down to the industry level are ultimately of less use than analyses that do. The third is that respondent perceptions of Australia's performance in a given driver can also vary by industry. This can be due in part to the fact that the same driver might play out in very different ways in different industries (Government Policy in the iron ore and the higher education industries for example) or because the industries face different competitors or comparators and therefore use different benchmarks.

The fourth is that from a policy and strategy standpoint, the IPCA charts allow us to home in quickly on the advantages and disadvantages faced by these industries. Respondents from the stronger industries—iron ore, wine, and higher education—indicate that Australia has advantages in all or nearly all of the drivers of competitiveness, indicating that improving competitiveness is perhaps more a matter of leveraging existing advantages and making sure they are not squandered than overcoming core disadvantages. The automotive industry, on the other hand, faces several disadvantages, indicating that trying to make this industry internationally competitive would be like trying to push a very big rock up a very steep hill. The fifth conclusion is that the individual IPCA charts also give industry-specific views on the important drivers that should be leveraged and those that should be improved in order to improve Australia's competitiveness in the industries. Again, this provides a much finer analysis than that provided by aggregate competitiveness measures that do not allow for industry-specific conclusions, policy implications, and strategic directions.

Moving Ahead

In this chapter, we have introduced a framework, the Five Level Competitiveness Framework™, and have shown how it can be incorporated into an Importance-Performance Competitiveness Analysis™ that allows us not only to understand competitiveness for sharply defined drivers in particular industries, but also allows us to identify key drivers and generate priorities for action by governments and firms. We have shown that the analysis generates sensible conclusions for a set of well-known Australian industries. The next task is to apply this process across the entire Australian economy, a task we take up in the next chapter.

Notes

1. Observers will note that the FLCF™ incorporates many features that are addressed in the sources described in Chapter 2. The FLCF™ also has features similar to that found in Michael E. Porter, *The Competitive Advantage of Nations* (New York: The Free Press, 1990). Michael Enright was Research Director for the Harvard Business School project that generated the material for that book and remains to this day the only person who has seen all of the input research. While clearly owing a major debt to previous work, the present framework and methodology were developed specifically to extend, change, and re-orient previous approaches based on the authors' experience of what drives competitiveness in the real world.
2. We note that Michael J. Enright holds the copyright on the survey instrument, in whole and in part, and the intellectual property within.
3. Australian Bureau of Statistics, *Year Book Australia*, May 2012.
4. IBISWorld, *Iron Ore Industry in Australia 2011*, August 2011.
5. International Monetary Fund, *IMF Primary Commodity Prices*. Note that converting USD into AUD at prevailing rates for each date gives a price of AUD 193.19 for February 2011 and AUD 102.88 for September 2012 and thus a decline in price that is also nearly 47 percent, though fractionally less than the decline in prices when measured in USD.
6. IBISWorld, *Iron Ore Industry in Australia 2011*, August 2011.
7. See Naomi Edwards, *Foreign Ownership of Australian Mining Profits*, Australian Greens, 2011; and Matthew Stevens, "Dodgy figures behind Brown's wrong-headed views on mining sector," *The Australian*, 30 June 2011 for two very different views.
8. Australian and New Zealand Standard Industrial Classification (ANZSIC), 2006.
9. Australian Bureau of Statistics, *Australian Wine and Grape Industry 2010–2011*, February 2012.
10. IBISWorld, various industry reports.
11. Winebiz Pty Ltd, *The Australian and New Zealand Wine Industry Directory, 2012*.
12. Project analysis; Winebiz Pty Ltd website; Individual wine company websites.
13. Australian and New Zealand Standard Industrial Classification (ANZSIC), 2006.
14. IBISWorld, *Motor Vehicle Manufacturing in Australia*, January 2012.

15. Australian Department of Foreign Affairs and Trade, *STARS Database*; Australian Department of Innovation, Industry, Science and Research, July 2011.

16. IBISWorld, *Motor Vehicle Manufacturing in Australia*, January 2012.

17. IBISWorld, *Motor Vehicle Manufacturing in Australia*, January 2012.

18. Australian Government, *Background Paper for the Higher Education Base Funding Review*, December 2010.

19. Australian Department of Education, Employment and Workforce Relations, *Overseas Student, Higher Education*, June 2012.

20. The Times Higher Education, *World University Rankings 2011–2012*, London, 2012.

21. QS Intelligence Unit, *World University Rankings 2011*, London, 2011.

22. We note that resource endowments are subject to direct analysis, so we tend to deal with those directly rather than incorporate them into a survey.

23. At the time of the survey the Australian Government had plans to implement a carbon tax, and it subsequently was introduced in July 2012.

CHAPTER 4

Drivers of Competitiveness in Australia

I n the last chapter, we introduced a method for assessing a nation's competitiveness on an industry-by-industry basis and used it to examine the competitiveness of four Australian industries. In this chapter, we use the same method and the broader survey results to examine the drivers of competitiveness across the entire Australian economy. To do so, we aggregate the survey responses up to the one-digit level in the Australian and New Zealand Standard Industrial Classification (ANZSIC) 2006 code, except for manufacturing, where we aggregate to the two-digit level. The result gives us a total of 32 sectors.[1] In this process, we lose some of the fine structure that we were able to show for the industries in Chapter 3. Even so, data on the importance of the competitiveness drivers and Australia's performance in these drivers on a sector-by-sector basis still provides a wealth of information on Australia's competitiveness. A large amount of data is provided in this chapter. The text provides the highlights for the general reader, while those that are interested can delve into the details.

In this chapter, we have chosen to organise the information according to the drivers of competitiveness in order to highlight drivers whose importance cuts across the economy and that provide indicators of issues that require more detailed analysis. We could have organised the material by industry to focus on the competitiveness and advantages and disadvantages of individual industries or of groups of related industries. The reader can easily reorganise the data in this chapter to focus on sectors.

Firm and Industry Drivers

Table 4.1 shows the mean responses of the survey respondents for the importance and performance of the firm- and industry-level drivers of competitiveness for the primary and manufacturing industries. All of the drivers in this set are viewed as important (above 4 = neutral on a 1 to 7 scale), with Level of Technology Employed the most important on average, followed by Government Incentives for Your Industry; Sector Targeting, Government Support Policies; Knowledge of Asian Markets; and Capabilities of Companies from the Country. The least important on average were Co-operation among Local Firms, Tough Local Competition, and Industry Associations or Organisations. This indicates that the companies tend to view both competition and co-operation among firms as less important drivers of competitiveness, which in turn might be due to an aversion to considering competition as potentially beneficial, and limited interaction and co-operation compared to what one might find elsewhere.

TABLE 4.1 Importance and Performance, Firm- and Industry-Level Drivers; Primary and Manufacturing Sectors[2]

Driver	A0	B0	C11	C12	C13	C14	C15	C16	C17	C18	C19	C20	C21	C22	C23	C24	C25	AVE
Number of Responses	*141*	*134*	*77*	*17*	*40*	*16*	*18*	*20*	*15*	*27*	*27*	*9*	*33*	*57*	*29*	*81*	*53*	*47*
Importance																		
Level of Technology Employed	5.54	5.59	5.54	5.58	5.15	5.64	5.38	5.47	5.57	**6.05**	5.76	5.44	5.67	5.87	5.85	5.93	5.75	5.63
Government Incentives for Your Industry	5.81	5.26	5.53	5.82	5.58	5.15	5.45	5.00	5.50	**6.15**	5.95	5.44	5.52	5.88	5.62	5.69	5.43	5.58
Sector Targeting, Government Support Policies	5.69	5.18	5.50	5.64	5.58	4.62	5.36	5.35	5.50	5.85	5.80	5.22	5.35	5.47	5.81	5.72	5.44	5.48
Knowledge of Asian Markets	5.48	5.52	5.33	5.75	5.09	5.07	5.33	5.44	5.71	**6.24**	5.30	4.67	5.65	5.53	5.80	5.65	5.45	5.47
Capabilities of Companies from the Country	5.26	5.25	5.54	5.42	4.97	5.43	5.46	5.44	5.57	5.95	5.71	5.22	5.21	5.40	5.60	5.86	5.52	5.46
Leading Companies that Drive Competitiveness	5.23	5.34	5.55	5.25	4.97	4.86	5.08	5.40	5.43	5.85	5.70	5.11	5.00	5.43	5.92	5.70	5.43	5.37
Strategies Used by Firms from the Country	5.13	5.02	5.38	5.58	5.23	5.57	4.92	5.38	5.21	5.60	5.48	4.56	4.92	5.43	5.72	5.64	5.43	5.31
Tough Local Competition	4.99	4.37	5.36	5.75	4.61	4.79	5.38	5.38	5.29	5.35	5.05	5.11	5.17	5.44	4.80	5.46	5.22	5.15
Industry Associations or Organisations	5.45	5.08	5.28	4.75	5.00	4.57	5.00	5.27	5.36	5.45	5.43	4.89	4.96	5.36	5.16	5.35	5.13	5.15
Co-operation among Local Firms	5.21	4.75	4.97	5.10	5.29	5.14	5.15	5.18	5.36	5.60	4.90	4.56	4.87	4.90	5.32	5.31	5.07	5.10
Performance																		
Level of Technology Employed	**5.08**	**5.02**	4.71	**5.27**	**5.00**	**5.54**	**5.64**	**5.07**	4.92	4.86	**5.20**	4.67	**4.91**	**5.22**	4.65	**5.22**	4.74	5.04
Industry Associations or Organisations	4.92	4.70	4.83	4.90	4.59	**5.58**	5.00	4.88	**5.15**	**5.00**	**5.21**	**5.00**	4.86	4.56	**4.88**	**5.08**	4.31	4.91
Capabilities of Companies from the Country	4.93	4.90	4.92	4.90	4.54	**5.33**	4.80	4.80	**5.08**	**5.35**	4.95	4.78	4.74	4.76	4.72	4.94	4.43	4.87
Leading Companies that Drive Competitiveness	4.74	4.90	4.95	4.55	4.46	4.69	4.64	4.87	**5.00**	**5.15**	**5.05**	**5.00**	4.50	4.45	4.63	4.78	4.45	4.75
Strategies Used by Firms from the Country	4.77	4.58	4.88	**5.20**	4.53	**5.54**	4.91	4.60	4.85	4.75	4.60	4.56	4.57	4.50	4.36	4.80	4.39	4.73
Knowledge of Asian Markets	4.95	4.78	4.63	**5.25**	3.77	4.69	**5.08**	4.53	4.54	4.86	4.05	**5.33**	4.41	4.28	4.56	4.91	4.57	4.66
Co-operation among Local Firms	4.67	4.44	4.56	4.56	4.59	**5.46**	**5.09**	4.33	**5.08**	4.65	4.58	4.11	4.38	4.10	4.28	4.76	4.25	4.58
Tough Local Competition	4.77	4.43	4.79	4.70	4.46	4.85	**5.00**	4.60	4.62	4.75	4.50	4.00	4.35	4.19	4.29	4.92	4.34	4.56
Sector Targeting, Government Support Policies	4.38	4.03	4.79	3.91	4.31	3.58	4.89	4.06	4.85	4.45	4.32	4.44	4.18	3.95	4.31	4.35	4.14	4.29
Government Incentives for Your Industry	4.04	3.77	4.47	3.73	4.44	3.25	4.44	3.94	4.38	4.50	3.72	4.67	3.90	3.62	4.27	4.40	4.07	4.09

Notes:

1 = very unimportant/much worse than competitors/comparators, 4 = neutral, 7 = very important/much better than competitors/comparators.

A0 = Agriculture/Forestry/Fishing; B0 = Mining; C11 = Food Product Manufacturing; C12 = Beverage and Tobacco Product Manufacturing; C13 = Textile, Leather, Clothing, and Footwear Manufacturing; C14 = Wood Product Manufacturing; C15 = Pulp, Paper, and Converted Paper Product Manufacturing; C16 = Printing; C17 = Petroleum and Coal Product Manufacturing; C18 = Basic Chemical and Chemical Product Manufacturing; C19 = Polymer Product and Rubber Product Manufacturing; C20 = Non-Metallic Mineral Product Manufacturing; C21 = Primary Metal and Metal Product Manufacturing; C22 = Fabricated Metal Product Manufacturing; C23 = Transport Equipment Manufacturing; C24 = Machinery and Equipment Manufacturing; C25 = Furniture and Other Manufacturing.

Sources: Michael J. Enright and CPA Australia.

88

The importance of different drivers differs by sector, with the highest single value given to Knowledge of Asian Markets by respondents in the Chemical sector, presumably because that is where the main market potential lies, and the lowest to Tough Local Competition by respondents in the Mining sector, which is ramping up output to serve burgeoning international markets and where the local market is a small portion of total sales. We note that respondents in only two industries, Wood Products and Printing, viewed Strategies Used by Firms as more important to competitiveness than Sector Targeting and Government Incentives. This strikes us as perhaps reflecting an unhealthy emphasis on what government can do and a lack of sufficient emphasis on what firms can do for themselves and their industries.

The respondents rate Australia on average as ahead of competitors and comparators in the firm and industry-level drivers (again with 4 = neutral on a 1 to 7 scale), but only slightly, with Level of Technology Employed, Industry Associations or Organisations, Capabilities of Companies from the Country, and Leading Companies that Drive Competitiveness showing the best performance, and Government Incentives, Sector Targeting, Government Support Policies, Tough Local Competition, and Co-operation among Local Firms having the weakest performance. Respondents in seven of the industries rated Australia as worse than the competition in Government Incentives, and respondents from three rated it as worse than the competition in Sector Targeting. These are not particularly surprising given that Australia tends not to have aggressive incentive or support programmes.

We note that the range of response means for performance is relatively narrow, ranging from just above neutral to a moderate advantage, and that all of the importance values are higher than all of the performance values. This would indicate that Australia could stand improvement in all of these drivers.

Table 4.2 shows the importance and performance of the firm and industry level drivers of competitiveness for utilities, construction, and the service sectors. Only two cells in the table have mean responses below neutral (below 4.0), Knowledge of Asian Markets for the Healthcare and Social Assistance sector and Tough Local Competition for the Public Administration and Safety sector. The former serves domestic customers and the latter is monopolistic, so there are no surprises there. All of the other cells report mean responses above neutral, so each of the other drivers is important to competitiveness or effectiveness in each of the industries indicated.

On average, the most important driver in the set is Level of Technology Employed, indicating that firms will only be up to date in service sectors if they are using up-to-date technology. This is particularly true for the Information, Media, Telecommunications, and Finance and Insurance Sectors. Government Incentives and Sector Targeting were viewed as the next most important, particularly in sectors in which government dominates (Education and Training, and Health Care and Social Assistance, for example), but also in Transport, Postal, Warehousing and Rental, Hiring, Real Estate Services. The least important driver in the set on average is Knowledge of Asian Markets, again because several of the sectors serve only domestic markets. Co-operation among Local Firms was on average the second least important, particularly for service sectors with extensive government involvement.

Australia's performance in these drivers is reported as above neutral (Australia being better than its competitors or comparators) for these sectors except for Government Incentives, which were viewed as disadvantages in the Wholesale Trade; Transport, Postal, Warehousing; and Arts and Recreation sectors, reflecting a view that

TABLE 4.2 Importance and Performance, Firm- and Industry-Level Drivers; Utilities, Construction, and Service Sectors[3]

Driver	D0 & E0	F0	G0	H0	I0	J0	K0	L0	M0	N0	O0	P0	Q0	R0	S0	AVE
Number of Responses	*464*	*231*	*456*	*166*	*227*	*359*	*636*	*104*	*641*	*209*	*168*	*334*	*309*	*117*	*721*	*343*
Importance																
Level of Technology Employed	5.66	5.52	5.55	5.41	5.65	5.84	5.80	5.43	5.73	5.64	5.68	5.72	5.64	5.06	5.35	5.58
Government Incentives for Your Industry	5.53	5.31	5.36	5.48	5.56	5.22	5.27	5.67	5.19	5.12	5.09	5.56	5.61	5.36	5.16	5.37
Sector Targeting, Government Support Policies	5.46	5.19	5.28	5.33	5.44	5.21	5.37	5.60	5.16	4.97	5.23	5.44	5.42	4.95	4.99	5.27
Capabilities of Companies from the Country	5.38	5.30	5.36	5.31	5.44	5.34	5.50	5.25	5.36	5.15	4.78	5.28	5.10	5.00	5.02	5.24
Strategies Used by Firms from the Country	5.21	5.22	5.24	5.42	5.31	5.09	5.30	5.18	5.13	4.94	4.50	5.26	4.95	4.78	4.88	5.09
Industry Associations or Organisations	5.16	5.11	5.13	5.15	5.25	4.96	5.24	5.03	5.18	4.81	4.88	5.17	5.16	5.03	4.89	5.08
Leading Companies that Drive Competitiveness	5.22	5.45	5.33	5.25	5.31	5.24	5.48	5.12	5.12	4.75	4.35	5.00	4.84	4.85	4.82	5.08
Tough Local Competition	5.21	5.40	5.43	5.54	5.29	4.97	5.22	5.59	4.99	5.07	3.74	5.21	4.70	4.74	4.90	5.07
Co-operation among Local Firms	5.19	5.03	5.04	5.34	5.21	4.85	4.82	4.91	4.94	4.93	4.50	5.15	4.90	4.79	4.83	4.96
Knowledge of Asian Markets	4.92	5.39	5.14	4.92	5.15	5.12	5.28	4.60	4.93	4.48	4.16	4.81	3.98	4.10	4.42	4.76
Performance																
Level of Technology Employed	4.93	4.93	4.85	4.80	4.78	4.83	4.84	4.73	4.86	4.91	4.56	4.82	4.88	4.64	4.82	4.81
Industry Associations or Organisations	4.83	4.81	4.73	4.78	4.63	4.60	4.79	4.71	4.69	**5.01**	4.66	4.80	4.76	4.23	4.63	4.71
Capabilities of Companies from the Country	4.83	4.80	4.62	4.65	4.66	4.66	4.80	4.58	4.69	4.86	4.71	4.67	4.62	4.43	4.67	4.68
Tough Local Competition	4.59	4.55	4.61	4.87	4.60	4.56	4.84	4.94	4.51	4.90	4.63	4.71	4.64	4.41	4.73	4.67
Strategies Used by Firms from the Country	4.73	4.62	4.57	4.65	4.65	4.60	4.71	4.70	4.56	4.89	4.69	4.68	4.62	4.26	4.63	4.64
Leading Companies that Drive Competitiveness	4.74	4.74	4.59	4.64	4.64	4.59	4.74	4.75	4.57	4.83	4.53	4.71	4.59	4.18	4.53	4.62
Knowledge of Asian Markets	4.59	4.64	4.54	4.56	4.73	4.73	4.67	4.59	4.57	4.54	4.67	4.72	4.60	4.59	4.58	4.62
Co-operation among Local Firms	4.59	4.47	4.43	4.70	4.48	4.46	4.69	4.55	4.35	4.81	4.67	4.58	4.58	4.16	4.61	4.54
Sector Targeting, Government Support Policies	4.38	4.21	4.25	4.41	4.23	4.55	4.44	4.25	4.28	4.74	4.69	4.58	4.28	4.02	4.34	4.38
Government Incentives for Your Industry	4.21	3.97	4.03	4.25	3.96	4.40	4.27	4.15	4.06	4.57	4.57	4.38	4.16	3.94	4.24	4.21

Notes:

1 = very unimportant/much worse than competitors/comparators; 4 = neutral, 7 = very important/much better than competitors/comparators.

D0&E0 = Utilities and Construction; F0 = Wholesale Trade; G0 = Retail Trade; H0 = Accommodation and Food Services; I0 = Transport, Postal, Ware-housing; J0 = Information, Media, Telecommunications; K0 = Finance and Insurance Services; L0 = Rental, Hiring, Real Estate Services; M0 = Professional, Scientific, and Technical Services; N0 = Administrative and Support Services; O0 = Public Administration and Safety; P0 = Education and Training; Q0 = Health Care and Social Assistance; R0 = Arts and Recreation; S0 = Other Services.

Sources: Michael J. Enright and CPA Australia.

the sectors received more support in other nations than in Australia. Australia performed best on average in Level of Technology Employed, which was also considered the most important driver of competitiveness across these sectors. Australia's industry associations were viewed as stronger than those in competing nations, as was the situation in Capabilities of Companies, Tough Local Competition, and Strategies Used by Firms.

What is interesting is that while Australia is viewed as having advantages versus competitors, these were mostly marginal, and, other than in Level of Technology, the biggest advantages tended to be in the drivers with lesser importance. The performance results are in an even narrower range than in Table 4.1, and all but one of the drivers had a higher mean importance value higher than all the mean performance values. Clearly there is substantial room for improvement across all of these drivers. Another interesting observation is that in many sectors respondents rated Sector Targeting and Government Incentives as more important than Strategies Used by Firms or Capabilities of Companies in determining competitiveness, which might again reflect an unhealthy reliance on government to solve competitiveness issues rather than firms taking matters into their own hands.

Meso or Cluster-Level Drivers

Meso or cluster-level drivers are those that operate at the level of the ecosystem surrounding an industry, including drivers related to inputs and suppliers, customers and demand, and related industries. In this chapter, we have divided the cluster-level drivers into two groups for clarity and ease of exposition. These groups are land, labour, and infrastructure; and inputs, demand, and linkages. In each case, we provide the mean of the responses for importance and performance in competitiveness drivers for the primary and manufacturing sectors in one table, and the utilities, construction, service sectors in another.

Land, Labour, and Infrastructure

Tables 4.3 and 4.4 show the survey results for drivers that reflect land, labour, and infrastructure. In Tables 4.3 and 4.4, with regard to the workforce, we see that all of the drivers are viewed as important across all of the sectors, with some reaching very important. In most cases, the mean ratings are well above 5, indicating relatively high levels of importance. The most important workforce-related drivers in the primary and manufacturing sectors are Staff Costs, Access to Appropriate Staff Skills, and Other Employment Costs. The most important workforce drivers for utilities, construction, and service sectors on average are Access to Appropriate Staff Skills, Staff Costs, and Other Employment Costs. In both sets, these are followed by Managerial Skills and Scientific and Technical Skills. The least important in both sets is Access to Multilingual Staff. Staff skills and costs are clearly major concerns, with companies more exposed to international trade focusing more on costs, and those less subject to international trade focusing more on skills.

In the primary and manufacturing sectors, Australia is seen as having reasonably strong positions across most sectors in Scientific and Technical Skills, Access to Local Managerial Skills, and Access to Appropriate Staff Skills. It is in Staff Costs and Other

TABLE 4.3 Importance and Performance; Cluster-Level Drivers; Land, Labour, Infrastructure; Primary and Manufacturing Sectors

Driver	A0	B0	C11	C12	C13	C14	C15	C16	C17	C18	C19	C20	C21	C22	C23	C24	C25	AVE
Importance																		
Staff Costs	5.80	5.74	5.67	6.55	5.57	6.00	5.77	5.81	5.50	5.90	5.76	5.63	5.48	6.13	5.92	5.88	5.58	5.81
Access to Appropriate Staff Skills	5.54	5.84	5.79	6.17	5.23	6.07	5.93	5.29	5.71	5.90	5.77	5.56	5.96	5.98	6.19	5.91	5.60	5.79
Other Employment Costs	5.71	5.51	5.71	5.91	5.59	6.07	5.69	5.81	5.07	6.05	5.67	5.56	5.42	5.98	5.88	5.86	5.33	5.70
Transportation Infrastructure	5.64	5.57	5.96	6.25	4.85	5.21	6.00	5.06	6.00	6.14	5.77	5.56	5.58	5.90	6.04	5.48	5.67	5.69
Scientific and Technical Skills	5.47	5.43	5.71	5.73	4.74	4.21	5.87	5.27	5.21	6.19	5.86	5.67	5.73	5.76	5.96	5.85	5.59	5.54
Access to Local Managerial Skills	5.25	5.37	5.52	5.92	4.88	5.46	5.80	5.24	5.36	5.67	5.55	5.22	5.54	5.44	5.96	5.70	5.35	5.48
Property or Land-Related Costs	5.68	5.17	5.55	5.40	5.32	5.93	4.62	5.82	5.29	5.79	5.52	5.50	5.00	5.67	5.56	5.60	5.21	5.45
Communication Infrastructure	5.08	5.27	5.50	5.33	4.79	5.20	5.27	5.35	5.50	5.71	5.64	5.00	5.31	5.84	5.38	5.55	5.39	5.36
Geographic Location	5.32	5.22	5.53	5.42	4.53	3.79	5.87	5.65	5.79	5.81	5.36	6.00	5.04	5.14	5.69	5.34	5.12	5.33
Other Costs	5.42	4.93	5.39	5.44	5.25	5.71	4.85	5.12	5.50	5.37	5.22	5.25	4.96	5.64	5.65	5.63	5.23	5.33
IT and Internet Infrastructure	4.83	5.26	5.43	5.33	4.61	5.29	5.33	5.53	5.29	5.81	5.48	4.67	5.50	5.53	5.54	5.59	5.29	5.31
Access to Multilingual Staff	4.72	5.10	4.83	5.42	5.39	4.43	5.00	5.33	5.57	5.95	5.05	4.11	5.46	4.95	5.28	5.51	5.04	5.13
Other Infrastructure	4.96	5.01	5.03	5.00	4.70	4.69	4.67	5.00	5.21	5.52	5.00	4.63	5.13	5.13	5.08	5.14	4.81	4.98
Performance																		
Communication Infrastructure	4.88	5.00	5.00	4.50	4.76	4.86	5.57	5.06	4.85	5.14	5.15	5.33	4.83	5.42	4.50	5.06	4.98	4.99
Scientific and Technical Skills	5.19	5.06	5.00	4.91	4.84	4.86	5.50	4.60	4.69	5.24	5.33	4.88	4.74	5.19	4.68	5.14	4.87	4.98
Access to Local Managerial Skills	5.07	5.02	5.02	4.50	4.88	4.86	5.36	5.07	5.23	4.90	5.00	4.89	4.57	5.08	4.76	5.26	4.91	4.96
Access to Appropriate Staff Skills	4.86	4.92	5.00	4.50	5.03	4.86	5.21	5.13	5.00	4.95	4.79	4.44	4.78	5.13	4.40	5.10	4.83	4.88
IT and Internet Infrastructure	4.76	4.89	4.69	4.25	4.62	4.86	5.64	5.06	4.46	5.14	4.89	5.00	4.57	5.19	4.46	5.03	4.67	4.83
Transportation Infrastructure	4.74	4.88	4.70	4.42	4.84	5.00	5.71	4.75	4.85	4.76	5.00	4.44	4.70	4.89	4.81	5.00	4.49	4.82
Other Infrastructure	4.68	4.75	4.63	4.36	4.55	4.79	5.21	4.67	4.69	4.90	4.68	4.00	4.70	4.84	4.73	4.89	4.56	4.68
Geographic Location	4.72	4.87	4.86	4.17	4.48	5.29	5.21	4.75	4.46	4.67	4.62	4.56	4.52	4.63	4.24	4.75	4.60	4.67
Access to Multilingual Staff	4.59	4.44	4.15	4.27	4.06	4.77	4.77	4.59	4.46	4.52	4.55	3.67	4.83	4.47	4.44	4.44	4.27	4.43
Other Costs	4.09	4.18	4.31	3.78	3.80	4.31	5.00	3.35	4.62	4.29	3.94	3.63	4.05	3.57	4.12	4.34	3.96	4.08
Property or Land-Related Costs	4.09	3.98	4.41	3.89	3.90	4.46	4.64	3.65	4.69	4.14	3.95	3.63	3.87	3.76	3.88	4.36	4.02	4.08
Other Employment Costs	3.76	3.86	4.30	4.36	3.71	4.00	5.07	3.82	4.85	4.00	3.95	3.33	3.68	3.58	3.56	4.46	3.98	4.02
Staff Costs	3.71	3.75	4.14	3.45	3.90	3.92	5.07	3.82	4.54	3.90	3.47	3.78	3.74	3.64	3.58	4.34	3.96	3.92

Notes:

1 = very unimportant/much worse than competitors/comparators; 4 = neutral; 7 = very important/much better than competitors/comparators.

A0 = Agriculture/Forestry/Fishing; B0 = Mining; C11 = Food Product Manufacturing; C12 = Beverage and Tobacco Product Manufacturing; C13 = Textile, Leather, Clothing, and Footwear Manufacturing; C14 = Wood Product Manufacturing; C15 = Pulp, Paper, and Converted Paper Product Manufacturing; C16 = Printing; C17 = Petroleum and Coal Product Manufacturing; C18 = Basic Chemical and Chemical Product Manufacturing; C19 = Polymer Product and Rubber Product Manufacturing; C20 = Non-Metallic Mineral Product Manufacturing; C21 = Primary Metal and Metal Product Manufacturing; C22 = Fabricated Metal Product Manufacturing; C23 = Transport Equipment Manufacturing; C24 = Machinery and Equipment Manufacturing; C25 = Furniture and Other Manufacturing.

Sources: Michael J. Enright and CPA Australia.

TABLE 4.4 Importance and Performance; Cluster-Level Drivers; Land, Labour, Infrastructure; Utilities, Construction, Services

Driver	DO & EO	FO	GO	HO	IO	JO	KO	LO	MO	NO	OO	PO	QO	RO	SO	AVE
Importance																
Access to Appropriate Staff Skills	5.86	5.59	5.52	5.62	5.77	5.80	5.86	5.26	5.99	5.79	5.99	**6.12**	**6.08**	5.33	5.50	5.74
IT and Internet Infrastructure	5.41	5.60	5.61	5.35	5.73	**6.16**	**6.01**	5.57	5.97	5.94	5.81	5.83	5.55	5.42	5.43	5.69
Staff Costs	5.71	5.82	5.92	5.88	5.81	5.68	5.74	5.42	5.83	5.48	5.61	5.84	5.80	5.28	5.42	5.68
Communication Infrastructure	5.56	5.63	5.48	5.31	5.77	**6.00**	5.90	5.48	5.87	5.85	5.75	5.76	5.64	5.19	5.43	5.64
Other Employment Costs	5.64	5.66	5.73	5.94	5.67	5.51	5.56	5.36	5.65	5.39	5.31	5.63	5.66	5.20	5.35	5.55
Access to Local Managerial Skills	5.42	5.39	5.32	5.36	5.49	5.43	5.55	5.19	5.50	5.40	5.53	5.48	5.50	4.88	5.10	5.37
Property or Land-Related Costs	5.46	5.45	5.47	5.61	5.43	5.04	5.03	5.74	4.96	5.17	4.51	5.16	5.20	4.47	4.94	5.18
Other Costs	5.35	5.41	5.29	5.67	5.36	5.07	5.06	5.19	4.92	4.98	4.74	5.26	5.05	4.95	4.94	5.15
Scientific and Technical Skills	5.41	5.24	4.78	4.49	5.13	5.66	4.91	4.44	5.54	5.09	5.45	5.41	5.69	4.73	4.86	5.12
Geographic Location	5.03	5.09	5.09	5.80	5.41	4.76	4.84	5.41	4.91	4.82	4.69	5.08	5.02	4.75	4.74	5.03
Transportation Infrastructure	5.28	5.71	5.39	5.38	5.98	4.35	4.21	5.07	4.37	4.65	4.76	4.85	4.80	4.60	4.65	4.94
Other Infrastructure	5.03	4.94	4.93	4.98	5.34	4.90	4.92	4.80	4.86	4.96	5.11	5.11	4.77	4.44	4.64	4.92
Access to Multilingual Staff	4.89	5.06	4.85	5.01	4.72	5.06	5.13	4.28	4.93	4.58	4.95	5.15	4.68	4.01	4.61	4.79
Performance																
Access to Local Managerial Skills	**5.03**	**5.22**	4.99	4.92	4.88	4.89	4.99	4.90	4.84	**5.04**	4.69	4.93	4.94	4.61	4.89	4.92
Access to Appropriate Staff Skills	4.91	**5.23**	4.94	4.83	4.92	4.85	**5.04**	4.71	4.77	**5.03**	4.74	4.97	**5.00**	4.74	4.87	4.90
Scientific and Technical Skills	4.97	**5.08**	4.75	4.92	4.75	4.83	4.87	4.80	4.84	**5.03**	4.69	4.87	**5.01**	4.75	4.72	4.86
Communication Infrastructure	4.91	**5.21**	4.86	4.99	4.80	4.61	4.92	4.54	4.76	4.87	4.47	4.69	4.89	4.52	4.81	4.79
IT and Internet Infrastructure	4.79	**5.16**	4.81	4.84	4.73	4.56	4.86	4.27	4.71	4.80	4.46	4.67	4.72	4.43	4.74	4.70
Geographic Location	4.84	4.55	4.56	4.94	4.65	4.32	4.63	**5.10**	4.53	4.88	4.59	4.72	4.66	4.25	4.66	4.66
Other Infrastructure	4.91	4.95	4.67	4.77	4.64	4.60	4.66	4.40	4.46	4.70	4.48	4.66	4.55	4.37	4.62	4.63
Transportation Infrastructure	4.87	4.83	4.67	4.73	4.72	4.35	4.40	4.43	4.36	4.71	4.32	4.36	4.57	4.23	4.56	4.54
Access to Multilingual Staff	4.41	4.37	4.44	4.39	4.48	4.50	4.44	4.27	4.30	4.60	4.52	4.54	4.45	4.11	4.47	4.42
Other Costs	4.31	4.05	4.13	4.18	4.43	4.26	4.34	4.05	4.09	4.35	4.37	4.43	4.37	4.10	4.22	4.25
Property or Land-Related Costs	4.34	4.01	4.08	4.05	4.36	4.16	4.24	4.25	4.04	4.31	4.38	4.33	4.38	4.02	4.25	4.21
Staff Costs	4.24	3.79	4.02	3.99	4.05	4.13	4.35	4.01	4.03	4.33	4.26	4.28	4.30	4.30	4.35	4.16
Other Employment Costs	4.17	3.79	3.94	4.01	4.13	4.16	4.26	4.03	4.00	4.28	4.34	4.25	4.32	4.27	4.33	4.15

Notes:

1 = very unimportant/much worse than competitors/comparators, 4 = neutral, 7 = very important/much better than competitors/comparators. DO&EO = Utilities and Construction; FO = Wholesale Trade; GO = Retail Trade; HO = Accommodation and Food Services; IO = Transport, Postal, Warehousing; JO = Information, Media, Telecommunications; KO = Finance and Insurance Services; LO = Rental, Hiring, Real Estate Services; MO = Professional, Scientific, and Technical Services; NO = Administrative and Support Services; OO = Public Administration and Safety; PO = Education and Training; QO = Health Care and Social Assistance; RO = Arts and Recreation; SO = Other Services.

Sources: Michael J. Enright and CPA Australia.

93

Employment Costs that Australia is seen to be lagging, with respondents in 13 out of the 17 sectors indicating Australia has disadvantages (mean rating below 4) in terms of Staff Costs and respondents in 10 out of 17 sectors indicating disadvantages in Other Employment Costs. In the utilities, construction, and service sector set, Australia's position is seen as strongest in Access to Local Managerial Skills, Access to Appropriate Staff Skills, and Scientific and Technical Skills. Again, Staff Costs and Other Employment Costs are viewed as the least positive, though respondents in only two sectors indicated Australia is disadvantaged in each of these drivers. In any case, the advantages in workforce-related drivers are moderate (none averaging more than 5), and the disadvantages in cost are considered important.

The same tables also show the mean importance and performance responses for the two sets of sectors regarding infrastructure. All infrastructure drivers are viewed as important in all sectors. For the primary and manufacturing sectors, Transportation Infrastructure is viewed as substantially more important than Communication Infrastructure, which is only slightly more important than IT and Internet Infrastructure. For the utilities, construction, services set, IT and Internet Infrastructure is the most important infrastructure variable, followed closely by Communications Infrastructure, with Transportation Infrastructure lagging these two, but still considered important. The differences are not surprising. We note the critical importance of Transportation Infrastructure to the first set of sectors and that of IT, Internet, and Communications Technologies to the second.

With respect to performance, respondents from all sectors rated Australia on average as ahead of competitors and comparators in all infrastructure drivers. Respondents from both sets of sectors generally regard Australia's performance in key infrastructure as solid, but not spectacular, with respondents from the primary and manufacturing sectors giving Australia somewhat higher ratings, perhaps because the competitors or comparators for those sectors include a number of developing or middle-income countries, while the competitors or comparators for many of the latter set include some of the world's most advanced economies. In any case, infrastructure is viewed as more of an advantage by the primary and manufacturing sector respondents than the utilities, construction, and service sector respondents. Given Australia's distance from world markets and its dispersed population, one would imagine that Australia would have to have substantial infrastructure advantages, that is, larger than those reported, to overcome the disadvantages of distance and dispersion.

Geographic location is viewed as important by respondents in both sets of sectors, with respondents in the primary and manufacturing sectors viewing location as slightly more important on average than those in the utilities, construction, and service sectors, which again makes sense since the former need to ship physical product and the latter tend to locate near customers. Interestingly, Geographic Location is viewed as an advantage by respondents in all sectors. This may reflect respondents whose companies serve domestic markets in which distance from other nations affords natural protection, or companies that serve markets in the Asia-Pacific region for which Australia is reasonably well-positioned, or companies that do not particularly concern themselves with serving global markets, or all of the above. Land Costs were viewed as more important than Geographic Location by respondents in most sectors. Respondents in 9 of the 17 primary and manufacturing sectors claimed Australia had disadvantages in Land Costs versus competitors or comparators, while respondents in all of the utilities, construction, and service sectors on average believed Australia had a very slight advantage versus competitors and comparators in Land Costs.

The overall situation in land, labour, and infrastructure is that Australia is viewed as having advantages in skills, but either disadvantages or only slight advantages when it comes to staff costs. The results suggest that skill levels are appropriate, but that the supply of skilled personnel might be limited in a way that drives up costs. In addition, other costs associated with employing people that do not go directly into the pay packet should receive greater attention given the importance and perceived weak performance in this area. Australia performs reasonably well in terms of infrastructure, but one wonders if just scoring a bit above competitors is sufficient given Australia's distance from other markets and the dispersion of its population. Property or Land-Related Costs are also viewed as relatively weak, suggesting that the incentives to invest in land and property in Australia, which might drive up prices versus other investments, should be examined.

The results also show the importance of breaking down the economy into industries or sectors. Australia's competitive position in land, labour, and infrastructure drivers is considerably different in the service sector from the manufacturing sector, for example. This is due in part to the fact that competitors in the primary and manufacturing sectors are just as likely to be middle income or developing nations as advanced nations, while in much of the service sector, Australia's competitors or comparators tend to be advanced economies. Again, on average the importance scores are significantly higher than the performance scores, indicating slight advantages at best, and substantial room for improvement.

Inputs, Demand, and Linkages

Tables 4.5 and 4.6 show the results for drivers involving inputs, demand, and inter-firm and inter-industry linkages. Inputs here include financial inputs, information inputs, goods and services, industrial inputs, and capital equipment. Demand refers to the size, sophistication, and future potential for the domestic market. Linkages refer to support from related industries and the clustering of firms in the same or related industries.

Among the inputs included in the tables, Access to Capital Equipment, Access to Input Goods and Services, and Access to Business Relevant Information are rated the most important by respondents in the primary and manufacturing sectors on average, ahead of drivers related to capital and finance. The most important inputs for the utilities, construction, service sectors are Access to Business-Relevant Information, Access to Input Goods and Services, and Access to Capital Equipment, again ahead of the financial drivers. In both cases, Availability of Venture Capital is important, but far down the list. Australia is seen as having advantages against competitors and comparators in all of the input-related drivers. Strength of the Local Banking System is the strongest performer for both sets of sectors, followed by Access to Business-Relevant Information and Access to Debt Finance for the primary and manufacturing sectors, and by the same two drivers, but in reverse order, for the utilities, construction, and service sectors.

With respect to demand, the Future Local Market Potential and Size of Local Market are rated as more important in influencing competitiveness by respondents on average in both sets of sectors than the input categories in Tables 4.5 and 4.6. While

TABLE 4.5   Importance and Performance; Cluster-Level Drivers; Inputs, Demand, and Linkages; Primary and Manufacturing Sectors

Driver	A0	B0	C11	C12	C13	C14	C15	C16	C17	C18	C19	C20	C21	C22	C23	C24	C25	AVE
Importance																		
Future Local Market Potential	5.69	4.78	5.82	5.92	4.90	5.50	5.92	5.06	5.64	5.90	**6.00**	5.56	5.50	**6.14**	**6.04**	5.87	5.72	5.64
Size of Local Market Demand	5.71	4.52	5.68	5.45	4.75	5.86	**6.17**	5.33	5.71	5.86	5.71	5.78	5.50	**6.00**	**6.12**	5.89	5.77	5.64
Access to Capital Equipment	5.51	5.59	5.52	5.33	5.41	5.64	5.75	5.63	5.36	**6.00**	5.76	5.25	5.29	**6.02**	5.88	5.79	5.40	5.60
Access to Input Goods and Services	5.55	5.54	5.67	5.36	5.36	5.86	5.69	5.47	5.64	5.76	5.57	5.22	5.54	5.68	5.77	5.90	5.44	5.59
Access to Business Relevant Information	5.69	5.43	5.53	5.25	4.94	5.57	5.77	5.29	5.71	5.86	5.62	5.11	5.21	5.81	5.81	5.63	5.53	5.52
Availability of Equity Capital	5.29	5.18	5.51	5.78	4.81	5.54	5.62	5.29	5.50	5.57	5.62	5.25	5.48	5.85	5.62	5.55	5.13	5.45
Cost of Debt Finance	5.42	5.21	5.52	5.50	5.06	5.43	5.38	5.47	5.43	5.71	5.57	5.14	5.29	5.85	5.69	5.67	5.13	5.44
Support from Related Industries	5.14	5.42	5.26	5.33	5.35	5.07	5.58	5.35	5.43	**6.10**	5.35	5.11	5.13	5.60	5.76	5.75	5.23	5.41
Sophistication of Local Demand	5.52	4.40	5.41	5.58	4.74	5.43	5.42	5.06	5.71	5.76	5.57	5.00	4.92	5.53	5.58	5.73	5.38	5.34
Access to Debt Finance	4.98	4.99	5.11	5.00	4.80	5.14	5.46	5.27	4.93	5.90	5.05	5.00	5.00	4.92	5.65	5.22	4.85	5.13
Availability of Venture Capital	5.17	5.05	5.25	5.20	4.84	5.38	4.77	5.35	4.93	5.43	5.48	3.88	4.92	5.46	5.35	5.45	4.94	5.11
Strength of the Local Banking System	5.03	4.70	5.07	5.09	4.70	4.64	5.20	4.93	5.43	5.85	4.82	5.00	5.15	5.24	5.35	5.17	4.92	5.08
Clustering of Firms in Your Industry	4.73	4.76	4.84	5.10	5.16	4.71	5.25	5.31	5.36	5.29	5.10	4.33	4.65	4.93	5.08	5.25	4.74	4.98
Performance																		
Strength of the Local Banking System	**5.25**	**5.27**	**5.08**	**5.00**	4.77	4.93	**5.50**	4.73	**5.00**	**5.24**	**5.05**	**5.25**	4.91	**5.25**	4.68	**5.48**	4.91	5.08
Access to Business-Relevant Information	4.92	**5.01**	**5.03**	**5.00**	4.84	**5.31**	**5.64**	**5.33**	**5.08**	**5.05**	**5.10**	4.67	4.52	**5.18**	4.96	**5.06**	**5.00**	5.04
Access to Debt Finance	4.92	4.79	4.86	4.91	4.65	4.93	**5.62**	4.86	**5.00**	**5.00**	**5.20**	**5.00**	4.62	4.96	4.68	**5.20**	4.77	4.94
Access to Input Goods and Services	4.84	**5.01**	4.84	4.75	4.59	**5.31**	**5.71**	4.56	**5.46**	4.76	4.53	4.56	**5.00**	4.98	4.46	**5.16**	4.70	4.90
Access to Capital Equipment	4.79	4.86	4.71	4.70	4.83	**5.46**	**5.50**	4.56	**5.31**	4.75	4.53	4.50	4.91	**5.07**	4.64	**5.02**	4.61	4.87
Sophistication of Local Demand	4.97	4.44	4.89	4.92	4.32	4.85	**5.46**	4.63	4.38	4.43	4.53	4.67	4.50	4.51	4.56	4.70	4.47	4.66
Availability of Equity Capital	4.52	4.46	4.81	4.45	4.23	4.92	**5.71**	4.53	**5.00**	4.29	4.79	4.25	4.59	4.49	4.40	4.88	4.64	4.64
Support from Related Industries	4.66	4.55	4.53	4.82	4.00	**5.00**	4.92	4.75	**5.00**	4.43	4.33	4.56	4.87	4.49	4.36	4.70	4.28	4.60
Availability of Venture Capital	4.43	4.43	4.72	4.73	4.17	4.92	**5.43**	4.40	4.69	4.29	4.63	**5.00**	4.36	4.42	4.25	4.71	4.66	4.60
Cost of Debt Finance	4.45	4.40	4.68	4.27	4.07	4.77	**5.43**	4.53	4.85	4.29	4.37	4.00	4.18	4.30	4.23	4.61	4.41	4.46
Future Local Market Potential	4.66	4.30	4.77	4.55	4.28	4.77	**5.31**	4.41	4.08	4.48	4.40	4.22	4.17	4.19	4.08	4.63	4.35	4.45
Clustering of Firms in Your Industry	4.58	4.55	4.30	4.60	3.97	4.46	4.69	4.06	4.85	4.71	4.67	4.22	4.32	4.35	4.24	4.46	4.31	4.43
Size of Local Market Demand	4.55	4.29	4.69	4.67	4.03	4.31	**5.54**	4.18	4.38	4.52	3.95	4.44	3.70	4.05	3.96	4.45	4.13	4.34

Notes:

1 = very unimportant/much worse than competitors/comparators, 4 = neutral, 7 = very important/much better than competitors/comparators.

A0 = Agriculture/Forestry/Fishing; B0 = Mining; C11 = Food Product Manufacturing; C12 = Beverage and Tobacco Product Manufacturing; C13 = Textile, Leather, Clothing, and Footwear Manufacturing; C14 = Wood Product Manufacturing; C15 = Pulp, Paper, and Converted Paper Product Manufacturing; C16 = Printing; C17 = Petroleum and Coal Product Manufacturing; C18 = Basic Chemical and Chemical Product Manufacturing; C19 = Polymer Product and Rubber Product Manufacturing; C20 = Non-Metallic Mineral Product Manufacturing; C21 = Primary Metal and Metal Product Manufacturing; C22 = Fabricated Metal Product Manufacturing; C23 = Transport Equipment Manufacturing; C24 = Machinery and Equipment Manufacturing; C25 = Furniture and Other Manufacturing.

Sources: Michael J. Enright and CPA Australia.

TABLE 4.6 Importance and Performance; Cluster-Level Drivers; Inputs, Demand, and Linkages; Utilities, Construction, Services

Driver	DO & EO	FO	GO	HO	IO	JO	KO	LO	MO	NO	OO	PO	QO	RO	SO	AVE
Importance																
Future Local Market Potential	5.84	5.81	5.96	5.9	5.83	5.68	5.73	**6.04**	5.62	5.53	4.77	5.69	5.59	5.81	5.49	5.69
Size of Local Market Demand	5.83	5.66	5.93	5.85	5.81	5.58	5.66	**6.07**	5.56	5.58	4.64	5.62	5.53	5.83	5.51	5.64
Access to Business-Relevant Information	5.59	5.61	5.58	5.58	5.65	5.53	5.8	5.72	5.61	5.61	5.21	5.33	5.43	5.18	5.19	5.51
Sophistication of Local Demand	5.38	5.39	5.58	5.44	5.39	5.42	5.52	5.69	5.41	5.29	4.61	5.37	5.30	5.58	5.04	5.36
Access to Input Goods and Services	5.54	5.54	5.61	5.53	5.50	5.18	4.97	5.12	5.04	5.21	4.98	5.15	5.33	4.89	5.04	5.24
Access to Capital Equipment	5.45	5.33	5.30	5.36	5.63	5.20	4.86	4.95	4.88	5.02	4.95	5.08	5.47	4.71	4.94	5.14
Support from Related Industries	5.31	5.20	5.18	5.27	5.28	5.22	5.21	4.78	4.99	5.07	5.03	5.13	5.18	4.96	4.99	5.12
Cost of Debt Finance	5.47	5.33	5.33	5.44	5.41	4.86	5.50	5.67	4.79	4.94	4.20	4.48	4.83	4.28	4.80	5.02
Availability of Equity Capital	5.45	5.24	5.31	5.38	5.32	4.95	5.44	5.70	4.86	4.90	4.21	4.52	4.94	4.29	4.71	5.01
Strength of the Local Banking System	5.12	5.02	5.16	4.80	5.16	4.88	5.88	5.34	5.00	5.14	4.45	4.62	4.69	4.20	4.81	4.95
Availability of Venture Capital	5.26	4.99	5.21	5.21	5.15	5.00	5.01	5.33	4.72	4.84	3.99	4.49	4.74	4.44	4.62	4.87
Access to Debt Finance	5.25	4.91	4.81	4.67	5.13	4.68	5.33	5.32	4.68	4.56	4.06	4.28	4.29	3.94	4.52	4.70
Clustering of Firms in Your Industry	4.78	4.70	4.77	4.58	4.85	4.78	4.9	4.38	4.57	4.46	4.11	4.64	4.5	4.24	4.37	4.58
Performance																
Strength of the Local Banking System	**5.23**	**5.34**	**5.07**	**5.15**	**5.14**	**5.14**	**5.47**	**5.24**	**5.08**	**5.18**	4.97	**5.06**	4.92	4.78	**5.06**	5.12
Access to Debt Finance	**5.04**	**5.09**	4.78	**5.02**	4.96	4.84	**5.04**	4.76	4.67	4.86	4.84	4.83	4.79	4.55	4.75	4.85
Access to Business-Relevant Information	4.97	4.92	4.91	4.88	4.8	4.83	**5.05**	4.70	4.83	**5.04**	4.77	4.90	4.86	4.53	4.79	4.85
Access to Input Goods and Services	4.86	4.88	4.74	4.76	4.72	4.65	4.74	4.62	4.59	4.82	4.72	4.80	4.80	4.42	4.65	4.72
Access to Capital Equipment	4.85	4.70	4.71	4.84	4.65	4.75	4.73	4.70	4.55	4.87	4.56	4.76	4.77	4.54	4.70	4.71
Availability of Equity Capital	4.77	4.63	4.60	4.78	4.75	4.54	4.64	4.76	4.50	4.78	4.63	4.62	4.72	4.41	4.65	4.65
Sophistication of Local Demand	4.67	4.69	4.65	4.79	4.68	4.66	4.76	4.56	4.57	4.82	4.58	4.59	4.63	4.27	4.66	4.64
Future Local Market Potential	4.71	4.39	4.57	4.80	4.75	4.48	4.72	4.61	4.36	4.75	4.43	4.57	4.63	4.09	4.68	4.57
Availability of Venture Capital	4.66	4.58	4.49	4.68	4.53	4.44	4.54	4.59	4.29	4.71	4.49	4.51	4.67	4.32	4.57	4.54
Cost of Debt Finance	4.63	4.46	4.52	4.59	4.64	4.53	4.49	4.40	4.37	4.60	4.76	4.62	4.53	4.35	4.58	4.54
Support from Related Industries	4.62	4.43	4.51	4.58	4.51	4.53	4.70	4.35	4.42	4.82	4.54	4.56	4.65	4.23	4.61	4.54
Size of Local Market Demand	4.50	4.03	4.44	4.62	4.66	4.34	4.59	4.60	4.24	4.68	4.35	4.49	4.56	4.02	4.53	4.44
Clustering of Firms in Your Industry	4.51	4.40	4.42	4.40	4.48	4.42	4.56	4.28	4.31	4.64	4.39	4.58	4.56	4.20	4.38	4.44

Notes:

1 = very unimportant/much worse than competitors/comparators, 4 = neutral, 7 = very important/much better than competitors/comparators.

DO&EO = Utilities and Construction; F0 = Wholesale Trade; G0 = Retail Trade; H0 = Accommodation and Food Services; I0 = Transport, Postal, Warehousing; J0 = Information, Media, Telecommunications; K0 = Finance and Insurance Services; L0 = Rental, Hiring, Real Estate Services; M0 = Professional, Scientific, and Technical Services; N0 = Administrative and Support Services; O0 = Public Administration and Safety; P0 = Education and Training; Q0 = Health Care and Social Assistance; R0 = Arts and Recreation; S0 = Other Services.

Sources: Michael J. Enright and CPA Australia.

97

Australia is rated above the competition/comparators on average in both of these drivers in both sets of sectors, they were among the lowest performers among the drivers shown in the tables. This is not surprising given the moderate size of the domestic market compared to some major economies around the world.

Support from Related Industries and Clustering of Firms are viewed as moderately important by respondents in the two sets of sectors and generally as less of an advantage to Australian competitiveness than other drivers in the two tables. This could represent a lack of efforts to organise and co-ordinate the activities of Australian companies to improve their competitiveness and their ability to penetrate international markets. This would be consistent with the responses reported for industry association activities earlier. In any case, this represents an interesting area for further analysis in the Australian context.

The picture that emerges is one in which local markets are important in many industries, but not likely to be a big advantage, reasonably good service support for industries (with finance and information particularly strong), and linkages that are marginal advantages or are disadvantages. Again, few of the drivers have average performance scores above 5, which indicates only moderate advantages, so all of the drivers in these tables could use improvement.

Macro or National-Level Drivers

Several macro or national-level drivers were shown to be important to the industries described in Chapter 3. Here we have divided the analysis of the survey responses on national-level drivers of competitiveness into three groups, including macroeconomics, taxes, and regulation; government policy; and society and institutions.

Macroeconomics, Taxes, and Regulation

Responses on macroeconomic, tax, and regulation-related drivers are found in Tables 4.7 and 4.8. Respondents in both sets of sectors view all of the drivers listed as important and the top few as approaching very important. According to respondents in the primary and manufacturing sectors, the most important macroeconomic drivers are Exchange Rates, Overall Local Economic Conditions, Inflation Rates, and Interest Rates. For the utilities, construction, service sectors, the most important macroeconomic drivers are Overall Local Economic Conditions, Strength of Government Finances, Interest Rates, and Inflation Rates.

Australia is viewed as performing better than competitors in all of the macroeconomic drivers by respondents in both sets of sectors, and by a significant margin in general. On average, respondents from both sets of sectors give Australia relatively high marks for Macroeconomic Stability, Overall Local Economic Conditions, Strength of Government Finances, and Inflation Rates, in precisely the same order. Respondents in several primary and manufacturing sectors shown in the tables claim that Australia has disadvantages versus competitors when it comes to Exchange Rates and Interest Rates, though this is not the case for the utilities, construction, service sectors. The overall sense one gets is that Australia is doing well in the important macroeconomic drivers, which has certainly been the case in recent years versus major Western economies and many developing economies as well.

TABLE 4.7   Importance and Performance; National-Level Drivers; Macroeconomics, Taxes, Regulation; Primary and Manufacturing Sectors

Driver	A0	B0	C11	C12	C13	C14	C15	C16	C17	C18	C19	C20	C21	C22	C23	C24	C25	AVE
Importance																		
Exchange Rates	5.78	5.89	5.78	**6.20**	5.72	5.57	**6.00**	5.50	**6.00**	**6.35**	**6.24**	**6.00**	5.74	**6.51**	**6.12**	**6.03**	5.72	5.95
Overall Local Economic Conditions	5.59	5.29	5.60	5.75	5.19	5.79	5.75	5.60	5.57	**6.11**	5.95	**6.44**	5.58	**6.30**	5.96	5.86	5.87	5.78
Inflation Rates	5.75	5.53	5.75	**6.18**	5.69	5.57	**6.00**	5.39	5.54	**6.00**	5.81	5.67	5.43	**6.07**	5.96	5.80	5.89	5.77
Interest Rates	5.76	5.24	5.69	**6.18**	5.65	**6.00**	5.67	5.17	5.29	**6.15**	5.81	5.56	5.48	**6.21**	5.96	5.84	5.72	5.73
Regulatory and Legal Framework	5.74	5.74	5.76	5.92	5.44	4.93	5.92	5.29	5.86	**6.05**	5.76	5.89	5.83	**6.09**	5.69	5.95	5.51	5.73
Macroeconomic Stability	5.47	5.30	5.62	5.50	5.13	5.64	5.67	5.50	5.46	**6.32**	5.53	**6.11**	5.48	**6.00**	5.96	5.73	5.69	5.65
Strength of Government Finances	5.63	5.22	5.46	5.64	5.31	5.07	5.83	5.59	5.86	5.50	5.60	**6.11**	5.70	**6.00**	**6.12**	5.84	5.42	5.64
Corporate Tax Rate	5.59	5.52	5.67	5.67	5.52	5.29	5.64	5.11	5.79	5.95	**6.00**	5.56	5.35	**6.07**	5.73	5.75	5.64	5.64
Tax Regime (Overall)	5.68	5.48	5.67	5.58	5.63	5.79	5.55	5.11	5.50	5.85	5.81	5.44	5.27	5.91	5.58	5.91	5.67	5.61
Other Taxes and Charges	5.75	5.42	5.75	5.33	5.67	5.15	5.64	5.24	5.57	5.85	5.70	5.22	5.13	5.88	5.81	5.75	5.45	5.55
Payroll Taxes	5.65	5.32	5.75	5.17	5.69	5.38	5.73	5.17	5.50	5.70	5.75	5.56	4.83	5.78	5.65	5.62	5.19	5.50
Carbon Tax/Emission Trading Scheme	5.48	5.20	5.33	5.50	5.58	4.93	5.42	5.06	5.21	5.80	5.71	**6.22**	4.57	5.88	5.81	5.29	5.30	5.43
Personal Income Tax Rate	5.46	4.98	5.44	5.25	5.38	5.36	5.55	5.28	5.57	5.65	5.33	5.33	4.83	5.74	5.54	5.52	5.35	5.39
Performance																		
Macroeconomic Stability	**5.12**	4.78	**5.20**	**5.22**	4.07	**5.54**	**5.09**	4.80	**5.54**	4.95	4.95	4.67	4.73	4.70	**5.04**	4.98	4.66	4.94
Overall Local Economic Conditions	**5.00**	4.80	**5.06**	**5.55**	4.33	**5.31**	5.27	4.56	**5.23**	**5.15**	4.74	**5.00**	4.30	4.88	**5.08**	**5.06**	4.71	4.94
Strength of Government Finances	4.85	4.49	4.98	**5.18**	4.59	4.62	**5.91**	4.56	4.85	4.53	**5.11**	**5.56**	4.91	4.71	4.88	4.95	4.88	4.92
Regulatory and Legal Framework	4.91	4.57	4.84	4.75	4.83	4.62	**5.45**	4.72	4.69	4.79	**5.26**	**5.33**	**5.00**	4.57	4.85	**5.06**	4.98	4.90
Inflation Rates	4.72	4.21	**5.04**	3.75	4.48	4.69	**5.73**	4.82	**5.00**	4.16	4.80	4.78	4.50	3.93	4.31	4.85	4.50	4.60
Interest Rates	4.38	4.03	4.75	3.58	4.21	3.77	**5.55**	4.53	4.54	4.47	4.21	**5.11**	4.09	4.00	4.27	4.60	4.30	4.38
Exchange Rates	4.35	4.06	4.64	4.73	4.48	4.69	**5.27**	4.47	4.54	4.26	3.65	4.38	3.77	3.74	4.16	4.68	4.20	4.36
Tax Regime (Overall)	4.43	3.70	4.37	4.18	4.24	4.18	4.40	3.81	4.08	4.50	4.58	4.33	4.33	3.60	4.23	4.63	4.30	4.23
Corporate Tax Rate	4.36	3.84	4.30	4.00	4.23	3.82	4.20	4.00	4.15	4.45	4.37	4.44	4.14	3.57	4.28	4.52	4.12	4.16
Personal Income Tax Rate	4.26	3.56	4.11	3.91	4.30	3.91	4.40	3.88	4.31	4.05	4.58	4.00	4.27	3.41	4.04	4.56	3.98	4.09
Other Taxes and Charges	4.21	3.49	4.39	4.00	4.32	3.45	3.50	3.59	4.62	4.20	3.72	4.33	4.05	3.18	4.24	4.32	3.79	3.96
Payroll Taxes	4.19	3.47	4.18	4.09	4.07	3.70	3.30	3.71	4.31	4.25	4.00	4.13	4.23	3.18	4.24	4.27	3.86	3.95
Carbon Tax/Emission Trading Scheme	3.83	3.15	4.07	3.75	3.93	2.77	4.55	3.94	4.54	3.89	4.05	4.33	3.59	2.98	3.27	4.33	4.07	3.83

Notes:

1 = very unimportant/much worse than competitors/comparators, 4 = neutral, 7 = very important/much better than competitors/comparators.

A0 = Agriculture/Forestry/Fishing; B0 = Mining; C11 = Food Product Manufacturing; C12 = Beverage and Tobacco Product Manufacturing; C13 = Textile, Leather, Clothing, and Footwear Manufacturing; C14 = Wood Product Manufacturing; C15 = Pulp, Paper, and Converted Paper Product Manufacturing; C16 = Printing; C17 = Petroleum and Coal Product Manufacturing; C18 = Basic Chemical and Chemical Product Manufacturing; C19 = Polymer Product and Rubber Product Manufacturing; C20 = Non-Metallic Mineral Product Manufacturing; C21 = Primary Metal and Metal Product Manufacturing; C22 = Fabricated Metal Product Manufacturing; C23 = Transport Equipment Manufacturing; C24 = Machinery and Equipment Manufacturing; C25 = Furniture and Other Manufacturing.

Sources: Michael J. Enright and CPA Australia.

TABLE 4.8 Importance and Performance; National-Level Drivers; Macroeconomics, Taxes, Regulation; Utilities, Construction, Services

Driver	DO & EO	FO	GO	HO	IO	JO	KO	LO	MO	NO	OO	PO	QO	RO	SO	AVE
Importance																
Regulatory and Legal Framework	5.81	5.68	5.52	5.61	5.78	5.55	5.99	5.75	5.88	5.45	5.89	5.71	5.96	5.09	5.42	5.67
Overall Local Economic Conditions	5.75	5.89	5.79	5.80	5.81	5.43	5.89	5.95	5.53	5.38	4.88	5.61	5.46	5.69	5.39	5.62
Strength of Government Finances	5.79	5.53	5.54	5.55	5.66	5.33	5.71	5.80	5.47	5.34	5.73	5.62	5.82	4.80	5.20	5.53
Tax Regime (Overall)	5.78	5.70	5.57	5.55	5.74	5.38	5.65	5.89	5.60	5.39	4.89	5.21	5.44	5.09	5.26	5.48
Interest Rates	5.88	5.75	5.64	5.82	5.60	5.24	5.80	**6.16**	5.26	5.33	4.47	5.14	5.22	5.01	5.15	5.43
Inflation Rates	5.72	5.72	5.71	5.69	5.66	5.20	5.67	5.90	5.41	5.34	4.52	5.19	5.34	5.11	5.18	5.42
Other Taxes and Charges	5.72	5.52	5.53	5.71	5.57	5.31	5.38	5.89	5.50	5.28	4.69	5.14	5.37	5.32	5.27	5.41
Macroeconomic Stability	5.49	5.76	5.51	5.50	5.57	5.40	5.73	5.58	5.58	5.16	4.85	5.40	5.22	5.19	5.14	5.41
Personal Income Tax Rate	5.67	5.49	5.49	5.62	5.48	5.20	5.50	5.63	5.46	5.35	4.61	5.23	5.40	5.17	5.17	5.36
Payroll Taxes	5.65	5.49	5.48	5.73	5.52	5.31	5.36	5.49	5.41	5.31	4.73	5.12	5.32	5.02	5.12	5.34
Corporate Tax Rate	5.69	5.62	5.41	5.46	5.76	5.41	5.62	5.76	5.53	5.34	4.50	4.69	5.19	4.66	5.18	5.32
Exchange Rates	5.49	**6.03**	5.82	5.50	5.60	5.41	5.59	5.16	5.36	5.18	4.18	5.08	4.70	5.12	4.99	5.28
Carbon Tax/Emission Trading Scheme	5.38	5.20	4.98	5.12	5.45	4.60	4.73	5.04	4.53	4.89	4.24	4.35	4.50	4.04	4.66	4.78
Performance																
Macroeconomic Stability	4.84	**5.04**	4.76	4.95	4.83	4.97	**5.26**	4.88	4.98	**5.15**	4.95	**5.08**	4.83	4.77	4.70	4.93
Overall Local Economic Conditions	4.79	4.98	4.79	4.93	4.73	4.93	**5.20**	**5.03**	4.93	**5.23**	4.94	**5.01**	4.90	4.68	4.79	4.92
Strength of Government Finances	4.81	4.70	4.69	4.87	4.57	4.99	**5.15**	4.91	4.83	**5.15**	**5.03**	**5.13**	4.83	4.40	4.68	4.85
Regulatory and Legal Framework	4.74	4.86	4.61	4.74	4.59	4.96	**5.19**	4.59	4.90	**5.11**	**5.02**	**5.06**	4.84	4.34	4.65	4.81
Inflation Rates	4.59	4.71	4.52	4.61	4.44	4.62	4.81	4.72	4.56	4.79	4.63	4.91	4.61	4.25	4.51	4.62
Exchange Rates	4.80	4.65	4.72	4.53	4.57	4.67	4.57	4.66	4.41	4.71	4.78	4.65	4.64	4.42	4.50	4.62
Interest Rates	4.43	4.24	4.30	4.39	4.20	4.51	4.55	4.28	4.22	4.50	4.54	4.74	4.49	4.23	4.40	4.40
Tax Regime (Overall)	4.20	3.99	4.19	4.49	4.00	4.37	4.17	4.32	4.05	4.58	4.66	4.30	4.24	4.00	4.15	4.25
Corporate Tax Rate	4.15	3.92	4.14	4.34	4.01	4.30	4.24	4.16	4.00	4.51	4.58	4.27	4.18	3.98	4.10	4.19
Personal Income Tax Rate	4.05	3.75	4.09	4.41	3.71	4.06	4.01	3.96	3.78	4.43	4.48	4.27	4.00	3.96	4.04	4.07
Other Taxes and Charges	4.02	3.78	3.93	4.22	3.73	4.23	3.96	3.87	3.80	4.38	4.48	4.20	4.01	3.85	3.95	4.03
Payroll Taxes	4.02	3.70	3.92	4.29	3.65	4.15	4.02	3.94	3.66	4.30	4.45	4.21	4.03	3.87	3.97	4.01
Carbon Tax/Emission Trading Scheme	3.95	3.78	3.77	4.14	3.53	4.02	3.90	3.49	3.85	4.25	4.43	4.02	3.97	3.72	3.87	3.91

Notes:

1 = very unimportant/much worse than competitors/comparators, 4 = neutral, 7 = very important/much better than competitors/comparators.

DO&EO = Utilities and Construction; FO = Wholesale Trade; GO = Retail Trade; HO = Accommodation and Food Services; IO = Transport, Postal, Warehousing; JO = Information, Media, Telecommunications; KO = Finance and Insurance Services; LO = Rental, Hiring, Real Estate Services; MO = Professional, Scientific, and Technical Services; NO = Administrative and Support Services; OO = Public Administration and Safety; PO = Education and Training; QO = Health Care and Social Assistance; RO = Arts and Recreation; SO = Other Services.

Sources: Michael J. Enright and CPA Australia.

Respondents' views on taxes are another matter; all of the tax-related drivers are viewed as important by respondents in both sets of sectors, but they are generally considered less important than macroeconomic drivers. Australia's position in taxes is considered a disadvantage in many, but not all, of the sectors in the tables. Australia is seen as performing worst in Carbon Tax/Emissions Trading, Payroll Taxes, Other Taxes and Charges, and Personal Income Tax Rates. It is clear that the Carbon Tax is not popular with respondents in most sectors.[4] Respondents in 11 of 17 primary and manufacturing sectors, and 9 of 15 of the utilities, construction, service sectors view it as a competitive disadvantage. While average performance on some tax-related drivers, such as Tax Regime (overall), is slightly positive, taxes and the tax system are clearly concerns for respondents. Of course, we have never met managers that want their company's taxes increased, and while tax drivers are viewed as somewhat less important than macroeconomic drivers by respondents, they remain a cause for concern.

The Regulatory and Legal Framework is viewed as important by respondents in all sectors. On average, respondents give Australia positive (above neutral) marks on the Regulatory and Legal Framework, which is interesting, because while in our experience Australians take a great deal of pride in the nation's legal system, they take far less pride in the nation's regulatory system.

The picture that emerges from the responses for macroeconomic, tax, and regulation drivers is one of strong macroeconomic performance, reasonably good regulatory and legal systems, and less favourable tax regimes. These results show broad agreement with those from the international assessments in Chapter 2 with the exception of views on the regulatory environment. Australia's macroeconomic performance has already been discussed in Chapter 1. Its tax and regulatory regimes will be discussed further below. Again, we note that all of the drivers for the primary and manufacturing sectors and all but two for the construction, utilities, service sectors received average importance ratings ahead of all of the performance ratings for these drivers. Again, the indication is that there is much work to do.

Government Policy

Several of the most important national-level drivers are those involving government policy. In Tables 4.9 and 4.10, we see that respondents in all sectors view all of the government policy drivers identified as important, with some approaching very important. On average, respondents in the primary and manufacturing sectors view government policies as more important than respondents in the utilities, construction, service sectors. Respondents in both sets of sectors identify Overall Government Policy, Industrial and Workplace Relations/Labour Laws, and Competition Policy as the three most important government policy drivers. Environmental Policies, Science and Technology Policy, and Planning Laws are viewed as the least important by the primary and manufacturing respondents, while Science and Technology Policy, Foreign Trade and Tariff Policy, and Foreign Investment Policy are viewed as the least important by the utilities, construction, service sector respondents. It is interesting that Science and Technology Policy, while viewed as important in the sense of above neutral in importance, is far down the overall list.

In terms of performance, respondents in both sets of sectors indicate that Australia has advantages versus competitor and comparator economies in most of the drivers.

TABLE 4.9 Importance and Performance, National-Level Drivers, Government Policy; Primary and Manufacturing Sectors

Driver	A0	B0	C11	C12	C13	C14	C15	C16	C17	C18	C19	C20	C21	C22	C23	C24	C25	AVE
Importance																		
Overall Government Policy	5.82	5.73	5.60	5.83	5.76	4.93	5.67	5.67	5.93	**6.15**	5.75	**6.00**	5.78	**6.14**	**6.12**	5.88	5.64	5.79
Industrial, Workplace Relations/Labour Laws	5.70	5.55	5.79	5.75	5.74	5.07	**6.00**	5.41	5.36	**6.15**	5.65	**6.00**	5.30	**6.09**	**6.04**	5.69	5.36	5.69
Competition Policy	5.69	5.01	5.60	5.42	5.58	5.31	5.55	5.41	5.64	**6.00**	5.68	5.56	5.57	5.60	**6.00**	5.69	5.43	5.57
Foreign Trade and Tariff Policy	5.79	5.43	5.86	5.50	5.34	4.85	5.82	5.25	5.50	**6.05**	5.95	5.22	5.39	5.49	5.88	5.69	5.31	5.55
Policies to Encourage R&D	5.67	5.33	5.39	4.92	5.41	4.79	5.64	5.06	5.36	**6.10**	5.52	5.33	5.04	5.59	5.88	5.69	5.39	5.42
Foreign Investment Policy	5.54	5.36	5.72	5.00	5.30	4.77	5.91	5.14	5.86	5.55	5.42	5.22	5.22	5.50	5.52	5.56	5.32	5.41
Environmental Policies	5.65	5.40	5.07	5.17	5.32	5.14	5.82	4.75	5.57	**6.15**	5.53	5.38	4.78	5.33	5.65	5.49	5.20	5.38
Science and Technology Policy	5.42	5.25	5.14	4.50	5.14	4.64	5.82	5.13	5.21	5.79	5.26	5.22	4.87	5.30	5.50	5.67	5.11	5.23
Planning Laws	5.39	5.38	5.19	4.27	5.17	4.93	5.00	4.94	5.43	5.50	5.28	5.33	4.87	5.07	5.31	5.33	5.00	5.14
Performance																		
Environmental Policies	4.87	4.88	4.86	**5.17**	4.70	4.92	**6.33**	4.81	4.54	5.05	5.22	5.22	5.10	5.02	5.00	**5.16**	4.63	5.03
Science and Technology Policy	4.63	4.61	4.72	4.09	4.64	**5.15**	5.00	4.87	4.85	4.85	4.65	4.56	4.59	4.33	4.80	4.59	4.38	4.67
Policies to Encourage R&D	4.60	4.52	4.86	4.27	4.64	4.54	**5.11**	4.67	4.62	4.75	4.72	4.44	4.27	4.23	4.62	4.51	4.36	4.57
Planning Laws	4.48	4.45	4.39	4.00	4.56	**5.08**	**5.00**	4.07	4.92	4.80	4.41	4.44	4.27	4.07	4.68	4.73	4.31	4.51
Competition Policy	4.46	4.28	4.68	4.27	4.52	4.42	4.40	3.83	**5.00**	4.50	4.47	4.63	4.41	3.90	4.15	4.50	4.18	4.39
Foreign Investment Policy	4.33	4.57	4.64	3.91	4.26	4.31	4.75	4.25	4.62	4.55	4.06	4.67	4.14	4.15	4.24	4.35	4.39	4.36
Foreign Trade and Tariff Policy	4.38	4.41	4.56	3.91	4.31	4.69	**5.22**	4.31	4.46	4.55	3.79	4.44	4.27	3.95	4.12	4.35	4.37	4.36
Overall Government Policy	4.24	3.92	4.50	3.82	4.45	4.08	**5.09**	4.06	4.85	4.42	4.05	4.44	4.09	3.66	4.08	4.61	4.40	4.28
Industrial, Workplace Relations/Labour Laws	4.25	3.63	4.57	4.09	4.10	4.17	4.80	3.94	4.69	4.25	3.84	4.22	3.90	3.80	4.42	4.61	4.29	4.21

Notes:

1 = very unimportant/much worse than competitors/comparators, 4 = neutral, 7 = very important/much better than competitors/comparators.

A0 = Agriculture/Forestry/Fishing; B0 = Mining; C11 = Food Product Manufacturing; C12 = Beverage and Tobacco Product Manufacturing; C13 = Textile, Leather, Clothing, and Footwear Manufacturing; C14 = Wood Product Manufacturing; C15 = Pulp, Paper, and Converted Paper Product Manufacturing; C16 = Printing; C17 = Petroleum and Coal Product Manufacturing; C18 = Basic Chemical and Chemical Product Manufacturing; C19 = Polymer Product and Rubber Product Manufacturing; C20 = Non-Metallic Mineral Product Manufacturing; C21 = Primary Metal and Metal Product Manufacturing; C22 = Fabricated Metal Product Manufacturing; C23 = Transport Equipment Manufacturing; C24 = Machinery and Equipment Manufacturing; C25 = Furniture and Other Manufacturing.

Sources: Michael J. Enright and CPA Australia.

TABLE 4.10 Importance and Performance; National-Level Drivers; Government Policy; Construction, Utilities, Service Sectors

Driver	D0 & E0	F0	G0	H0	I0	J0	K0	L0	M0	N0	O0	P0	Q0	R0	S0	AVE
Importance																
Overall Government Policy	5.75	5.65	5.50	5.52	5.68	5.30	5.83	5.81	5.50	5.52	5.83	5.78	5.79	4.85	5.30	5.57
Industrial, Workplace Relations/Labour Laws	5.72	5.44	5.36	5.58	5.71	5.23	5.25	5.43	5.40	5.21	5.25	5.51	5.60	5.01	5.20	5.39
Competition Policy	5.53	5.38	5.44	5.41	5.45	5.33	5.51	5.42	5.31	4.94	4.55	5.03	5.06	5.00	5.01	5.22
Environmental Policies	5.46	5.37	5.07	5.05	5.38	4.92	4.86	5.25	4.98	4.97	4.75	5.06	5.09	4.52	4.99	5.05
Policies to Encourage R&D	5.13	5.03	4.89	4.65	4.95	5.16	4.67	4.51	5.15	4.72	5.00	5.26	5.47	4.34	4.63	4.90
Planning Laws	5.43	4.86	4.89	5.32	5.14	4.68	4.71	5.76	4.80	4.68	4.54	4.70	4.79	3.99	4.68	4.86
Science and Technology Policy	5.04	4.97	4.84	4.61	4.84	5.24	4.58	4.32	5.00	4.59	4.78	5.01	5.16	3.96	4.44	4.76
Foreign Trade and Tariff Policy	5.07	5.47	5.32	4.80	4.98	4.98	4.91	4.36	4.86	4.59	4.25	4.45	4.30	4.15	4.57	4.74
Foreign Investment Policy	5.10	5.20	4.98	4.79	4.93	4.91	5.27	5.09	4.80	4.47	4.25	4.32	4.25	4.04	4.50	4.73
Performance																
Environmental Policies	4.92	**5.02**	4.78	4.83	4.65	4.77	4.80	4.90	4.72	**5.10**	4.95	**5.02**	4.94	4.55	4.71	4.84
Science and Technology Policy	4.63	4.60	4.52	4.63	4.51	4.49	4.47	4.38	4.39	4.79	4.48	4.55	4.54	4.42	4.44	4.52
Planning Laws	4.50	4.58	4.42	4.58	4.55	4.48	4.47	4.57	4.37	4.82	4.54	4.68	4.49	4.18	4.43	4.51
Competition Policy	4.44	4.33	4.36	4.58	4.34	4.55	4.60	4.47	4.37	4.77	4.66	4.52	4.34	4.09	4.34	4.45
Policies to Encourage R&D	4.54	4.45	4.44	4.45	4.36	4.44	4.39	4.40	4.27	4.70	4.48	4.50	4.47	4.24	4.42	4.44
Foreign Trade and Tariff Policy	4.48	4.42	4.31	4.45	4.43	4.45	4.40	4.20	4.28	4.65	4.54	4.45	4.38	4.36	4.32	4.41
Foreign Investment Policy	4.39	4.48	4.32	4.28	4.41	4.48	4.46	4.29	4.28	4.65	4.40	4.49	4.40	4.28	4.26	4.39
Overall Government Policy	4.34	4.14	4.09	4.33	4.15	4.56	4.53	4.19	4.33	4.80	4.89	4.65	4.61	3.94	4.31	4.39
Industrial, Workplace Relations/Labour Laws	4.36	4.00	4.32	4.38	4.13	4.57	4.28	4.27	4.11	4.55	4.51	4.47	4.24	4.04	4.22	4.30

Notes:

1 = very unimportant/much worse than competitors/comparators; 4 = neutral; 7 = very important/much better than competitors/comparators.

D0&E0 = Utilities and Construction; F0 = Wholesale Trade; G0 = Retail Trade; H0 = Accommodation and Food Services; I0 = Transport, Postal, Warehousing; J0 = Information, Media, Telecommunications; K0 = Finance and Insurance Services; L0 = Rental, Hiring, Real Estate Services; M0 = Professional, Scientific, and Technical Services; N0 = Administrative and Support Services; O0 = Public Administration and Safety; P0 = Education and Training; Q0 = Health Care and Social Assistance; R0 = Arts and Recreation; S0 = Other Services.

Sources: Michael J. Enright and CPA Australia.

However, the lead in most cases is slight, and there are some drivers in which Australia is viewed as having disadvantages. Respondents in both sets of sectors indicate that Australia's performance on average is strongest in Environmental Policies and Science and Technology Policy (again areas viewed as of middling in importance). The next-best performance is in Policies to Encourage R&D, Planning Laws, and Competition Policy according to respondents in the primary and manufacturing sectors, and the same in a slightly different order according to respondents in the utilities, construction, service sectors. Both groups rate Overall Government Policy and Industrial and Workplace Relations/Labour Laws as Australia's weakest areas among the policies investigated, with a significant minority of sectors in the primary and manufacturing set viewing these as disadvantages, and most other sector respondents viewing them as mild advantages.

The survey responses indicate that all of the policy areas are considered important, and that Australia has advantages, on average, in all of them. However, the responses indicate that the advantages are weak, and the two policy drivers that are considered most important, Overall Government Policy and Industrial and Workplace Relations/Laws, have Australia's weakest performance among the drivers in the set. Again, the importance scores are generally higher than the performance scores. In addition, some of the policy areas that get a great deal of press, such as Science and Technology Policy, are viewed as less important than other areas that might get less attention. Government Policy is another area we will return to in subsequent chapters.

Society and Institutions

Tables 4.11 and 4.12 provide summaries of responses regarding the impact of drivers related to society and institutions on the competitiveness of Australian industries. Again, respondents in all of the sectors indicate that each of the drivers listed in the tables is important to competitiveness. This again suggests that any approach that leaves them out is fundamentally incomplete. Among respondents in the primary and manufacturing sectors, Government Freedom from Corruption, Political Stability, Social Stability, Transparency of Government, and Quality of Education & Training Institutions are viewed as the most important of these drivers. Respondents in the utilities, construction, and service sectors indicate that the most important drivers in this set are Quality of Life, Quality of Education & Training Institutions, Government Freedom from Corruption, Social Stability, and Transparency of Government. Both groups indicate that Community Institutions are the least important among these drivers, although again respondents in all of the sectors rate these as above neutral in importance.

We note that even though they did not reach the top in terms of importance in the society and institutions drivers, that Attitudes of Community toward Innovation, Attitudes of Community toward Business, Attitudes of Community toward Entrepreneurship, and Environmental Consciousness actually receive average importance ratings well above many drivers in other categories. This is interesting in that such soft drivers of competitiveness often receive far less attention than the hard drivers such as infrastructure, costs, inputs, and so on. The importance results indicate that concerted efforts to generate more positive attitudes towards innovation, business, and entrepreneurship could have a significant payoff in terms of enhanced competitiveness in Australia.

TABLE 4.11 Importance and Performance, National-Level Drivers, Society and Institutions; Primary and Manufacturing Sectors

Driver	A0	B0	C11	C12	C13	C14	C15	C16	C17	C18	C19	C20	C21	C22	C23	C24	C25	AVE
Importance																		
Government Freedom from Corruption	5.73	5.65	5.53	5.83	5.34	5.43	6.00	5.12	5.57	6.00	5.90	5.78	5.74	5.79	6.00	5.98	5.53	5.70
Political Stability	5.61	5.63	5.57	5.50	5.75	5.00	5.75	5.56	5.93	5.75	5.60	5.44	5.87	5.86	6.27	5.98	5.54	5.68
Social Stability	5.64	5.59	5.47	5.83	5.68	5.64	6.10	5.12	6.07	5.80	5.50	5.44	5.43	5.93	5.69	5.66	5.36	5.64
Transparency of Government	5.76	5.47	5.44	5.75	5.41	5.21	5.83	5.29	5.64	5.80	5.65	5.78	5.61	5.86	5.81	5.94	5.41	5.63
Quality of Education & Training Institutions	5.57	5.73	5.42	6.08	5.39	5.07	5.90	4.71	5.64	6.00	5.76	5.44	5.57	5.98	5.96	5.81	5.45	5.62
Quality of Research Institutions, Organisations	5.69	5.47	5.39	5.42	5.32	4.79	5.91	4.75	5.57	6.00	5.67	5.44	5.17	5.67	5.85	5.92	5.31	5.49
Quality of Life	5.62	5.38	5.19	5.75	5.13	5.23	5.82	5.13	5.64	5.35	5.45	5.67	5.17	5.72	5.77	5.57	5.27	5.46
Attitudes of Community toward Innovation	5.56	5.32	5.28	4.92	5.32	5.07	6.00	5.00	5.57	6.15	5.15	5.44	4.95	5.38	5.69	5.86	5.14	5.40
Attitudes of Community toward Business	5.60	5.54	5.43	5.25	5.43	5.14	5.56	4.94	5.57	6.10	4.95	5.11	4.87	5.43	5.42	5.57	5.49	5.38
Environmental Consciousness	5.49	5.35	5.07	5.42	5.13	4.93	5.82	4.81	5.79	5.90	5.25	5.33	4.78	5.40	5.62	5.64	5.07	5.34
Attitudes toward Entrepreneurship	5.46	5.10	5.29	4.83	5.41	4.80	5.80	4.88	5.57	5.95	4.90	5.11	4.74	5.48	5.23	5.61	5.20	5.26
Community Institutions	5.07	4.76	5.02	4.55	5.04	4.85	5.00	5.21	5.57	5.10	4.79	4.56	4.26	4.75	5.00	5.11	4.68	4.90
Performance																		
Quality of Life	5.42	5.33	5.51	6.08	5.00	5.91	6.33	5.20	4.92	5.65	5.42	5.44	4.77	5.52	5.40	5.38	4.98	5.43
Social Stability	5.37	5.26	5.54	6.00	4.86	5.77	6.00	5.07	4.92	5.25	5.37	5.56	4.95	5.42	5.12	5.29	4.65	5.32
Environmental Consciousness	5.15	5.09	5.24	5.42	4.81	5.23	6.13	5.07	4.38	5.10	5.28	5.44	5.05	5.35	4.96	5.34	4.79	5.17
Government Freedom from Corruption	4.97	4.89	5.12	5.00	4.82	4.46	5.91	4.76	5.38	4.95	5.37	6.22	5.05	4.95	5.15	5.07	5.14	5.13
Quality of Education & Training Institutions	5.19	4.90	5.11	5.00	4.67	5.69	6.13	5.27	4.77	5.10	5.60	4.78	5.05	5.07	4.92	5.14	4.65	5.12
Quality of Research Institutions, Organisations	5.11	4.82	5.07	5.00	4.73	5.38	6.00	4.86	4.46	5.25	5.37	4.78	4.64	5.14	4.88	5.21	4.35	5.00
Transparency of Government	4.81	4.32	4.96	4.75	4.59	4.77	5.91	4.59	5.08	4.89	5.16	5.78	5.09	4.59	5.00	5.08	4.95	4.96
Political Stability	4.81	4.47	5.23	4.50	4.73	4.46	5.82	4.94	5.15	4.79	5.00	5.56	4.82	4.71	4.88	4.81	4.77	4.91
Attitudes of Community toward Innovation	4.83	4.22	5.04	4.18	4.58	4.38	5.78	4.63	4.31	5.15	5.00	5.44	4.10	5.12	4.58	4.95	4.49	4.75
Attitudes of Community toward Business	4.87	4.45	4.95	3.92	4.61	4.69	5.86	4.31	4.38	4.75	5.17	5.11	4.24	5.05	4.56	5.16	4.60	4.75
Attitudes toward Entrepreneurship	4.69	4.21	4.78	3.58	4.62	4.54	5.25	4.63	4.23	4.70	4.89	5.22	4.05	4.98	4.62	4.92	4.35	4.60
Community Institutions	4.63	4.44	4.78	3.90	4.38	4.38	4.33	4.73	4.62	4.65	4.50	5.11	4.27	4.30	4.63	4.52	4.31	4.50

Notes:

1 = very unimportant/much worse than competitors/comparators, 4 = neutral, 7 = very important/much better than competitors/comparators.

A0 = Agriculture/Forestry/Fishing; B0 = Mining; C11 = Food Product Manufacturing; C12 = Beverage and Tobacco Product Manufacturing; C13 = Textile, Leather, Clothing, and Footwear Manufacturing; C14 = Wood Product Manufacturing; C15 = Pulp, Paper, and Converted Paper Product Manufacturing; C16 = Printing; C17 = Petroleum and Coal Product Manufacturing; C18 = Basic Chemical and Chemical Product Manufacturing; C19 = Polymer Product and Rubber Product Manufacturing; C20 = Non-Metallic Mineral Product Manufacturing; C21 = Primary Metal and Metal Product Manufacturing; C22 = Fabricated Metal Product Manufacturing; C23 = Transport Equipment Manufacturing; C24 = Machinery and Equipment Manufacturing; C25 = Furniture and Other Manufacturing.

Sources: Michael J. Enright and CPA Australia.

TABLE 4.12 Importance and Performance; National-Level Drivers; Society and Institutions; Utilities, Construction, Service Sectors

Driver	D0 & E0	F0	G0	H0	I0	J0	K0	L0	M0	N0	O0	P0	Q0	R0	S0	AVE
Importance																
Quality of Life	5.62	5.49	5.65	5.77	5.62	5.43	5.63	5.85	5.55	5.35	5.30	5.91	5.96	5.87	5.42	5.63
Quality of Education & Training Institutions	5.68	5.48	5.38	5.54	5.58	5.59	5.69	5.55	5.87	5.43	5.38	**6.29**	**6.15**	5.42	5.37	5.63
Government Freedom from Corruption	5.74	5.66	5.50	5.65	5.77	5.45	5.81	5.79	5.74	5.45	5.75	5.68	5.66	5.00	5.41	5.60
Social Stability	5.54	5.44	5.52	5.62	5.66	5.49	5.66	5.85	5.50	5.28	5.29	5.89	5.84	5.44	5.39	5.56
Transparency of Government	5.74	5.46	5.47	5.56	5.80	5.36	5.71	5.67	5.63	5.45	5.71	5.57	5.76	4.97	5.29	5.54
Political Stability	5.76	5.55	5.47	5.50	5.71	5.34	5.79	5.66	5.62	5.42	5.68	5.60	5.60	4.74	5.25	5.51
Attitudes of Community toward Business	5.49	5.32	5.49	5.58	5.54	5.15	5.48	5.54	5.36	5.13	4.87	5.44	5.42	5.22	5.31	5.36
Quality of Research Institutions, Organisations	5.42	5.32	5.16	4.92	5.32	5.38	5.39	4.99	5.53	5.18	5.19	5.87	**6.06**	4.74	5.11	5.31
Attitudes of Community toward Innovation	5.37	5.35	5.50	5.34	5.43	5.35	5.32	5.39	5.34	5.06	4.85	5.54	5.33	5.10	5.15	5.29
Attitudes toward Entrepreneurship	5.27	5.17	5.44	5.29	5.33	5.20	5.30	5.46	5.19	5.03	4.62	5.33	5.12	5.23	5.10	5.21
Environmental Consciousness	5.41	5.30	5.15	5.13	5.43	5.05	4.86	5.36	4.98	5.04	4.70	5.22	5.18	4.65	5.07	5.10
Community Institutions	4.85	4.59	4.68	4.68	4.80	4.55	4.72	4.67	4.53	4.52	4.72	5.19	5.14	4.39	4.60	4.71
Performance																
Quality of Life	**5.30**	**5.47**	**5.34**	**5.32**	**5.20**	**5.33**	**5.52**	**5.47**	**5.35**	**5.36**	**5.20**	**5.58**	**5.32**	**5.16**	**5.22**	**5.34**
Social Stability	**5.19**	**5.31**	**5.20**	**5.28**	**5.03**	**5.17**	**5.34**	**5.35**	**5.24**	**5.28**	**5.20**	**5.41**	**5.22**	**5.08**	**5.07**	**5.22**
Environmental Consciousness	**5.09**	**5.18**	4.96	**5.19**	4.98	4.91	5.02	5.18	4.90	**5.14**	5.02	**5.10**	**5.11**	4.77	4.90	5.03
Quality of Education & Training Institutions	4.99	**5.07**	4.82	4.82	4.81	4.84	5.08	5.09	4.96	**5.03**	4.88	**5.01**	**5.03**	4.61	4.82	4.92
Government Freedom from Corruption	4.87	4.95	4.75	4.86	4.79	4.97	**5.20**	4.86	4.95	**5.03**	**5.06**	**5.14**	4.94	4.43	4.76	4.90
Quality of Research Institutions, Organisations	4.89	4.94	4.85	4.79	4.77	4.81	4.92	4.95	4.86	4.97	4.88	4.90	4.91	4.71	4.76	4.86
Attitudes of Community toward Business	4.84	4.80	4.73	4.91	4.51	4.73	4.73	4.73	4.63	4.96	4.72	4.84	4.77	4.42	4.68	4.73
Political Stability	4.57	4.55	4.51	4.72	4.62	4.84	4.89	4.74	4.77	**5.04**	4.77	4.97	4.72	4.31	4.60	4.71
Attitudes of Community toward Innovation	4.81	4.64	4.71	4.83	4.69	4.67	4.73	4.68	4.49	4.82	4.75	4.77	4.67	4.30	4.68	4.68
Transparency of Government	4.65	4.56	4.49	4.63	4.58	4.82	4.93	4.53	4.68	4.93	4.95	4.92	4.74	4.25	4.53	4.68
Attitudes toward Entrepreneurship	4.70	4.71	4.66	4.82	4.46	4.70	4.67	4.72	4.46	4.84	4.63	4.69	4.67	4.31	4.57	4.64
Community Institutions	4.51	4.48	4.52	4.62	4.45	4.38	4.58	4.51	4.48	4.67	4.66	4.70	4.68	4.25	4.44	4.53

Notes:

1 = very unimportant/much worse than competitors/comparators, 4 = neutral, 7 = very important/much better than competitors/comparators.
D0&E0 = Utilities and Construction; F0 = Wholesale Trade; G0 = Retail Trade; H0 = Accommodation and Food Services; I0 = Transport, Postal, Warehousing; J0 = Information, Media, Telecommunications; K0 = Finance and Insurance Services; L0 = Rental, Hiring, Real Estate Services; M0 = Professional, Scientific, and Technical Services; N0 = Administrative and Support Services; O0 = Public Administration and Safety; P0 = Education and Training; Q0 = Health Care and Social Assistance; R0 = Arts and Recreation; S0 = Other Services.

Sources: Michael J. Enright and CPA Australia.

Respondents from all of the sectors indicate that on average, Australia performed better than competitor and comparator countries in all of the drivers in the set. In fact, several of these drivers show Australia's best overall performance across all levels of analysis. Only Attitudes of Community toward Business, Attitudes of Community toward Entrepreneurship, and Community Institutions are rated as worse than competitors in any sector and these are all rated worse than competitors by respondents in the Beverage and Tobacco Product Manufacturing sector. Respondents from both sets of sectors indicate, on average, that Australia performed best in Quality of Life, Social Stability, Environmental Consciousness, Government Freedom from Corruption, and Quality of Education & Training Institutions, with only the ordering of the last two changing from the primary and manufacturing sectors set to the utilities, construction, service sectors set.

The primary and manufacturing sector respondents indicate that the worst performing drivers in the set were Attitudes of Community toward Innovation, Attitudes of Community toward Business, Attitudes of Community toward Entrepreneurship, and Community Institutions. The utilities, construction, and service sector respondents indicate that the worst performing drivers in the set were Attitudes of Community toward Innovation, Transparency of Government, Attitudes of Community toward Entrepreneurship, and Community Institutions. These would appear to be areas that would benefit from some considered action. We note in both cases that even the worst performing drivers are viewed as being better in Australia than in competitor nations.

We note that this is the only set of drivers so far in which Australia's performance, as indicated by respondents, approximates the importance of the drivers. We note also that the range of mean performance responses is comparable across the primary and manufacturing sectors, where competitors include some middle income and developing nations as well as some advanced nations, and the service sectors, in which competitors and comparators are often drawn from advanced economies. Australia's strong performance in the drivers related to society and institutions echoes its ratings in similar dimensions from the international sources on competitiveness described in Chapter 2. The difference here is that the assessment of the importance of these drivers by sector allows one to target industries that might be amenable to using these drivers as competitive weapons. For example, according to survey respondents the importance of Quality of Life as a driver of competitiveness varies substantially across sectors. To the extent that these drivers are not just good things to have, but actually affect decision making in industries, Australia will have advantages versus many competitors. Australia's strong position in these drivers also indicates that any deterioration in the political or social system, perhaps due to political paralysis and the politicisation of social issues, could be a severe blow to Australia's competitiveness.

Meta or Supranational-Level Drivers

Supranational-level drivers are those that are beyond the scope of a single country. While these drivers tend to be less direct in their influence on competitiveness than drivers at other levels, they can still be important as they influence the opportunity set for Australia and Australian companies and industries.

In Tables 4.13 and 4.14, respondents in all of the sectors indicate that all of the supranational drivers are above neutral in importance, though they differ in terms that

TABLE 4.13 Importance and Performance, Supranational-Level Drivers; Primary and Manufacturing Sectors

Driver	A0	B0	C11	C12	C13	C14	C15	C16	C17	C18	C19	C20	C21	C22	C23	C24	C25	AVE
Importance																		
Access to the China Market	5.50	5.69	5.06	5.82	5.09	4.79	5.67	5.28	5.71	**6.10**	4.90	4.89	5.67	5.11	5.92	5.58	5.36	5.42
Access to Other Asia-Pacific Markets	5.46	5.46	5.00	**6.00**	5.27	4.50	5.67	5.17	5.64	**6.05**	5.45	4.67	5.46	5.34	5.76	5.71	5.32	5.41
Foreign Government Support for Foreign Companies	5.29	5.20	5.42	4.92	5.47	5.00	5.82	5.07	5.79	5.40	5.47	5.33	5.26	5.60	5.65	5.56	5.07	5.37
Strategies of International Companies	4.95	5.27	5.50	5.08	4.68	4.79	5.08	5.67	5.64	**6.05**	5.16	4.78	4.75	5.22	5.76	5.68	5.20	5.25
International Companies in the Country	4.78	5.04	5.08	4.83	4.50	5.07	5.08	5.19	5.57	5.70	5.15	4.78	4.92	5.21	5.48	5.56	5.15	5.12
Activities of Multilateral Agencies	4.89	4.61	5.03	4.45	5.33	4.92	5.09	5.20	5.50	5.15	5.00	4.67	4.35	4.85	5.20	4.95	4.44	4.92
Performance																		
International Companies in the Country	4.81	4.84	4.97	4.64	4.45	4.69	**5.18**	4.67	4.77	**5.05**	4.65	**5.11**	4.52	4.26	4.64	4.84	4.35	4.73
Strategies of International Companies	4.67	4.81	4.83	4.30	4.52	4.77	4.82	4.73	4.77	**5.25**	4.95	**5.00**	4.43	4.54	4.36	4.67	4.44	4.70
Access to Other Asia-Pacific Markets	4.90	4.94	4.72	4.82	4.35	4.77	**5.46**	4.94	4.69	**5.05**	4.15	4.22	4.45	4.23	4.44	4.84	4.63	4.68
Access to the China Market	4.99	**5.03**	4.58	**5.00**	4.03	4.62	4.85	**5.12**	4.46	4.86	3.74	4.67	4.41	4.12	4.32	4.80	4.46	4.59
Activities of Multilateral Agencies	4.56	4.46	4.50	4.00	4.21	4.15	4.11	4.13	4.33	4.45	4.38	**5.00**	4.32	4.49	4.54	4.45	4.33	4.38
Foreign Government Support for Foreign Companies	4.47	4.41	4.33	4.00	4.00	4.38	4.44	4.13	4.23	4.65	4.28	4.67	4.00	4.13	4.36	4.36	4.46	4.31

Notes:

1 = very unimportant/much worse than competitors/comparators, 4 = neutral, 7 = very important/much better than competitors/comparators.

A0 = Agriculture/Forestry/Fishing; B0 = Mining; C11 = Food Product Manufacturing; C12 = Beverage and Tobacco Product Manufacturing; C13 = Textile, Leather, Clothing, and Footwear Manufacturing; C14 = Wood Product Manufacturing; C15 = Pulp, Paper, and Converted Paper Product Manufacturing; C16 = Printing; C17 = Petroleum and Coal Product Manufacturing; C18 = Basic Chemical and Chemical Product Manufacturing; C19 = Polymer Product and Rubber Product Manufacturing; C20 = Non-Metallic Mineral Product Manufacturing; C21 = Primary Metal and Metal Product Manufacturing; C22 = Fabricated Metal Product Manufacturing; C23 = Transport Equipment Manufacturing; C24 = Machinery and Equipment Manufacturing; C25 = Furniture and Other Manufacturing.

Sources: Michael J. Enright and CPA Australia.

TABLE 4.14 Importance and Performance; Supranational-Level Drivers; Utilities, Construction, Service Sectors

Driver	D0 & E0	F0	G0	H0	I0	J0	K0	L0	M0	N0	O0	P0	Q0	R0	S0	AVE
Importance																
Strategies of International Companies	4.90	5.43	5.15	4.97	5.17	5.19	5.24	4.57	4.95	4.53	4.19	4.71	4.33	4.33	4.56	4.81
International Companies in the Country	4.93	5.28	5.01	4.97	5.03	5.09	5.13	4.62	4.91	4.54	4.13	4.65	4.16	4.09	4.46	4.73
Access to Other Asia-Pacific Markets	4.78	5.36	5.08	4.80	5.01	4.99	5.21	4.38	4.87	4.32	4.05	4.75	3.81	4.02	4.35	4.65
Access to the China Market	4.77	5.39	5.08	4.83	5.00	4.93	5.25	4.33	4.82	4.37	3.97	4.78	3.73	3.99	4.33	4.64
Foreign Government Support for Foreign Companies	4.92	5.16	4.80	4.59	4.87	4.88	4.97	4.55	4.65	4.33	4.14	4.33	4.09	3.99	4.47	4.58
Activities of Multilateral Agencies	4.77	4.66	4.66	4.56	4.65	4.51	4.81	4.32	4.40	4.21	4.11	4.24	4.13	3.63	4.31	4.40
Performance																
Access to Other Asia-Pacific Markets	4.54	4.71	4.61	4.59	4.79	4.78	4.79	4.59	4.64	4.53	4.65	4.75	4.56	4.53	4.55	4.64
Access to the China Market	4.54	4.66	4.65	4.42	4.74	4.68	4.66	4.48	4.59	4.50	4.77	4.75	4.49	4.48	4.52	4.60
Strategies of International Companies	4.62	4.72	4.53	4.43	4.59	4.55	4.65	4.65	4.52	4.78	4.56	4.61	4.40	3.97	4.41	4.53
International Companies in the Country	4.61	4.82	4.49	4.55	4.57	4.57	4.62	4.52	4.56	4.66	4.43	4.57	4.43	4.04	4.42	4.52
Activities of Multilateral Agencies	4.46	4.51	4.39	4.45	4.31	4.41	4.44	4.45	4.35	4.58	4.58	4.59	4.36	4.21	4.35	4.43
Foreign Government Support for Foreign Companies	4.38	4.54	4.31	4.34	4.27	4.46	4.43	4.29	4.35	4.61	4.55	4.48	4.32	4.11	4.26	4.38

Notes:

1 = very unimportant/much worse than competitors/comparators, 4 = neutral, 7 = very important/much better than competitors/comparators.

D0&E0 = Utilities and Construction; F0 = Wholesale Trade; G0 = Retail Trade; H0 = Accommodation and Food Services; I0 = Transport, Postal, Warehousing; J0 = Information, Media, Telecommunications; K0 = Finance and Insurance Services; L0 = Rental, Hiring, Real Estate Services; M0 = Professional, Scientific, and Technical Services; N0 = Administrative and Support Services; O0 = Public Administration and Safety; P0 = Education and Training; Q0 = Health Care and Social Assistance; R0 = Arts and Recreation; S0 = Other Services.

Sources: Michael J. Enright and CPA Australia.

109

are considered the most important. Access to the China Market, Access to Other Asia-Pacific Markets, and Foreign Government Support for Foreign Companies are considered the most important drivers in the set by respondents in the primary and manufacturing sectors. This is not surprising in that the primary and manufacturing sectors tend to be subject to international competition and access to foreign markets is crucial to their ability to compete, and foreign government support can provide advantages for foreign firms in either defending their home markets, penetrating the Australian market, or penetrating third-country markets in competition with Australian firms.

For the utilities, construction, service sectors, the most important of the supranational drivers are Strategies of International Companies, International Companies in the Country, and Access to Other Asia-Pacific Markets. Again, market access is important, but in many cases these industries are domestically focused and in some cases are dominated by, or have lead firms that are, major multinational companies. In such cases, the presence of such multinationals can raise the game of an entire industry, or it can result in a branch office mentality that limits the international operations of the Australian office, or both. Thus, there are clear differences in the relative importance of these drivers across sectors. It is not surprising that the Activities of Multilateral Agencies tends to be the least important of these drivers, as multilaterals are more important in developing countries and in specific regional blocs, like the European Union, than in Australia.

In terms of performance, for the primary and manufacturing industries, Australia's best performance among the supranational-level drivers is in International Companies in the Country, Strategies of International Companies, and Access to Other Asia-Pacific Markets. For the utilities, construction, service sectors, the best performance is seen in Access to other Asia-Pacific Markets, Access to the China Market, and Strategies of International Companies. Respondents in the first set of sectors see the international companies active in Australia as advantages for the country more so than the second set. Respondents in the second set see access to regional markets as being better than that of competitors to a greater extent, perhaps because many of their competitors are not from the Asia-Pacific region.

In any case, it would appear that Australia can and should leverage both the presence of many international firms in the country, and its favourable position in the Asia-Pacific region to raise the game of industries within Australia and to internationalise activities to the region. We do note that the advantages reported here are relatively small, so to the extent that these drivers are important, Australia should extend, develop, and leverage them going forward.

Competitiveness Drivers in Perspective

There are a number of conclusions that come out of the analysis of the survey responses on the drivers of competitiveness in Australia. All of the drivers examined are viewed as important to competitiveness by respondents in the vast majority of sectors of the Australian economy. Most of the drivers are viewed as important in all of the sectors. This means that any competitiveness analysis that does not include all of the drivers examined here is incomplete.

Overall, the responses indicate a high level of satisfaction in many parts of the economy. Respondents in the primary and service sectors appear to be doing well and believe that Australia has numerous advantages across the drivers of competitiveness. On the other hand, respondents in several of Australia's manufacturing sectors report substantial challenges in several drivers related to cost and government policy, where they believe they are disadvantaged. The results do seem to reflect a view that on average Australia is in a reasonably good position in many of the sectors reported. However, the advantages tend to be relatively modest, and very few seem to be large enough and important enough to guarantee prosperity going forward. In fact, the results indicate that there is room for improvement virtually across the board.

Table 4.15 combines responses from all of the sectors to provide overall importance and performance scores for the drivers of competitiveness. Taken together with the sectoral data presented earlier, the table provides an overview of the competitiveness drivers, but this time rooted firmly in assessments based on relevant competitors in specific industries. We do note, however, that aggregation does tend to average out differences across industries in a way that reduces the sharpness of the survey results.

TABLE 4.15   Importance and Performance, All Sectors

Driver	Importance	Performance
Firm and Industry-Level Drivers		
Level of Technology Employed	5.62	4.86
Government Incentives for Your Industry	5.38	4.18
Sector Targeting, Government Support Policies	5.30	4.36
Knowledge of Asian Markets	4.93	4.63
Capabilities of Companies from the Country	5.30	4.72
Leading Companies that Drive Competitiveness	5.16	4.65
Strategies Used by Firms from the Country	5.14	4.65
Tough Local Competition	5.09	4.65
Industry Associations or Organisations	5.11	4.74
Co-operation among Local Firms	4.98	4.54
Cluster-Level Drivers—Land, Labour, Infrastructure		
Staff Costs	5.72	4.14
Access to Appropriate Staff Skills	5.78	4.92
Other Employment Costs	5.59	4.13
Transportation Infrastructure	4.97	4.58
Scientific and Technical Skills	5.24	4.88
Access to Local Managerial Skills	5.40	4.95
Property or Land Related Costs	5.21	4.19
Communication Infrastructure	5.63	4.84
Geographic Location	5.02	4.65
Other Costs	5.16	4.23

(Continued)

TABLE 4.15   **Continued**

Driver	Importance	Performance
IT and Internet Infrastructure	5.65	4.76
Access to Multilingual Staff	4.89	4.43
Other Infrastructure	4.92	4.66
Cluster-Level Drivers—Inputs, Demand, and Linkages		
Future Local Market Potential	5.68	4.57
Size of Local Market Demand	5.63	4.44
Access to Capital Equipment	5.21	4.74
Access to Input Goods and Services	5.29	4.75
Access to Business Relevant Information	5.52	4.90
Availability of Equity Capital	5.09	4.64
Cost of Debt Finance	5.11	4.52
Support from Related Industries	5.17	4.56
Sophistication of Local Demand	5.35	4.66
Access to Debt Finance	4.80	4.86
Availability of Venture Capital	4.93	4.53
Strength of the Local Banking System	5.02	**5.14**
Clustering of Firms in Your Industry	4.67	4.45
National-Level Drivers—Macroeconomics, Taxes, Regulation		
Exchange Rates	5.42	4.57
Overall Local Economic Conditions	5.63	4.92
Inflation Rates	5.49	4.61
Interest Rates	5.48	4.40
Regulatory and Legal Framework	5.71	4.84
Macroeconomic Stability	5.45	4.93
Strength of Government Finances	5.54	4.85
Corporate Tax Rate	5.41	4.17
Tax Regime (Overall)	5.52	4.21
Other Taxes and Charges	5.45	4.00
Payroll Taxes	5.38	3.98
Carbon Tax/Emission Trading Scheme	4.88	3.88
Personal Income Tax Rate	5.38	4.04
National-Level Drivers—Government Policy		
Overall Government Policy	5.61	4.37
Industrial, Workplace Relations/Labour Laws	5.44	4.28
Competition Policy	5.30	4.43
Foreign Trade and Tariff Policy	4.93	4.39
Policies to Encourage R&D	5.03	4.45
Foreign Investment Policy	4.88	4.38
Environmental Policies	5.11	4.85
Science and Technology Policy	4.89	4.53
Planning Laws	4.91	4.49

TABLE 4.15   Continued

Driver	Importance	Performance
National-Level Drivers—Society and Institutions		
Government Freedom from Corruption	5.63	4.94
Political Stability	5.56	4.73
Social Stability	5.57	**5.23**
Transparency of Government	5.56	4.71
Quality of Education & Training Institutions	5.65	4.95
Quality of Research Institutions, Organisations	5.40	4.88
Quality of Life	5.59	**5.35**
Attitudes of Community toward Innovation	5.34	4.69
Attitudes of Community toward Business	5.39	4.74
Environmental Consciousness	5.14	**5.03**
Attitudes toward Entrepreneurship	5.23	4.63
Community Institutions	4.75	4.52
Supranational-Level Drivers		
Access to the China Market	4.83	4.61
Access to Other Asia-Pacific Markets	4.84	4.66
Foreign Government Support for Foreign Companies	4.75	4.37
Strategies of International Companies	4.93	4.56
International Companies in the Country	4.84	4.57
Activities of Multilateral Agencies	4.52	4.42

Notes:
1 = very unimportant/much worse than competitors/comparators, 4 = neutral, 7 = very important/much better than competitors/comparators.
Sources: Michael J. Enright and CPA Australia.

For the firm and industry-level drivers, the survey responses indicate a view that Australia is doing reasonably well at the firm level. However, this result must be viewed with caution because in these drivers business people are essentially rating themselves. Here we should temper the conclusions with information from the international assessments of Chapter 2, which show a less positive picture.

At the industry level, the lack of co-operation among firms is understandable for competition in the domestic market, but could be a hindrance in international markets. The importance placed on government incentives and industry targeting, and the view that this is more important to competitiveness than firm strategies in many sectors is a cause for concern. It does lead us to suspect that Australian managers and business people might be overestimating their own capabilities and potentially pushing responsibility for competitiveness off on government rather than focusing on how they can improve their own operations to enhance the competitiveness of their industries. The activities of industry associations, interaction with related industries, and clustering of firms is not seen at present to either be that important or a substantial advantage in Australia's industries. This is interesting in that regional cluster approaches have become a dominant approach to economic development in many

OECD nations, but an approach that has not generated widespread interest in Australia to date.

With respect to cluster-level drivers, in land, labour, and infrastructure, land costs are seen as high, as are staff costs and other employment costs. The picture is one of a labour market that has the level of skills required for most sectors, but perhaps not the quantity or cost to make these skills even greater advantages. Infrastructure is generally seen as providing advantages, but again the advantages are mostly moderate, and one wonders if that is enough. The input side of Australia's economy is seen as beneficial, but the demand side is seen as weaker (perhaps unavoidably), and linkages among firms and between industries seem not as robust as they might be for a nation with many small and medium-sized enterprises that is hoping to internationalise its economy further.

In national-level drivers, Australia's macroeconomic performance is regarded as both important and strong, which is a significant advantage for Australian firms. Exchange rates are not viewed as negatively as we expected, though they are not viewed as very beneficial either. Some of the worst performing drivers of the whole study are those having to do with tax, with specific taxes being viewed as negative by respondents in many sectors. Of course, managers always want lower taxes, but the number of sectors that report tax as an issue remains a cause for concern. Some of Australia's best performing drivers are those related to Australia's basic social and political fabric, and quality of life. The high performance rating in these drivers is not surprising, given the results reported in Chapter 2. What is surprising is the importance to competitiveness that respondents indicate for these drivers. This implies that such drivers could be leveraged for advantage in a range of industries. Results for attitudes towards business and entrepreneurship indicate that these are areas that could potentially be improved to the benefit of the economy.

Finally, among the supranational drivers, we see importance of both access to regional markets and the presence of multinational companies in Australia. The question arises to what extent Australia and Australian firms can leverage these to extend their international positions to the benefit of Australia's economy.

The present chapter contains a wealth of information that the discussion only begins to describe. There are clear advantages and some disadvantages. The information on importance and performance can allow for a sector-by-sector approach to improving competitiveness as well as identifying drivers that merit further investigation and analysis across the economy. In particular, the results on drivers concerning the workforce, infrastructure, government policy, regulation, and taxation would appear to be of particular interest. So too are drivers that reflect the ability of Australia and Australian companies to be ahead of the curve in the knowledge-innovation economy. So too are drivers that reflect the growing importance of Asia and the ability of Australia and Australian companies to penetrate those markets. It is to these issues that we will turn in the next chapters.

Notes

1. For clarity, we will refer to "industries" at the four-digit level of the ANZSIC 2006 classification and "sectors" at the one or two-digit levels.
2. The number of responses for each industry as shown in Table 4.1 applies to each of the exhibits for the primary and manufacturing sectors. The average in the far right column is the simple average, so every sector counts the same.
3. The number of responses for each industry as shown in Table 4.2 applies to each of the exhibits for the utilities, construction, and service sectors. The average in the far right column is the simple average, so every sector counts the same.
4. At the time of the survey the Australian Government had plans to implement a carbon tax, and it subsequently was introduced in July 2012.

CHAPTER 5

Workforce, Infrastructure, and Natural Resources

The analysis of earlier chapters shows that there are a number of key issues that cut across Australia's economy that must be understood, and dealt with, in order to improve Australia's competitiveness. Space considerations preclude us from addressing all of these key issues. Among the cluster-level drivers, inputs to industries are particularly important. In this chapter, we will focus on three types of inputs: the workforce, infrastructure, and natural resources. The workforce and infrastructure have arisen repeatedly as crucial to Australia's competitiveness across a broad range of industries. In addition, no discussion of Australia's economy would be complete without reference to natural resources and natural resource sectors, which are particularly prominent in Australia.

The prosperity of any economy depends on the effectiveness and productivity of its workforce. Australia is no exception. In a world in which more and more countries have the basic levels of infrastructure to compete globally, technology is available on international markets, knowledge and information flow more freely than ever before, and multinational companies can divide up their activities into finer and finer pieces and place each piece in its optimal location, a nation's workforce is perhaps more critical to its competitiveness than ever before. As an advanced economy with a high standard of living and high aspirations, Australia has to continue to move ahead in terms of workforce development, or it will fall behind. How far Australia can go will be determined in large part by the skills and capabilities of its workforce, and the system in which that workforce is deployed.

The analysis in earlier chapters indicates that infrastructure represents a challenge for Australia. As a nation with a small population in a huge land mass, and one that is distant from many of the world's traditional economic centres, Australia faces distinctive infrastructure challenges, which in turn create issues about priorities and funding. According to a variety of international sources, Australia does not measure up to the world's best when it comes to infrastructure. The question is whether Australia's multiple levels of government and administration can set the right strategy, develop the right priorities, fund sufficient investment, and execute the investment programme necessary to provide the nation with the infrastructure necessary to support future prosperity.

Natural resource abundance used to be the main if not sole determinant of a nation's prosperity. Recent history has shown us, however, that countries can become prosperous without significant natural resource advantages and that countries can become and remain poor even if they have sizable resource endowments. Australia has benefitted greatly from its distinctive resource abundance, but that very abundance has also created a range of challenges. While Australia might be the lucky country when it comes to natural resources, luck will only get Australia so far. Instead, it will be sound policies and strategies that will allow Australia, Australian businesses, and Australians to obtain the greatest possible benefit from Australia's resource advantages.

Workforce

The nature of the workforce in any country is crucial to its competitiveness and development potential. Major attributes of the workforce include its quantity, quality, outlook, fit with the needs of the economy, and the industrial and workplace relations situation within which it operates. Workforce development is influenced heavily by the education and training system in a nation, including all levels of the traditional education system, vocational training, and company-based training, as well as the ability of the nation to provide opportunities for life-long learning. Enhancing workforce capabilities has become even more important in a world of rising competition, rising input prices, and increasing customer demands, as has developing workplace relations in which management and workers can find common ground to enhance overall prosperity within the country.

Australia's Workforce

There were 12,098,400 people in Australia's workforce as of April 2012. Roughly 17.5 percent were in the 15 to 24 age group, 22.4 percent in the 25 to 34 group, 43.1 percent in the 35 to 54 age group, 13.8 percent in the 55 to 64 age group, and 3.2 percent were 65 or above.[1] Australia's workforce participation rate was 65.2 percent in April 2012[2] and its rate in recent years has been higher than many comparable OECD countries (see Table 5.1). Unemployment in Australia was 5.1 percent in April 2012, lower than the OECD average of 8.2 percent.[3] The combination of higher participation and lower unemployment has represented a healthy trend for the Australian economy. Approximately one-third of Australia's labour force was tertiary qualified in 2008, 38.9 percent had a secondary education, and 27.3 percent had a primary education. This was comparable to several of the OECD nations in Table 5.1.

Assessments of Australia's Workforce

Several international sources on competitiveness rank countries according to workforce-related variables. The World Economic Forum ranked Australia 10th in Health and Primary Education (out of 142 economies), 11th in Higher Education and Training, and 13th in Labour Market Efficiency in 2011 (see Table 5.2). In individual items, Australia ranked particularly well in secondary enrolment, measures of rigidity of employment, redundancy costs, quality of primary education, and reliance on

TABLE 5.1   Workforce Statistics, Selected Countries

Country	Size of Workforce (million)	Participation Rate (%)	Unemploy-ment Rate (%)	By Qualification		
				Primary Education (%)	Secondary Education (%)	Tertiary Education (%)
Australia	11.8	65.5	5.2	27.3	38.9	33.8
Canada	19.0	66.6	8.0	13.5	40.0	46.5
Denmark	2.9	64.6	7.4	25.9	41.3	29.3
Finland	2.7	60.2	8.4	17.9	46.8	35.3
France	29.9	56.4	9.3	25.1	44.8	30.0
Germany	42.2	59.6	7.1	15.8	58.9	25.0
Japan	66.7	60.4	5.0	58.6	NA	41.4
New Zealand	2.4	67.7	6.5	17.9	41.2	36.2
United Kingdom	31.8	61.9	7.8	21.9	45.2	32.2
United States	157.5	63.7	9.6	9.5	29.4	61.1

Notes:
Statistics for the size of workforce, participation rate, and unemployment rate are for 2010. Statistics for workforce qualifications are for 2008, except for the United States, which are for 2007.
Source: World Bank, *World Development Indicators*, April 2012.

professional managers. It ranked far lower in Labour Relations, Flexibility of Wage Determination, Pay and Productivity, Brain Drain, and Female Participation. According to the International Institute for Management Development (IMD), Australia ranked 12th in Labour Market, 8th in Education, and 2nd in Attitudes and Values in 2011 (out of 59 economies). Strong points were found in Finance Skills, Attracting and Retaining Talents, Foreign High-Skilled People, Competent Senior Managers, Educational System, University Education, and Management Education. Several features of Attitudes and Values should also be positive for the workforce. The downsides were found in Labour Relations, Skilled Labour, International Experience, and Language Skills. The overall assessments should indicate a high-quality workforce, though with some gaps and definite issues with respect to workforce relations, employment systems, and skill levels.

Australia is well-situated when it comes to its universities. In 2011, the *Times* ranked the University of Melbourne, the Australian National University, the University of Sydney, and the University of Queensland among the top 100 universities in the world.[4] In 2011 QS ranked the Australian National University, the University of Melbourne, the University of Sydney, the University of Queensland, and the University of New South Wales among the top 50 in the world.[5] The Australian National University ranked in the top 10 in the world according to QS in modern languages, philosophy, geography and area studies, earth and marine

TABLE 5.2   Assessments of Australia's Workforce

World Economic Forum (out of 142 economies)		IMD (out of 59 economies)	
Indicators	**2011 Rank**	**Indicators**	**2011 Rank**
Health and Primary Education	**10**	**Labour Market**	**12**
Quality of Primary Education	10	Labour Relations	24
Primary Education Enrolment, Net %	36	Worker Motivation	13
		Employee Training	14
Higher Education and Training	**11**	Skilled Labour	35
Secondary Education Enrolment, Gross %	1	Finance Skills	4
Tertiary Education Enrolment, Gross %	14	Attracting and Retaining Talents	7
Quality of the Education System	13	Brain Drain	14
Quality of Math and Science Education	19	Foreign High-Skilled People	4
Quality of Management Schools	15	International Experience	20
Internet Access in Schools	19	Competent Senior Managers	9
Availability of Research and Training Services	14		
Extent of Staff Training	17	**Education**	**8**
		Educational System	6
Labour Market Efficiency	**13**	Science in Schools	14
Co-operation in Labour-Employer Relations	39	University Education	7
Flexibility of Wage Determination	116	Management Education	9
Rigidity of Employment Index, 0–100 (Worst)	1	Language Skills	27
Hiring and Firing Practices	97		
Redundancy Costs, Weeks of Salary	6	**Attitudes and Values**	**2**
Pay and Productivity	40	Attitudes toward Globalisation	15
Reliance on Professional Management	10	Value System	5
Brain Drain	28	National Culture	6
Women in Labour Force, Ratio to Men	45	Flexibility and Adaptability	3

Sources: The Global Competitiveness Report 2011–2012, World Economic Forum, Switzerland, 2011; International Institute for Management Development, *IMD Competitiveness Online 1995–2011*.

sciences, politics and international studies, environmental sciences, and linguistics, and the University of Melbourne ranked in the top 10 globally for psychology and law. Both the Australian School of Business and Melbourne Business School ranked in the top 50 in the world in the 2012 Financial Times Global MBA Rankings.[6] The fact that Australia runs a sizeable trade surplus in educational services also shows the strength of the university system.

We also note that these assessments need to be combined with those reported in the previous chapter, in which Australian survey respondents found Australia tended to have advantages in managerial and technical skills, moderate advantages in other staff skills, and minimal advantages or disadvantages in staff costs and other employment costs, results that bode well for Australia, but not so well as to allow for complacency.

Issues in Australia's Workforce

Australians recognise the importance of having a workforce that can drive the economy forward. According to the Australian Chamber of Commerce and Industry, "It is critical we plan for future skill needs so that Australia has the required pool of skills and knowledge to drive productivity and economic growth."[7] However, there are a number of issues with respect to the workforce that indicate there are gaps or disadvantages to overcome.

> ***Skills Gap:*** According to the Australia Industry Group and Deloitte, a shortage of skills in Australia has been a major drag on the economy.[8] Skills shortages are seen in many fields in Australia, with shortages in science and mathematics viewed as particularly acute.[9] The Australian Industry Group found that employers identified the inability to secure skilled staff as the greatest single barrier to remaining competitive.[10] This view was seconded by the Business Council of Australia, which found that shortages in skilled labour would continue for a number of years and argued that a lack of skilled workers was a significant challenge to improving national prosperity.[11] A St George-Australian Chamber of Commerce And Industry (ACCI) business survey found the lack of suitably qualified employees to be the biggest constraint on small, medium, and large businesses in Australia.[12] A report by Skills Australia estimated that Australia needs 3 percent growth in tertiary enrolments per annum through to 2025 to address its skills gap[13] and this would need to be combined with other measures such as improving job-readiness and improving workforce participation among older citizens to combat the effect of an ageing population.
>
> ***Workforce Participation:*** Australia compares well with other OECD economies when it comes to workforce participation. However, the Grattan Institute estimates that an increase in the mature age labour force participation rate by 7 percent would increase GDP by approximately AUD 25 billion a year by 2022. It recommends that this could be achieved by increasing the pension age to 70 and by restricting access to superannuation until workers reach pension age. It estimates another AUD 25 billion a year in GDP could be realised by 2022 by increasing female workforce participation.[14] It argues that women can be encouraged to enter or remain in the workforce by making childcare more affordable and through tax incentives. Having women remain in the workforce becomes even more significant when one considers that more women than men have studied at Australian universities since 1987 and that this trend looks likely to continue.[15]
>
> ***Job-Readiness:*** The job-readiness of school-leavers and university graduates also is an issue, with Australian employers claiming that they have difficulty recruiting employees with appropriate levels of soft skills[16] and with surveys of employers suggesting that the core job-relevant skill levels of university graduates need to improve.[17] The Australian Labor Party has acknowledged that training has not matched up with the needs of employers.[18] Overall, it appears that the growth in job opportunities in Australia is not being matched by the skills of underemployed or unemployed workers. As a result, Australia is increasingly facing the problem of a lack of effective workers rather than a lack of jobs.[19]

Gaps in Private Sector Training: Gaps have also been found in private sector efforts in workforce development. A Task Force convened by the Business Council of Australia found that gaps in engagement between business and secondary schools affected the job-readiness of students.[20] A report commissioned by the Australian Government's Department of Innovation, Industry, Science and Research found that many Australian enterprises need to improve their ability to attract, develop, and retain talent, and need to find innovative and practical ways to develop their workforce so as to improve their performance.[21] The report also found that Australian firms in a high-skill environment have better human capital management practices than those in a low-skill environment, indicating that the Australian businesses doing a better job in managing their workforce might serve as lessons for others. The ACCI argues that the business community does have a commitment to training and found in 2011 that a majority of Australian companies in the services industry provide in-house training, though the informal nature of such training makes it hard to measure the investment being made.[22]

Wage Costs and Geographic Mismatches: Australia's resource boom and strong economic performance have resulted in an appreciating exchange rate and upward pressure on wages. As a result, Australia has recorded large increases in manufacturing unit labour costs on a US dollar basis, making Australian manufacturing less cost competitive.[23] This has resulted in calls to mitigate exchange rate appreciation and to support manufacturing industry. In Western Australia, shortages in the labour force and the remoteness of some sites mean that people are flown in and out of their worksite. In some cases, semi-skilled workers are making several times the starting salaries of new college graduates elsewhere in the country, perhaps influencing incentives to stay in school or to seek higher qualifications.

Emigration: Concerns are expressed that a brain drain is working against Australia's competitiveness. This brain drain is particularly noticeable in the professions and must be considered in the light of Australia's relatively high tax rates (as well as significant capital gains taxes and a tax on dividend income), a lack of senior employment opportunities in multinational companies (who have their more senior positions outside Australia), the higher income-earning potential and career advancement opportunities on offer in other countries, and cultural and other factors such as the often mentioned tall-poppy syndrome that is cited by many as an explanation as to why a large number of successful Australians choose to live and work abroad. Most Australians working overseas are highly qualified and are in high demand. A study by the Lowy Institute for International Policy in 2004 found that 45 percent of Australian expatriates hold a postgraduate degree compared to 9 percent of the domestically based Australian workforce.[24] A question that arises is why an educated professional should remain in Australia when the United States represents a much larger market, or when Hong Kong and Singapore offer lower income tax rates (see Table 5.3); fewer taxes on capital gains, dividends, or interest; and a greater opportunity to work in a more senior role in a more global organisation? This is something that Australia will need to address to remain competitive.

Immigration: While is it true that a large number of Australians leave to work overseas, and that a majority of them are skilled workers, the net overseas

TABLE 5.3   Top Personal Income Tax Rates for Selected Countries, 2011

Country	Top Rate of Personal Income Tax (%)	Income Level Threshold for Top Rate of Personal Income Tax (AUD)
Australia	45	180,000
Hong Kong	15	15,415
Singapore	20	254,865
United States	35	378,251
New Zealand	33	54,643
United Kingdom	50	240,456

Note:
Income level threshold for top rate of personal income tax in AUD as at May 2012; the top rate of personal income tax for the United Kingdom will be reduced to 45 percent in 2013.
Source: KPMG, *KMPG's Individual Income Tax and Social Security Rate Survey 2011.*

migration statistics suggest that they are replaced by workers from overseas. This is important since there would be little to no growth in Australia's labour supply without international migration.[25] There are strong incentives for people to want to move to Australia. In recent years, these have included a strong Australian dollar, a solid economy, and a high quality of life. Disincentives include relatively high taxation, a lack of opportunities in senior management roles with multinational companies, the remoteness of Australia, difficult workforce relations, and perceptions of racism against some ethnic groups. In any case, as long as Australia is bringing in more qualified talent than goes overseas, and that talent is in the right occupations, then Australia will gain economically. For 2009–2010, net overseas migration is estimated at 215,600 persons, and the majority of arrivals from overseas were of working age with the median age being 26.5 years.[26] During the period 2007–2011, an average of 57.9 percent of immigrants were in the labour force, with the most common occupations being professionals, managers, technicians and trades workers, and clerical and administrative workers.[27]

Workplace Relations: Australia has a reputation for difficult workplace relations. High profile industrial disputes, such as Qantas's employee lock-out in 2011 and the 1998 Australian waterfront dispute, imposed substantial costs on the Australian economy. Some reforms have been made, but in assessing the impact of these the Grattan Institute[28] suggests that it is difficult to correlate industrial relations reforms with changes in labour productivity. Most recently, the focal issue has been the disagreements over how the fruits of Australia's resource boom should be shared, with labour demanding a higher share and management indicating that workforce relations were making Australia uncompetitive and unattractive for investment.[29] A history of comparable wages across Australia has caused concern that the high wages in some sectors in Western Australia will raise the expectations elsewhere in the nation.[30] In any case, workplace relations in Australia fall short of supporting employment, training, and workforce productivity to the extent one might hope. The danger is that poor workplace relations will exacerbate Australia's difficulties in industries in which it is relatively uncompetitive and prevent the optimal development of industries in which it is competitive.

Fair Work Australia, Solution or Problem? Fair Work Australia came into being in July 2009 to be an independent umpire in workplace negotiations with the power to make minimum wage orders, approve agreements, determine unfair dismissal claims, and make orders on industrial action to resolve workplace disputes. However, Fair Work Australia has been criticised for being inflexible, lacking neutrality, and causing harm both to employers and employees. Business interests claim that the Fair Work Act favours the interests of trade unions[31] and that Fair Work Australia is anti-employer and anti-business.[32] The organisation has become so controversial that the Australian Chamber of Commerce and Industry and the Fair Work Australia Chief Executive have called for the name of the organisation to be changed to deflect criticism and the Federal Opposition has vowed to overhaul Fair Work Australia if elected. Presently, the Government is undertaking a review of the Fair Work Act, and this would seem to be much needed.

Policies and Programs

Australia has introduced a raft of policies and programs that intend to support workforce development. Large investments are made in the education and training system. In addition, Job Services Australia was established with promised funding of AUD 4.7 billon. AUD 2.4 billon has been earmarked for the Digital Education Revolution in Australian Schools. The introduction of the Fair Work Act, the establishment of the Office of Early Childhood Education and Child Care, the founding of Australian Government Skills Connect to help businesses and industry organisations access workforce development-related funding, and the creation of the Investing in Experience Program to assist workers over the age of 50 with training are some of the initiatives. Major reviews of education have been carried out, the two most notable ones being the Review of Funding for Schooling in 2011 and the Bradley Review of Australian Higher Education in 2008. In addition, programs have been set up so foreign applicants for permanent residency in Australia can demonstrate job readiness in nominated occupations.[33] The Council of Australian Governments (COAG) in 2006 called for an increase in the proportion of adult workers who have the skills and qualifications needed to enjoy active and productive working lives,[34] but the goals have yet to find their way into policy.

For the policies, programs, and reviews to be effective, however, they must turn into action, be sufficiently resourced, and be properly promoted. It is not clear that this is happening. To many, the education revolution promised by the Government in 2008, and for which AUD 10 billon was budgeted, has yet to materialise. There has been criticism of the allocation of funds for new facilities rather than on additional teachers, teacher training, or other teaching resources.[35] The Review of Funding for Schooling completed in 2011 recommended significant increases in funding for schooling as a means of combating a decline in the performance of Australian students at all levels as observed from 2000 onwards.[36] However, the recommendations made by the Review Panel have not been acted upon to date and were not reflected in the 2012 Federal Budget, a situation that has disappointed many, including former senior ministers from the Australian Labor Party.[37] A report from the Grattan Institute[38] argues that reforms to education have the potential for enormous benefit, but that the payoff in improved productivity and higher GDP will take decades to realise, making it hard for governments to expend political capital on such reforms, regardless of their potential impact.

Australia's Workforce in Perspective

Workforce statistics and Australia's positive net overseas migration rate suggest that there is a sufficient quantity of workers in Australia. The question, however, is whether they are in the right places and have the right skills to meet Australia's needs going forward. Workforce capabilities must be aligned with the needs of Australia's economy, and there must be enough people in the workforce creating wealth, as opposed to merely redistributing it, in order for Australia to become and remain competitive.

International sources tend to rank Australia highly in terms of education, training, attitudes, and a variety of features related to the quality of the workforce. Leading Australian companies leverage home-grown talent to compete internationally. The talent that Australia produces does well internationally and is able to compete with the best in the world for the best jobs. Many Australian inventors, inventions, and innovations also highlight the potential of Australia's talent pool and its competitiveness globally in the development of human capital.

However, in Australia, there are many who believe that there are shortages or gaps in the workforce and in skills that hold Australia back. The quality of education is seen as falling and in need of improvement, the education system is seen as not providing sufficient job-ready personnel to meet the economy's needs, and the training system has yet to fill the gap. Many people come to Australia to work, but many leave Australia, and those that do are more highly trained than those that stay.[39] Australia's recent economic success has placed pressure on wages in sectors in which Australia is advantaged (like the resources sector) and where it is disadvantaged (as in much of manufacturing). Australia's workplace relations remain problematic, at times appearing to be in a time warp when compared with major competitors. The combination of high wages in some sectors and locations, challenging times in other sectors and locations, and a history of solidarity wages all seem to be exacerbating a deep mistrust between labour and management. Taxes are viewed as high and may be a disincentive to employment and to staff remaining in Australia.

Various business groups and commissions have identified the key issues with respect to Australia's workforce, but it is not clear that the resulting recommendations will be implemented, or implemented with sufficient resources and promotion. It is also not clear that the incentives for talented individuals to leave Australia, or come to Australia, have been sufficiently addressed. The result is a situation in which we can ask whether good is good enough, whether high scores for quality of life will offset concerns in other areas, and whether Australia's workforce is sufficient to foster greater prosperity in the future.

Infrastructure

Infrastructure[40] underpins economic development. High-quality infrastructure enables companies to grow, and it encourages them to invest. It also supports a quality of life that contributes to the desirability of a country. There is a long time lag to plan and build major infrastructure such as airports, ports, and roads, so planning and development of infrastructure needs to be done well in advance of when it is needed. Not doing so can drastically lower productivity and be a considerable drag on a country's competitiveness. Getting Australia's infrastructure right requires active engagement with government, businesses, and the community, and it will take concerted effort on the part of all involved to ensure that Australia's present and future infrastructure needs are met.

Australia's Infrastructure

Australia's population of 22.9 million[41] is dispersed across the nation but concentrated in coastal areas. New South Wales has the largest population (7.31 million) followed by Victoria (5.64 million), Queensland (4.59 million), Western Australia (2.36 million), South Australia (1.65 million), Tasmania (0.51 million), Australian Capital Territory (0.36 million), and Northern Territory (0.23 million).

Australia has 817,089 kilometres of roads.[42] Approximately 657,000 kilometres of roads are controlled by local governments, although state-controlled roads account for about three-quarters of all vehicle kilometres travelled.[43] In addition, there are private toll road, bridge, and tunnel operators collecting fees for use under agreements with governments in New South Wales, Queensland, and Victoria.[44] There also is a mix of government-owned and privately held utilities for water and electricity in each state and the Capital Territory.[45] New South Wales has taken the most recent move toward privatisation with plans to sell its electricity generators to raise AUD 3 billion for investment in other critical infrastructure.[46] Most major railways in Australia are government-owned with a few exceptions in the Northern Territory, Queensland, South Australia, and Western Australia, where privately owned railways are used to transport cargo including minerals and grain.[47]

Australia has more than 60 major ports, with 20 ports accounting for over 95 percent of volume.[48] Many ports are at or near capacity, with Sydney's port estimated to hit capacity by 2013,[49] Melbourne's by 2015 (a full 10 years before an alternative port at Hastings can be established[50]), and occupancy rates at the Dampier Cargo Wharf in Western Australia operating at or above full capacity since 2007.[51] Most ports in Australia are government-owned with privately owned ports in Brisbane, Adelaide, and Geelong.[52] Australia has 21 leased federal airports, by far the largest being Sydney Kingsford-Smith International Airport.[53] Several airports are at or near capacity, with demand forecast to exceed runway capacity in Brisbane by around 2014,[54] Perth by 2018,[55] and Sydney Kingsford-Smith for peak hour use as early as 2018.[56]

Australia has 10.59 million fixed telephone lines and 25.99 million mobile telephone subscribers.[57] Australia's mobile phone subscriber rate in per capita terms ranks it 69th in the world.[58] Australia's telecommunications sector has both public and private investment. All major telecommunication companies have national reach, and the largest of these is the former government-owned and now both public- and privately owned Telstra, which had a market capitalisation of AUD 43,920 million in May 2012 and revenue of AUD 24,983 million for 2011. Optus is the largest privately held company with revenues of AUD 9,284 million for 2011. Australia compares reasonably well to other OECD comparator nations in most measures of information and communication technology (ICT), and does particularly well in business use of broadband, where it has a relatively high usage rate among OECD nations.

Assessments of Australia's Infrastructure

The World Economic Forum (WEF) and IMD rank countries on infrastructure. The WEF ranked Australia 24th in Infrastructure in 2011 (see Table 5.4). Australia rated poorly compared to other OECD nations on all the individual items except in Airline Capacity per Capita. Results with respect to mobile phones, ports, roads, electricity, air transport, and overall quality of infrastructure should all be major sources of concern for Australia. IMD ranked Australia 17th in Basic Infrastructure in 2011 (out of 59 economies), with relatively poor performance versus competitor countries in all of the items in the table. Ranks in the twenties or thirties, or worse, for water, energy infrastructure, water transportation, and maintenance and development of infrastructure, among others, should again be major causes of concern.

This is interesting as the respondents to the business competitiveness survey reported in the previous chapter indicated that Australia had slight advantages versus competitors in infrastructure. This might be due to the fact that Australia's competitors in many industries are not the most advanced nations. In other cases, it could be that Australians do not have a complete picture of infrastructure in other countries and might be overestimating Australia's position. In any case, given the international assessments and the debates about infrastructure in Australia, this appears to be an area in which significant improvements are needed.

Infrastructure Issues in Australia

Australians are aware that world-class infrastructure is key to keeping Australia competitive, to increasing productivity and output, to creating employment opportunities, and to attracting local and foreign investment. The Australian Industry Group stated, "The provision of high-quality infrastructure is a key driver influencing

TABLE 5.4   **Assessments of Australia's Infrastructure**

World Economic Forum (out of 142 economies)		IMD (out of 59 economies)	
Indicators	**2011 Rank**	**Indicators**	**2011 Rank**
Infrastructure	**24**	**Basic Infrastructure**	**17**
Quality of Overall Infrastructure	37	Access to Water	47
Quality of Roads	34	Access to Commodities	23
Quality of Railroad Infrastructure	28	Urbanisation	29
Quality of Port Infrastructure	40	Quality of Air Transportation	21
Quality of Air Transport Infrastructure	29	Distribution Infrastructure	24
Available Airline Seat Kms/Week, Millions	6	Water Transportation	33
Quality of Electricity Supply	33	Maintenance and Development	33
Fixed Telephone Lines/100 Pop.	28	Energy Infrastructure	34
Mobile Telephone Subscriptions/100 Pop.	69	Future Energy Supply	28

Sources: The Global Competitiveness Report 2011–2012, World Economic Forum, Switzerland, 2011; International Institute for Management Development, *IMD Competitiveness Online 1995–2011*.

Engaging the Private Sector: The situation in Australia in which government owns and operates some infrastructure and acts as regulator for competing privately owned and operated infrastructure creates challenges.[81] A report for the Business Council of Australia suggests that a situation in which the private sector should run businesses and the public sector would focus on policy setting and regulation would generate benefits in terms of cost, choice, and flexibility.[82] However, the private sector is less inclined to invest if there is a real or perceived conflict of interest between the public and private sectors. Well-publicised cases where government action or inaction has caused private infrastructure investments to run into difficulty have soured the environment for private investment.[83] Government investment in public goods is a necessary feature in most economies, and in Australia, where the land is vast and the population is widely dispersed, government will need to make such investments. The question becomes how best to structure roles for the public and private sectors to encourage needed investment.

Harmonisation of Road and Rail Rules: The lack of consistency in the rules and regulations that apply to road and rail is an issue.[84] Australia's size and its low population density mean that transporting goods long distances and frequently interstate by road and rail is required in order to make many operations commercially viable. Different road and rail rules in different locations create inefficiencies, generate bureaucratic problems, and drive up the cost of doing business.[85]

Need for Infrastructure Finance: Engineers Australia notes that Infrastructure Australia has identified nationally significant priority projects that will cost tens of billions of dollars for which a funding solution needs to be found.[86] Project finance is a problem at national, state, and local levels. In commenting on the 2012–2013 Victorian State Budget, CPA Australia observed that there is a " . . . yawning gap in funding for the actual delivery of major infrastructure projects."[87] Public finance of needed projects is a challenge, given budget constraints, competing demand for funding from other sectors, and political issues. Private finance is also challenging with the amounts involved and the significant uncertainties and risks attached to large-scale, long-term projects.[88] In thinking through its infrastructure financing issues, Australia might find it useful to look to other countries to better understand which funding models work and which do not and learn from the experience of those nations.

Policies and Programs

Australia has many policies and programs that aim to support infrastructure development. The National Competition Policy (NCP) that came into effect in 1995 created the foundation for most of Australia's subsequent infrastructure policy reforms. The NCP and related legislation allowed private interests to compete in key infrastructure markets including rail, telecommunications, and electricity, and resulted in the structural reform of many public monopolies. In 2005, the Productivity Commission found that productivity had improved and cost had significantly decreased in relation to key infrastructure services, largely as a result of NCP reforms.[89]

In 2006, the Council of Australian Governments (COAG) agreed on a National Reform Agenda (NRA), which would build on the NCP to streamline, harmonise, and simplify infrastructure regulation. Infrastructure Australia, which reports to COAG through the Federal Minister for Infrastructure and Transportation, was established in April 2008 to advise on national infrastructure priorities and user needs, reforms to policy and regulation, the removal of obstacles to efficient national infrastructure, and financing.

The Australian Government used infrastructure spending to help Australia through the Global Financial Crisis that began in 2007, and it set up the Building Australia Fund in 2009 to fund infrastructure projects in the transport, communications, water, and energy sectors. Major projects have been funded in all Australian states and territories except the Northern Territory. The Australian Government set up the Major Cities Unit in 2008 to give advice on policy, planning, and infrastructure for cities and suburbs. The Government's Nation Building Program, which commenced in 2008 to invest in road and rail infrastructure, should harmonise road and rail regulations and make land transportation more efficient and cost-effective across the country. The Regional Infrastructure Fund was established in 2010 to invest in the development of the mining industry, regional economies, and export capacity.

Major infrastructure issues, including infrastructure finance, public-private partnerships, city planning, the future for ports, and water security, have been the subject of detailed analysis and strategic review in recent years. While great efforts have been made to understand Australia's infrastructure needs and priorities, there are gaps in translating this effort into action. Infrastructure Australia has called for Government to " . . . get on with the job"[90] and to present a strategic rationale for infrastructure investments, accusing them of adopting " . . . a 'magic pudding' approach to infrastructure planning."[91] The OECD has called for Infrastructure Australia to enhance transparency in evaluating projects, do more audits of projects, and improve the quality of its cost-benefit analyses—all suggestions being intended to improve the quality of policy making for large infrastructure investments.[92] The picture that emerges is one of policy makers acting too slowly, as over-promising and under-delivering, and as failing to co-operate to solve Australia's infrastructure problems.

Australia's Infrastructure in Perspective

Australia's large land mass and small population complicate infrastructure planning and investment. Imbalances in infrastructure between urban centres and rural and remote communities need to be addressed if key industries such as farming, livestock production, and resources and mining are to remain competitive, but all parts of Australia clearly cannot be provided the same service levels in a cost-effective fashion. This means difficult decisions about not extending infrastructure to some areas have to be made.

According to international sources, Australia does not measure up to the world's best when it comes to infrastructure. Analysts and business groups in Australia indicate that there are significant gaps and much of the existing infrastructure is at or near its limits. Efforts to improve Australia's infrastructure appear to be hampered by a lack of understanding and agreement as to key development needs and priorities, and a lack of funding. We note that the results of our business competitiveness survey indicate that most respondents do not believe that infrastructure has created significant competitive disadvantages as of yet. Instead, they indicate that Australia has slight advantages versus competitors and comparators in infrastructure. However, the gaps and imminent constraints identified in Australia suggest that this situation will not continue without concerted effort. In addition, as a remote country with a dispersed population, if Australia is not well ahead in terms of quantity and quality of infrastructure, it is behind, because its internal connectivity and connectivity to major markets are always going to be hampered by distance.

It would appear that much needs to be done by both the public and the private sectors, with clear needs to improve planning for infrastructure, enhance co-operation between various levels of government and other bodies, deal with inter-state rivalries, and reduce fragmentation that increases costs and adds inefficiencies. One solution would be to foster more private sector investment and management, as this has been shown to improve efficiency, enhance service levels, and reduce cost. This would require a further opening of infrastructure sectors and guidelines as to how potential conflicts of interest would be managed. This is vital, since world-class infrastructure will be crucial to making Australia more productive and more competitive.

Natural Resources

Australia is blessed with endowments of natural resources that help make the country one of the world's richest in terms of per capita national wealth. Australia's resource wealth has underpinned the country's economic development and has helped it achieve stronger GDP growth than most other OECD economies in recent years. However, this resource abundance is not without its challenges. The recent resource boom has contributed to the appreciation of the Australian dollar, a situation that has put other trade-exposed industries in Australia, particularly manufacturing, under pressure. A booming resource sector has attracted capital and personnel from the rest of the economy, in some cases competing up wages and other costs. The geographic asymmetry of Australia's resource sector means that some areas have benefitted from the resource boom to a greater extent than others. Questions have been raised about the distribution of resource wealth, and this has influenced Australia's political system to an extent that some would view as unhealthy. Meanwhile, some analysts warn that the resource boom will not go on forever and Australia needs to prepare for the bust that might follow.

The quantity of resources, their geographic distribution, the availability of capital and labour, and government policy are key factors that will determine the growth and development in the sector. In the context of the present situation and trends, the sustainability of Australia's resources is crucial to Australia's economy, and the way in which the resources are managed has huge implications for Australia's competitiveness. While Australia is blessed with a range of resource advantages, here we will focus on the extractive industries, as these have been important drivers of the Australian economy and the Australian economic debate over the last few years.

Australia's Resource Position

Australia has the world's largest reserves of uranium, second-largest reserves of bauxite, second-largest reserves of iron ore, and fifth-leading reserves of metallurgical and thermal coal. Australia also has substantial reserves of natural gas, diamonds and other gem stones, strategic minerals, and rare earths. In recent years, rapid growth in demand for resources, particularly in China, which is already the world's leading or near the world's leading consumer of numerous resources, has been pushing resource prices to record levels. This combination has resulted in record output and returns for resource firms operating in Australia.

Australia produced 433,452 thousand metric tons of iron ore and 235.4 million tons of coal in 2010. Natural gas production for 2009 was 1,915,880 terajoules. Australia was the largest iron ore producer in the world and one of the largest producers of coal and natural gas in these years.[93] More than half of Australia's total exports are from mining, and industry exports were equivalent to 11.5 percent of Australia's GDP in 2010.[94] The mining industry employs well over 100,000 workers, and supporting industries are likely to employ a similar number. Table 5.5 shows data for Australia and for selected OECD countries.

There has been an unprecedented increase in the prices of some resources in recent years in response to increasing demand in China and elsewhere. The export price of iron ore rose by nearly a factor of seven from 2005 to 2011, and then fell by approximately 47 percent from early 2011 to September 2012,[95] while metallurgical and thermal coal saw their export prices spike to eight times and more than three times 2005 levels, respectively, in 2008 only to fall to levels four and two times those of 2005 by 2011 (see Figures 5.1 and 5.2).

Extractive industries accounted for 8.7 percent of Australia's total GDP in 2010–2011. Australia's gross fixed capital formation in extractive industries from 2006

TABLE 5.5   Comparison of the Mining Industry across OECD Countries

	Mining Industries % of Total Exports, 2010[1]	Mining Industry Exports As a % of GDP, 2010[2]	% of Total Employment in Mining Industries, 2008	Employment in Mining Industries, 2008 ('000)
Australia	58.1	11.5	1.22	135.2
Canada	26.9	7.9	1.52	277.3
Denmark	9.2	4.6	NA	NA
Finland	8.7	3.5	0.18	5.0
France	4.7	1.2	0.09	25.5
Germany	2.7	1.3	0.26	109.0
Japan	2.3	0.4	0.04	30.0
New Zealand	5.6	1.6	0.18	4.0
United Kingdom	14.2	4.3	0.45[3]	133.2[3]
United States	8.6	1.1	0.54	845.0

Notes:

1. Exports of the mining industry includes commodities exported of Group 28 (Metalliferous Ore, Scrap) and Group 3 (Coal, Coke, Petroleum, Gas, Lubricants and Related Materials, and other related products).

2. Calculated from "mining industries export as a percentage of total exports" and "exports as a percentage of GDP" from World Bank indicators.

3. The most updated data for the United Kingdom are 2007 data.

Sources: UN Comtrade; World Bank; International Labour Organization; Australian Taxation Office; Australian Bureau of Statistics.

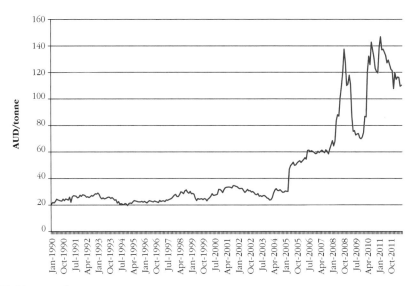

FIGURE 5.1 **Price for Iron Ore Exports, 1990 to June 2012**
Sources: Australian Bureau of Agricultural and Resource Economics and Sciences, *Australian Mineral Statistics*, June 2011; Bureau of Resources and Energy Economics, *Resources and Energy Quarterly*, 2012.

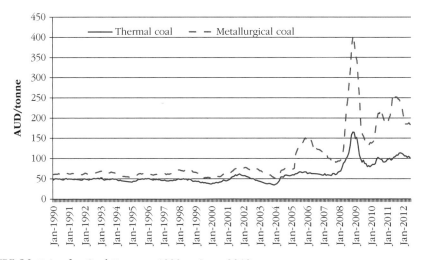

FIGURE 5.2 **Price for Coal Exports, 1990 to June 2012**
Sources: Australian Bureau of Agricultural and Resource Economics and Sciences, *Australian Mineral Statistics*, June 2011; Bureau of Resources and Energy Economics, *Resources and Energy Quarterly*, 2012.

to 2010 was AUD 121.7 billion, and tax receipts from extractive industries for 2009–2010 were AUD 4.1 billion. The sector is concentrated in Western Australia, with extractive industries making up 32.85 percent of Gross State Product (the state version of GDP), and in Queensland, where the sector accounts for 9.01 percent of GSP. Figures for the remaining states and territories are Australian Capital Territory

TABLE 5.6   Geographic Distribution of Resource Sector in Australia

State/ Capital Territory	Produced Value, 2009–2010 (AUD million)			Total Mineral Commodities	Total Exports 2010–2011 (AUD million)	Employment in Extractive Industries, 2009–2010
	Iron Ore	Black Coal	Gas			
Australia Total	**34,529**	**36,393**	**5,047**	**132,307**	**237,218**	**144,000**
Australian Capital Territory	n/a	n/a	n/a	n/a	2	n/a
New South Wales	n/a	13,216	n/a	16,560	36,369	23,000
Northern Territory	208	n/a	587	5,243	5,295	n/a
Queensland	n/a	22,790	275	31,456	49,353	39,000
South Australia	664	60	476	4,222	11,193	9,000
Tasmania	n/a	n/a	n/a	956	3,186	2,000
Victoria	n/a	n/a	1,740	5,115	19,648	9,000
Western Australia	33,657	326	1,968	68,043	112,171	60,000

Source: Australian Bureau of Statistics.

(0.08 percent of GSP), New South Wales (2.88 percent), Northern Territory (20.12 percent), South Australia (4.32 percent), Tasmania (1.37 percent), and Victoria (2.34 percent). Table 5.6 provides information on the geographic distribution of Australia's iron ore, coal, and gas.

Australia is home to two world-class, world-scale, globally competitive resource companies, BHP Billiton and Rio Tinto. In 2011, BHP Billiton's revenue was AUD 70.1 billion and it had 100,000 employees, and Rio Tinto's revenue was AUD 59.2 billion and it had 68,000 employees.[96] Australia is home to several smaller mining concerns that are significant companies in their own right. Australia also is home to Origin Energy and Woodside Petroleum, substantial producers of natural gas.

Issues in Australia's Resources Sector

Australia came out of the Global Financial Crisis that started in 2007 better than most countries, and much credit is given to the resources sector for protecting the rest of Australia from suffering as most of the rest of the world did.[97] There are significant issues facing the resources sector, including the sustainability of the recent resource boom, how the resource wealth should be managed and distributed, and the impact of the resource boom on the rest of the economy. Finally, opinions differ on how these issues should be managed and whether it is time for a rethink how resources are administered in Australia.

Impact of Rising Resource Prices: The rapid rise in resource prices has created an unprecedented windfall for resource companies, as well as huge
incentive to invest to expand resource output. This, in turn, has absorbed
substantial capital from Australian and external sources, has bid up labour
costs in parts of the country, and has influenced exchange rates. From
2004–2008 Australia's terms of trade rose by almost 50 percent due to
increases in non-rural commodity prices.[98] The Australian dollar appreciated
by more than 50 percent versus the US dollar from 2006 to late 2011, and
although it came down somewhat in 2012 the Australian dollar remains
higher valued than its historical average. The mining boom has also contributed to an inflationary environment that is putting upward pressure on
interest rates, with significant interest rate increases only being stemmed by
the weakness in the non-mining sectors of the economy.

One Speed, Two Speeds, or Three Speeds? Much discussion is focused on
whether Australia now has a two-speed or three-speed economy—a phenomenon that is not new to Australia, having previously been felt several
decades ago.[99] It is widely agreed that the resources boom that began in 2004
created a two-speed economy in Australia, with the resources sector racing
ahead of the rest of the economy. More recently, some have claimed that the
iron ore industry has further separated itself from the rest of the resources
sector.[100] The existence of a three-speed economy will only further complicate the issues that already are in play, and may in fact generate a
heightened sense that the resources sector and those working in it have
things too good and that something must be done to address the imbalance.
The multi-speed economy has had far-ranging impacts, with some claiming
that senior Treasury officials are finding it increasingly difficult to forecast
national economic growth and that managers of large equity portfolios in
Australia are fixating on the resources sector to the exclusion of other sectors.[101] The multi-speed economy also creates challenges for the Government, with the Liberal Party accusing the Government of outsourcing the
management of the multi-speed economy to the Reserve Bank to control via
interest rates.[102]

Impacts of the Multi-Speed Economy: Survey findings suggest that the ever
widening gap between the resources sector and other sectors is creating
pressure in the manufacturing, construction, and retail sectors in particular
and that confidence in those sectors is low.[103] The manufacturing sector is
frequently cited as being a victim of the mining boom and its associated
effects, with resource exports putting upward pressure on the Australian
dollar, making Australia's exporting manufacturers less competitive, and with
resource companies hiring workers and bidding up wages to uncompetitive
levels. The Australian Industry Group has estimated that 10 percent of Australia's manufacturing jobs disappeared from 2009 to 2011, in part as a
result.[104] The Prime Minister has acknowledged the effects that the mining
boom has had on other key sectors, including retail, agriculture, and
manufacturing, but claims that the strength in the resources sector will persist,
leaving Australia in better economic condition.[105]

Uneven Geographic Distribution of Benefits: In addition to uneven impacts
on industries, there are fears that the main mining states of Western Australia,

the Northern Territory, and Queensland will benefit while other states will feel the negative effects of higher exchange rates and higher interest rates. While mining states have had higher output and employment growth than non-mining states, there is also evidence that the benefits of the boom are spreading throughout Australia.[106] There are concerns, however, that the benefits are disproportionately skewed in favour of the mining states, that this might lead to imbalances that cause social disruption, and that the positive effects of the mining boom on non-mining states may not be sustainable.[107]

Sustainability of the Resource Boom: It has been asserted that the government is making "Pollyanna-type assumptions about future mining revenues," and there is no guarantee that the resource boom will go on forever.[108] Demand from China has been the major force driving the resources boom, and the large resource companies and mining analysts forecast that this will continue, with one mining analyst being quoted as saying, "China's right next door and they want to buy as much of our stuff as quickly as they can."[109] There are concerns, however, that a global slowdown, provincial debt, and other challenges in China might slow or reverse the resource boom.[110] The World Bank has expressed the view that China's economy might slow more than anticipated and that this would be a threat to Australia's economy.[111] Presently Australia would seem largely unprepared for such an outcome. The Grattan Institute, for one, has suggested that Australia needs to develop a range of internationally competitive industries in order to prepare for the risk of overreliance on a narrow set of export industries.[112] Indeed, a fall in commodity prices in 2012 indicated that the resource boom could be more fragile than many expected.

Labour Shortages: Rapid growth in mining has created labour shortages in the sector. One result has been the approval of 1,700 overseas guest workers in May 2012 under the first Enterprise Migration Agreement (EMA) to work in mining in Western Australia. Union leaders in Australia have been deeply unhappy, with one claiming that bringing in overseas workers is "sheer lunacy" when job losses are occurring in other sectors in Australia.[113] Others note that many displaced workers are distant from where the jobs are located and choose not to move to accept a job, and a recent online poll found that more than one third of workers would not consider moving to Western Australia for a job, citing family reasons and hardships in living and working in remote communities.[114] A survey of Australian workers in the mining, industrial, and construction sectors found that the mining boom is causing shortages in the manufacturing and retail sectors.[115]

Sharing the Wealth? Calls have for some time been made for the Government to give all Australians a fair share of the wealth that is being generated by the resources boom by imposing a tax on the industry and then investing the monies raised into productivity-enhancing reforms, into education, and into high value-adding industries. The Government has responded by introducing a Minerals Resource Rent Tax (MRRT), which came into effect 1 July 2012. Tough words have been used in relation to the MRRT, with the Prime Minister asserting that resource companies do not own the minerals in the ground, that they only are given the right to mine the resources, and that it is the Australian people who own the minerals and they deserve their share, while at the same time telling mining companies, "There's nowhere in the world you'd be better off investing."[116] Not surprisingly, the mining companies hold a different view and the CEO of BHP Billiton predicted there would be repercussions to the mining tax, claiming that a consequence of increased mining taxes in Australia might be that capital available for investment will eventually be redirected elsewhere.[117]

Foreign Investment in the Resource Sector: For an industry that has huge capital requirements that often can't attract sufficient domestic funding and has to look to foreign investment to fill the gap, the spectre that the investment pipeline might be tightening is disconcerting. Australia has been relatively open to foreign investment, and Japanese companies started making significant investments in Australia's coal and iron ore industries decades ago.[118] More recently, Chinese entities have become big investors and are estimated to have committed more than AUD 70 billion between 2007 and 2012. This has created tensions in China and in Australia, with the Chinese entities concerned about big losses in some of the projects in which they have invested[119] and Australia having concerns as to sovereignty and management control.[120] There is a growing recognition that China's investment strategy may be changing, with a former BHP Billiton China president stating, "The Chinese Government thinking is gradually evolving towards the conclusion that security of supply does not necessarily require ownership of these [resource] assets."[121]

Policies and Programs

Australia's natural resources are governed by a complex set of arrangements involving federal, state, and local governments. While the Crown (Commonwealth) owns most mineral resources under Australian laws, the administration of these resources is generally a matter for the states and territories. The Federal Government's jurisdiction over natural resources comes from its power in other areas (taxes, trade, external relations, and so on). States and territories in Australia grant concessions or leases for the exploration and development of individual tracts. In the case of several large projects, particularly in Western Australia, the concession arrangement becomes a contract that is ratified by the state or territorial parliament, giving it the force of law.

In general, policy in Australia has historically been in favour of development of resource industries. States and territories have seen natural resource sectors as sources of investment, employment, and tax revenue with which to meet other obligations. Foreign investment is prominent in the resource sectors. The two largest "Australian" mining companies, BHP and Rio Tinto, have the majority of their shares owned outside of Australia. Australia's large offshore natural gas projects have participation from Western and Japanese companies. In more recent times, Chinese companies have made significant investments in the resources sector.

The tax treatment of Australia's extractive industries has several components. There are the normal corporate income taxes, payroll taxes, a goods and services tax, and personal income taxes paid by corporations and individuals in the sector. In addition, there are royalties based on the volume or value of production. One of the major issues that developed subsequent to the dramatic rise in prices in some resources was whether and how the windfall should be treated from a tax standpoint. Meanwhile, the Henry Review of Australia's tax regime had suggested replacing royalties with a resource rent tax. Ultimately, the existing Petroleum Resource Rent Tax (PRRT) was extended to all onshore and offshore hydrocarbon sources, a Mining Resource Rent Tax (MRRT) was introduced, and existing royalty arrangements for other minerals were extended.[122] The MRRT has been controversial in Australia with strong arguments being put for and against. Many sections of the Australian community view a tax on resources as right, if not long overdue, with plans for the monies raised to be used to fund infrastructure projects and to help diversify the economy in ways that aim to ensure Australia's long-term prosperity. Mining companies, on the other hand, claim the tax is unfair and reduces Australia's attractiveness as an investment location.

Environmental concerns related to the resources sector are growing and are driving up the cost of doing business and the time taken to get project approval as environmental groups and others demand that resource companies better justify their activities from an environmental standpoint.[123] The carbon tax implemented on 1 July 2012, which falls on the resources sector to a greater extent than many other sectors, has been one manifestation of environmental concerns affecting the resources sector. Responding to the overall environmental regulatory situation, the Minerals Council of Australia has called for the environmental management of mining operations to be streamlined.[124] Most large firms in the resources sector actively invest in environmental protection programs and initiatives to combat criticisms that they are environmentally unfriendly.

Since the resources sector requires large-scale, long-term investment underpinned by long-term plans, uncertainty and delay are not conducive to long-term thinking, and present claims are that government policies, the MRRT included, combined with a slow approval process have been driving uncertainty and making resource companies nervous.[125] The Chairman of the Board of BHP Billiton stated, "I cannot overestimate how the level of uncertainty about Australia's tax system is generating negative investor reaction."[126] The Minerals Council of Australia has argued that the focus of policy should be on how to take advantage of global conditions to build up the resources sector further, not on how to extract concessions from the sector or create bottlenecks that delay its development and help competitors.[127] Opposition politicians have picked up this view as well, claiming that the Government needs to stop feeding uncertainty, and that it needs to get out of the way to allow the mining boom to develop while finding ways to drive productivity in other sectors.[128]

Australia's Natural Resources in Perspective

The size of the natural resources sector in general, and the extractive industries in particular, in Australia in terms of investment, employment, and wealth creation makes them a natural focus for robust discussion regarding the future. This includes addressing issues of ownership, contractual integrity, inclusion and equality, and concerns regarding a sharing of the wealth. Many claim that Australia is at risk of suffering the Dutch Disease in which resource wealth drives up the exchange rate while at the same time increasing domestic inflation, and that this will make Australia less competitive internationally and retard its prosperity in the long-term.[129] There is a fear that skilled workers from other sectors will switch to higher paid jobs in the resources sector and that a high currency and increased costs may cause other industries to disappear, particularly in the manufacturing sector.[130]

While there has been much discussion of the challenges posed by the resource boom, there are those who remind us that it is a boom after all. In a speech titled, "Australia's mining boom: what's the problem?"[131] Productivity Commission Chairman Gary Banks stated that the "pressures" felt were because Australia had become wealthier than it had been, which was a good thing, and that the adjustments that had taken place had simply amplified underlying trends and that the result was an overall expansion of employment, not a contraction, across the economy. According to this view, employment in the manufacturing sector started from an artificially high level due to past protection and had been in secular decline even before the latest resource boom. In this context, Australia's flexible exchange rate and decentralised labour market were really the only policies that were necessary to manage the boom, additional expenditures should be based on cost-benefit analysis, there is no particular reason for industrial support programs, and the challenge is to manage the adjustments, not to prevent them.

Resource companies have been quite vocal in their opposition to the carbon tax, the MRRT, and other aspects of government policy that they view as changing the game for the industry, making it less attractive, and making it more uncertain. The claims are that several forces are combining to create a high-cost, uncertain environment that will attract less investment in the resources sector with a resulting negative impact on Australia's prosperity. The fact remains, however, that the resources are physically located in Australia and that they will at some point be exploited for commercial gain. Most likely, companies will factor in the various challenges and will continue to invest as long as the overall economics of such investments look good. We do note that the fall in commodity prices in 2012 has caused much discussion about the sustainability of the resource boom in Australia and has put some companies that had committed to aggressive investment programs in difficulty.

Input Issues in Perspective

Australia's workforce, infrastructure, and resource endowments are key drivers of competitiveness. The analysis in earlier chapters indicates that workforce and infrastructure issues are crucial across a broad range of Australian industries. Australia has a range of advantages when compared to competitors in various aspects of the workforce and workforce development. However, the translation of these advantages into business development is not as direct and extensive as one might hope. Respondents to the business competitiveness survey indicated that Australia had at least mild advantages versus competitors in a variety of infrastructure-related drivers, but international assessments of Australia's infrastructure continue to tell a somewhat different story. While neither the workforce nor the infrastructure is in crisis, both are areas in which much work needs to be done to ensure Australia's competitiveness. Australia's resource endowment is a strength that has contributed greatly to Australia's prosperity. However, the sheer magnitude of the endowments has created a variety of challenges for the country. One of the challenges is to create a clear policy framework that will allow the sector and its companies to prosper, while taking into account the legitimate concerns of workers, other sectors, and the public in general.

While workforce, infrastructure, and resource development all have important private sector features, they are also important areas of public policy that show how government decisions have major implications throughout the Australian economy. The workforce is shaped by education and training investments and policies, as well as tax and immigration policies. Government is a major player in most forms and aspects of infrastructure, making polices as well as acting as an investor, operator, and regulator. The resources sector operates under specific agreements, federal and state level rules and regulations, foreign investment rules, and tax arrangements. Whether the policy regime in the resources sector helps or hinders the country is a matter of open debate.

Government policy clearly has numerous impacts on these and other drivers of competitiveness in the Australian context. We will continue with this theme by turning to the broader policy environment in Australia and its impacts on the economy in the next chapter.

Notes

1. Australian Bureau of Statistics, *Labour Force, Australia*, April 2012.
2. Australian Bureau of Statistics, *Labour Force, Australia*, April 2012.
3. OECD, *Labour Force Statistics, OECD. StatExtracts*, April 2012. The OECD harmonised unemployment rates for January, February, and March were all calculated as 8.2 percent.
4. Times Higher Education, *World University Rankings 2011–2012*, London, 2012.
5. QS Intelligence Unit, *World University Rankings 2011/2012*, London, 2012.
6. The Financial Times, *Global MBA Rankings 2012*.
7. Australian Chamber of Commerce and Industry, *2012–13 Pre-budget Submission to the Department of Treasury*, February 2012.
8. Australian Industry Group and Deloitte, *National CEO Survey—Skilling Business in Tough Time*, October 2009.
9. Ken Rowe, *Report of the National Enquiry into the Teaching of Literacy*, Commonwealth Department of Education, Science and Training, 2005.
10. Australian Industry Group and Allen Consulting Group, *World Class Skills for World Class Industries: Employers' Perspectives on Skilling in Victoria*, July 2006.
11. Business Council of Australia, *Restoring Our Edge in Education: Making Australia's Education System Its Next Competitive Advantage*, 2007.
12. St George and Australian Chamber of Commerce and Industry, *Business Expectations Survey: Identifying National Trends and Conditions for Australian Business*, August 2007.
13. Skills Australia, *Skills for Prosperity: A Roadmap for Vocational Education and Training*, 2011.
14. John Daley, Cassie McGannon, and Leah Ginnivan, *Game-changers: Economic Reform Priorities for Australia*, Grattan Institute, Melbourne, 2012.
15. Andrew Norton, *Mapping Australian Higher Education*, Grattan Institute, Melbourne, 2012.
16. Allen Consulting Group, *Assessment and Reporting of Employability Skills in Training Packages, Report to the Department of Education, Science and Training*, March 2006.
17. Graduate Careers Australia, *University & Beyond 2008: Snapshot*.
18. Kevin Rudd, Wayne Swan, Stephen Smith, and Penny Wong, *Skilling Australia for the Future*, Australian Labor Party, 2007.

19. Skills Australia, *Skills for Prosperity: A Roadmap for Vocational Education and Training*, 2011.

20. Business Council of Australia, *Restoring Our Edge in Education: Making Australia's Education System Its Next Competitive Advantage*, 2007.

21. Roy Green, Renu Agarwal, John Van Reenen, Nicholas Bloom, John Mathews, Christina Boedker, Danny Sampson, Paul Gollan, Phillip Toner, Hao Tan, and Paul Brown, *Management Matters in Australia: Just How Productive are We?*, Department of Industry, Innovation, Science and Research, Canberra, Australia, 2009.

22. Australian Chamber of Commerce and Industry, *ACCI Service Industries Blueprint*, 2011.

23. U.S. Department of Labor, Bureau of Labor Statistics, *International Comparisons of Manufacturing Productivity and Unit Labor Cost Trends, 2010*, October 2011.

24. Michael Fullilove and Chloë Flutter, *Diaspora: The World Wide Web of Australians*, Lowy Institute for International Policy, 2004.

25. Peter McDonald and Jeromey Temple, *Demographic and Labour Supply Future for Australia*, Australian Demographic and Social Research Institute, December 2008.

26. Australian Bureau of Statistics, *Migration, Australia, 2009–10*, 16 June 2011.

27. Australian Department of Immigration and Citizenship, *Immigration Update*, 2011.

28. John Daley, Cassie McGannon, and Leah Ginnivan, *Game-changers: Economic Reform Priorities for Australia*, Grattan Institute, Melbourne, 2012.

29. Elizabeth Knight and Phillip Coorey, "BHP Boss Threatens to Invest Offshore," *Sydney Morning Herald*, 17 May 2012.

30. Clancy Yates, "Real Skills Crisis Is Still to Come," *The Age*, 18 April 2011.

31. Deborah Snow, "Union Boss Rallies for the Battle to Come," *Sydney Morning Herald*, 12 May 2012.

32. Robert Gottliebsen, "Wrapped in a Red Tape Tangle," *Business Spectator*, 3 May 2012.

33. Australian Department of Education, Employment and Workplace Relations, *Trade Recognition Australia*, 2012.

34. Council of Australian Governments, *Council of Australian Governments' Meeting*, 10 February 2006.

35. "Abbott Demands Schools, Batts Inquiry," *Sydney Morning Herald*, 5 April 2010.

36. Australian Department of Education, Employment and Workplace Relations, *Review of Funding for Schooling*, 2011.

37. Jewel Topsfield, "Ex-premier Fires up over Canberra's Gonski Snub," *Sydney Morning Herald*, 26 May 2012.

38. John Daley, Cassie McGannon, and Leah Ginnivan, *Game-changers: Economic Reform Priorities for Australia*, Grattan Institute, Melbourne, 2012.

39. Although many that emigrate do eventually return and Australia's net immigration position is positive, this remains a concern.

40. The focus of this section is on hard infrastructure, including roads, railroads, ports, air transportation, energy, water, and communications.

41. Australian Bureau of Statistics, *National Statistics*, May 2012.

42. Australian Department of Infrastructure and Transport, *Australian Infrastructure Statistics Yearbook 2011*, March 2011.

43. Roads Australia.

44. For New South Wales: NSW Government, Transport Roads & Maritime Services. *Using Toll Roads FAQs*. For Queensland and Victoria: CityLink, *CityLink e-TAG Accepted Australia Wide: Australia Wide Roaming Fact Sheet*.

45. Australian Bureau of Statistics, *Engineering Construction Activity, Australia*, April 2012.

46. "NSW's Power Generators to Be Sold," *Sydney Morning Herald*, 30 May 2012.

47. Australian Department of Infrastructure and Transport, *Background—Organisation of Australia's Railways*, 1 June 2012.

48. Infrastructure Australia and the National Transport Commission, *National Port Strategy Background Paper*, December 2010.

49. "Sydney Ports Could Reach Capacity by 2013," *9News*, 25 August 2011.

50. Jason Dowling, "Boom Port to Bust by 2015," *The Age*, 10 December 2011.

51. Dampier Port Authority, *Port of Dampier Development Plan 2010–2020*, December 2010.

52. Infrastructure Australia and the National Transport Commission, *National Ports Strategy: Background Paper*, December 2010.

53. Australian Department of Infrastructure and Transport, *Airports, Aviation*, 6 January 2012.

54. Brisbane Airport Corporation, *New Parallel Runway Draft EIS/MDP for Public Comment*.

55. Geoffrey Thomas, "Watch Needed on Runway Capacity," *The West Australian*, 9 October 2011.

56. Heath Gilmore, "Sydney Airport to Hit Critical Capacity within Eight Years," *Sydney Morning Herald*, 8 November 2010.

57. Australian Department of Infrastructure and Transport, *Australian Infrastructure Statistics Yearbook 2011*, March 2011.

58. *The Global Competitiveness Report 2011–2012*, World Economic Forum, Switzerland, 2011.

59. Australian Industry Group, *Ai Group Industry Snapshot—Infrastructure Issues in Queensland: Industry's Views*, May 2009.

60. Leanne Hardwicke, *Infrastructure Report Card 2010*, Engineers Australia, November 2010.

61. Stephen Dziedzic, "ABC News, Australia's Infrastructure 'Barely Adequate'," *ABC News*, 4 July 2011.

62. National Farmers Federation Limited, *Federal Budget Submission 2011*, February 2011.

63. Australian Industry Group, *Ai Group Industry Snapshot—Infrastructure Issues in Queensland: Industry's Views*, May 2009.

64. John Daley, Cassie McGannon, and Leah Ginnivan, *Game-changers: Economic Reform Priorities for Australia*, Grattan Institute, Melbourne, 2012.

65. Port Jackson Partners Limited and Business Council of Australia, *Infrastructure Roadmap for Reform*, September 2007.

66. CPA Australia, *Enhancing Australia's Prosperity*, 2011.

67. Australian Industry Group, *Ai Group Industry Snapshot—Infrastructure Issues in Queensland: Industry's Views*, May 2009.

68. Port Jackson Partners Limited and Business Council of Australia, *Infrastructure Roadmap for Reform*, September 2007.

69. David Bartlett, *National Broadband Network (Tasmania) Bill 2010, Second Reading*, 2010.

70. Leanne Hardwicke, *Infrastructure Report Card 2010*, Engineers Australia, November 2010; and National Farmers Federation Limited, *Federal Budget Submission 2011*, February 2011.

71. Alan March, "Swan's Splurge Alone Can't Fix the Cracks in Infrastructure Australia," *The Conversation*, 13 May 2011.

72. Association of Consulting Engineers Australia, *Discussion Paper 1: Australia's Future Infrastructure Requirements*, October 2008.

73. Alan March, "Swan's Splurge Alone Can't Fix the Cracks in Infrastructure Australia," *The Conversation*, 13 May 2011.

74. Leanne Hardwicke, *Infrastructure Report Card 2010*, Engineers Australia, November 2010.

75. Port Jackson Partners Limited and Business Council of Australia, *Infrastructure Roadmap for Reform*, September 2007.

76. Alan March, "Swan's Splurge Alone Can't Fix the Cracks in Infrastructure Australia," *The Conversation*, 13 May 2011.

77. Leanne Hardwicke, *Infrastructure Report Card 2010*, Engineers Australia, November 2010.

78. OECD, *Economic Survey of Australia 2005*, Paris, 2005.

79. Port Jackson Partners Limited and Business Council of Australia, *Infrastructure Roadmap for Reform*, September 2007.

80. Frances Perkins, Chris Nadarajah, and Luke McInerney, *Australia's Infrastructure Policy and the COAG National Reform Agenda, Economic Round-up*, The Treasury, Summer 2007.

81. Frances Perkins, Chris Nadarajah, and Luke McInerney, *Australia's Infrastructure Policy and the COAG National Reform Agenda, Economic Round-up*, The Treasury, Summer 2007.

82. Port Jackson Partners Limited and Business Council of Australia, *Infrastructure Roadmap for Reform*, September 2007.

83. Jordan Baker, Jessica Irvine, and Anne Davies, "Cross City Tunnel Heads for the Bargain Basement Bin," *Sydney Morning Herald*, 17 November 2006.

84. Frances Perkins, Chris Nadarajah, and Luke McInerney, *Australia's Infrastructure Policy and the COAG National Reform Agenda, Economic Round-up*, The Treasury, Summer 2007.

85. Leanne Hardwicke, *Infrastructure Report Card 2010*, Engineers Australia, November 2010.

86. Leanne Hardwicke, *Infrastructure Report Card 2010*, Engineers Australia, November 2010.

87. CPA Australia, *Victorian Budget Puts Spotlight on Need for Serious National Tax Reform*, 1 May 2012.

88. Ernst & Young, *Financing Australia's Infrastructure Needs: Superannuation Investment in Infrastructure*, 2011.

89. Australian Productivity Commission, *Review of National Competition Policy Reforms (2005)*, February 2005.

90. Infrastructure Australia, *Press Release: Infrastructure Australia Pushes for Better Projects and Private Funding*, 4 July 2011.

91. Infrastructure Australia, *Press Release: Infrastructure Australia Pushes for Better Projects and Private Funding*, 4 July 2011.

92. Claude Giorno, "Meeting Infrastructure Needs in Australia," *OECD Economics Department Working Papers*, No. 851, March 2011.

93. British Geological Survey, *World Mineral Production*, 2010; IEA website.

94. "Equivalent to 11.5 percent of GDP" does not mean "responsible for 11.5 percent of GDP" as the GDP contribution of an industry is its value added, not its output or revenues.

95. International Monetary Fund Primary Commodity Prices show that the price per metric ton of iron ore imported into China fell to USD 99.47 by the end of September 2012 down from a high of USD 187.18 in February 2011, a drop of nearly 47 percent in less than 2 years.

96. Information obtained from company annual reports, Yahoo Finance, and public sources.

97. Tim Mazzarol, "Australia's Two Speed Economy—Who Wins, Who Loses?" *The Conversation*, 1 June 2011.

98. Australian Treasury, "The Resources Boom and the Two-speed Economy," *Economic Roundup*, Issue 3, 2008.

99. Gary Banks notes that previously it was labeled the "Gregory Effect" after Professor Bob Gregory. See Gary Banks "Successful Reform: Past Lessons, Future Challenges" (Keynote address to the Annual Forecasting Conference of The Australian Business Economists, Productivity Commission, Sydney, 8 December 2010).

100. Domain-b, *Australia's "Two-speed" Economy now a "Three-Speed" Economy: Rio Tinto*, 12 May 2012.

101. Christine St Anne, "How to Run a Two-speed Economy," *Morningstar*, 18 May, 2012.

102. The Western Australian Division of the Liberal Party, *Government Fails with Two-speed Economy—Opinion piece for the Australian*, 2012.

103. Sarah Falson, "Manufacturers Concerned about the Widening Gap in the Two-speed Economy," *Manufacturers' Monthly*, 16 May 2012.

104. David Lague, "China Boom Spurs 'Two-speed Economy' in Australia," *Financial Post*, 1 December 2011.

105. "PM Gillard: Mining Boom Brings Sustainable Benefits for Australia," *International Business Times*, 4 October 2011.

106. Australian Treasury, "The Resources Boom and the Two-speed Economy," *Economic Roundup*, Issue 3, 2008.

107. Tim Mazzarol, "Australia's Two Speed Economy—Who Wins, Who Loses?" *The Conversation*, 1 June 2011.

108. The Western Australian Division of the Liberal Party, *Government Fails with Two-speed Economy—Opinion piece for the Australian*, 2012.

109. Malcolm Maiden, "Singing from the Same Song Book," *Sydney Morning Herald*, 17 May 2012.

110. Shahar Hameiri and Toby Carroll, "The Political Consequences of Australia's Resources Boom," *ABC News*, 18 August 2011.

111. "China Slowdown Threatens Australia: World Bank," *Sydney Morning Herald*, 23 May 2012.

112. John Daley, Cassie McGannon, and Leah Ginnivan, *Game-Changers: Economic Reform Priorities for Australia*, Grattan Institute, Melbourne, 2012.

113. Judith Ireland, "Union fury over Rinehart Migration Deal," *Sydney Morning Herald*, 25 May 2012.

114. Julie Power, "Pulling in mining dollars takes frontier spirit—hard to find in the city," *Sydney Morning Herald*, 30 May 2012.

115. Sarah Falson, "Manufacturers Concerned about the Widening Gap in the Two-speed Economy," *Manufacturers' Monthly*, 16 May 2012.

116. Prime Minister Julia Gillard (Speech to the Minerals Council of Australia, 30 May 2012).

117. Malcolm Maiden, "Singing from the Same Song Book," *Sydney Morning Herald*, 17 May 2012.

118. Kate Penney, Jane Melanie, Clare Stark, and Terry Sheale, "Opportunities and Challenges Facing the Australian Resources Sector," *Australian Journal of Agricultural and Resource Economics* 56, no. 2 (April 2012): 152–170.

119. Peter Cai, "China Takes a Tougher Line," *Sydney Morning Herald*, 13 April 2012.

120. Sameera Anand, "Rio Tinto China Deal Faces Growing Opposition," *Bloomberg Businessweek*, 18 March 2009.

121. Peter Cai, "China Takes a Tougher Line," *Sydney Morning Herald*, 13 April 2012.

122. John Freebarin and John Quiggin, "Special Taxation of the Mining Industry," *Australian Public Policy Program Working Paper*. P10, No.3.

123. Charles Kennedy, "Australia's Proposed Coal-Seam Natural Gas Mining Controversial," August 2011: oilprice.com.

124. Sarah-Jane Collins, "Too Many Cooks in the Mining Kitchen," *Global Mail*, 6 February 2012.

125. AAP, *Australian Resources Boom Rolls on*, 7 July 2011.

126. Elizabeth Knight and Phillip Coorey, "BHP Boss Threatens to Invest Offshore," *Sydney Morning Herald*, 17 May 2012.

127. Ed Shann, *Maximising Growth in a Mining Boom*, Minerals Council of Australia, March 2012.

128. The Western Australian Division of the Liberal Party, *Government Fails with Two-speed Economy—Opinion piece for the Australian*, 2012..

129. Paul Cleary, "Mining boom could bust us," *The Age*, 11 November 2007.

130. Clancy Yeates, "Two-speed economy to widen," *The Age*, 24 April 2012.

131. Gary Banks, "Australia's Mining Boom: What's the Problem?" (Address to the Melbourne Institute and The Australian Economic and Social Outlook Conference, 30 June 2011).

CHAPTER 6

Economic Policy, Regulation, and Tax

Many aspects and types of government policies influence the competitiveness of nations and regions. While it is impossible to go into all aspects of government policy in this chapter, it is useful to at least outline some of the main features of Australia's economic policy, regulatory system, and tax policy, as they have come up repeatedly in both international assessments of Australia's competitiveness and in the business competitiveness survey results reported in Chapter 4. These policy areas set a context that either supports or does not support the ability of industries and businesses to develop and to prosper.

Economic policy, in particular fiscal policy, monetary policy, competition policy, exchange rate policy, industrial support policy, trade policy, and investment policy, influences the prices of goods and services, the extent to which businesses face domestic and foreign competition, as well as influencing the price of and access to funding. Each of these, in turn, affects the position of Australian companies, industries, and the economy as a whole.

Regulatory policy also has a broad range and broad impacts. Regulation on entry, product standards, safety standards, the workplace, the environment, and numerous other aspects of business provide the rules within which businesses can operate. The nature and details of individual regulations can be important to an economy, but so too can the number of regulations, the complexity of the regulatory environment, the cost of complying with regulations, and whether regulations across jurisdictions are distinct or overlapping, similar or different.

Finally, a nation's tax system influences its competitiveness in a variety of ways. Features of the tax system, including the number and type of taxes, tax rates, tax thresholds, compliance costs, and the way in which taxes are collected, are considered when businesses and individuals decide whether to invest, immigrate, or emigrate. If taxes are too high or kick in too early, people may work less, and productivity may decrease. If taxes are too low, government may not be able to fund essential services to a level that maintains a country's overall competitiveness and its standard of living. The right balance must be found if Australia is to compete in a sustainable way.

In a world in which more and more nations are trying to improve their competitiveness, develop their own firms, attract foreign investment, and attract highly skilled and geographically mobile professionals, we see more and more of what can only be termed competition in terms of economic policy, regulation, and taxation. Nations and governments must make their own choices in these areas, governed by the needs and norms of the country, but they cannot do so in a vacuum. Economic policy, regulatory policy, and tax policy are intertwined, and therefore should be considered together when attempting to understand a country's ability to compete.

Economic Policy

A broad range of economic policies influence a nation's competitiveness, and it will be important that Australia get these policies right if it is to maximise its prosperity. Here we will focus on a limited number of high-profile policy areas, including fiscal policy, monetary policy, currency and foreign exchange policy, trade policy, investment policy, and competition policy. Getting economic policies right in these areas in any advanced economy requires a concerted effort on the part of political leaders, businesses, and the community in general.

Australia's Economic Policy

Fiscal policy uses government spending and tax revenues to stabilise economic fluctuations or to achieve economic policy goals. For the past two decades, fiscal policy in Australia has focused on keeping debt down and retaining the flexibility to act when necessary. This was shown during the Global Financial Crisis when Australia instituted a range of fiscal measures, including direct transfer payments and a massive building program, to stimulate the economy—all while retaining debt to GDP levels far lower than most other OECD nations. Australian Government spending went from AUD 272 billion in 2007–2008 to AUD 371 billion in 2011–2012, while government net debt in the latter year was 9.6 percent of GDP.[1] By the 2012–2013 budget, the Government was attempting to return the country to surpluses to reduce debt levels and avoid the problems other OECD nations had faced.[2]

The Reserve Bank of Australia (RBA) is Australia's central bank responsible for monetary policy and the management of the nation's gold and foreign exchange reserves. The RBA is independent but accountable to the Federal Parliament for its actions. The Reserve Bank Act (1959) specifies the objectives of monetary policy as price stability, economic prosperity, and maintaining full employment. Since 1993, Australia's monetary policy has been focused on inflation, with consumer price index (CPI) inflation the main target and interest rates the main policy tool. The official interest rate is the cash rate set by the RBA. Historically, Australia's major banks tended to set their variable interest rates in lock-step with changes to the cash rate set by the RBA. In recent times, this has changed with the major banks in Australia passing on only part of interest rate cuts set by the RBA and also increasing their interest rates outside of the rate cycle set by the RBA due in part to increased wholesale funding costs. In recent years, given the strong growth dynamics and inflationary pressures due to the resource boom, Australia's interest rates have been fairly high compared to other OECD countries. The desire for flexibility is key to Australia's approach to monetary policy. Thus, during the Global Financial Crisis, the RBA pre-emptively cut interest rates, a move, which along with the fiscal measures described, was credited with helping Australia weather the storm without going into recession,[3] while retaining high enough rates to do more if necessary.

In 1983, Australia moved from a fixed to a floating exchange rate regime in which government generally does not attempt to intervene to control the exchange rate. Going to a floating exchange rate was designed to identify structural weaknesses and remove market distortions in Australia's economy.[4] In recent years, the effect of a strong Australian dollar on Australian exporters, and especially on manufacturers, has been often debated in Australia. The position of the Government seems to be that currency movements will be adverse for some parts of the economy but beneficial to other parts, and that the Government won't intervene on the exchange rate to try to counterbalance market forces. Rather, when there is specific need, it may address the negative effect that currency movements have on particular sectors by shoring up those sectors in other ways. The support being given to Australia's automotive industry at a cost of billions of dollars is a case in point.[5]

Australia has a limited number of industrial support programs. It provides support for research and development through tax concessions. It provides export support through Austrade. It provides support for small and medium-sized business through the Enterprise Connect program. The Australian Government also provides support for venture capital, providing favourable tax treatment for Australian venture capital providers as well as favourable tax treatment for foreign venture capital companies from selected nations. There is also direct support for the automotive, textile and garment, film, and tourism industries, among others. However, for the most part, the Australian Government takes a light-handed approach towards industrial support.

Australia introduced a National Competition Policy and related reforms in 1995 following an inquiry that was chaired by Professor Frederick Hilmer. The philosophy of increasing competition to improve Australia's efficiency, innovation, and productivity is one that has been followed by Australian governments since 1995. The Commonwealth Competition Policy Reform Act 1995 extended the trade practices laws prohibiting anti-competitive activities to all businesses.[6] It also introduced competitive neutrality to ensure that public ownership did not confer an advantage over privately owned businesses; it enabled businesses to access nationally significant infrastructure that might be owned by government or by other businesses; and it introduced various other reforms. The vision that inspired the National Competition Policy has been realised in many ways with increased competition and efficiencies in sectors where previously competition had been limited by regulatory barriers, such as in the telecommunications and energy sectors.

Australia started moving from a highly protected trade regime to a much more open regime with a view to increasing the competitiveness of Australian industry in the 1980s. The shift from protecting manufacturers at high and often not measured costs to finding ways to improve the competitiveness of the economy resulted in significant reductions to tariffs and the encouragement of exports through export promotion programs. Australia's trade policy was reorganised in 2011 to operate under five principles: (1) the pursuit of ongoing, trade-related economic reform without waiting for other countries to reform their trade policies; (2) non-discrimination among countries in trade negotiations; (3) foreign policy considerations not overriding trade policy; (4) transparency in free trade negotiations; and (5) the seamless execution of trade policy and wider economic reform.[7] The present Government asserts that it will champion multilateral trade liberalisation, but since progress on multilateral agreement has been slow, it will work on bilateral and regional trade agreements that are supportive of the multilateral system. In a speech to the Committee for Economic Development of Australia (CEDA) in March 2012, Australia's Trade Minister reaffirmed the Government's commitment to multilateral trade and further commented that Australia's trade activities are being refocused towards emerging and frontier markets where commercial opportunities can be very large.[8]

Until the late 1970s, foreign investment into Australia was highly regulated and often discouraged. Helped by the establishment of the Foreign Investment Review Board in 1976 and the structure and rigour that it brought to thinking on foreign investment proposals, the Australian Government began to liberalise controls on foreign investment in the 1980s. At present, the Australian Government states that it welcomes foreign investment and views it as important to Australia's economic growth and prosperity.[9] There is some control in place in the form of the Foreign Acquisitions and Takeovers Act 1975 (FATA), which provides for Australia's Treasurer or his delegate to review investment proposals from foreign parties and block foreign investment proposals that are contrary to the national interest.[10] Proposals are evaluated on a case-by-case basis, and the vast majority are allowed, although there are a few high-profile cases in which foreign investment has been blocked by this mechanism.[11]

International Assessments

Australia gets mixed marks on its economic policies in international comparisons. In 2011, the World Economic Forum ranked Australia 26th in Macroeconomic Environment, 86th in Government Budget Balance, and 43rd in Gross National Savings, though it should be said that the Government Budget Balance was in an extraordinary year in which a massive fiscal stimulus was implemented, and in most years the government budget balance is quite strong. In 2011, IMD ranked Australia 13th in Economic Performance and 7th in Government Efficiency. Australia was ranked 18th (out of 100 economies) for Economic Efficiency, and 72nd for Economic Growth by the Chinese Academy of Social Sciences for 2009–2010.

TABLE 6.1   Australia's Ranking, Features Related to Economic Policy, WEF and IMD

World Economic Forum, 2011 (out of 142 economies)		IMD, 2011 (out of 59 economies)	
Item	Rank	Item	Rank
Property Rights	23	Resilience of the Economy	2
Wastefulness of Government Spending	31	Inflation	27
Inflation, Annual Change	1	Exchange Rates	34
Interest Rate Spread	32	International Investment	17
General Government Debt	29	Public Finance	17
Intensity of Local Competition	7	Management of Public Finances	27
Extent of Market Dominance	25	Fiscal Policy	19
Effectiveness of Anti-Monopoly Policy	22	Central Bank Policy	10
Prevalence of Trade Barriers	14	Adaptability of Government Policy	15
Trade Tariffs	45	Government Decision	23
Prevalence of Foreign Ownership	10	Customs Authorities	9
Business Impact of Rules on FDI	47	Protectionism	6
Burden of Customs Procedures	20	Investment Incentives	27
Government Balance, % of GDP	86	Competition Legislation	4

Sources: The Global Competitiveness Report, 2011–2012, World Economic Forum, Switzerland, 2011; IMD, *World Competitiveness Online*, 1995–2011.

Australia ranked 3rd out of 184 nations in the 2012 Heritage Foundation Index of Economic Freedom, behind only Hong Kong and Singapore. It was ahead of all of the comparison set countries, and behind only 2 of 13 other Asia-Pacific economies. In the sub-indexes, Australia receives a high rank for Financial Freedom (1st), Monetary Freedom (11th), Business Freedom (13th), and Investment Freedom (4th). It ranked closer to the middle in Trade Freedom (37th), and did not perform well at all in Government Spending (85th) and Fiscal Freedom (160th), again, however, reflecting an extraordinary year in these dimensions. Australia ranked 5th (out of 141 economies) in the Fraser Institute Economic Freedom of the World Index for 2009, behind Hong Kong, Singapore, New Zealand, and Switzerland. In the sub-indices, Australia ranked 60th in Size of Government, 38th in Money Growth, 43rd in Inflation, 95th in Government Consumption, and 83rd in Transfers and Subsidies.

To the international assessments, we should add the results of the business competitiveness survey carried out for this project. Respondents from most industries indicated that Australia has advantages versus competitor and comparator countries in most dimensions of economic policy, including competition policy, trade policy, and foreign investment policies. Advantages were reported in all of these drivers in all of the service sectors shown in Chapter 4. Disadvantages were reported in mining and a few manufacturing sectors in foreign investment policy, trade policy, and overall government policy. Modest advantages were also reported for access to and cost of debt finance, which is influenced by interest rate policies. Australia was rated as having very modest advantages in terms of government support programs for industries and government incentives for industries, with several manufacturing and a few service industries reporting disadvantages. Interestingly, Australia's exchange rate and interest rates were viewed as disadvantages only in a few of the manufacturing industries analysed.

Economic Policy Issues in Australia

Australians understand that Australia must have economic policies that foster competitiveness and that a consistent mix of policies that reinforce each other is needed to properly manage the Australian economy.[12] While Australia generally gets good marks in terms of economic policy, there are a number of issues and challenges that have arisen with respect to economic policy in recent years.

> ***Fiscal Policy, Too Much, Too Little, or Just Enough?*** Australia's fiscal policy has been credited as saving Australia from the worst of the economic problems that many other nations have endured since 2007.[13] However, some in Australia have argued that the Government's policies in relation to tax and spending have in recent years been fiscally irresponsible and will harm Australia's economic performance in the long term, even going so far as to suggest that new legislation be put in place to force politicians in Australia to be fiscally responsible.[14] Others have observed that the present political imperative to bring the government budget back to surplus in 2012–2013 is not good economics, that some debt is to be expected if capital investment is to be made, and that the effects of fiscal policy changes on economic activity must be considered.[15] Australia's treasurer, Wayne Swan, received an endorsement from *Euromoney* in 2011 when it chose him Finance Minister of the Year, and in relation to that award he defended his fiscal policies by

saying, "The fiscal rules that we put in place to deal with the global recession when we moved to stimulate the economy were ahead of the rest of the world."[16] Quibbles over the crisis period spending would seem to be best directed to whether the specific spending items will generate long-term benefits or not; in the latter event this would represent lost opportunity. With respect to views that Government is trying to return to surplus too soon, conservatism in the face of the debt situation is probably a good thing, and if global conditions change, there is room for adjustment.

Is Monetary Policy Making Australia Uncompetitive? In an address to the Australian Industry Group, the deputy governor of the Reserve Bank of Australia noted that the main role for monetary policy is to keep inflation low and stable and that Australia's relatively high interest rates are needed in combination with a robust exchange rate in order to maintain overall macro-economic stability.[17] Critics of RBA policy claim that the high Australian dollar is diminishing Australia's competitiveness across many sectors and that more needs to be done to get the dollar down.[18] Supporters of RBA policy claim that the RBA has helped to bring about financial stability during a period when many other countries have failed to do so, and that if the RBA were to lower interest rates to a level that would materially reduce the value of the currency then this might help some industries but it would create problems for others, particularly in the light of high commodity prices.[19] Again, it would seem to us that a policy shift that would substantially change the value of the currency would have distorting impacts that could be hard to reverse.

Enhancing Competition Policy: The Productivity Commission reviewed the National Competition Policy Reforms in 2005 and found that it had delivered significant benefits but that more could be done.[20] Consequently, the Council of Australian Governments (COAG) in 2006 agreed to continue competition reform and regulatory reform as part of the National Reform Agenda, and in 2007 the COAG agreed that the COAG Reform Council would monitor progress.

Is Trade Policy Consistent with Other Policies? It is claimed by some that Australia has no choice but to have a free trade policy, but that this means the costs imposed on business by government must be limited, leaving no room for a payroll tax and a carbon tax that increase the cost of doing business in Australia. The present Government's focus on multilateral trade negotiations has been criticised as potentially getting in the way of reducing trade barriers on a bilateral basis.[21] There also is a view that the timing is not presently right for delivering and sustaining trade liberalisation given conditions in the global and national economies.[22] We do note in this context, that the World Trade Organization in 2011 observed that Australia's continuing process on trade liberalisation was an integral part of the structural reforms that have contributed to Australia's impressive economic performance.[23]

Government and Commercial Decisions: Australia's overall economic philosophy has been that government should stay out of commercial decisions in the vast majority of cases. Market-orientation and openness to inward investment have helped to make Australia one of the of world's economic success stories.[24] Openness to investment in all sectors, but particularly in the resources sector, has been crucial for Australia's development. There are some who argue that the Government should limit the market for corporate control in Australia and that the resources sector in particular should be structured along Norwegian lines wherein resource ventures are publicly owned and the sector presumably operates for public rather than private benefit.[25] This view tends to overlook the fact that foreign investors in Australia have to live by Australia's laws, rules, and regulations; that most investments and resource investments in particular are already subject to numerous approvals and negotiations with Government; that Government can reject any individual bidder if it concludes that the national interest would be damaged; that Government could negotiate specific conditions and safeguards in return for approving any particular investment; and that the Government shares in the financial success of any business by way of existing taxes.

Limited Impact of Industrial Support Programs: Drawing on data from the Productivity Commission,[26] the Grattan Institute argues that in spite of the Australian Government spending nearly AUD 14 billion on industry support, such as R&D tax concessions, export assistance, and direct assistance given to the automotive, textile, clothing and footwear, and film industries, among others, there is little evidence that this aids productivity growth in any meaningful way.[27] The Enterprise Connect program does appear to be successful, having served over 7,500 companies in its first three years (it was founded in 2008), with its model of providing information, advice, and networking opportunities.

Lack of Cluster Development Initiatives: Industrial clusters are groups of firms in the same and related industries whose performance is in some way interdependent. Regional clusters are industrial clusters that are concentrated in relatively small geographic areas that, depending on the industries involved, can be a small part of a city (leading financial and professional service clusters, for example), around a city (many manufacturing clusters), or throughout a region within a country (resource-based and some heavy industrial clusters).[28] Cluster-based development policies have been used with success in many countries around the world, including France, Germany, Italy, Spain, Sweden, Denmark, Brazil, Singapore, India, and others.[29] While Australia is home to numerous regional clusters, in the wine, resource, marine, financial, and professional service industries, programs to foster or leverage clusters have a mixed history, with starts and stops and limited cumulative experience compared to many other countries.[30] This is due in part to the dominance of the Federal Government in economic development initiatives in Australia and the time horizon for success. Cluster initiatives are best carried out locally within communities and over extended periods of time.

Is the Foreign Investment Environment Too Restrictive? The Foreign Investment Review Board (FIRB) works with interested parties to ensure that the national interest is protected. The FIRB has blocked a number of investments, including a bid by state-owned China interests to buy a controlling stake in a rare earth deposit in Western Australia,[31] but it also approved AUD 60 billion in Chinese investment to the end of 2010.[32] Though not a universally held view, there are some who argue that Australia's foreign investment regime is too restrictive and that this discourages significant foreign investment.[33] In an OECD assessment, Australia was found to be less restrictive on foreign investment than Canada, Iceland, Japan, Korea, Mexico, and New Zealand, but more restrictive than the 27 other OECD nations.[34] Among non-OECD nations, Argentina, Brazil, and South Africa were termed less restrictive than Australia, whereas China, India, and Russia were more restrictive. This would indicate that if Australia is to conform more closely with norms in the most advanced economies then it should be considering reducing restrictions on foreign investment, not increasing them.

According to the United Nations Conference on Trade and Development (UNCTAD), in 2010, the stock of foreign investment in Australia was equivalent to 39.9 percent of GDP, well above the world average of 30.4 percent, making Australia relatively reliant on foreign investment in international terms.[35] It has been noted in Australia that foreign investment has driven strong economic growth, increased employment, and resulted in higher income levels than otherwise would have been realised and that on this basis greater foreign investment should be allowed.[36]

Australia's Economic Policy in Perspective

Overall, Australia performs relatively well in most areas of economic policy, and in some areas where it is ranked poorly in international assessments, this was due to extraordinary circumstances and policy moves that have been considered appropriate generally inside and outside of Australia. Again, this shows the importance of moving beyond the headline rankings and ratings to understand important drivers of competitiveness in detail. The results indicate that Australia provides appropriate policy conditions for the economy as a whole. The sources also suggest that Australia gets many of the basic conditions regarding government, openness, and flexibility right, although there are some issues in terms of bureaucracy costs, government consumption, transfers and subsidies, and trade taxes.

Australia's fiscal and monetary policies have been prudent, avoiding the excesses of many other countries, and providing flexibility to respond in times of global economic crisis. Australia's competition, exchange rate, trade, and investment policies have given the country the resilience to adjust to changing global and national economic circumstances, as well as the ability to leverage its advantages in key sectors of the economy. The results have been strong and stable growth, a dramatic reduction of distortions and inefficiencies since the 1980s, large increases in trade, and large increases in inward investment.

The positives of Australia's economic policy are evident when one considers that Australia's economy is in good shape compared with the rest of the developed world, with relatively low unemployment rates and fairly stable and positive GDP growth. The Australian dollar is high against historical averages, and its volatility is an issue both for exporting and importing businesses, but the strength of the dollar is a sign of a robust economy that has benefitted from sound policy initiatives. Australia's fiscal policy is primed to bring Australia back to a surplus. Combined with the present expansionary monetary policy, there would seem to be a fair level of flexibility to manoeuvre to meet changing global circumstances.

While Australia has performed well in the areas of government policy we have assessed here versus other OECD nations, we should recall that there are other economies in the Asia-Pacific region that have performed as well or even better in recent times in terms of economic performance and in terms of assessments of their economic policies. In addition, while a good economic policy regime would appear to be a necessary condition, it is unlikely to be a sufficient condition to improve competitiveness on its own. Strengths in economic policy will have to be combined with other strengths in order to improve Australia's competitiveness.

Regulation

Businesses operate under a range of regulations in any nation. Regulation supports the safety of products and workplaces, limits the environmental damage that can be done by economic activities, protects workers and businesses from the acts of others, and sets standards for products and professions. The content of regulation usually reflects the values of society and the trade-offs that nations choose in order to advance their various agendas. How regulations are set and administered reflects the nature of the political and jurisdictional system within a country.

While the content and administration of regulations will vary greatly across nations, a common objective should be to understand the impacts of regulation on the competitiveness of the economy, as well as on other aspects of society, and to achieve valid regulatory ends through the most effective and efficient means possible. This is particularly true in a rapidly changing world in which the competition between nations is heating up, and in which an effective and efficient regulatory regime can be a strong competitive advantage. Thus, while regulation is necessary and important, it is vital that there be a clear understanding of the purpose and intent, that regulations be sensible and fair, and that they do not needlessly shackle businesses. Getting the balance right will require focus and co-operation by governments at all levels, and consultation with the corporate sector and the community.

Regulation in Australia

Regulations in Australia are set at the federal, state, and local levels. There are approximately 60 Commonwealth regulators and national standard-setting bodies in Australia. There are a further 40 federal ministerial councils that set and administer regulations. There is a huge volume of standards in Australia, too, with 6,873 existing standards in place maintained by Standards Australia.[37] According to Australia's Productivity Commission, it is estimated that federal regulatory agencies employ over 34,000 people, with a combined annual budget of well over AUD 4.5 billion; from 2000 to 2006, a total of 40,266 pages of Commonwealth Acts were passed by the Federal Parliament (and in FY2007 a further 8,198 pages were passed); and the average number of pages per Act went from 9 pages in the 1970s to 35 pages by the mid-2000s.[38] At the local level, there are 560 government areas in Australia delivering policies and setting regulations that impact businesses and individuals.[39] Australia's states and territories also have regulatory bodies. The result is a great deal of duplication and contradictions in regulation at the local and state level. This redundancy in setting regulations is a significant time and cost burden.

Total government spending on administering regulations in Australia is estimated at AUD 5.3 billion per year.[40] It is estimated that the cost of the regulatory burden on Australian individuals is at least 8 percent of GDP, representing a cost of some AUD 16 billion (or AUD 826 per Australian) per annum, and this may be a conservative esti-mate.[41] The total cost of regulation on businesses in Australia (taking into account the cost of the time it takes to deal with regulation) is estimated to be AUD 16.9 billion, of which around 85 percent is borne by small and medium-sized enterprises.[42]

The Business Council of Australia 2010 scorecard on Australia's regulatory system graded overall performance as well as the principles of good regulation making, and the accountability, transparency, and review of regulations. Australia overall was given a grade of adequate to good. Victoria was the best performing state, with an overall grade of good (see Table 6.2).

Australia is ahead of many other nations, including the United States and the United Kingdom, in having a legislated body, the Productivity Commission, which has the responsibility of reporting on matters related to industry and productivity, including regulation, in a way that aims to improve economic performance. The Productivity Commission has produced numerous reports in recent years that provide an overview of regulation in Australia and offer suggestions for improvement and for reform.[43]

International Assessments

Several international sources rate countries on features related to the regulatory sys-tem. Table 6.3 lists selected results from the World Economic Forum and the Inter-national Institute for Management Development (IMD). In the World Economic Forum results, Australia ranks within the top 10 in features related to starting a business, the legal system, and securities regulation, but ranks not well at all in features related to regulation, and practices related to hiring, firing, and wage determination.

The IMD results rank Australia highly in features related to starting companies, financial regulation, government efficiency, and the legal and regulatory framework. The last apparently contradicts the WEF results. Among the items in the table, only in Government Decisions was Australia outside the top 20.

The IFC Ease of Doing Business Index and the Heritage Foundation and Fraser Institute indices of economic freedom also include several features related to the regulatory environment that are used as a tool for policymakers and investors to assess the state of, and need for, reform in different economies. Australia ranked 15th out of 183 economies in the 2012 Ease of Doing Business Index. It ranked 2nd for Starting a Business, 8th for Getting Credit, 17th for Enforcing Contracts, 17th for Resolving Insolvency, 38th for Registering Property, 42nd for Dealing with Construction Permits, and 65th for Protecting Investors.[44] Australia ranked 3rd out of 184 countries in the Heritage Foundation Index of Economic Freedom in 2012. In terms of the sub-indexes, Australia does well in Financial Freedom (1st), Property Rights (2nd), Free-dom from Corruption (8th), Labour Freedom (8th), Monetary Freedom (11th), Busi-ness Freedom (13th), and Investment Freedom (14th).[45]

The 2009 Economic Freedom of the World Index published by The Fraser Insti-tute in the *2011 Economic Freedom of the World Report*[46] ranked Australia 5th out of 141 countries. Australia scored highly in the sub-index Regulation of Credit, Labour, and Business (9th), coming first in the underlying components in Ownership of Banks, Private Sector Credit, Interest Rate Controls/Negative Real Interest Rates, Hiring Regulations and Minimum Wage, Hour Regulations, Mandated Cost of Worker Dis-missal, Conscription, and Starting a Business. Sub-indexes that detracted from the

TABLE 6.2 Summary Result of Business Council of Australia Scorecard, 2010

	Overall Assessment	Principles of Good Regulation-making	Accountability	Transparency	Review
Commonwealth	Adequate/Good	Good	Adequate/Good	Adequate/Good	Adequate/Good
Victoria	Good	Good	Good	Adequate/Good	Good—with some improvement shown
New South Wales	Adequate/Good	Good	Adequate/Good	Adequate/Good	Good
Queensland	Adequate/Good	Good	Adequate/Good	Adequate—but with clear room for improvement	Good
Western Australia	Adequate/Good	Good	Adequate/Good	Adequate/Good	Adequate/Good
South Australia	Adequate/Good	Good	Adequate/Good	Adequate—but with clear room for improvement	Good—with some improvement shown
Northern Territory	Adequate/Good	Good	Adequate—but with clear room for improvement	Adequate/Good	Adequate
Tasmania	Adequate—but with clear room for improvement	Adequate/Good	Adequate/Good	Adequate—but with clear room for improvement	Adequate—but with clear room for improvement
Australian Capital Territory	Adequate—but with clear room for improvement	Good	Adequate—but with clear room for improvement	Adequate/Good	Poor

Note:
Rating: Excellent 9–10, Good 7–8, Adequate/Good 5–6, Adequate—but room for improvement 3–4, Poor 0–2.
Source: Business Council of Australia, *2010 Scorecard of Red Tape Reform: Summary*, 2010.

TABLE 6.3   Australia's Ranking, Features Related to Regulation, WEF and IMD

World Economic Forum, 2011 (out of 142 economies)		IMD, 2011 (out of 59 economies)	
Item	Rank	Item	Rank
Favouritism in Decisions of Government Officials	21	Government Efficiency	7
Burden of Government Regulation	75	Legal and Regulatory	3
Efficiency of Legal System in Challenging Regulations	16	Framework	
Strength of Auditing and Reporting Standards	13	Government Decisions	23
Strength of Investor Protection	47	Transparency	12
Procedures to Start a Business	3	Bureaucracy	10
Days to Start a Business	2	Ease of Doing Business	7
Flexibility in Wage Determination	116	Creation of Firms	8
Hiring and Firing Practices	97	Start-Up Days	2
Regulation of Securities Exchanges	10	Start-Up Procedures	3
Legal Rights	8	Personal Security and Private Property Rights	6
		Financial Institution Transparency	5
		Finance and Banking Regulation	7
		Shareholders' Rights	7

Sources: The Global Competitiveness Report, 2011–2012, World Economic Forum, Switzerland, 2011; IMD, *World Competitiveness Online*, 1995–2011.

good performance were Hiring and Firing Regulations (69th), Centralised Collective Bargaining (98th), and Bureaucracy Costs (114th). Australia did fairly well in Legal Structure and Security of Property Rights (11th). Of the sub-components of Legal Structure and Security of Property Rights, Australia performed well in Judicial Independence (8th), Military Interference in Rule of Law and Politics (1st), and Integrity of Legal System (11th).[47]

Again, we should add perspectives from the business competitiveness survey. As seen in Chapter 4, Australia's regulatory and legal framework were viewed as advantages by all of the industries reported. Australia's environmental policies, planning laws, transparency of government decision making, and institutions were also viewed as advantages.

Regulation Issues in Australia

Australians understand that the nation must have regulations to govern business activity and to instil confidence in all parties as to the orderly functioning of business and government. Several issues arise in relation to regulation that indicate challenges that need to be addressed.

Too Many Regulations: The Productivity Commission recommends that new regulations and the existing stock of regulation should be appropriate, effective, and efficient, and it points out that to achieve this there must be robust vetting of regulation and a focus on key areas for reform.[48] More than 100 entities in Australia set regulations and standards, and there are nearly 7,000 existing standards in Australia. This is a huge volume of regulations and standards for businesses to understand and to meet. Small businesses in particular feel the burden.

Regulations Are Too Costly: The New South Wales Chamber of Commerce estimated that the average business in NSW spends 400 hours a year complying with regulations or meeting legal obligations.[49] In 2011, in a survey of Chief Executive Officers by the Australian Industry Group, they estimated that on average the costs of meeting regulation were almost 4 percent of their total annual expenditure.[50] This is just too big a cost for companies that hope to be competitive in the face of tough international competition.

Needless Regulatory Complexity, Duplication, and Redundancy: The Government Taskforce on Reducing Regulatory Burdens on Business in its report *Rethinking Regulation* noted that different arms of government often request similar information, that they make demands that are either excessive or unnecessary, and that their demands are rarely co-ordinated and are often duplicative.[51] The upshot of this is that businesses incur needless compliance costs both in time and money and this is a drag on their competitiveness.[52] There are inconsistent laws and regulations around occupational health and safety, workers' compensation, environmental regulation, property transfers, taxes, company law, and consumer protection. It is estimated that, if each of these areas was consistent across Australia and, where appropriate, consistent with international obligations, significant costs would be saved and productivity improvements would result.[53] The Government has encouraged reform, announcing a commitment to continuous improvement in regulatory quality and has reaffirmed the commitment to best-practice regulation requirements.[54] There is an opportunity to remove some of the duplication as sunset requirements requiring the review of legislative instruments take effect, but there is a concern that the volume of legislation that is coming up for review under these requirements may overwhelm those responsible for doing the review and this may undermine the usefulness of the review in terms of dispensing with duplication and reducing the volume of regulation.[55]

Australia's Regulation in Perspective

Australia gets good marks overall from international sources that compare regulation across countries and from the business competitiveness survey carried out for this project. Glaring exceptions are a very low rank for Burden of Regulation from IMD, and a range of features associated with labour market regulation. In addition, while it appears that Australia is a very easy place to set up a business, the regulatory environment could be more difficult for growing existing businesses. We note that most of the Western benchmark countries in Chapter 2 perform better than Australia in the Ease of Doing Business Index and that four of the economies that do better than

Australia in the Index, Singapore, Hong Kong, New Zealand, and Korea, are in the Asia-Pacific region, and are, apart from New Zealand, far more tightly woven into the rapidly growing economies of East Asia. Thus, it is not clear that Australia has any advantage over some places that might be viewed as business alternatives by some entrepreneurs in the Asia-Pacific region.

Looking at the regulatory situation within Australia, it is clear that there is an understanding that Australia is heavily regulated and that this comes at a significant cost, but it is less clear that enough is being done in a timely manner to help alleviate the regulatory burden on businesses, and tardiness in this regard will undermine Australia's competitiveness to some extent. We do note that the Australian Government issued a final response to *Rethinking Regulation* in August 2006 in which it agreed to work to reduce the burden of regulation by streamlining a number of regulatory activities, by conducting a more thorough cost-benefit analysis when considering new regulations, by adopting a whole-of-Government policy on consultation on developing regulation, by providing clearer guidance to regulators on policy objectives, by reviewing areas with significant jurisdictional overlap, by developing a framework for national harmonisation of regulation, by assessing regulations that are not subject to sunset clauses every 5 years, and by having the Productivity Commission do a study of how to benchmark regulatory performance across jurisdictions.[56] A total of 158 of the Taskforce's 178 recommendations were accepted by the Government in part or in full, and although significant progress has been made in implementing the recommendations, there is room for more to be done, with the Business Council of Australia calling on COAG in April 2012 to use the recommendations made in *Rethinking Regulation* to inform its approach to regulation.[57]

In November 2008, as part of a new agenda for Commonwealth-State relationships directed toward building a seamless national economy, 27 priority areas of regulatory reform where overlapping and inconsistent regulatory regimes are impeding economic activity and 8 competition reforms were cited in a National Partnership Agreement. Support for reducing regulation in the form of an AUD 100 million facilitation payment, and a further AUD 450 million in reward payments are scheduled for the period to 2012–2013, with the reward payments being contingent on states' performance in making progress toward regulatory reform.[58]

Substantial progress has been made, but we do note that the chairman of the Productivity Commission has cautioned that in spite of achieving some good international rankings in recent and past years, Australia should not become complacent because as a moderate-scale economy far from many major markets it is in a different position to some of its competitors, and therefore the continued mission must be to rid the Australian economy of any unnecessary costs.[59]

Tax and Tax Policy

Taxation needs to be considered against a backdrop of global financial challenges, tougher markets, nations competing for investment and talent, the ability of companies and individuals to choose location, and greater accountability being demanded of governments. The amount of tax and how it is levied thus involve not just social choices; it involves competitiveness as well.

Taxation in Australia

According to Australia's Department of the Treasury at the time of the Henry Review, Australians paid at least 125 different taxes, with 99 being levied by the Australian Government, 25 by state governments, and 1 by local governments.[60] Since then a resource tax (MRRT) and a carbon tax have been introduced. All income tax, and a portion of other taxes are levied and collected by the Commonwealth Government. State governments levy taxes on property, employers' payroll, and on the use of goods and services. In New South Wales there are 24 major state taxes, while in Victoria there are 21, in Western Australia there are 16, and in Tasmania there are 21.[61] Local governments tax only property in the form of council rates. In 2010–2011, combined total taxation revenue for all levels of government was AUD 357,917 million, with taxes on income making up 57.3 percent, employers' payroll taxes 5.0 percent, taxes on property 9.3 percent, taxes on the provision of goods and services 25.7 percent, and taxes on use of goods and performance of activities 2.7 percent.[62] According to the Australian Bureau of Statistics (ABS), total taxation was 26 percent of GDP in 2010–2011, with Commonwealth tax revenue accounting for 21 percent of GDP, State Government revenues 4 percent, and Local Government revenues for 1 percent.[63]

In 2009–2010, individuals accounted for 67.7 percent of net tax paid to the Commonwealth Government, companies 28.3 percent, and superannuation funds 4.0 percent. For resident individuals, the first AUD 18,200 earned is not taxed, and the top marginal tax rate of 45 percent starts at an annual income of AUD 180,000. For non-resident individuals, all income is taxed starting at 32.5 percent of the first AUD 80,000 earned and topping out at 45 percent at an annual income of AUD 180,000. In addition, individual taxpayers must also pay an additional tax in the form of a Medicare levy of 1.5 percent of their taxable income. Most of the companies (77.3 percent) that paid tax in 2009–2010 fell into the "micro" category and had a total annual income of less than AUD 2 million. Only 0.2 percent of companies were "large" or "very large," having a total annual income exceeding AUD 100 million.[64]

Australia's total tax take is relatively light compared to most other OECD countries. According to the OECD, in 2010, Australia's total tax take as a percentage of GDP (25.6 percent) was only higher than Mexico, Chile, the United States, and South Korea among OECD countries.[65] We note, however, that the estimated tax burdens as a percentage of GDP for Taiwan (8.4 percent of GDP), the Philippines (12.8 percent), Singapore (13.4 percent), Hong Kong (13.9 percent), Thailand (14.9 percent), Malaysia (15.7 percent), China (17.5 percent), Vietnam (22.3 percent), and South Korea (25.6 percent) were lower than Australia (27.1 percent of GDP) according to the Heritage Foundation in 2012.[66] To the extent that tax competition is with the United States, or with other Asia-Pacific economies, Australia's position is not as strong as one might assume given its standing versus most of the rest of the OECD. As shown in Table 6.4, Australia's tax receipts per capita are comparable to Canada and Germany but much higher than the United States, New Zealand, and Japan.

When one looks at specific tax rates, Australia's capital gains tax rate is relatively high, but the corporate tax rate, the top rate of personal income tax, and the tax on dividends are comparable to several of the OECD nations in Table 6.4. It is worth noting that the threshold for Australia's top personal income tax rate is relatively low, at AUD 180,000 compared to countries such as Singapore, where the threshold

TABLE 6.4 **Taxation Statistics for Selected Countries**

Country Year	Corporate Tax Rate (%) 2010	Top Rate of Personal Income Tax (%)[2] 2011	Top Rate of Capital Gains Tax (%) 2011	Top Integrated Dividend Tax[3] (%) 2011	Taxes on Goods and Services (% of Revenue)[4] 2010	Tax Receipts Per Capita (AUD) 2010	Total Tax Receipts % of GDP[5] 2011
Australia	30.0	45.0	45.0	45.0	24.3	15,944	25.6 (2010)
Canada	31.0	46.4	50 percent of regular tax rate	48.0	15.0	15,863	31.0
Germany	29.4	47.5	25.0	48.6	24.7	15,714	37.1
Japan	40.87	50.0	Varies	45.6	34.4	7,408	27.6 (2010)
New Zealand	30.0	33.0	No Capital Gains Tax	33.0	27.1	11,255	31.7
United Kingdom	28.0	50.0	18.0 basic but 28.0 for higher and additional rate taxpayers	52.7	29.9	14,030	35.5
United States	40.0	41.9	0.0 or 15.0 depending on income	50.8	3.0	12,685	25.1

Notes:

1. Tax payments by businesses are the total number of taxes paid by businesses, including electronic filing.

2. For countries that tax income at different levels, only the top level of tax that is paid by resident taxpayers is presented. With the exception of Canada, where the figure quoted includes Ontario's provincial rate, amounts reported do not include state/provincial rates. The top rates listed also exclude additional levies, for example in Australia, taxpayers are required to pay a Medicare Levy of 1.5 percent on taxable income, hence taking the top rate of personal income tax from 45.0 percent to 46.5 percent.

3. Weighted average. It includes both central government and subnational tax rates.

4. Taxes on goods and services (percent of revenue) include general sales and turnover or value added taxes, selective excises on goods, selective taxes on services, taxes on the use of goods or property, taxes on the extraction and production of minerals, and profits of fiscal monopolies.

5. Unweighted average.

6. German corporate tax rate—the overall rate includes federal corporate income tax at a rate of 15 percent, solidarity surcharge at a rate of 5.5 percent of the corporate income tax and local trade tax. The local trade tax generally varies between 7 percent and 17.15 percent, assuming a municipality multiplier (Hebesatz) ranging normally from 200 percent to 490 percent (the average multiplier for 2010 was 390 percent).

7. Japanese corporate tax rate—according to the Japan External Trade Organization, the Japanese corporate tax rate for companies with over 8 million yen in taxable income is made up of a corporate rate of 30 percent, prefectural tax of 1.5 percent, municipal tax of 3.69 percent, enterprise tax of 5.3 percent, and special local corporate tax of 4.3 percent, giving an effective rate of 40.87 percent (prefectural and municipal tax is based on Tokyo).

8. US corporate tax rate is approximately 40 percent; however, it may vary significantly depending on the locality in which a corporation conducts business. The highest federal corporate tax rate is 35 percent. State and local governments also impose corporate taxes ranging from less than 1 percent to 12 percent. A corporation may deduct its state and local income tax expense when computing its federal taxable income, generally resulting in a net effective rate of approximately 40 percent.

Sources: World Bank, *World Development Indicators,* 2012; KPMG, *Individual Income Tax and Social Security Rate Survey 2011;* KPMG, *KPMG's Corporate and Indirect Tax Survey 2010;* OANDA; OECD, *Revenue Statistics—OECD Member Countries,* 2012; Ernst & Young, *Corporate Dividend and Capital Gains Taxation: A Comparison of the United States to Other Developed Nations,* 2012.

income for the top tax rate to apply is AUD 254,865, and the top tax rate is much lower at 20 percent. Hong Kong also has a much lower top marginal tax rate on personal income tax (15 percent), though the threshold at which taxpayers start paying the top rate is much lower at AUD 15,415.[67]

Australia's total business tax take as a percentage of commercial profits (47.7 percent) is second-highest among the Western OECD economies in Table 6.5, with only Sweden (52.8 percent) having a higher percentage. Against Asia-Pacific economies, Australia is ahead of China (63.5 percent), India (61.8 percent), and Japan (49.1 percent) on this measure, but well behind most other economies, including Hong Kong (23.0 percent) and Singapore (27.1 percent). Australia rates well against most of the economies in the table when it comes to the time it takes to prepare and pay major taxes, though it is behind Switzerland, Norway, Finland, Hong Kong, and Singapore on this measure.

Australia does not offer many tax incentives. The most significant from an investment standpoint is the research and development tax incentive, which the Government introduced in July 2011 and which provides for a refundable tax offset of 45 percent (equivalent to a deduction of up to 150 percent) for small companies, and a refundable tax offset of 40 percent (equivalent to a deduction of up to 133 percent) for larger companies. The R&D tax incentive has been criticised as being open to distortion and gaming by companies, but Australia's Industry Minister has described it as the biggest reform to business support in more than a decade.[68]

International Assessments

While Australia's tax system appears similar to several comparators, the picture in more comprehensive international rankings is not as good. The World Economic Forum ranked Australia 88th out of 142 countries for the Extent and Effect of Taxation and 99th for Total Tax Rate. In the 2011, IMD *World Competitiveness Yearbook*, Australia ranked 43rd out of 59 countries for Corporate Tax Rate on Profit, 21st for Real Personal Taxes, and 24th for Real Corporate Taxes. The World Bank rated Australia 53rd out of 183 economies in the 2012 Ease of Doing Business Index in terms of Paying Taxes. The Fraser Institute's 2009 Economic Freedom of the World Index had Australia 78th out of 141 countries for Top Marginal Tax Rate, 13th for Taxes on International Trade, and 13th for Cost of Tax Compliance.[69] These rankings indicate that the tax system is potentially a significant disadvantage for Australia's economy when it comes to competitiveness.

Again we must combine the international assessments with those of the business competitiveness survey carried out for this project in Australia. Here we found various tax-related drivers, including the overall tax regime, corporate tax rates, personal income tax rates, other taxes and charges, and payroll taxes as among the worst-performing drivers in the Australian context. In most cases, however, the respondents indicated that Australia's performance on these dimensions was more or less comparable to major competitors. The mining sector, several manufacturing industries, and several service industries (wholesale, transport, professional, and arts and culture) gave Australia its worst ratings on these dimensions.

TABLE 6.5   Business Tax Indicators, Selected Economies

Country	Total Business Tax as % of Commercial Profits, 2011[1]	Tax Time Burden / Time Spent Doing Taxes in 2011 (hours)[2]
Australia	47.7	109
Canada	28.8	131
Denmark	27.5	135
Finland	39.0	93
Ireland	26.3	132
Israel	31.2	235
Netherlands	40.5	127
New Zealand	34.4	172
Norway	41.6	87
Sweden	52.8	122
Switzerland	30.1	63
United States	46.7	187
China	63.5	398
Hong Kong	23.0	80
India	61.8	254
Indonesia	34.5	266
Japan	49.1	330
Korea	29.7	225
Malaysia	34.0	133
New Zealand	34.4	172
Philippines	46.5	195
Singapore	27.1	84
Taiwan	N/A	N/A
Thailand	37.5	264
Vietnam	40.1	941

Notes:
1. Total business tax measures the amount of taxes and mandatory contributions payable by businesses after accounting for allowable deductions and exemptions as a share of commercial profits. Taxes withheld (such as personal income tax) or collected and remitted to tax authorities (such as value added taxes, sales taxes, or goods and service taxes) are excluded.
2. Time to prepare and pay taxes is the time in hours per year it takes to prepare, file, and pay (or withhold) three major types of business taxes: the corporate income tax, the value added or sales tax, and labour taxes, including payroll taxes and social security contributions.
Sources: The World Bank, "Total tax rate (% of commercial profits)," *World Development Indicators*, 2011; The World Bank, "Time to Prepare and Pay Taxes (Hours)," *World Development Indicators*, 2011; OECD, *Taxing Wages 2011*.

Tax Issues in Australia

A great deal of work has been done on Australia's taxation system over the last 30 years. The most significant in recent history has been the Australia's Future Tax System Review, otherwise known as "The Henry Review." There is a widely expressed view that Australia's taxation system is burdensome and less efficient than it should be, that it detracts from Australia's competitiveness, and that changes to the tax system could result in an increase in workforce participation, improvements in savings levels, greater investment by businesses, and better prospects for innovation and high value-added industries.[70] In looking at the need for tax reform and at the implications for local government in particular, it has been claimed that the "current tax arrangements are unstable and cannot survive in their current form much longer."[71]

Overall Tax Burden Too Great: Numerous business leaders have expressed concerns that Australia's overall tax burden is too high and that the mix of taxes is wrong. The former chairman of Australia's Future Fund, for example, claimed that the tax burden should be shifted from individual and corporate income taxes to taxing consumption.[72] The Australian Industry Group has suggested that workforce participation incentives should be created by lowering effective rates of individual income tax and that the company tax rate be reduced to 25 percent as soon as possible.[73] The Business Council of Australia observes that even at 25 percent, the company tax rate barely puts Australia at the average of its trading partners and it claims that this is a minimum requirement for staying competitive.[74]

Different Levels of Tax and Inefficiency: CPA Australia notes that taxes are levied by three levels of government, many of the taxes are inefficient, and the taxation system in its present form means that states do not have sufficient taxing powers to meet their expenditure responsibilities.[75] The authority to tax rests largely at the Commonwealth level, but many expenditure responsibilities are those of the states, leaving the states dependent on the Commonwealth for the funds to deliver core services. This limits the ability of the states to reform taxes that the Henry Review, and others, found to be inefficient.[76]

Costly and Complex Compliance: The Australian Chamber of Commerce and Industry claims that Australia's taxation system is too complicated and that compliance costs are too high and should be reduced. It also suggests that there are too many levels of personal income tax, that the number of tax thresholds should be reduced to two instead of the present four, and that the top marginal personal tax rate should be reduced to the same level as the corporate tax rate.[77] The Henry Review recommends a move to a more efficient tax base with four taxes as the foundation—personal income, business income, private consumption, and economic rent—noting that simplification is key to achieving a more competitive taxation system.[78] Respondents to CPA Australia surveys have consistently reported tax compliance costs to be too high, in one case finding that a majority of small business respondents wondered whether the cost of compliance outweighed the benefits of staying in business,[79] and in another that the costs of compliance for businesses are substantial but hard to quantify, with key stakeholders not knowing how much compliance was costing their business.[80]

Carbon Tax: The Australian Government asserts that it wants to take a leadership role in setting a carbon tax as one step to improving the environment and to address global climate change issues.[81] Many business leaders and business groups are opposed to the tax, or to the form in which the tax has been implemented. There are claims that a carbon tax will be excessively burdensome to business[82] and that it was making Australia unviable for many international investors before it was even levied.[83] As long as Australia imposes a carbon tax and competing countries do not, the tax will be a potential disadvantage for Australian industries and companies trying to compete internationally. Respondents to the business competitiveness survey singled out the carbon tax as particularly disadvantageous to Australian businesses.

Resources Tax: In early 2010, the Government first proposed the introduction of a Resources Super Profits Tax (RSPT) as part of its response to the Henry Review. This led to massive lobbying efforts on the part of the resources sector and was cited as a factor in the removal of Prime Minister Kevin Rudd by his own political party in June 2010. The name of the tax was changed to the Minerals Resource Rent Tax (MRRT), and the existing Petroleum Resource Rent Tax (PRRT) was extended, with the tax changes to take effect from 1 July 2012. The change in name does not change the fact that the MRRT is a new tax that applies to the resources sector and that it has become a highly politicised issue. Proponents claim that the resources belong to the country and that windfall profits should be shared with the public. Mining companies, such as BHP Billiton,[84] and business groups including the Business Council of Australia,[85] claim that the tax will reduce Australia's desirability as an investment location.

Payroll Tax: Australia's payroll tax has been labelled narrow and inefficient. The point often is made that the payroll tax creates a drag on employment and is not aligned with maximising productivity and business growth.[86] Calls have been made to remove the payroll tax altogether with a compromise position being the harmonisation of payroll taxes across Australia's states.[87] The Australian Chamber of Commerce and Industry wants the Federal Government to pressure the states to reduce payroll taxes and eventually to abolish them.[88] CPA Australia agrees that the payroll tax should be abolished.[89] The Henry Review suggested that a broad-based consumption tax, such as a cash flow tax, would provide additional revenue, providing scope to remove current payroll taxes.

Shift to a Consumption Tax: The Henry Review found that a private consumption tax should be an important part of Australia's taxation system.[90] One challenge for the Henry Review was that its terms of reference ruled out any changes to the Goods and Services Tax, so the issue was not considered. CPA Australia has noted that Australia's reliance on consumption taxes is at the lower end of all OECD nations.[91] Consistent with its message that fewer and simpler taxes are better, CPA Australia argues that the Goods and Services Tax should either be raised or broadened, and points to scenario modelling commissioned by CPA Australia that suggests that a rate of 15 percent represents the best option of the four scenarios modelled.[92] The Grattan Institute[93] recommends that the Goods and Services Tax be broadened to cover all consumption including education, health, and fresh food. It suggests that personal income taxes and corporate taxes be reduced to offset changes to the Goods and Services Tax, resulting in no net revenue impact to the Commonwealth budget. It claims that rebalancing the tax base in favour of a consumption tax will lead to greater workforce incentives and participation, higher productivity, greater savings, administrative efficiencies, and other improvements that could increase Australia's GDP over time by AUD 25 billion a year.

Taxation in Australia in Perspective

Australia is not taxed excessively when compared to most other OECD nations. However, compared to those nations the burden appears to fall disproportionately on business and high-income individuals, and the tax burden is substantially higher than in several other Asia-Pacific economies. It is this burden, combined with the complexity of the system and the large number of individual taxes that lead to Australia's poor rankings in some of the international comparisons when it comes to taxation. The competitiveness survey carried out for this project reinforces the notion that Australia's taxes are too burdensome on the whole and supports the view that specific items, such as employment taxes, are a drag on Australia's competitiveness.

There have been several calls to significantly reduce the number of taxes, rebalance the system, improve the tax relationship across levels of government, and simplify tax administration. Leading business groups and business figures in Australia argue that personal income tax rates are too high and that corporate tax rates are uncompetitive, particularly when compared against key competitors and potential investment partners. With respect to business centres in the Asia-Pacific region, Hong Kong and Singapore have fewer taxes, lower corporate and individual tax rates, low or no taxes on capital gains and dividends, and much simpler tax systems overall. Given their positions in the Asia-Pacific region, they provide attractive locations for Australian professionals and companies. Other places, like the United States, have larger markets, more opportunities, and lower taxes. This raises the question as to how Australia's competitiveness will fare with skills shortages, large distances to many markets, and the increasing importance of entrepreneurship and mobile professionals to modern competition.

The Henry Review, the most comprehensive review of Australia's tax system in recent memory, made 138 recommendations. In making its recommendations, the Henry Review argued for all taxes (nearly 125 of them) other than those related to personal income, business income, private consumption, and economic rents to be abolished over time. At the time of release in May 2010, the Government adopted, or indicated that it would adopt, just four of the recommendations, it removed no taxes, and it put in place the new resource tax. The response of the Government disappointed many and surprised others.[94] The Business Council of Australia acknowledged the Henry Review as laying out a "comprehensive blueprint to redesign Australia's tax system" and criticised the Government for its narrow response and for its failure to deliver the tax reform that was promised.[95] The strong response led the Government to announce that it would consider some of the other recommendations as part of a "mature tax debate" in the fullness of time.[96] However, it is not clear when this debate will commence and when it will result in an improved tax system.

Policy Areas in Perspective

There are several common themes that emerge across Australia's economic policy, regulatory environment, and tax system. One theme is that the overall philosophy of Australia's Government in recent years has for the most part been reasonable and appropriate. There is a tendency towards prudence, towards not trying to shape markets to too great an extent, and to fostering an economy in which the framework conditions are positive and consistent with the nation's overall objectives. There is a tendency to be willing to make difficult decisions to ensure flexibility and to use the flexibility afforded by this approach when necessary.

However, there is another theme of duplication, inefficiency, and high compliance costs that cuts across these areas as well. These are due in part to a history in which the costs of compliance with policies, rules, regulations, and taxes were not a primary focus, and were therefore not often addressed. They are also due in part to unresolved tensions between different levels of government that sometimes have overlapping jurisdiction and sometimes appear to have opposite interests.

Another theme is that there has been a great deal of analysis of Australia's challenges in the areas of economic policy, regulation, and taxation. The Reserve Bank, Treasury, and other government and private organisations do ongoing analyses of a range of economic policy areas. The Productivity Commission and others have done extensive reviews of the regulatory system and made recommendations to improve it. The Henry Review of the tax system, and responses to the Review, has made a substantial contribution to understanding issues surrounding Australia's tax system. In many areas, particularly regulatory and tax reform, it appears that what needs to be done is known, it is just a matter of getting on with it.

Notes

1. Ernst J. Weber, *Australian Fiscal Policy in the Aftermath of the Global Financial Crisis*, University of Western Australia Discussion Paper, quoting the *2012–2013 Budget Overview* and Historical Australian Government Data.
2. Wayne Swan (Speech to Australian Chamber of Commerce in Hong Kong & Macau, 11 July 2012).
3. OECD, *Economic Surveys: Australia*, November 2010.
4. Gary Banks, "Successful Reform: Past Lessons, Future Challenges" (Keynote address to the Annual Forecasting Conference of The Australian Business Economists, Sydney, 8 December 2010).
5. Emma Griffiths, "Holden Gets $275m to Stay in Australia," *ABC News*, 22 March 2012.
6. Australian Government, *National Competition Policy*: ncp.ncc.gov.au.
7. Australian Minister for Trade and Competitiveness, *Gillard Government reforms Australia's trade policy*, 12 April 2011.
8. The Hon. Dr Craig Emerson, Australian Minister for Trade and Competitiveness, "Boosting Australia's Trade and Competitiveness" (Keynote address to CEDA, 6 March 2012).
9. Treasurer of the Commonwealth of Australia, *Australia's Foreign Investment Policy*, January 2012.
10. Treasurer of the Commonwealth of Australia, *Australia's Foreign Investment Policy*, January 2012.
11. These include a proposed bid by the Singapore Exchange for Australia's ASX Ltd, the blocking of state-linked China Minmetals' bid for Oz Minerals, and the blocking of China Non-Ferrous Metal Mining Co. from buying a controlling stake in Lynas Corp, a rare earths company.
12. Peter Reith, "Australia needs an integrated and coherent economic plan," *The Drum*, 20 September 2011.
13. Peter Hartcher, "European Chief Praises Australia's Fiscal Policy," *Sydney Morning Herald*, 7 September 2011.

14. Robert Carling and Stephen Kirchner, "End the Budget Sideshow," *The Australian*, 15 July 2009.

15. Kevin Davis, "Don't Forget the Debt: There's More to Fiscal Prudence than a Return to Surplus," *The Conversation*, 2 May 2012.

16. Eric Ellis, "Finance Minister of the Year 2011: Swan Confounds his Domestic Skeptics," *Euromoney*, September 2011.

17. Philip Lowe, "The Changing Structure of the Australian Economy and Monetary Policy" (Address to the Australian Industry Group 12th Annual Economic Forum, Sydney, 7 March 2012).

18. Laura Tingle, "Dollar Dictates Focus on Monetary Policy," *Australian Financial Review*, 13 April 2012.

19. Paul Brennan and Josh Williamson, "RBA Strikes a Delicate Balance," *Australian Financial Review*, 1 May 2012.

20. Australian Productivity Commission, "Review of National Competition Policy Reforms," *Productivity Commission Inquiry Report*, No. 33, 28 February 2005.

21. Liberal Party of Australia, *Concerns about Trade Policy*, 12 April 2011.

22. Neville R. Norman, "Australia's Trade Liberalization Prospects in Hostile Conditions," *East Asia Forum*, 26 May 2011.

23. World Trade Organization, "Trade Policy Review," Report by the Secretariat, Australia, 1 March 2011.

24. Business Council of Australia, *Foreign Attraction: Building on Our Advantages through Foreign Investment*, April 2010.

25. Shahar Hameiri and Toby Carroll, "Resource Sector Chipping Away at Australian Prosperity," *The Drum*, ABC News, 7 March 2012.

26. Productivity Commission, *Trade and Assistance Review 2010–11*, 2012.

27. John Daley, Cassie McGannonn, and Leah Ginnivan, *Game-Changers: Economic Reform Priorities for Australia*, Grattan Institute, Melbourne, 2012.

28. Michael J. Enright, "Regional Clusters: What we know and what we should know," in *Innovation Clusters and Interregional Competition*, ed. Johannes Bröcker, Dirk Dohse, and Rüdiger Soltwedel, 99–129 (Berlin: Springer, 2003).

29. Economist Intelligence Unit, *Fostering Innovation-Led Clusters: A Review of Leading Global Practices, 2011*. Ivory Tower, *Cluster Initiative Greenbook*, 2004.

30. Michael J. Enright and Brian H. Roberts, "Industry Clusters in Australia: Recent Trends and Prospects," *European Planning Studies* 12 no. 1 (2004): 99–121.

31. "Australia Blocked China Investment on Supply Concerns," *Sydney Morning Herald*, 15 February 2011.

32. Alan Kohler, "Investment Board Keeps Foreign Raiders at Bay," *Inside Business*, ABC News, 14 November 2010.

33. Mark Thirwell, "Five Points on Foreign Investment (part 55)," *The Interpreter*, Lowy Institute for International Policy, 12 May 2009..

34. Blanka Kalinova, Angel Palerm, and Stephen Thomsen, "OECD's FDI Restrictiveness Index: 2010 Update," OECD Working Papers on International Investment, No. 2010/3, OECD Investment Division.

35. UNCTAD, *Inward and Outward Foreign Direct Investment Flows, Annual, 1970–2010*, July 2011; UNCTAD, *GDP by Type of Expenditure and Value Added by Kind of Economic Activity, Annual, 1970–2010*, February 2012.

36. Business Council of Australia, *Foreign Attraction: Building on Our Advantages through Foreign Investment*, April 2010.

37. Standards Australia, *Annual Report*, 2011.

38. Institute of Public Affairs, *Policy without Parliament—The Growth of Regulation in Australia*, November 2007.

39. Australian Productivity Commission, *Business Regulation Benchmarking—Role of Local Government*, September 2011.

40. *Regulation and Its Review* (Productivity Commission 2005) reported that the administration expenses of 15 dedicated Australian Government regulatory agencies approached AUD 2 billion in 2003–2004 (equivalent to AUD 2.5 billion in current dollars), with the Australian Tax Office accounting for a further AUD 2.3 billion in the same year (AUD 2.8 billion in current dollars), quoted from *Regulatory Impact Analysis: Benchmarking*, Productivity Commission Issues Paper, March 2012.

41. Michael Ronaldson, *Fighting Australia's Over-Regulation*, Australian Government, Regulation Taskforce, 2005.

42. An early study by Productivity Commission researchers (R. Lattimore, B. Martin, A. Madge, and J. Mills, *Design Principles for Small Business Programs and Regulations*, Productivity Commission Staff Research Paper, 1998) estimated the administrative compliance costs on business from regulation at around AUD 11 billion in 1994–1995 (AUD 16.9 billion in current dollars), of which around 85 percent was borne by small and medium-sized enterprises, quoted from *Regulatory Impact Analysis: Benchmarking*, Productivity Commission Issues Paper, March 2012.

43. This includes most recently the publication *Identifying and Evaluating Regulation Reforms*, December 2011, with most of the suggested reforms yet to be adopted or decided upon by the Government.

44. International Finance Corporation, *Ease of Doing Business Index*, 2011.

45. The Heritage Foundation and the Wall Street Journal, *2011 Index of Economic Freedom*, 2012.

46. The gap in years is due to the time lag in the availability of some data.

47. James Gwartney, Robert Lawson, and Joshua Hall, *Economic Freedom of the World: 2011 Annual Report*, Fraser Institute, 2011.

48. Australian Productivity Commission, *Identifying and Evaluating Regulation Reforms*, Productivity Commission Research Report, December 2011.

49. *Rethinking Regulation*, Report of the Taskforce on Reducing Regulatory Burdens on Business, January 2006; see also Australian Productivity Commission, *Regulatory Impact Analysis: Benchmarking*, Productivity Commission Issues Paper, March 2012.

50. Australian Industry Group, *National CEO Survey: Business Regulation*, September 2011, quoted from *Regulatory Impact Analysis: Benchmarking*, Productivity Commission Issues Paper, March 2012.

51. *Rethinking Regulation*, Report of the Taskforce on Reducing Regulatory Burdens on Business, January 2006.

52. *Rethinking Regulation*, Report of the Taskforce on Reducing Regulatory Burdens on Business, January 2006.

53. *Rethinking Regulation*, Report of the Taskforce on Reducing Regulatory Burdens on Business, January 2006.

54. OECD, *Australia: Moving to a Seamless National Economy*, February 2010.

55. Australian Productivity Commission, *Identifying and Evaluating Regulation Reforms*, Canberra, 2011.

56. Australian Government, *Rethinking Regulation: Report of the Taskforce on Reducing Regulatory Burdens on Business, Australian Government's Response*, 15 August 2006.

57. Business Council of Australia, *Discussion Paper for the COAG Business Advisory Forum*, 10 April 2012.

58. OECD, *Australia: Moving to a Seamless National Economy*, February 2010.

59. Gary Banks, "Reducing the Regulatory Burden: The Way Forward" (Public lecture, Monash Centre for Regulatory Studies, University Law Chambers, Melbourne, 17 May 2006).

60. Australian Treasury, *Architecture of Australia's Tax and Transfer System, Many Australian Taxes*. 2008 estimate with the Department noting that for various definitional differences and other reasons the exact number of taxes is difficult to determine and may be higher than these estimates.

61. ESA Analysis; The Treasury, NSW Government, *Interstate Comparison of Taxes 2010–11*, Office of Financial Management Research and Information Paper, December 2010.

62. Australian Bureau of Statistics, *Taxation Revenue, Australia, 2010–11—Taxation for All Levels of Government*, 16 April 2012.

63. Australian Bureau of Statistics, *Taxation Revenue, Australia, 2010–11—Taxation for All Levels of Government*, 16 April 2012.

64. Australian Taxation Office, *Taxation Statistics 2009–2010*, Canberra, April 2012.

65. OECD, *Tax Database*, October 2012.

66. Heritage Foundation and the Wall Street Journal, *2012 Index of Economic Freedom*, Washington D.C., 2012.

67. KPMG International, *KPMG's Individual Income Tax and Social Security Rate Survey 2011*, September 2011.

68. Michael Owen, "Companies 'Rorting' R&D Tax Credits," *The Australian*, 27 March 2012.

69. The gap in years is due to the time lag in the availability of some data.

70. Australian Industry Group, *Tax Reform Priorities, A position Statement for the Tax Forum*, October 2011.

71. John Passant and John McLaren, "The Henry Review of Australia's Future Tax System: Implications for Local Government," Australian Centre of Excellence for Local Government, Working Paper No. 3, June 2011, p.6.

72. Eli Greenblat, "Investors 'say no to Australia'," *Sydney Morning Herald*, 25 May 2012.

73. Australian Industry Group, *Tax Reform Priorities, A Position Statement for the Tax Forum*, October 2011.

74. Business Council of Australia (Speech to the Australian Government 2011 Tax Forum, 4 October 2011).

75. CPA Australia, *Tax Reform—Next Steps for Australia*, 9 September 2011.

76. Australian Chamber of Commerce and Industry, *Australia's Future Tax System, ACCI Submission to the Department of Treasury*, October 2008; Commonwealth of Australia, *Australia's Future Tax System Consultation Paper*, December 2008; Adam Creighton, *The Henry Tax Review: A Liberal Critique, Issue Analysis*, No. 130, March 2012.

77. Australian Chamber of Commerce and Industry, *Australia's Future Tax System*, ACCI Submission to the Department of Treasury, October 2008.

78. Commonwealth of Australia, *Australia's Future Tax System Consultation Paper*, December 2008.

79. CPA Australia, *Compliance Burden, CPA Australia Small Business Survey*, May 2003.

80. CPA Australia, "Record Keeping: Its Effect on Tax Compliance," *Small Business Survey Program*, May 2005.

81. Tim Leslie, "Gillard Unveils Carbon Price Details," *ABC News*, 24 February 2011.

82. Australian Chamber of Commerce and Industry, *Australia's Future Tax System, ACCI Submission to the Department of Treasury*, October 2008.

83. Eli Greenblat, "Investors 'Say No to Australia'," *Sydney Morning Herald*, 25 May 2012.

84. Elizabeth Knight and Philip Coorey, "BHP Boss Threatens to Invest Offshore," *Sydney Morning Herald*, 17 May 2012. The chairman of the board of BHP Billiton stated, "I cannot overestimate how the level of uncertainty about Australia's tax system is generating negative investor reaction."

85. Robert Milliner, "Henry Taxation Review and the Resource Super Profits Tax," media release, Business Council of Australia, 2 June 2010. At the time the RSPT was first raised, the Business Council of Australia strongly objected claiming that its adoption would lead to increased sovereign risk associated with investing in Australia.

86. PricewaterhouseCoopers, *Tax Talk, Tax Reform*, Issue 7, May 2010.

87. Australian Industry Group, *Tax Reform Priorities, A Position Statement for the Tax Forum*, October 2011.

88. Australian Chamber of Commerce and Industry, *Australia's Future Tax System, ACCI Submission to the Department of Treasury*, October 2008.

89. CPA Australia, *Tax Reform—Next steps for Australia*, 9 September 2011.

90. Adam Creighton, "The Henry Tax Review: A Liberal Critique," *Issue Analysis*, No. 130, March 2012.

91. CPA Australia, *Australia's Future Tax System Review—Issues Paper*, 2008.

92. Garry Addison, "Tax Reform is Vital for Growth," *In the Black*, 1 February 2012.

93. John Daley, Cassie McGannon, and Leah Ginnivan, *Game-Changers: Economic reform priorities for Australia*, Grattan Institute, Melbourne, 2012.

94. Adam Creighton, "The Henry Tax Review: A Liberal Critique," *Issue Analysis*, No.130, March 2012.

95. Business Council of Australia, "Henry Taxation Review and the Resource Super Profits Tax," media release, 2 June 2010.

96. John Passant and John McLaren, "The Henry Review of Australia's Future Tax System: Implications for Local Government," Australian Centre of Excellence for Local Government, Working Paper No. 3, June 2011. Comments by the Federal Treasurer Wayne Swan cited in the paper.

CHAPTER 7

The Knowledge Economy, the Asia-Pacific Region, and the Role of Cities

The rise of the knowledge economy and the Asia-Pacific region provides distinctive opportunities and challenges for Australia. The knowledge economy involves generating value through the intellectual property that is embedded in high-value goods and services. The resulting products and services tend to have high value per weight or volume, or in some cases like software and digital media, potentially no weight or volume at all. The advent of this particular form of the knowledge economy, sometimes called the *weightless economy*, has the potential of freeing Australian companies from the tyranny of distance. Leveraging the knowledge economy in this way requires the ability to generate new knowledge, or to bundle existing knowledge into new combinations, in ways that create value for customers. It also requires sufficient connectivity to assimilate valuable information from abroad, and to deliver products or services at a distance.

At the same time, the rise of Asia-Pacific economies also provides distinct opportunities for Australia. Historically, Australia has been far from the world's leading markets. With greater openness in the region, and with the world's economic weight shifting towards Asia, Australia's traditional disadvantages may be diminishing. As many of the Asia-Pacific economies are less developed than Australia's, one might expect that Australia should be able to sell not just resources, but high value products and services as well, into the rapidly growing markets. In order to do so, Australia and Australian businesses must be able to understand the markets and outcompete companies from Asia and other regions to serve those markets.

The role of cities is increasingly important in generating commercially valuable knowledge and leveraging such knowledge into international markets. Cities bring together complementary skills and capabilities; they are sources of information; and they are places where ideas come together in new ways. Cities are also the nodes that connect countries to the rest of the world and are the points through which goods, information, people, and finance flow within and between countries. Thus, Australia's cities will be crucial to the country's efforts to generate and leverage knowledge and to inject itself into trade and investment flows within the Asia-Pacific region and beyond.

Australia and the Knowledge-Innovation Economy

In a world economy in which routine tasks can be performed in an increasing number of developing economies at a fraction of the cost they would require in more advanced economies, the latter increasingly have to rely on knowledge and innovation in order to enhance their prosperity and improve their incomes. No nation or region today can hope to become truly prosperous unless it develops a knowledge-innovation economy. This fact has enormous implications and poses enormous challenges for Australia.

The knowledge-innovation economy is ill-defined and little understood. Many analysts equate the term with participation in a limited number of high-technology industries, or to specific activities like R&D, but the knowledge-innovation economy also involves innovation in business systems, business processes, standards, training, and market development, and also encompasses knowledge-intensive professional services, creative industries, and the managerial activities of large companies. Knowledge and innovation can be competitive weapons in any industry, and while R&D activities may be knowledge-intensive, they are not the only knowledge-intensive activities that firms perform, nor necessarily the most important.

A knowledge-innovation economy is enabled by a highly developed education system; a talented workforce with qualified managers and professionals; the presence of high-quality research institutes, universities, and think tanks; high levels of information and communication technology (ICT); and by opportunities to commercialise innovations and leverage knowledge capabilities. It is also enabled by technology adoption, cultural diversity, and by networking and collaboration among knowledge workers and across industries. Finally, a knowledge-innovation economy cannot succeed unless it is sufficiently linked with source of information, with markets, and with sources of supply inside and outside the country. Thus, connectivity, particularly through ICT systems, is crucial to the success of the knowledge-innovation economy.

The Knowledge-Innovation Economy in Australia

Given the wide range of the knowledge-innovation economy, there are several ways of measuring a nation's position in this economy. These include employment in professional and managerial activities, exports of knowledge-intensive services, exports in high-tech manufacturing, R&D expenditures, patents and other measures of innovative output, and ICT utilisation.

The number of managers and professionals in Australia's workforce increased from 2,412,868 in 2001 to 3,152,895 in 2011, a rise of 30.7 percent.[1] Knowledge-intensive occupations accounted for 29.2 percent of Australia's workforce in 2008,[2] and 33.5 percent was in knowledge-intensive industries in 2010.[3] Typically, workers in knowledge-intensive roles in Australia are paid an estimated 40 percent more on average than those not working in knowledge-intensive roles.[4]

Another way of looking at the knowledge economy is to examine the knowledge-intensity of a nation's exports. According to the Australian Bureau of Statistics, Australia's exports of knowledge-intensive services accounted for 25.2 percent[5] of total service exports in 2011, a slight increase from 24.0 percent[6] in 2000. In 2010, 11.9 percent of Australia's manufactured exports were in high-tech industries. R&D expenditures equalled 2.24 percent of GDP in 2008, up from 1.43 percent in 1998.[7] Public R&D spending in 2008 was 34 percent of total R&D versus 62 percent private spending. The number of patents registered by Australian entities during the period 2001 to 2010 was 10,899.[8]

In Table 7.1, we compare Australia to a set of comparison countries in a range of variables related to the knowledge economy. We see that Australia was above most of the comparison countries in the percentage of employment in professional and managerial occupations, was substantially lower than most in knowledge-intensive service exports as a percent of service exports (in part due to a large tourism sector), was relatively low in high-tech exports as a percent of manufactured exports, was middling in terms of R&D spending as a percent of GDP, was somewhat higher than most in government's share of R&D spending, and was on par with the other countries in the sample with respect to ICT indicators. From the table, we can see that Australia is a bit behind several of the countries in the sample on most measures.

International Assessments

Several international sources on competitiveness rank countries on knowledge and innovation capabilities and environments. The World Bank ranked Australia 8th globally in its weighted Knowledge Index in 2009 out of 146 economies (see Table 7.2). Australia ranked highly in Education, but less well in terms of ICT Environment and Innovation. Australia was in the upper echelon of countries in terms of Internet users and computer penetration, and ranked highly in Science and Engineering Articles, but less well in Telephone Connections, Payments and Receipts (usually technology or IP licensing), and Patents Granted.

In the World Economic Forum's competiveness rankings, Australia ranked 22nd in terms of Innovation Capacity. Australia ranked first in Secondary School Enrolment, and in the upper echelon of nations in Quality of Science and Research Institutions, University-Industry Collaboration in R&D, Higher Education and Training, Tertiary Enrolment, and Availability of Research Training Services. On the other hand, Australia ranked further down in Capacity for Innovation, Technological Readiness, Business Sophistication, and Company Spending on R&D. It also ranked far down the list in technological infrastructure measures as well as availability of scientists and engineers. These views are echoed by the assessments of the International Institute for Management Development (IMD), which gave Australia high marks for education, moderate marks for features having to do with technology, but lower marks for most features related to the workforce and technological infrastructure.

To these assessments, we should add those from the business competitiveness survey reported in Chapter 4. Respondents to that survey indicated that Australia had modest advantages versus competitors and comparators in most sectors when it came to Level of Technology Employed, Firm Capabilities, Scientific and Technical Skills, and IT Infrastructure. There were also slight advantages in Access to Business-Relevant Information and Venture Capital. The picture from the survey mirrored that of international sources in indicating that Australia has a reasonably good position in the knowledge economy, but not a world-beating one by any stretch of the imagination.

Knowledge-Innovation Issues in Australia

Australians understand that knowledge and innovation are crucial for development in all industries. In 2006, the Business Council of Australia in collaboration with the

TABLE 7.1   Indicators or Knowledge and Innovation, Selected Countries

Country	Percent of Total Employment in Professional and Managerial Occupations, 2008[1]	Exports of Knowledge-Intensive Services (% of Total Service Exports), 2010[2]	High-Tech Exports (% of Total Manufactured Exports), 2010	R&D (% of GDP), 2010[3]	R&D Spend, Public Vs. Private (% Public/% Private), 2010[4]	No. of Patent Registrations 2001–2010[5]	Total Communication Access Paths per 100 Inhabitants, 2009[6]	% of Households with Access to the Internet, 2010	Business Use of Broadband, 2010 (% of Businesses with 10 Or More Employees)	Share of ICT-Intensive Occupations in the Total Economy, 2010, %
Australia	29.2	25.2[7]	11.9	2.24[8]	34/62[8]	10,899	173.5	78.9	96.6[9]	22.1[9]
Canada	26.9	53.3	14.0	1.80	34/48[8]	35,521	155.6	77.8[9]	94.3[10]	21.2
Denmark	22.0	26.4	14.2	3.06	28/60	4,419	201.9	86.1	86.6[9]	27.3
Finland	27.8	72.5	10.8	3.87	26/66	8,675	197.7	80.5	93.9	25.5
France	21.9	35.2	24.9	2.26	40/51	35,505	158.2	73.6	93.3	20.7
Germany	21.5	52.1	15.3	2.82	30/66[9]	103,106	202.7	82.5	89.3	22.5
Japan	17.6	53.2	18.0	3.36[9]	18/75[9]	353,446	147.0	67.1[9]	79.7[11]	N/A
New Zealand	30.5	20.2	9.0	1.30[9]	46/38[9]	1,312	176.4	75.0[9]	94.7[11]	N/A
United Kingdom	28.2	69.1	20.9	1.77	32/45	35,482	205.4	79.6	87.9	28.1
United States	36.3	57.4	19.9	2.90[9]	31/62[9]	858,416	162.8	71.1	N/A	20.3

Notes:

1. Employment data by occupation reported by International Labour Organization. Including all persons employed in occupations in Major Group 1 (Legislators, Senior Officials, and Managers) and Major Group 2 (Professionals) by ISCO-88. Most recent data available are 2008 data.

2. Knowledge-intensive services as defined for this chapter include: Insurance Services; Financial Services; Computer and Information Services; Royalties and License Fees; Other Business Services; and Personal, Cultural, and Recreational Services.

3. OECD Average for 2008 is 2.33%.

4. The percentage does not add to 100 because "other national" and "abroad" sources are not included.

5. Number of patents granted by United States Patent and Trademark Office, World Intellectual Property Organization.

6. Total Communication Access Paths includes analogue lines, ISDN lines, DSL, cable modem, fibre, other, and mobile.

7. 2011 data.

8. 2008 data.

9. 2009 data.

10. 2007 data.

11. For Japan, businesses with 100 or more employees. For New Zealand, businesses with 6 or more employees and with a turnover exceeding NZD 30,000.

Sources: OECD; World Bank; United Nations Service Trade Database; Australian Bureau of Statistics; World Intellectual Property Organization.

TABLE 7.2 Selected Knowledge and Innovation-Related Measures from International Sources

World Bank, Knowledge Economy (out of 146)		World Economic Forum, Competitiveness (out of 142)		IMD, Competitiveness (out of 59)	
Item	Rank	Item	Rank	Item	Rank
Weighted Knowledge Index	8	Innovation	22	Education System	6
Education	4	- Capacity of Innovation	27	- University Education	7
ICT	18	- Company Spending on R&D	27	- Management Education	9
- Internet Users	15	- Technological Readiness	22	- Science in Schools	14
- Computers	15	- Quality of Scientific Research Institutions	13	Technology	19
- Telephones per 1000	31	- University-Industry Collaboration in R&D	14	- Innovative Capacity	23
Innovation	20	- Business Sophistication	29	- Funding for Technological Development	11
- Payments and Receipts	18	- Availability of Scientists and Engineers	60	- Intellectual Property Rights	17
- Patents Granted	20	Education	11	- Scientific Research	17
- Science and Engineering Journal Articles per Million People	10	- Higher Education and Training	1	- Knowledge Transfer	19
		- Secondary Education Enrolment	14	- Technological Regulation	7
		- Tertiary Education Enrolment	13	- Development and Application of Technology	15
		- Quality of Education System	19	Technology	8
		- Quality of Math and Science Education	15	- Public and Private Sector Ventures	27
		- Quality of Management Schools	14	Workforce	32
		- Availability of Research Training Services	19	- Researchers and Scientists	35
		Infrastructure	28	- Language Skills	20
		- Internet Access in Schools	69	- Information Technology Skills	46
		- Fixed Telephone Lines	50	- Skilled Labour	36
		- Mobile Telephone Subscriptions		- International Experience of Labour	
		Government Procurement of Advanced Technology Products		Infrastructure	
				- Communications Technology	
				- Connectivity	

Sources: World Bank, *Knowledge Index 2009*, October 2011; *The Global Competitiveness Report 2011–2012*, World Economic Forum, Switzerland, 2012; International Institute for Management Development, *World Competitiveness Yearbook 2011*, Lausanne, 2011.

177

Society for Knowledge Economics called for the creation of a National Innovation Framework, claiming that knowledge and innovation are the basis for competition in modern developed economies.[9] This call was followed by a review of Australia's National Innovation System that was commissioned by the Federal Government in 2008,[10] and the Government's response, which established a 10-year reform agenda to make Australia more innovative, productive, and competitive.[11] Extensive consultation with a wide range of individuals and groups in these reviews, and further analysis, has identified a number of issues that Australia will need to address to become a world-class knowledge-innovation economy.

Lack of Innovative Activity: In 2008–2009, only just over a third of firms in Australia introduced an innovation to their business, with the most frequently implemented innovation being the introduction of new or significantly improved organisational or managerial processes: 44 percent of businesses in the wholesale trade, 42 percent of manufacturing businesses, and 26 percent of businesses in the construction industry introduced an innovation in 2008–2009, and larger businesses were found to be more likely to innovate than smaller businesses.[12] This would indicate only a small portion of Australia's businesses are innovative.

Shallow Innovation System: Suggestions for improvement in the national innovation system include establishing a National Innovation Council and a Research Coordination Council to better coordinate innovation and research efforts,[13] streamlining access to government programs and support,[14] and promoting strategic policy objectives that bring about innovation-relevant linkages at a national level.[15] According to the Business Council of Australia–Society for Knowledge Economics study, fewer than 7 percent of Australian businesses got ideas for innovation from government research institutes or universities.[16] This would indicate that much of the R&D that is carried out by government and educational institutions is divorced from the business reality of the vast majority of Australian companies.

Research and Development: Many in Australia claim that more should be spent on R&D, noting that Australia lags many other nations in government and business investment in R&D.[17] Some suggest the size and structure of R&D expenditure partly explain why Australia's productivity went from ahead of the OECD average to significantly behind since 2000.[18] There are issues of scale and focus. Australia can't hope to match larger nations, such as the United States, Japan, and Germany, that have larger GDPs, spend a higher portion of their GDP on R&D, have much better established international linkages, and have much larger companies doing R&D within their borders. There is a question of how much effort should be focused on high-tech versus low- and medium-tech industries, how much should be done by the private as opposed to the public sector, and the mix of basic and applied research.[19]

Limited Capacity and Technology: Australia's capacity to support a knowledge-innovation economy is limited by its infrastructure and by poor levels of technology adoption in some sectors. Presently, Australia does not have a national broadband network, nor does it have the research and educational infrastructure that will support innovation at a world-class level in most areas.

These limitations and others are driving calls for a long-term integrated approach toward investments in knowledge infrastructure and to upgrade technology to retain competitiveness and support innovation.[20] It has been found that many Australian companies are not aware of and do not invest in relevant supporting technologies.[21] It is suggested that improvements in ICT are needed and that better utilisation of technology is needed.[22]

Filling the Skills Gap: Australia's Productivity Commission claims that a highly skilled workforce is an essential foundation for Australia's innovation system, noting that it is crucial not only for the generation and application of new knowledge, but also to being able to use and adapt knowledge produced elsewhere.[23] *Powering Ideas—An Innovation Agenda for the 21st Century* concludes that innovation requires skills of all kinds, including leadership and management skills. There are skills deficiencies at the managerial level in particular and calls for the Australian Government to explicitly incorporate support for management and leadership development into its productivity agenda.[24] This is echoed by the Australian Industry Group in reporting that key areas of knowledge and innovation capability are not widely embedded in Australian workplaces.[25]

The Job-Readiness Imperative: The rise in the number of knowledge workers indicates that the knowledge economy is already developing in Australia. The question is whether Australia's workforce is ready for this economy. To make graduates more job-ready from a knowledge and innovation standpoint, it has been suggested that Australia's education and training system focus on skills in communication, teamwork, problem solving, entrepreneurship, and leadership, in addition to providing industry-relevant technical skills.[26]

Matching the Market: There is a need to match market needs with new knowledge and new ideas. The chairman of the Productivity Commission has stated ". . . it is important to remember that our success in innovation and adaptation will depend both on the skills and attitudes of our people, and on how well they are utilised in enterprises of all kinds throughout the country."[27] The Australian Business Foundation observes that innovation policy in Australia has supported research into new products without properly considering the demand-pull dimensions of innovation. It calls for the application of knowledge that meets the existing needs of customers and that solves problems that are evident in the community.[28] This view is supported by the Australian Industry Group, which has called for a shift from a research-driven approach to innovation to one that is more market-facing.[29]

Incentives to Innovate: There is an incentives gap that inhibits innovation in Australia and results in innovations and knowledge assets being taken offshore. The Business Council of Australia and the Society for Knowledge Economics suggest tax reforms and the institution of other financial incentives to support innovation including loan subsidies and income-contingent loans.[30] A survey for the Society for Knowledge Economics by Open Forum into innovation attitudes in Australia quotes the view of a respondent that "Conditions need to be established where it is either necessary or lucrative to innovate."[31] Australia has a domestic market that is small compared to markets in the United States, Europe, and Asia; a regulatory regime viewed as burdensome for small businesses; and a tax system seen as regressive, with many entrepreneurs citing the taxation of stock options at time of issue as a reason for leaving Australia.[32] In addition, universities tend to reward researchers for publishing in academic journals rather than for doing work that contributes to the development of a knowledge-innovation economy.

Need to Fill the Funding Gap: It is widely agreed that there is insufficient investment and capital for innovative activity, technology development, and entrepreneurs in Australia.[33&34] Technology entrepreneurs are reported to be leaving Australia due to an inability to obtain early-stage funding in Australia, with one successful entrepreneur who left Australia for the United States labelling venture capital in Australia "a joke," and others observing that unless a business involves mining or property it tends not to attract investors in Australia.[35] One way to address this is to adopt Cutler's (2008) recommendation that Government attract international venture capital fund(s) to Australia, and to put in place his suggested improvements to Australia's capital market to support investment in knowledge and innovation.[36] The Australian Industry Group proposes that a corporate venturing program be developed as a means of getting larger and better funded companies to invest in smaller and less well funded companies.[37] Others have suggested tax reforms including reduced capital gains tax for technology innovators as a means of attracting more venture capital.[38]

Need to Enhance Commercialisation: There are gaps in commercialising ideas in Australia. The Australian Government notes that too many Australian discoveries end up being commercialised overseas, with the value captured abroad.[39] The establishment of Commercialisation in Australia by the Government in 2010 is a step in the right direction, but to date it appears not to have stemmed the flow of Australian innovations abroad.[40] If Australian ingenuity is to be turned into economic and business success, progress needs to be made in commercialising research that is done in universities and institutes, promoting research that can be commercialised,[41] focusing on commercial outcomes from innovation,[42] seeking substantially higher contributions from industry in support of innovation-related research, and achieving greater industry involvement and networking with universities and researchers.

Need to Foster Collaboration: The Australian Government cites greater collaboration internationally, within the research sector, and between researchers and industry as being national innovation priorities. Australia performs poorly in measures of collaboration versus OECD countries, particularly for collaboration between public researchers and private industry.[43] Greater collaboration is needed domestically between government and business, between universities and business, and between public researchers and private industry.[44] Greater international collaboration also is needed.[45] Green and colleagues (2009) note that only through collaboration with all stakeholders will Australian public policy and Australia's enterprises remain competitive, and they suggest that Enterprise Connect could facilitate partnerships with enterprises, research, educational institutions, and other public sector agencies when formulating new initiatives.[46]

Need to Leverage the Public Sector: The lack of government support for Australian companies through procurement practices is an issue, with claims that small changes in government procurement could have an enormous impact on innovation in Australia, particularly among small and medium-sized enterprises (SMEs).[47] Leveraging public sector spending to foster private sector innovation is an idea that is endorsed by the private sector[48] and is supported in principle by Government.[49] Calls also have been made for Government to lead by example by innovating in its own activities and by improving service delivery through innovation, with the suggestion that an advocate for government innovation be established to promote innovation in the public sector.[50]

Lack of an Innovation Culture: The lack of a culture of innovation in Australia is noted by many, including the Australian Industry Group, which has called for developing a culture of innovation by highlighting success stories and lessons learned in Australian innovation practice.[51] A survey for the Society for Knowledge Economics by Open Forum found that the so-called tall-poppy syndrome, risk aversion, short-termism, and complacency are key impediments to innovation.[52] Another survey indicated that Australian manufacturers fail to see innovation as a tool for their business and have not responded positively to the opportunities presented by a globalised knowledge-intensive marketplace. Australian firms also tend to rate innovation and technology as factors of low importance in driving competitiveness in contrast to their European counterparts. This led to a conclusion that Australian firms lack a strategic approach to innovation and that "they are fighting yesterday's war."[53]

Policies and Programs

In response to a review of Australia's National Innovation System in 2008,[54] the Government established a 10-year reform agenda with significant new budget commitments at the federal level. This agenda, which has as its priorities commitments to additional public research funding, developing a strong base of skilled researchers both in the public and private sectors, developing industries of the future that can benefit from the commercialisation of Australian R&D, improving the dissemination of new ideas across the economy, improving R&D collaboration domestically and internationally, and improving policy development and service delivery in support of innovation, has become the basis for other policies aimed at developing Australia's knowledge-innovation economy.

Australia has a great many policies and programs that intend to support the development of the knowledge-innovation economy. These include the Workforce Innovation Program to help make graduates of knowledge and creative industries job-ready; the establishment of Innovation & Business Skills Australia (IBSA) to build innovative capacity in Australia's workforce in ICT, in printing, and in graphic arts; the Australia Council's ArtStart program, which makes funds available to recent arts graduates to help them pursue a career as professional artists; and training and development programs through Indigenous Business Australia and the National Arts and Crafts Industry Support program, as well as the Indigenous Contemporary Music Action Plan for Australia's Indigenous community.

To support academic research into innovation and the creative industries, the Federal Government established the Australian Research Council Centre of Excellence for Creative Industries and Innovation in addition to providing grants in support of research linkages and funding for universities to be more focused on R&D. Structural reform of the university sector is underway to create additional university places to support growth in disciplines, including those related to knowledge-intensive and creative industries. In addition, the Government is funding the Creative Industries Innovation Centre and the Centre of Excellence for Creative Industries and Innovation to create links between industry and universities.

Initiatives to develop infrastructure include the commitment to build a superfast National Broadband Network (NBN) at an estimated cost of up to AUD 43 billion so that a majority of Australian premises, including those in rural and regional areas, have high-speed globally competitive Internet connections, and funding for the Digital Education Revolution (DER) to better prepare students to live and work in a digital world and to ensure that all students have access to a computer. The Government also has committed significant funds to National ICT Australia to support ICT research and to develop ICT platforms that will aid the DER, and it has set up the Information Technology Industry Innovation Council to promote the IT sector and to advise government on innovation issues.

Financial policies in support of knowledge and innovation include an R&D Tax Credit to encourage companies to undertake increased levels of business R&D in Australia. The Government also has an Innovation Investment Fund that matches public funds with private capital, as well as the Export Market Development Grants scheme to support the export of intellectual property. For creative industries, the Government supports investment in Australian-created content by funding the Australian Broadcasting Corporation as well as the Australia Network, by offering tax incentives to Australian filmmakers, and via the Export Finance and Insurance Corporation, which provides financial support to Australian film and television productions that have international distribution agreements.

Commercialisation Australia was established in 2010 to help researchers, entrepreneurs, and innovative businesses to commercialise their ideas. This is something that Enterprise Connect's Creative Industries Innovation Centre also aims to do as well as fostering collaboration between businesses, university, industry, and government. More broadly, Enterprise Connect aims to build capabilities in SMEs and to help them transform to become more innovative and competitive.

However, it is not clear that all of these policies and programs have sufficient funding, or have been promoted extensively enough, meaning that awareness of the opportunities they represent may be low. There also is a view that the government support programs are too complex and confusing, and that there is duplication and overlap at the state and federal levels, leading to calls for a single portal for innovation-related support.[55]

Knowledge and Innovation in Australia in Perspective

Australia's desire to be a world leader in knowledge and innovation is well documented and is an ambition that has the support of both government and business. Significant reviews of Australia's innovation performance have led to a raft of recommendations for performance improvement, and many already have been addressed to some extent by government policy. The question, however, is whether Australia's ambitions can be satisfied in the context of its limited financial resources, its limited number of large companies, and its relatively low exports of knowledge-intensive services and high-technology manufacturers. For Australia to advance its knowledge-innovation economy, there is a need to focus limited resources on doing a few things well rather than trying to do everything. This means having a workforce with the right skills and capabilities, doing the right types of R&D, and creating the right incentives for collaboration, greater international linkages, and commercialisation of R&D. It also means making maximum use of knowledge created abroad. Otherwise the investment made in funding the infrastructure for the knowledge-innovation economy will not achieve the desired outcomes.

While Australia scores well in high-level aggregate view of the knowledge-innovation economy, more detailed analysis shows Australia performing relatively poorly in several measures associated with connectivity, entrepreneurship, information technology skills, R&D spending, innovative capacity, skilled labour, and international experience of labour. The findings of the competitiveness survey carried out for this project agree with the international rankings on Australia's education levels, managerial capabilities, and the presence of research and scientific capabilities. The concern is that the ability to innovate might be constrained by Australia's middling performance in access to funds in the form of venture capital and equity capital, in the clustering of firms, and science and technology policy in most service and manufacturing sectors.

There are enough success stories of innovation in Australia to suggest that the knowledge-innovation economy exists and that home-grown innovation with global reach is achievable. Well-known examples of this include the Hills Hoist, Cochlear's bionic ear, and the orbital engine, but there are many others, and there also are many examples of individual Australians based in Australia who are leaders in the global knowledge-innovation economy. However, for every Australian innovation or individual that has achieved success in Australia there appear to be others who felt the need to leave Australia in order to make it. Reasons for leaving include a lack of access to funding, the lack of an innovation culture in Australia, poor linkages within Australia and between Australia and the rest of the world in knowledge and innovation, cost barriers including bureaucratic obstacles and relatively high levels of taxation, an insufficient supply of talent, difficulties in commercialising ideas and knowledge in Australia, and poor infrastructure.

Various business groups have identified the key issues in relation to Australia's knowledge-innovation economy and have in many instances offered suggestions as to how these issues might be dealt with. It is clear that the Government has on the whole been receptive to these views, but it is not clear that, with the exception of funding for the National Broadband Network, adequate funds are available to close the gaps that presently exist.

The Rise of the Asia-Pacific Region

Asia has become a major growth engine for the world economy and an even more important growth engine for Australia. The rise of Asian economies has the potential to shift the economic balance in global terms and specifically for Australia. This creates a major opportunity, in that Australia has long been hampered by the fact that it has been distant from most of the world's leading economies. As the global economic balance shifts more toward Asia and the Asia-Pacific region, this traditional disadvantage is being sharply reduced.

There is an understanding in Australia that Asian nations and the Asia-Pacific region are vitally important to Australia's economic future, and that regional markets and regional competitors are likely to be of more direct importance to Australia than far away countries that are neither direct competitors nor major markets for Australia's vital industries. The Australian Government and the general public recognise the importance of Asia to Australia's future and the Australian Government's White Paper *Australia in the Asian Century* considers how best to position Australia in Asia and the economic and strategic changes that will take place with the emergence of Asian economies.[56]

The key question for Australia is the extent to which the nation can capitalise on the rise of Asian economies, not just in terms of selling commodities and educational services, but in terms of selling other high-value goods and services and becoming an important part of the managerial, communication, and financial fabric of the region. This will require not only closer linkages with the rest of the Asia-Pacific region, but also the ability to outcompete Asian countries and companies, as well as other countries and companies for a portion of the regional business.

Asia-Pacific Markets and Australia

Asia has long been the world's dominant region when it comes to population. In 2010, Asia accounted for 54.6 percent of global population, with East Asia accounting for 23.6 percent, South Asia for 23.1 percent, and Southeast Asia for 7.9 percent. By 2030, the US Government projects that Asia will account for 52.2 percent of a much larger world population, with East Asia accounting for 19.5 percent, South Asia for 24.7, and Southeast Asia for 8.0 percent (see Table 7.3).

While Asia had the world's leading economies in the days before the Industrial Revolution in the West, its share of world economic output fell dramatically starting around 1820. This began to turn around in the 1960s and 1970s, but even so, by 2010, Asia's share of global GDP at market exchange rates was only 20.90 percent, or well under half its population share. However, Asia's rapid economic growth raised its share of global GDP to 25.28 percent by 2010 and US Government projects that it will reach 35.17 percent by 2030, with East Asia (25.44 percent) accounting for the lion's

TABLE 7.3 **Projected Population, Millions**

	2000	**2005**	**2010**	**2015**	**2020**	**2025**	**2030**
World	6,009	6,388	6,772	7,151	7,521	7,871	8,199
North America	313	328	344	359	374	389	403
Latin America	519	555	589	622	653	682	708
Europe	529	538	547	552	556	558	557
Former Soviet Union	282	279	278	277	275	273	270
Africa	799	902	1,017	1,143	1,276	1,417	1,567
Oceania	30	32	35	37	39	41	43
Middle East	240	263	289	312	334	355	374
Asia	3,296	3,490	3,673	3,850	4,014	4,157	4,277
East Asia	1,469	1,506	1,540	1,572	1,594	1,602	1,596
Southeast Asia	469	505	539	571	602	630	657
South Asia	1,358	1,479	1,593	1,707	1,817	1,924	2,024

Source: US Department of Agriculture, *International Macroeconomic Database*, October 2012.

TABLE 7.4   Projected Share of World GDP, Real 2005 USD, Percent

	2000	2005	2010	2015	2020	2025	2030
North America	30.86	30.26	28.14	26.87	25.92	24.95	23.81
Latin America	6.17	6.13	6.55	6.86	7.12	7.34	7.50
Europe	33.49	31.95	29.88	27.88	26.08	24.23	22.31
Former Soviet Union	1.83	2.20	2.39	2.51	2.58	2.62	2.62
Africa	1.96	2.14	2.44	2.55	2.72	2.86	2.96
Oceania	1.93	1.97	2.02	1.97	1.93	1.86	1.77
Middle East	2.86	3.05	3.30	3.55	3.69	3.79	3.85
Asia	20.90	22.30	25.28	27.82	29.95	32.35	35.17
East Asia	17.21	18.04	20.01	21.60	22.73	23.95	25.44
Southeast Asia	1.78	1.97	2.26	2.52	2.70	2.85	2.98
South Asia	1.91	2.29	3.00	3.69	4.53	5.55	6.75

Source: US Department of Agriculture, *International Macroeconomic Database*, October 2012.

share (see Table 7.4). In 2000, just one Asian economy, Japan, was in the top four in the world in terms of GDP. By 2030, three Asian countries, China, India, and Japan, were projected to be in the top four (see Table 7.5).[57] The opening of Asian economies, improvements in transportation and communication, international flows of knowledge and technology, the advent of modern logistics systems, and the evolution of major multinational companies that slice up their activities into finer and finer parts and place each part in its optimal location have spread economic activity around the world to the point where shares of global GDP might eventually revert to shares of population, at least for countries that are sufficiently open and able to enter the global economic system. If this is the case, we would expect that Asia will only become more important in relative terms in the coming years.

We note that some analysts prefer to compare country GDP by purchasing power parity (PPP) exchange rates rather than market exchange rates. PPP exchange rates were developed to correct for different price levels across countries to provide better comparisons between actual standards of living than market exchange rates. At PPP exchange rates, China, India, and Japan already had the second, third, and fourth largest economies in the world in 2010. By this measure, PriceWaterhouseCoopers (PwC) projects that China will pass the United States by 2020 and India will pass the United States by 2050 (see Table 7.6). In our view, when comparing the economic size or economic power of nations, however, GDP at market exchange rates is a more appropriate measure, as countries cannot spend or invest at their purchasing power parities.[58]

Australia is already closely linked to Asian economies in its trade. The Asia-Pacific economies listed in Table 7.7 accounted for 74.3 percent of Australia's exports of goods and services in 2011 and 49.3 percent of imports. Primary products accounted for 69.2 of Australia's exports to East Asia, 81.8 percent of exports to China, 78.6 percent of exports to South Korea, and 70.7 percent of exports to Japan, compared to Australia's global average of 62.9 percent.

TABLE 7.5   Top Countries by Projected Share of Global GDP, 2000–2030, Percent

Rank	Country	2000	Country	2010	Country	2020	Country	2030
1	United States	28.33	United States	25.77	United States	23.75	United States	21.86
2	Japan	10.78	Japan	9.12	China	11.84	China	16.58
3	Germany	6.75	China	7.55	Japan	7.28	India	5.98
4	United Kingdom	5.09	Germany	5.77	Germany	4.96	Japan	5.44
5	France	4.98	United Kingdom	4.56	United Kingdom	4.11	Germany	4.10
6	Italy	4.31	France	4.34	India	3.86	United Kingdom	3.60
7	China	3.58	Italy	3.44	France	3.75	France	3.17
8	Canada	2.53	India	2.44	Italy	2.73	Brazil	2.64
9	Spain	2.43	Canada	2.37	Brazil	2.41	Italy	2.13
10	Mexico	1.96	Spain	2.32	Canada	2.17	Russia	1.96
11	Brazil	1.94	Brazil	2.15	South Korea	2.09	Canada	1.95
12	South Korea	1.71	South Korea	2.00	Spain	1.93	South Korea	1.92
13	Australia	1.65	Mexico	1.83	Russia	1.90	Mexico	1.92
14	Netherlands	1.51	Russia	1.78	Mexico	1.90	Spain	1.62
15	India	1.49	Australia	1.74	Australia	1.67	Australia	1.53

Source: US Department of Agriculture, *International Macroeconomic Database*, October 2012.

We note the portion of primary products in Australia's exports is understated due to the way that gold and confidential items are treated in the trade statistics. Gold appears in the category "Other" because for many countries shipments of gold are financial transactions. For Australia, it makes more sense to think of gold as another primary product. The vast majority of Australia's exports in the "Other" category for Hong Kong, India, Singapore, Thailand, and Vietnam are gold. For the rest of the economies, the "Other" category is dominated by "Confidential Transactions." According to the Australian Department of Foreign Affairs and Trade, items to which confidentiality might exist for specific trade partners or overall include natural gas, a variety of minerals and mineral sands, a range of (mostly strategic) metals, non-industrial diamonds, uranium, a variety of food products, and ships.[59] Thus the vast majority of Australia's exports in the "Other" category in Table 7.7 can be reasonably assumed to be primary products, bringing the primary portion of exports to East Asia to well over 70 percent.

Australia's imports from the Asia-Pacific region, on the other hand are mostly manufactured goods. 62.1 percent of Australia's imports from East Asia, 91.7 percent of imports from China, 73.3 percent of imports from Japan, 75.4 percent of imports from Taiwan, and 68.3 percent of imports from South Korea were manufactured goods. The clear picture is that of Australia exporting primary goods and importing manufactured and processed goods from the region.

When we break down the trade, we see that East Asia absorbed 70.4 percent of Australia's merchandise (goods) exports in 2011. Adding in New Zealand and India brings the total to 79.2 percent. East Asia was the source of 50.1 percent of Australia's merchandise imports in 2011. Adding in New Zealand and India brings the total to

TABLE 7.6 Leading Nations by GDP at PPP Exchange Rates, 2010–2050

Rank	Country	2010	Country	2020	Country	2030	Country	2040	Country	2050
1	US	14,655	China	20,010	China	30,538	China	42,613	China	57,785
2	China	9,786	US	18,750	US	23,767	US	30,475	India	41,374
3	India	4,067	India	8,006	India	14,400	India	25,496	US	38,061
4	Japan	4,263	Japan	5,095	Japan	5,956	Brazil	6,979	Brazil	9,772
5	Russia	2,822	Russia	4,051	Russia	5,249	Japan	6,664	Japan	7,641
6	Brazil	2,168	Germany	3,604	Brazil	4,792	Russia	6,448	Russia	7,422
7	UK	2,293	Brazil	3,269	Germany	4,052	Mexico	4,918	Mexico	6,638
8	Germany	3,059	UK	2,887	UK	3,556	Germany	4,776	Indonesia	5,788
9	France	2,205	France	2,725	Mexico	3,522	UK	4,475	Germany	5,629
10	Italy	1,943	Mexico	2,391	France	3,393	France	4,229	UK	5,617
11	Spain	1,485	Italy	2,332	Italy	2,738	Indonesia	3,970	France	5,339
12	Canada	1,324	Korea	1,982	Indonesia	2,624	Turkey	3,776	Turkey	5,303
13	Australia	886	Spain	1,824	Turkey	2,589	Italy	3,155	Nigeria	4,478
14	Korea	1,403	Turkey	1,715	Korea	2,423	Korea	2,833	Vietnam	3,910
15	Mexico	1,606	Canada	1,706	Spain	2,244	Canada	2,655	Italy	3,806

Source: PWC, The World in 2050, 2011.

TABLE 7.7 Australia's Trade with Asia-Pacific Economies, 2011

Country	Exports	% of Australia Total	5 year Growth Rate %	% Primary Goods	% Manufacturing	% Other Goods	% Services
China	77,117	24.6	28.1	81.8	5.1	5.7	7.3
Hong Kong	4,765	1.5	0.7	26.1	29.2	8.6	36.1
Indonesia	6,662	2.1	4.9	47.6	23.9	9.5	19.0
Japan	52,384	16.7	7.4	70.7	4.6	21.0	3.7
Malaysia	6,134	2.0	7.1	37.8	31.0	4.4	26.8
Philippines	1,984	0.6	8.9	49.5	26.7	1.6	22.2
Korea	25,024	8.0	11.7	78.6	8.9	5.7	6.8
Singapore	9,526	3.0	3.7	37.1	15.5	14.6	32.8
Taiwan	9,670	3.1	7.5	70.4	18.5	5.6	5.5
Thailand	7,725	2.5	8.5	31.4	19.8	36.4	12.5
Vietnam	2,958	0.9	9.6	37.9	16.9	14.3	30.9
East Asia	204,392	65.2	13.2	69.2	9.5	11.4	9.8
India	17,386	5.6	13.1	57.8	4.5	25.3	12.3
New Zealand	11,010	3.5	−3.2	14.8	48.2	6.8	30.2
Total World	313,255	100.0	8.0	62.9	13.3	7.7	16.1

Country	Imports	% of Australia Total	5 year Growth Rate %	% Primary Goods	% Manufacturing	% Other Goods	% Services
China	43,938	14.9	10.3	2.6	91.7	1.6	4.1
Hong Kong	3,151	1.1	−1.2	2.9	32.8	0.4	63.9
Indonesia	8,167	2.8	9.2	38.8	26.5	7.0	27.6
Japan	20,076	6.8	0.4	10.9	73.3	5.4	10.5
Malaysia	9,891	3.4	5.2	44.0	38.8	3.8	13.4
Philippines	965	0.3	−3.3	7.4	35.9	2.0	54.8
Korea	7,644	2.6	2.2	21.2	68.3	3.8	6.8
Singapore	18,157	6.2	1.7	52.3	21.0	4.6	22.1
Taiwan	3,977	1.3	−3.5	10.1	75.4	9.5	5.0
Thailand	10,732	3.6	8.5	10.4	60.2	8.0	21.3
Vietnam	3,586	1.2	−9.1	52.7	26.0	0.1	21.2
East Asia	131,882	44.7	4.5	20.3	62.1	3.9	13.7
India	2,952	1.0	8.6	10.9	64.0	0.4	75.4
New Zealand	10,579	3.6	5.7	38.6	25.1	8.1	28.2
Total World	294,933	100.0	4.9	18.4	56.2	4.8	20.6

Sources: Australian Department of Foreign Affairs and Trade; Australia Bureau of Statistics.

54.0 percent. East Asia absorbed 40.1 percent of Australia's service exports in 2011. Adding New Zealand and India brings the total to 50.9 percent. East Asia was the source of 30.6 percent of Australia's service imports in that year. Adding New Zealand and India brings the total to 36.9 percent. In individual products, Australia's top exports to China, Japan, and South Korea have been iron ore and coal. Its top exports to India are coal and gold. On the other hand, Australia's leading imports from China are telecommunications equipment and parts, and computers. From Japan it is passenger motor vehicles and refined petroleum. From Korea it is passenger motor vehicles and refined petroleum. And from India it is pearls and gems, and jewellery.[60] Again, the picture that emerges is of an Australia that imports manufactured and refined goods from Asia and exports resources.

Asia looms large in Australia's service trade.[61] In fiscal 2010–2011, 50.5 percent of Australia's service exports were to Asia, and 36.9 percent of Australia's imports came from Asia. Europe was the next-most-important region, accounting for 19.4 percent of Australia's service exports and 27.7 percent of service imports. Education was the single largest category of service exports to Asia, accounting for 50.6 percent of Australia's service exports to Asia in 2010–2011. Asia accounted for AUD 12.9 billion out of Australia's AUD 15.8 billion in education exports in 2010–2011. Other personal travel, essentially personal tourism, accounted for 18.4 percent, and transportation services accounted for 10.6 percent. Asia accounted for 39.4 percent of Australia's non-education personal travel export revenues in 2010–2011. Australia's largest services imports from Asia were transportation services (41.7 percent), personal tourism (37.1 percent), and other business services (6.2 percent).

Australia's foreign investment position with respect to economies of the Asia-Pacific region is shown in Table 7.8. By 2011, the European Union (mostly the UK) and the United States dominated Australia's international investment flows and positions. Australia's investment position in New Zealand, by far the largest destination within the Asia-Pacific region, was dwarfed by that in the EU and United States. The EU and United States accounted for well over half of the foreign investment position in Australia in 2011, with Japan having by far the largest position among Asia-Pacific economies. Both Australia's outbound and inbound investment positions with respect to leading Asian economies have been growing much faster than those with the European Union and the United States (with the exception of Australia's investment position in Japan). While Chinese investment has received a great deal of press coverage, as of 2011, China was well down the list of foreign investors into Australia.[62]

Various measures of connectivity between Australia and Asia-Pacific economies are provided in Table 7.9. The Asia-Pacific nations and regions in the table accounted for the destination of 50.2 percent of Australia's emigrants, and were the source of 55.5 percent of Australia's immigrants, 56.3 percent of temporary visitors, and 76.1 of foreign university students studying in Australia. While from a time zone standpoint Australia is in the Asia-Pacific region, we note that the flight times between Sydney and most of the region's major cities are in excess of eight hours. Although this leaves Australia closer to major Asian markets than North America or Europe, there are still vast distances between Australia and most Asian markets, and Australia's distance advantage when it comes to Asian economies versus Europe and the Americas is perhaps not as great as many might think.

TABLE 7.8 Foreign Direct Investment Australia and Asia-Pacific Countries and Regions

	Australian Investment Abroad			Foreign Investment into Australia		
	Flow[1]	Position		Flow[1]	Position	
	2011	2011	CAGR 2006–2011 (%)	2011	2011	CAGR 2006–2011 (%)
China	−5,712	−16,994	41.1	929	19,047	40.3
Hong Kong	4,373	−20,386	4.3	−1,372	39,416	0.3
India	−668	−4,299	12.0	−1,708[2]	10,954	78.2
Indonesia	−264	−5,405	11.9	32	454	−2.5
Japan	−4,570	−34,595	−3.6	10,183	123,410	19.0
Korea	−1,155	−7,633	2.0	802	12,772	20.8
Malaysia	−1,379	−5,692	44.6	1,436	13,987	20.4
New Zealand	−1,923	−74,267	1.4	−2,669	29,707	−3.6
Philippines	−1,630	−5,335	39.7	−5	430	−31.7
Singapore	5,712	−21,350	7.2	1,318	48,709	12.2
Taiwan	430	−3,726	3.9	−46	4,866	7.2
Thailand	−400	−2,106	14.2	976	13,408	114.7
Vietnam	125	−716[3]	12.3	31	184	40.2
EU	14,414	−356,141	5.5	−37,941	637,176	6.5
US	−38,489	−410,612	11.5	36,932	555,868	11.2
Global Total	−55,411	−1,175,380	6.7	86,721	2,030,032	5.1

Notes:

1. Negative entries indicate an increase of outward direct investment by Australia to the country or a decrease in the foreign country's investment in Australia.

2. 2009 data.

3. 2010 data.

Source: Australian Bureau of Statistics, *International Investment Position, Australia: Supplementary Statistics, Calendar Year 2011,* released 2012.

TABLE 7.9 Connectivity Statistics, Australia and Asia-Pacific Countries

Country	Emigration from Australia, FY2011 (no. of persons)[1]	Immigration to Australia, FY2011 (no. of persons)[2]	No. of Visitors to Australia, 2011[3]	No. of University Students studying in Australia, FY 2011[4]	Approx. Flight time between Sydney and the Selected Cities
China	5,741	14,611	542,000	38,999	11:50 hours/Beijing10:20 hours/Shanghai
Hong Kong	6,635	1,097	166,300	3,730	9:20 hours/Hong Kong
India	632	10,566	148,200	9,180	NA
Indonesia	1,740	1,373	140,400	4,427	7:50 hours/Jakarta
Japan	1,374	483	332,700	1,050	9:35 hours/Tokyo
Korea	797	1,979	198,000	4,959	10:30 hours/Seoul
Malaysia	1,393	2,737	241,200	7,608	8:30 hours/Kuala Lumpur
New Zealand[5]	14,596	25,772	1,172,700	8,986	3:15 hours/Wellington
Philippines	630	5,048	56,800	1,326	8:30 hours/Manila
Singapore	6,952	1,095	318,500	3,618	8:10 hours/Singapore
Taiwan	913	599	84,400	1,656	9:10 hours/Taipei
Thailand	1,725	2,096	85,400	2,362	9:20 hours/Bangkok
Vietnam	1,291	3,339	33,700	4,825	9:00 hours/Ho Chi Minh City[6]
Selected A-P nations, regions	44,419	70,795	3,520,300	92,726	
Selected A-P %	50.2%	55.5%	56.3%	76.1%	
Global Total	88,461	127,458	6,254,735	121,770	

Notes:

1. Permanent departures by intended region/country of residence, 2010–2011.

2. Settlers arrivals by birthday and state/territory of intended residence, 2010–2011.

3. Number of short-term movement of visitor arrivals by countries of residence.

4. Number of visa applications granted by citizenship country of subclasses including "573 Higher Education" and "574 Postgraduate Research" sectors.

5. New Zealand citizens are entitled to study at Australian tertiary institutions without requiring a student visa. Number of New Zealand students in all higher education providers in Australia, 2010.

6. No direct flight from Hanoi to Sydney.

Sources: Australian Department of Immigration and Citisenship; Australian Department of Education, Employment and Workplace Relations; Bureau of Infrastructure, Transport and Regional Economics; Australian Department of Infrastructure and Transport; Official Website of Sydney Airport.

Assessments of Australia's Position in the Asia-Pacific Region

One question that arises is the extent to which Australia is linked to the markets of the Asia-Pacific region in terms of trade, investment, tourism, education, and migration. Another question is whether Australia is actually more competitive than other economies in the Asia-Pacific region. There is a tendency for Australia to be viewed as a more advanced economy than those of the other Asia-Pacific nations and regions. If so, then Australia presumably should be able to sell high-value goods and services into those markets.

Several international sources provide information on Australia's competitive position and related issues against other Asia-Pacific countries. Australia ranked 20th (out of 142 economies) overall in the World Economic Forum's 2011 Global Competitiveness Index (see Chapter 2). Among Asia-Pacific economies, Australia ranked behind Singapore, Hong Kong, Japan, and Taiwan, but ahead of Malaysia, Korea, New Zealand, China, Thailand, Indonesia, India, Vietnam, and the Philippines. In the 2011 IMD *World Competitiveness Yearbook*, Australia ranked behind Hong Kong, Singapore, and Taiwan, but ahead of Malaysia, China, New Zealand, Korea, Japan, Thailand, India, Indonesia, and the Philippines. Australia prides itself on the ease of doing business in the country, but Australia ranked behind Singapore, Hong Kong, New Zealand, and Korea (and ahead of other Asia-Pacific economies) in the World Bank's 2012 Ease of Doing Business Index. Australia ranked 8th globally, but behind New Zealand and Singapore, in the 2011 Transparency International Corruption Perceptions Index.

Australia ranked 3rd globally in the 2012 Heritage Foundation Index of Economic Freedom and 5th in the Fraser Institute Economic Freedom of the World in 2009, but in the former case both of the economies ahead of Australia, Hong Kong and Singapore, are also in the Asia-Pacific region, and in the latter case, three of the four economies ranked ahead of Australia (Hong Kong, Singapore, and New Zealand) are also in the region. Australia ranked 6th in the 2010 GMI ratings Global Corporate Governance Country Ranking, putting it behind New Zealand, but ahead of all other countries in the region. Australia did unambiguously rank ahead of all other Asia-Pacific economies in the World Bank Knowledge Indices and the UN's Human Development Index.

Australia ranks well in most sub-indices associated with international sources on competitiveness (see Chapter 2), but in most cases, it ranks behind several economies in the Asia-Pacific region. This leads to a conclusion that Australia's physical and cultural distance from most Asia-Pacific markets, and the fact that it is behind a number of Asia-Pacific economies in nearly all indices or sub-indices that purport to measure competitiveness, might make it more difficult for Australia to leverage the rise of Asian economies to the extent many in Australia might hope.

These assessments are supplemented by those from the business competitiveness survey carried out for this project and reported in Chapter 4. Geographic location, knowledge of Asia markets, access to the China market, access to Asia-Pacific markets, and access to multilingual staff were considered important for the vast majority of Australia's sectors, particularly manufacturing sectors. Australia was viewed as having better performance than competitors and comparators in each of these drivers in the vast majority of cases. This indicates that respondents not only think the markets are important, but view Australia as being better positioned to leverage these markets than competitors.

Issues in Positioning Australia as Part of the Asia-Pacific Region

The importance of the Asia-Pacific region to Australia's economic future has been recognised by governments led by both major political parties, by Australia's business community, and by the population at large. A 2011 survey by the Australian Industry Group and Asialink found that nearly half of the businesses surveyed planned to start or expand their businesses in Asia within 12 months.[63] The growth of the Asia-Pacific region holds out the potential for new and larger markets for Australian companies and industries, new sources of supply for Australian businesses and consumers, new investment sources and destinations, and new sources and destinations for travellers and migrants. There are a number of issues and challenges that Australia must deal with if it is to become an even more integral part of the Asia-Pacific region.

Need for a Better Understanding of the Asia-Pacific Region: Integrating more closely with the Asia-Pacific region requires an understanding of the cultures, societies, and business practices in the region. Very few main board directors and senior executives in Australia have direct experience in the Asia-Pacific region, with notable exceptions including Mike Smith of ANZ Bank and Sir Roderick Eddington.[64] According to a survey by Australian Industry Group and Asialink, 65 percent of businesses indicated that none of their board members have worked in Asia.[65] The problem is compounded by the fact that few recruiters in Australia have a detailed working knowledge of the Asia-Pacific region and are therefore not well positioned to identify talent that would help Australian businesses develop the region.

Need for a More Asia-Focused Education System: Part of the problem is that there has not been a focus in the Australian education system on Asia literacy. A 2010 report on language instruction in schools found that only 18 percent of Australian school students overall were studying an Asian language and that by the final year of high school only 6 percent of students were doing so,[66] and often the learning of the language was rudimentary and limited to fundamentals. Broader knowledge of the political, economic, and social systems in Asia is lacking as well. The Australian Industry Group and Asialink have recommended that an "Asia-ready" workforce strategy be developed to ensure that the skills that are needed to do well in Asia are in place in Australian businesses and in the community more broadly.[67]

Adjusting for Socio-Political Differences: Australia is a Western-style, English-speaking, democratic nation with a multicultural population, with an independent judicial system, and well established institutions that draw on its historical links with the United Kingdom. New Zealand aside, it is surrounded by countries with significant and fundamental social, political, and religious differences. These differences need to be understood if Australia is to align more closely with the Asia-Pacific region. The former Minister for Foreign Affairs and Trade made this explicit in a speech in 2010 when he noted various challenges in Australia's dealings with China and India, emphasising that any issues and differences must be successfully managed in focusing on "the much broader range of issues where our interests coincide."[68] The Australia-China Council agrees that the differences in world view, political systems, cultural, and social traditions between China in particular and

Australia are significant, but calls for a greater focus on the opportunities for Australia and on Australia's capacity to respond to those opportunities.[69]

Opposition to Foreign Investment in Australia: A 2012 poll conducted by the Lowy Institute for International Policy found that a majority of Australians think that the Australian Government is allowing too much investment from China. A majority of respondents also thought that Australian mining and agricultural companies need to be kept in Australian hands and that "China has so much money to invest it could end up buying and controlling a lot of Australian companies."[70] China was not the sole focus of opposition to foreign investment, with nearly half of the respondents agreeing that the Australian Government is allowing too much foreign investment from all countries. Concerns such as this had led to Australia's Trade Minister stating that investment from overseas is beneficial to Australia's interests and to saying that fears in relation to investment from China in agricultural assets in particular are being driven by political interests that are contrary to the interests of Australians.[71] We note that while Chinese investment in Australia has been growing rapidly, investment from China is still very small in terms of the total stock of foreign investment in the country.

Economic and Policy Factors: According to the Australia Industry Group and Asialink, economic and policy factors, including the exchange rate, the economy in general, and government policy, were 3 of the top 4 factors (out of a total of 18 factors) that adversely affect Australian companies expanding Asia-related activities.[72] The Australia-China Council suggests that Australian business engagement with Asia has been cyclical and profit-driven instead of partnership-driven and that this needs to change if Australian enterprises are to succeed in business in Asia. It notes that the present approach is unsustainable in the long term and that government policies in support of increasing Australian skills relevant to Asia are either non-existent or "fairly aimless."[73]

Free Trade Agreements: A 2011 survey by AFG Venture Group in Australia found that fewer than one third of Australian respondents felt that existing free trade agreements between Thailand and Australia, ASEAN and India, ASEAN and China, Australia and New Zealand, and Australia and the United States had positively affected their commercial relationships, and only 36 percent indicated the ASEAN-Australia and Australia–New Zealand agreements had had a positive impact.[74] Respondents were more positive on proposed free trade agreements between Australia and Indonesia (56 percent), Australia and China (40 percent), Australia and Japan (34 percent), and Australia and India (32 percent).[75] In each case, the challenge will be what to do after the agreements are reached and how more Australian businesses can leverage the agreements into business opportunities.

Need for Proactive Asia-Pacific Mindset: Believing that there are opportunities in the Asia-Pacific region and seeking out and exploiting those opportunities are very different things. In the 2011 Australian Industry Group and Asialink survey, fewer than half of the businesses presently involved in Asia described their involvement as being on a proactive basis; 12 percent rated their involvement as proactive and reactive; and 40 percent rated it either as reactive or undefined.[76] If Australian businesses are to maximise their potential in the Asia-Pacific region, then they will need to be proactive in addressing customers, partners, and competitors in those markets; CPA Australia has suggested putting much greater weight to benchmarking Australia's performance against Asia countries, rather than the small and mid-sized OECD countries that have been the case in the past.[77]

China Is Important, but Other Countries Are Too: Given the prominence of the resource sector in Australia and China's importance as a resource market, many Australians appear to focus on China to the exclusion of the rest of the Asia-Pacific region. While China is a key player, government and others are keen to ensure that Australian businesses do not ignore opportunities in other parts of the region. In 2009, the Australian Minister for Foreign Affairs and Trade stated, "The rise of India, the weight of the ASEAN economies combined, the great individual potential of Indonesia and the enduring economic strengths of Japan and South Korea, must also be acknowledged."[78] This view is echoed by the findings of the Australian Industry Group and Asialink survey, which found that 13 Asian economies (including China) were significant to the actual business plans of respondents and that Japan and Thailand, in particular, were important to their business success.[79]

Expanded Business and Political Ties to the Asia-Pacific Region: Australia's former Ambassador to China, Geoff Raby, observes that Australia's diplomatic footprint in China has not changed since 1995, that several of China's provinces would be among Australia's top 10 trading partners if they were countries, and that there is an urgent need for Australia to expand its diplomatic presence in China. He concludes that Austrade's "so-called outrider offices" in China are poor substitutes for official consulates.[80] The Australia-China Council submits that Australia has a significant representation in Europe and the Americas at the expense of Asia, where economic opportunities are manifest.[81] CPA Australia has called for funding to expand Austrade's presence in Asia and to develop a small business exchange program with Asia.[82] The Australian Industry Group calls for more trade missions that are targeted at specific geographical areas and economic sectors.[83] We agree and observe that Australia's official footprint in other parts of the Asia-Pacific region should also be expanded.

Policies and Programs

The Australian Government has engagement with Asia as one of the three fundamental pillars of its foreign policy.[84] The commissioning of the White Paper *Australia in the Asian Century* is evidence of the government's ongoing commitment to ensuring that Australia is and remains a vital and important part of Asia in coming decades.[85]

Australia gives significant development assistance to East Asia, with nearly AUD 1 billion in assistance being given in 2008–2009 alone. Alongside this, labour migration programs such as the Pacific Seasonal Workers Scheme exist to help develop a labour force that can return to their home country with skills that help them develop their nation, and with close ties to Australia that will hopefully deliver business and social benefits to Australia over the long term. There is the potential for similar benefits to result from the recently established Enterprise Migration Agreements, although the focus of that scheme is on addressing a shortage of workers in relation to particular projects.

Recognising the need to foster a better understanding of Asia, the Government has put in place a national school education policy to encourage Asia literacy, and the new school curriculum has as priorities Australia's engagement with Asia as well as Asian languages. A total of AUD 62.4 million up to June 2012 has been committed to the National Asian Languages and Studies in Schools Program (NALSSP). This is a start, but if there is to be a serious push for students to learn Asian languages to some reasonable level of fluency then much more money will need to be committed.

The Australian Government also is seeking to develop and strengthen trade between Australia and the Asia-Pacific region through a series of economic partnerships and free trade agreements. Agreements in place include those between Thailand and Australia, the Association of Southeast Asian Nations (ASEAN) and India, ASEAN and China, Australia and New Zealand, Australia and the United States, and ASEAN-Australia and New Zealand. Australia is pursuing bilateral partnership or free trade agreements with Indonesia, China, Japan, and India. The Australian Government has policies related to the development of export capabilities, such as the Australian Government Export Market Development Grants scheme, that hopefully will enhance the ability of Australian businesses to leverage the agreements.

The Australian Government views participation in regional groupings that aim to shape the future of the Asia-Pacific region as an important part of its policy of engagement. Australia is an important partner of ASEAN, becoming ASEAN's first dialogue partner in 1973. It participates in the ASEAN Regional Forum, is a founding member of the East Asia Summit, and participates in the Asia-Europe Meeting (ASEM), being invited to join ASEM in 2010—this has been taken as a sign of the increasing strength of Australia's engagement with Asian countries.

In October 2012, the Australian Government released a long-awaited White Paper, *Australia in the Asian Century*.[86] The White Paper recognises the unique opportunities for Australia associated with Asia's rise. It focuses on Australia's need to build on its strengths, develop its capabilities, develop collaborative relationships with others in the region, work to maintain regional security, and strengthen Australia's relationships in the region. The White Paper sets 25 national objectives for 2025. Several are generic in the sense that they are considered good things to do, but do not have any specific links to Asia per se. Objectives specifically focused on Asia include expanding exposure to Asian content and languages in school, more educational and research exchanges, greatly expanding the number of Asia-capable leaders in business and institutions, expanding government-business interchange to enhance Australia's ability to compete in the region, working toward comprehensive regional trade and investment agreements, enhanced trade links with the region, among others. A comprehensive review of this document is beyond the scope of the present work, though we note that it represents a strong positive step, and we look forward to the details that will be put forward in support of reaching the objectives.

Australia and the Asia-Pacific in Perspective

Australia recognises that it is part of the Asia-Pacific region, and government, industry groups, and businesses have demonstrated a clear commitment to engaging more closely with Asia politically, in business, and in other ways. The trade numbers highlight Asia's importance to Australia and vice versa, but Australia's exports to Asia are presently heavily weighted towards primary products resources, with little being exported in the way of value-added businesses except for education. Despite recent press focus, investment into Australia from the Asia-Pacific region is still dwarfed by that from the West. Migration statistics, visitor numbers, and the number of university students from the Asia-Pacific region all point to closer integration between Australia and countries in the Asia-Pacific region than has been the case to date. This is particularly the case for China, where all indicators suggest a rapidly growing and vital business and trade relationship. This, of course, will require adjustment on the part of Australia if it is to manage these relationships successfully.

According to international sources, Australia outperforms most Asia-Pacific economies on many dimensions related to competitiveness, but perhaps not in as many dimensions as people in Australia might think. Japan, Singapore, and Hong Kong tend to rank as high if not higher than Australia on most dimensions. In addition, Australia's ranking behind Malaysia and Korea in terms of overall innovation capacity and business sophistication in some sources should be a cause for concern. The business competitiveness survey results, on the other hand, indicate that business respondents in Australia recognise the importance of the wider region and believe Australian industries have advantages in accessing those markets versus their competitors and comparators.

Information on business opportunities and practices in Asia is already available through Austrade and other agencies. The overall approach in terms of information provided and the level at which it is pitched is well done. However, there is a great deal of difference between information being available and business experience being shared. Developing networks of service providers that can advise Australian companies on entry strategies for the main markets around the region is something to consider. There is a wide range of expertise in the region that can be leveraged to help Australian businesses penetrate Asian markets. Bringing such expertise to Australia to provide seminars and basic advice in collaboration with business groups to enhance Australia's businesses' knowledge of the region could be done more often.

There are a number of issues that must be dealt with if Australia is to leverage the rise of the Asia-Pacific region to the extent possible. Australians need to know the region better, including its political, social, and business systems, as well as its languages. Australia needs to start benchmarking itself more against nations that represent regional opportunities, as well as regional competitors. Australian businesses should understand that the challenges of entering and doing business in Asian markets are similar to those faced by companies from other countries. Australian businesses need to understand that the markets in the region differ greatly in almost every dimension. This means the decision to enter the region for Australian businesses should involve a careful consideration of which markets are the right ones to approach. While Australia should continue to expand trade opportunities for Australian businesses in the region, free trade agreements are not viewed as a particular advantage by many Australian companies.

At present, Australia does not appear to be fully leveraging its position as a more advanced economy than many in the region into business opportunities. Australia appears to be selling commodities to Asia, not much in the way of more advanced manufactured goods. Tourism and education are the main service exports to Asia. Presumably, the other high-value products and services that could be exported to

Asia are the ones that are already being exported to the United Kingdom, the United States, and other places. These presumably are being targeted for entry into Asia. The question here is whether Australian companies can improve their capabilities in order to take advantage of the opportunities. The recent White Paper on Asia is an important document in that it should help focus the minds of Australians, Australian business, and Australian governments at all levels on the importance of the region and on some of the steps that will be necessary for Australia to benefit from Asia's rise.

Competitiveness and Australia's Cities

Cities are increasingly important to the competitiveness of nations. Cities are major generators of knowledge across a wide range of activities and industries; cities perform the high-value supporting services that the innovation and internationalisation process require; and cities tend to be the nodes that connect national markets to international markets. Cities are therefore particularly important for the development of the knowledge economy and for the internationalisation of national economies. Thus, an assessment of Australia's ability to compete in the knowledge economy or to penetrate Asia-Pacific markets is incomplete without assessing the extent to which Australia's leading cities are up to that task. A report by the Australian Business Foundation, for example, concluded that cities are key drivers of innovation and that achieving innovation at a national level means innovating in cities where most people live, where there are the strongest global connections, and where most knowledge is concentrated.[87]

Australia's Cities

Australia has one of the world's highest urbanisation rates, on the order of 89 percent. Australia's major cities alone accounted for 69 percent of the nation's population in 2011.[88] Australian cities account for roughly 80 percent of Australia's economic activity, with Sydney, Melbourne, and Brisbane accounting for more than 50 percent.[89] It has been estimated that just five cities, Sydney, Melbourne, Brisbane, Perth, Adelaide, and Canberra, accounted for 58 percent of Australia's GDP growth from 1999–2000 to 2009–2010 and 67 percent of GDP growth from 2009–2010 to 2010–2011.[90] Australia's cities are clearly crucial to the nation's development. We would claim that Australia's distance to many world markets makes it even more important that Australia's cities are actively developed as connectors to the global economy than would be the case in most countries.

Assessments of Australia's Cities

In Chapter 2, we discussed Australia's city competiveness. Here we provide a somewhat more detailed analysis. As seen in Table 7.10, the top ranked Australian city in the Global Urban Competitiveness Index was Sydney, followed by Melbourne, Brisbane, Canberra, Hobart, and Adelaide. In addition to trailing the world leaders, Sydney (ranked 46th out of 500) also trailed Tokyo, Singapore, Seoul, Hong Kong, Shanghai, and Taipei among Asia-Pacific cities. In the Performance Indicators used in the study, Sydney, Melbourne, and Brisbane ranked relatively well in terms of GDP,

TABLE 7.10   Global Urban Competitiveness Index Rankings, 2009–2010

	Sydney	Melbourne	Brisbane	Canberra	Hobart	Adelaide
Global Urban Competitiveness Index (Out of 500 Cities)	46	91	136	229	238	243
Performance Indicators						
GDP	10	13	35	205	293	80
GDP per Capita	97	110	121	53	52	162
GDP per Sq Km	108	307	199	295	305	297
GDP Growth	414	283	352	338	281	430
Patent Applications	281	237	260	292	244	257
Multinational Enterprise	13	49	92	186	270	158
Explanatory Factors						
Enterprise Quality	14	35	102	258	304	138
Domestic Factors	65	44	186	340	256	148
Domestic Demand	106	170	217	244	159	160
Internal Structure	3	4	18	8	72	37
Public System	82	82	82	82	82	82
Global Linkages	20	72	73	215	307	175
Industrial Chains	9	53	96	220	320	183

Source: Peter Karl Kresl and Ni Pengfei, *Global Urban Competitive Report 2009–2010, Innovation: Sustainable Urban Competitiveness*, Chinese Academy of Social Sciences, 2010.

and Sydney ranked well in terms of Presence of Multinational Enterprises, but in the other measures, even Patent Applications, the Australian cities were well behind the leaders. In the Explanatory Factors used in the study, the Australian cities ranked among the world leaders in Internal Structure, a measure that includes inflation, multilingual capability, and political stability. Other than Sydney in Enterprise Quality, Global Linkages, and Industrial Chains, none of the Australian cities scored well in any of the other dimensions. Even in Public System, a measure based on ease of doing business, economic freedom, and government policy, and for which the same value is assigned for every city in a country, the Australian cities did not measure up to the world's best.

The Globalization and World Cities Study Group and Network at Loughborough University in the UK describes "world cities" as those that are best linked to the rest of the world, as indicated by the locations of headquarters of multinational companies, and the presence of offices of major multinational professional service firms. In 2010, Sydney ranked 10th in the Loughborough World City Index, with Melbourne 31st, Brisbane 87th, and Perth 105th.[91] This would indicate that only Sydney really has a position among the world's leading cities.

We note, however, that the presence of offices of major international companies and service providers does not necessarily mean that Sydney plays a leading role for such companies. In order to determine Sydney's global roles and its capabilities in the knowledge economy, Michael Enright, Richard Petty, and Suresh Cuganesan carried out a research project with the support of the Australian Business Foundation.[92] In this report, the researchers examined the role of Sydney in the strategies and organisations of major multinational companies, Sydney's position in the knowledge flows of these companies, and the ability of Sydney-based firms to enter into the supply chains of those companies.

Analysis of the importance of Sydney for multinational corporations is reported in Table 7.11. Sydney was most important for Sales, Customer Service, Marketing,

TABLE 7.11   The Importance of Sydney to the Parent Company as a Centre for the Performance of Various Activities (1 = Very Unimportant; 2 = Unimportant; 3 = Neutral; 4 = Important; 5 = Very Important)

Activity	Mean Response
Corporate Co-ordination	
Supporting Regional Operations (n = 82)	3.9
Co-ordination of Other Operations within Region (n = 82)	3.8
Reporting Regional Activities to Parent Company (n = 80)	3.7
Regional Liaison Centre for Parent Company (n = 81)	3.7
Monitoring of Other Regional Operations (n = 81)	3.3
Central Management Functions	
Competitor Intelligence (n = 83)	4.0
Regional Strategy Formulation (n = 83)	4.0
Business Process Development (n = 81)	3.5
Senior Personnel Management (n = 79)	3.5
Product/Service Development and Design (n = 80)	3.3
Regional Information Technology Management (n = 80)	3.2
Non–Raw Materials Procurement (n = 66)	2.5
Finance and Accounting	
Accounting/Auditing (n = 77)	3.3
Trade Finance (n = 73)	2.8
Insurance (n = 73)	2.6
Capital-Investment Finance (n = 72)	2.5
Sales, Marketing, and Customer Service	
Sales Planning and Execution (n = 79)	4.2
Customer Servicing and Support (n = 78)	4.2
Marketing Planning and Execution (n = 79)	4.1
Sales and Marketing Related Procurement (n = 76)	3.8
Market Research (n = 77)	3.6
Distributional Activities	
Order Processing (n = 59)	3.7
Warehousing Finished Goods (n = 50)	3.5
Trade Documentation (n = 58)	3.5
Land Distribution (n = 54)	3.5

Activity	Mean Response
Co-ordinating Regional Distribution (n = 58)	3.3
Air Distribution (n = 50)	3.2
Packaging (n = 50)	3.1
Sea Distribution (n = 46)	3.0
Co-ordinating Global Distribution (n = 54)	2.4
Production Activities	
Quality Control (n = 44)	3.2
Testing/Certification (n = 42)	3.0
Assembly/Processing (n = 40)	2.8
Manufacturing (n = 40)	2.5
Raw Materials Sourcing (n = 40)	2.4
Research and Development	
New Product Development (n = 60)	2.9
Basic Research (n = 58)	2.8
Applied Research (n = 57)	2.7
Process Technology Development (n = 54)	2.5

Source: Michael J. Enright, Richard Petty, and Suresh Cuganesan, *Global Connections: a Study of Multinational Companies in Sydney*, Australian Business Foundation, 2009.

Competitor Intelligence, and Regional Administrative roles. However, further study indicated that these were mostly for a "region" encompassing Australia and New Zealand. In most Production, Distribution, and Research and Development activities, the Sydney operations were just not important to the companies. Table 7.12 shows that Sydney operations were more *knowledge makers* than *knowledge takers*, but again subsequent analysis not reported here indicated that this knowledge was mostly used in Australia, relatively little was useful outside of the country. Finally, Table 7.13 shows that the foreign multinationals indicated that Sydney companies need significant improvement in essentially all of the capabilities investigated if they are to take part in the multinationals' global networks. These results, for Australia's leading business city, show that the global rankings, by focusing on presence of activities rather than the nature of activities carried out in Sydney, tend to overstate its importance. The conclusion is that Australia's cities are further behind the world leaders and Asia-Pacific regional leaders than the aggregate sources would suggest.

Issues for Australia's Cities

Australians recognise the importance of vibrant and dynamic cities to the nation's competitiveness. According to the 2010 *Our Cities* discussion paper, "The development and management of our cities affects national prosperity and the wellbeing of all Australians–no matter where they live." The document went on to quote a Council of Australian Governments (COAG) objective launched in December 2009, "to ensure Australian cities are globally competitive, productive, sustainable, liveable and socially

TABLE 7.12   Source of Knowledge Held by the Sydney Operation (1 = Strongly Disagree to 7 = Strongly Agree)

Category	Mean Response
Learned in Sydney in the Course of Day-to-Day Operations (n = 83)	5.3
Learned in Sydney by Working Together with Local Companies (n = 80)	4.1
Imported from Overseas Units of Your Corporation (n = 82)	4.0
Other Sources (Please Specify) (n = 12)	4.0
Learned in Sydney by Working with Other Multinational Companies (n = 80)	3.4
Learned from Companies Located Elsewhere in Asia-Pacific (n = 80)	2.9

Source: Michael J. Enright, Richard Petty, and Suresh Cuganesan, *Global Connections: a Study of Multinational Companies in Sydney*, Australian Business Foundation, 2009.

TABLE 7.13   The Extent of Improvement Required by Sydney-Based Companies in Order to Be Introduced to the Foreign Multinational Firm's International Business Network (1 = Not at all to 7 = Intense Improvement)

Category	Mean Response
Customer Service and Support	4.3
Strategic Thinking	4.2
Supplier Engagement	4.0
Marketing Activities	4.0
Cultural Sensitivity	3.9
Research and Development	3.8
Corporate Coordination Activities	3.8
Management Skill	3.8
General Attitude and Work Ethic	3.8
Output and Productivity Levels	3.7
Risk Management	3.6
Distributional Activities	3.6
Staff and Workplace Relations	3.5
Technology	3.5
Finance and Accounting Activities	3.3

Source: Michael J. Enright, Richard Petty, and Suresh Cuganesan, *Global Connections: a Study of Multinational Companies in Sydney*, Australian Business Foundation, 2009.

inclusive and are well placed to meet future challenges and growth."[93] However, there are a number of issues with respect to Australia's cities that will need to be addressed if they are to be engines of growth for the Australian economy they will need to be in the future.

Recognise the Importance of Cities: In recent years, Australia has recognised the importance of cities to competitiveness and has begun to put city development at the core of public policies. The first National Urban Policy was released in 2011. A Major Cities Unit has been set up within the Department of Infrastructure and Transport to focus on issues faced by the 18 cities in Australia with more than 100,000 in population. The COAG Reform Council has been asked to review strategic planning in Australia's major cities and to develop guidelines for development strategies. A Liveable Cities Program has been instituted to help raise the quality of living in Australia's major cities.

Invest in Urban Infrastructure: Cities connect local communities, other cities, and countries to the rest of the world. They are home of the concentrations of capabilities that often drives the innovation process. In order to carry out these roles, a nation's cities must have world-class infrastructure. Infrastructure Australia has stated, " . . . to maintain the economic success and environmental sustainability of Australia's cities, the time has come for an unprecedented commitment to the creation of world-class public transport in our cities."[94] As a result, Infrastructure Australia has recommended significant Australian Government investment in public transport in the nation's cities. While the National Broadband Network should improve the communications and IT connectivity of Australian cities, there is much work to be done to ensure that the local and international transportation connectivity of Australia's cities is enhanced. As of 2009, estimates were that congestion costs in Sydney were AUD 8 billion per year, while those in Melbourne were AUD 6 billion, and those in Brisbane AUD 3 billion.[95]

Urban Sprawl: Most major Australian cities suffer from urban sprawl. In fact, Australian cities are some of the worst exemplars of urban sprawl in the world. Instead of building vertically, Australia has historically built its cities horizontally. The result is sprawling cities, a preference for fringe development over infill development, increased reliance on automobiles, traffic congestion that reduces efficiency and quality of life, higher energy utilisation, fragmentation of demand for social and cultural services, an inability to create the critical mass associated with denser cities, and even in obesity due to time spent in automobiles. Government has recognised the problem and in its 2011 report indicated that there would be more reliance on infill development and that Australians would need to adjust expectations and lifestyles.[96] The 2011–2012 Commonwealth Budget included AUD 20 million to state, territory, and local governments for projects to improve affordability and liveability in Australia's cities.

Rethink CBDs: Australian cities have central business districts (CBDs) that allow them to provide services and support to their regional economies, but that do not have the scale and scope necessary to make them substantial international players. The high-end activities in leading world cities are generally found in compact, dense CBDs that bring together a depth and breadth of capabilities that allow the cities to have international reach. Australia's cities tend to have CBDs that are more spread out and therefore do not have the same concentration and critical mass as the CBDs in world leading cities.

Improve Planning: In an August 2011 communiqué, COAG indicated that, "Efficient and effective planning of our cities and towns is vital to productivity and investment. Governments at all levels have responsibility for approvals and it is important each jurisdiction administers its approvals processes well and in a co-ordinated manner with other levels of government."[97] The Business Council of Australia has stated, "The successful development of our cities will be facilitated by systematic, integrated, long-term strategic planning to address economic, social and environmental factors and provide for long-term infrastructure needs."[98] COAG's review of capital city planning systems released in 2012 indicated that none of the cities had planning systems consistent with all of COAG's guidelines, noting in particular insufficient attention paid to demographic change, housing affordability, and social inclusion. COAG further recommended that urban planning in Australia become far more strategic than has been the case.[99]

Governance and Collaboration: Urban policy and planning in Australia are for the most part functions of the cities and states. However, the importance of the Commonwealth Government in terms of funding means that all three levels of government are involved. This creates governance challenges and a strong need for co-operation across different levels of government. As is the case for many issues, when it comes to Australia's cities the involvement of several different levels of government complicates things because the policies that are developed often are inconsistent and poorly integrated, frequently being developed under pressure from groups with misaligned vested interests.[100] While improvements in collaboration have been made,[101] there is still a long way to go before the different levels of government operate in a seamless fashion.

Other Cities Are Better Situated to Take Advantage of the Rise of Asia: Australia has benefitted greatly from the economic rise of Asian nations, but its cities have not become hubs for Asia-Pacific development nearly as much as cities like Hong Kong, Singapore, Shanghai, and others. While this is natural, given the geography of the region, Australia's cities will need to integrate better into the region if they are to provide knowledge-intensive activities and services that could spur their own development.

Local Firms Need to Up Their Game: Australia has few major multinational companies outside the resources sector, and foreign multinationals operating in Australia indicate that local firms have to up their game almost across the board in order to be suitable to join the international networks of the foreign firms. This means that substantial improvements are needed at the company level if any Australian city is to become a more important contributor to the global economy and better at supporting the internationalisation of the Australian economy.

A Need to Work with Major Multinationals to Understand How to Get into MNC Networks: Australia and Australian states encourage foreign investment into the country. Investment promotion agencies have frequent contact with foreign multinationals. These contacts should be used to understand the skills and capabilities that are necessary to become part of the global networks of the foreign multinational companies (MNCs) already present in Australia and to attract higher value activities into Australian cities.

Policies and Programs

City development in Australia has been historically the responsibility of local and state governments and has received less attention at the national level. In recent years, this has changed substantially. The introduction of the National Urban Policy, the creation of a Major Cities Unit at the Department of Infrastructure and Transportation, and the focus of the Council of Australian Governments (COAG) on urban planning and urban development represent major changes and major steps forward.

The National Urban Policy is outlined in *Our Cities, Our Future*, which was released in May 2011.[102] The main focal points are enhancing productivity, advancing sustainability, enhancing the liveability of Australia's cities, and instituting better governance in the planning and management of cities. Productivity is to be improved by improving labour and capital productivity, integrating land use and infrastructure, and improving the efficiency of urban infrastructure. Sustainability is to be advanced by protecting the environment, reducing greenhouse gas emissions, managing resources, and increasing resilience to climate change and emergencies. Liveability is to be enhanced by facilitating the supply of mixed income housing, supporting affordable living, improving accessibility and reducing auto dependence, and supporting community well-being. Governance is to be improved by improving the planning and management of cities, streamlining administrative processes, and continuously evaluating progress.

The introduction of the National Urban Policy represents a landmark in terms of national policy attention for Australia's cities. We do note that much of the policy and related work appear to be reactions to major issues. There is a reaction to changing demographics, to issues of sustainability, to congestion, to housing issues, to challenges of urban governance, to past lack of investment, and to a past lack of detailed attention at the national level. All of these are certainly worth reacting to, but we would also like to see a more proactive approach to how Australia's cities can be engines of development and internationalisation for the Australian economy as a whole. While there has been work done on the nature of agglomeration and the productivity gains it can generate, and cities from other countries have been examined, there appears to have been little work done on how other cities leverage national capabilities into global markets and how cities rise in the hierarchy in the global city system. We would suggest that these are essential to understanding what Australia's cities could be and then helping them reach their potential. We also note that the initiative is housed in the Department of Infrastructure and Transport, when we might expect participation from the Department of Industry, Innovation, Science, Research, and Tertiary Education as well.

Australia's Cities in Perspective

Overall, Australia's cities do not compare favourably in terms of city level competitiveness under the analysis performed by the Chinese Academy of Social Sciences and to a lesser extent by the Globalization and World Cities Study Group and Network. Australia's cities tend to lag behind the world leaders and the leaders in the Asia-Pacific region. The Australian city that scores best in city competitiveness or world city measures, Sydney, turns out not to play as important a role in the international economy or in the strategies of multinational companies as some of the aggregate results would suggest. It essentially is a centre for managing Australia and New Zealand, and while it is able to generate sufficient knowledge locally to carry out that task, it is not for the most part able to generate knowledge sufficient to influence Asia-Pacific or global operations significantly. As others have noted, when it comes to the Asia-Pacific region, Australia could lose out in competitiveness as cities from other Asia-Pacific nations grow and develop, or could gain if Australian cities find ways of collaborating, tackling joint challenges, and providing growing Asian economies with knowledge-intensive services.[103]

The position of Australia's cities is due in part to the fact that Australia has a moderately sized economy, moderately sized population, and is distant from other countries. Cities tend to manage flows of goods, services, finance, and people. Large countries with widely dispersed small populations, particularly those far from large markets, tend to perform these functions at much lower scale than cities in larger countries with denser populations, or that are next to larger countries with whom they trade and interact on other dimensions. Australia does not have the scale or scope sufficient to support or generate a city like New York, London, Tokyo, or Shanghai. But it also appears to be due in part to internal issues of city structure, urban planning, infrastructure investment (or lack thereof), lack of high-level skills, and complex governance. While it is not possible to change the scale of Australia or its economy substantially in the medium term, it is possible to overcome some of the internal barriers that have prevented Australia's cities from reaching their full potential.

While Australian cities are modern cities that handle the service requirements of an advanced and growing economy, that is different from being able to get ahead of the curve internationally when it comes to the knowledge economy or in inter-nationalising Australian companies and Australia's economy. These require more advanced skill sets and more extensive international networks. The analysis reported in this chapter calls into question the ability of Australia's leading cities to play those important roles at this time. This does not mean that Australia's key cities cannot become more competitive. It is the case, however, that Australia is likely to rely more on innovation and on innovative ways for becoming more competitive at a city level than on scale; and that given moderate size and distance from large markets, Australia will have to be better than other countries at planning, managing, and connecting its cities, within the country and to the rest of the world, if its cities are to contribute as much as we might hope to national competitiveness.

The Knowledge Economy, Asia, and Cities in Perspective

The increasing importance of the knowledge-innovation economy, the rise of Asia-Pacific economies, and the emergence of cities as major sources of competitiveness provide distinct opportunities and challenges for Australia. The increasing importance of the knowledge-innovation economy allows a nation like Australia that is well-situated when it comes to knowledge resources to access information from around the world, develop new knowledge, and then leverage this knowledge into global markets. The rise of the Asia-Pacific economies and the shift in global economic weight towards the region means that Australia is not as disadvantaged as it has historically been by being geographically distant from major markets. The growing importance of cities as sources of competitiveness and as connectors between nations and the global economy gives Australia the chance to use its cities to help it connect to global markets, sources of information, capital providers, and other countries in the region. However, these opportunities will only be realised if Australia can learn from the world, generate commercially valuable knowledge, diversify the international portion of its economy, understand and penetrate new markets, and use its cities to maximum effect. Though Australia is well-positioned in many ways to take advantage of the trends outlined in this chapter, it is not a world-beater when it comes to the knowledge-innovation economy, it still has deficiencies in connectivity, it does not understand its regional neighbours enough to obtain the maximum benefit from new markets, and its cities generally lag behind the world's best. Thus, there is a great deal of work yet to be done, because as we will see in the next chapter, those that are not able to take full advantage of the global trends run the risk of falling behind.

Notes

1. Australian Bureau of Statistics, *Labour Force, Australia, Detailed, Quarterly*, March 2012.
2. International Labour Organization, *Labour Statistics Database*, May 2012. Including all persons employed in occupations, which are classified under Major Group 1 (legislators, senior officials, and managers) and Major Group 2 (professionals) by ISCO-88, International Labour Organization.
3. Australian Bureau of Statistics, *Labour Force, Australia, Detailed, Quarterly*, March 2012. Industries defined for the purpose of this chapter as being knowledge intensive include Information Media and Telecommunications; Financial and Insurance Services; Professional, Scientific, and Technical Services; Education and Training; Health Care and Social Assistance; and Arts and Recreation Services.
4. Australian Bureau of Statistics, *Employee Earnings and Hours, Australia*, May 2010.
5. Australian Bureau of Statistics, *International Trade in Goods and Services, Australia*, December 2011.
6. United Nations, *United Nations Service Trade Statistics Database*, May 2012.
7. OECD, *Main Science and Technology Indicators, OECD. StatExtracts*, January 2012.
8. World Intellectual Property Organization (WIPO), *WIPO Statistics Database*, December 2011. Number of patents granted by United States Patent and Trademark Office.
9. Business Council of Australia and Society for Knowledge Economics, *New Pathways to Prosperity: A National Innovation Framework for Australia*, November 2006.
10. Cutler & Company Pty Ltd, *Venturous Australia: Building Strength in Innovation*, September 2008.
11. Commonwealth of Australia, *Powering Ideas—An Innovation Agenda for the 21st Century*, 2009.
12. Australian Bureau of Statistics, *Summary of IT Use and Innovation in Australian Business, 2008–09*, June 2010.
13. Cutler & Company Pty Ltd, *Venturous Australia: Building Strength in Innovation*, September 2008.
14. Innovation Review Steering Group, *Innovation: New Thinking—New Directions*, Australian Industry Group, October 2010.
15. Business Council of Australia and Society for Knowledge Economics, *New Pathways to Prosperity*, November 2006.
16. Australian Bureau of Statistics, *Innovation in Australian Business, 2008–09*, August 2010.

17. Commonwealth of Australia, *Powering Ideas—An Innovation Agenda for the 21st Century*, 2009.

18. Innovation Review Steering Group, *Innovation: New Thinking—New Directions*, Australian Industry Group, October 2010.

19. Keith Smith and Jonathan West, *Australia's Innovation Challenges: The Key Policy Issues*, House of Representatives Standing Committee on Science and Innovation, April 2005.

20. Keith Smith and Jonathan West, *Australia's Innovation Challenges: The Key Policy Issues*, House of Representatives Standing Committee on Science and Innovation, April 2005.

21. Mark Dodgson and Peter Innes, *Australian Innovation in Manufacturing: Results from an International Survey*, Australian Business Foundation, July 2006.

22. Innovation Review Steering Group, *Innovation: New Thinking—New Directions*, Australian Industry Group, October 2010; Business Council of Australia and Society for Knowledge Economics, *New Pathways to Prosperity: A National Innovation Framework for Australia*, November 2006.

23. Australian Productivity Commission, *Public Support for Science and Innovation*, March 2007.

24. Roy Green, Renu Agarwal, John Van Reenen, Nicholas Bloom, John Mathews, Christina Boedker, Danny Sampson, Paul Gollan, Phillip Toner, Hao Tan, and Paul Brown, *Management Matters in Australia: Just How Productive Are We?*, Department of Industry, Innovation, Science and Research, Canberra, Australia, 2009.

25. Innovation Review Steering Group, *Innovation: New Thinking—New Directions*, Australian Industry Group, October 2010.

26. Business Council of Australia and Society for Knowledge Economics, *New Pathways to Prosperity*, November 2006.

27. Gary Banks, "Advancing Australia's 'Human Capital Agenda'" (The Fourth Ian Little Lecture, Melbourne, 13 April 2010).

28. Australian Business Foundation, *Submission to the Review of the National Innovation System*, April 2008.

29. Innovation Review Steering Group, *Innovation: New Thinking—New Directions*, Australian Industry Group, October 2010.

30. Business Council of Australia and Society for Knowledge Economics, *New Pathways to Prosperity*, November 2006.

31. Society for Knowledge Economics and Open Forum, *Innovation Attitudes in Australia*, 2008.

32. Asher Moses, "Children of the Revolution," *Sydney Morning Herald*, 21 May 2012.

33. Business Council of Australia and Society for Knowledge Economics, *New Pathways to Prosperity*, November 2006; Cutler & Company Pty Ltd, *Venturous Australia: Building Strength in Innovation*, September 2008; Keith Smith and Jonathan West, *Australia's Innovation Challenges: The Key Policy Issues*, House of Representatives Standing Committee on Science and Innovation, April 2005.

34. Commonwealth of Australia, *Powering Ideas—An Innovation Agenda for the 21st Century*, 2009.

35. Asher Moses, "Children of the Revolution," *Sydney Morning Herald*, 21 May 2012.

36. Cutler & Company Pty Ltd, *Venturous Australia: Building Strength in Innovation*, September 2008.

37. Innovation Review Steering Group, *Innovation: New Thinking—New Directions*, Australian Industry Group, October 2010.

38. Keith Smith and Jonathan West, *Australia's Innovation Challenges: The Key Policy Issues*, House of Representatives Standing Committee on Science and Innovation, April 2005.

39. Commonwealth of Australia, *Powering Ideas—An Innovation Agenda for the 21st Century*, 2009.

40. Asher Moses, "Children of the Revolution," *Sydney Morning Herald*, 21 May 2012.

41. Business Council of Australia and Society for Knowledge Economics, *New Pathways to Prosperity: A National Innovation Framework for Australia*, November 2006.

42. Innovation Review Steering Group, *Innovation: New Thinking—New Directions*, Australian Industry Group, October 2010.

43. Commonwealth of Australia, *Powering Ideas—An Innovation Agenda for the 21st Century*, 2009.

44. Business Council of Australia and Society for Knowledge Economics, *New Pathways to Prosperity*, November 2006.

45. Innovation Review Steering Group, *Innovation: New Thinking—New Directions*, Australian Industry Group, October 2010.

46. Roy Green, Renu Agarwal, John Van Reenen, Nicholas Bloom, John Mathews, Christina Boedker, Danny Sampson, Paul Gollan, Phillip Toner, Hao Tan, and Paul Brown, *Management Matters in Australia: Just How Productive Are We?*, Department of Industry, Innovation, Science and Research, Canberra, Australia, 2009.

47. Innovation Review Steering Group, *Innovation: New Thinking—New Directions*, Australian Industry Group, October 2010.

48. Cutler & Company Pty Ltd, *Venturous Australia: Building Strength in Innovation*, September 2008.

49. Commonwealth of Australia, *Powering Ideas—An Innovation Agenda for the 21st Century*, 2009.

50. Cutler & Company Pty Ltd, *Venturous Australia: Building Strength in Innovation*, September 2008.

51. Innovation Review Steering Group, *Innovation: New Thinking—New Directions*, Australian Industry Group, October 2010.

52. Society for Knowledge Economics and Open Forum, *Innovation Attitudes in Australia*, 2008.

53. Mark Dodgson and Peter Innes, *Australian Innovation in Manufacturing: Results from an International Survey*, Australian Business Foundation, July 2006.

54. Cutler & Company Pty Ltd, *Venturous Australia: Building Strength in Innovation*, September 2008.

55. Innovation Review Steering Group, *Innovation: New Thinking—New Directions*, Australian Industry Group, October 2010.

56. Commonwealth of Australia, *Australia in the Asian Century*, 2012.

57. These projections are at market exchange rates, not purchasing power parity exchange rates.

58. In some cases, we believe analysts use PPP exchange rates to hype the rise of Asian economies to an unreasonable extent, often in the context of claiming a relative decline of Western economies. We think the rise of Asian economies is extremely important and does not need any hype.

59. Australian Department of Foreign Affairs and Trade, *Confidentiality in Australian Merchandise Export Statistics*, 2011.

60. Australian Department of Foreign Affairs and Trade.

61. Australian Department of Foreign Affairs and Trade, *Trade in Services Australia, 2010–2011*, 2011. Note that Australia keeps some statistics on a calendar year basis, some on a fiscal year basis, and some on both.

62. Note that the figures for Hong Kong for both outbound and inbound investment include some investments that relate to the Chinese Mainland, but are funnelled through Hong Kong.

63. Australian Industry Group and Asialink, *Engaging Asia: Getting It Right for Australian Business: Australian Industry Group & Asialink Survey*, March 2011.

64. Rowan Callick, "Knowledge of Asia Sadly Lacking on Boards," *The Australian*, 8 December 2011.

65. Australian Industry Group and Asialink, *Engaging Asia: Getting It Right for Australian Business: Australian Industry Group & Asialink Survey*, March 2011.

66. Kathe Kirby, "Learning to Live in the Asian Century," *The Conversation*, 13 October 2011.

67. Australian Industry Group and Asialink, *Engaging Asia: Getting It Right for Australian Business: Australian Industry Group & Asialink Survey*, March 2011.

68. The Hon. Stephen Smith, Australian Minister for Foreign Affairs and Trade, *Australia and the Asia-Pacific Century*, paper presented to the South Australian Branch of the Australian Institute of International Affairs, 12 April 2010.

69. Australia-China Council, *Australia-China Council's Submission to the Australia in the Asian Century White Paper*, 24 February 2012.

70. Lowy Institute for International Policy, *The 2012 Lowy Poll: Opposition to Chinese Investment*, 2012.

71. The Hon. Dr. Craig Emerson, *Radio Interview*, ABC Radio Australia, 8 June 2012.

72. Australian Industry Group and Asialink, *Engaging Asia: Getting It Right for Australian Business: Australian Industry Group & Asialink Survey*, March 2011.

73. Australia-China Council, *Australia-China Council's Submission to the Australia in the Asian Century White Paper*, 24 February 2012.

74. AFG Venture Group, *Asian Perceptions 2011*.

75. AFG Venture Group, *Asian Perceptions 2011*.

76. Australian Industry Group and Asialink, *Engaging Asia: Getting It Right for Australian Business: Australian Industry Group & Asialink Survey*, March 2011.

77. CPA Australia, *Submission to the Australia in the Asian Century Taskforce*, March 2012.

78. The Hon. Stephen Smith, Australian Minister for Foreign Affairs and Trade "Australia and the Asia-Pacific Century" (Speech for the Griffith Asia Institute, Brisbane, 14 August 2009).

79. Australian Industry Group and Asialink, *Engaging Asia: Getting It Right for Australian Business: Australian Industry Group & Asialink Survey*, March 2011.

80. Geoff Raby, and Geoff Raby & Associates, *Submission to the White Paper on Australia in the "Asian Century,"* March 2012.

81. Australia-China Council, *Australia-China Council's Submission to the Australia in the Asian Century White Paper*, 24 February 2012.

82. CPA Australia, *Submission to the Australia in the Asian Century Taskforce*, March 2012.

83. Australian Industry Group, *Australian Industry Group Submission to Australia in the Asian Century*, March 2012.

84. The Hon. Stephen Smith, Australian Minister for Foreign Affairs and Trade "Australia and the Asia-Pacific Century" (Speech for the Griffith Asia Institute, Brisbane, 14 August 2009).

85. Commonwealth of Australia, *Australia in the Asian Century*, 2012.

86. Commonwealth of Australia, *Australia in the Asian Century*, 2012.

87. Anand Kulkarni, George Bougias, and Tim Black, *Building Australia's Future Cities*, Australian Business Foundation, May 2012.

88. Australian Bureau of Statistics, *Regional Population Growth, Australia, 2010—11*, 2011.

89. Australian Department of Infrastructure and Transport, *State of Australian Cities 2011*, 2011.

90. SGS Economics and Planning, *Australian Cities Accounts*, December 2011.

91. Globalization and World Cities (GaWC) Research Network, *The World According to GaWC 2010*.

92. Michael J. Enright, Richard Petty, and Suresh Cuganesan, *Global Connections: A Study of Multinational Companies in Sydney*, Australian Business Foundation, 2009.

93. Australian Department of Infrastructure and Transport, *Our Cities*, 2010, p.3.

94. *Infrastructure Australia—Cities*, October 2012

95. "Challenges Facing Australia's Cities," *The Australian*, 3 September 2009.

96. Australian Department of Infrastructure and Transport, *Our Cities, Our Future—A National Urban Policy for A Productive, Sustainable and Liveable Future*, May 2011.

97. Council of Australian Governments, *Communiqué*, 19 August 2011.

98. Business Council of Australia, *Submission to the Department of Infrastructure and Transport on National Urban Policy*, March 2011.

99. Council of Australian Governments, *Review of Capital City Strategic Planning Systems*, April 2012.

100. Anand Kulkarni, George Bougias, and Tim Black, *Building Australia's Future Cities*, Australian Business Foundation, May 2012.

101. Council of Australian Governments, *Review of Capital City Strategic Planning Systems*, April 2012.

102. Australian Department of Infrastructure and Transport, *Our Cities, Our Future—A National Urban Policy for A Productive, Sustainable and Liveable Future*, May 2011.

103. Anand Kulkarni, George Bougias, and Tim Black, *Building Australia's Future Cities*, Australian Business Foundation, May 2012.

CHAPTER 8

Scenarios for Australia's Economic and Business Future

Australia's economic and business future is not pre-ordained. It will be determined by a complex interaction of supranational (meta-level), national (macro-level), cluster (meso-level), industrial (micro-level), and firm-level drivers and forces. The number of drivers and the complexity of their interaction make predicting Australia's business and economic future difficult. Instead of trying to predict a single future for Australia, we will map out several potential futures, or scenarios, some positive and some negative, and then try to determine what will be necessary to maximise the likelihood that Australia will experience the positive futures and to minimise the likelihood that Australia will experience the negative futures. This, in turn, will provide insights into the drivers that Australia needs to improve and the ones it needs to leverage in order to improve overall competitiveness.

Key Trends

Scenarios are built around uncertainties and different potential outcomes to these uncertainties. However, the number of uncertainties needs to be manageable; we cannot assume that everything is uncertain or unpredictable. So first we will focus on trends that we believe can be identified and projections that can reasonably be made in terms of the international context within which Australia will be operating in the future.

Global Trends

One set of trends that we will take as given is the set of global trends that we identified in Chapter 1 involving the Global Financial Crisis and its aftermath, the rise of Asia-Pacific economies, the further development of modern information and communication technology, the rise of the knowledge-innovation economy, and the globalisation of companies and the flat world.

THE GLOBAL FINANCIAL CRISIS AND ITS AFTERMATH   Here we project that the global economy will take an extended period of time to recover from the Global Financial Crisis and its aftermath, that Europe will take time to get its house in order, that the

United States and many other countries will have to bring their debt levels under control, that financial sector deleveraging will be required and will take time, and that a new, more conservative system of public and private finance eventually comes into being. In this world, growth in aggregate demand in advanced economies remains slower than in the years preceding the crisis, resulting in slower trade growth, and tougher international competition. This has a ripple effect in developing countries, which will face smaller international markets than they had hoped, and tougher international financial markets than they might have anticipated. In such a world, improved competitiveness and productivity at home and internationally are vital in order to do more with less, compete in more difficult markets, and deal with a changed financial landscape.

THE RISE OF ASIA-PACIFIC ECONOMIES   We project that the Asia-Pacific economies will continue to grow in importance, both in absolute terms and relative terms. The path will not always be easy, but the combination of the region's population, policies that have created market-oriented economies, globalisation that has provided markets as well as technology and finance, improvements in infrastructure and education, the growth of local consumption and the development of domestic markets, and increasing links between economies within the region will allow the region's economies to continue to grow faster than the world average. One result will be a continuation of the shift in global economic weight from West to East. Another will be a quasi-decoupling in which the Asia-Pacific economies are still linked to and affected by events in the West, but where the growth dynamics of individual economies in the region will depend more on domestic forces and developments in other economies in the Asia-Pacific region than on developments elsewhere in the world.

THE DEVELOPMENT OF INFORMATION AND COMMUNICATION TECHNOLOGY   Here we project a continuation of trends toward ubiquitous use of modern information and communication technology, including the continued miniaturisation of electronic components, rapid increases in information transmission speeds, further development of the Cloud, on-everywhere use of smart phones and other portable communication devices, the continued spread of modern technologies through developing Asia, and increased connectivity almost across the board. Results of these trends would include increased interpersonal communication, increases in importance of social media, new channels for marketing and sales, new potential in terms of corporate management and information systems, and an increasing ability to operate remotely from customers, suppliers, colleagues, and partners. While we do not project that distance will die in this future, its importance in many dimensions will diminish, at least for those that can leverage the technologies for maximum effect.

THE RISE OF THE KNOWLEDGE-INNOVATION ECONOMY   We project that there will be a further spread of basic industrial capabilities and infrastructure in Asia, Latin America, and Africa. In addition, improved transportation and communication will mean that productive resources will be mobilised in more places than ever before. Resource constraints will force countries and companies to innovate to increase the value that can be added to resources. Countries and companies from around the world will try to imitate the most successful countries and companies, which will be the leaders in the knowledge-innovation economy. As a result, there will be even more pressure for advanced economies, and incentive for leading developing economies, to earn their living by creating and leveraging commercially valuable knowledge. Increasingly, the global leaders will do this by *learning from the world*,[1] not restricting themselves to inputs and information from their home countries, but rather seeking out, absorbing, and incorporating cutting edge knowledge wherever it might be found.

THE GLOBALISATION OF COMPANIES AND THE FLAT WORLD   The trends identified previously will provide companies with greater and greater opportunities to slice up their activities into finer and finer pieces and place each in its optimal location. This, in turn, will bring more and more nations, companies, and employees into direct competition with each other. The result will be a flattening[2] of the world in the sense that people of a given skill level in many cases will find their potential earnings capped by competition from others of similar skill levels elsewhere. While this may be a bleak prospect for many in the developed world, it should be a strong positive for many people in the developing world. In addition, as we have earlier stated, such an environment allows the individuals, companies, regions, and nations that can generate valuable ideas and knowledge to source and leverage productive resources on a competitive basis all over the world. The result is that those that cannot generate valuable ideas and knowledge will have limited potential, while those that can generate valuable ideas and knowledge and can source and leverage productive resources anywhere in the world will have almost unlimited potential.

Trends in Competitiveness

There are also a number of trends in drivers of competitiveness that we should note. In particular, we project that there will be an evolution in terms of the types of drivers that are important to overall competitiveness in the future. In broad terms, we can divide drivers of competitiveness into what we might call *traditional* or *basic* drivers, *advanced* drivers, and *new age* drivers. Traditional or *basic* drivers involve the basic conditions that allow a nation to enter into the global economy and compete, at least on a limited basis. These drivers have long been a focus of policymakers, analysts, and companies interested in improving competitiveness. They are the drivers at the core of the competitiveness of developing countries and are likely to stay so in the future. *Advanced* drivers are those that allow a limited number of nations to compete at a higher level in the global economy, including those involving innovation, advanced knowledge creation, and the ability to establish and manage complex global organisations. These are currently the focus of programs and policies in most developed economies. *New age* drivers are those we see emerging due to more recent evolution in the global economy. They include quality of life, sustainability, resource constraints, and related social issues, drivers that are expected to become more important in the future, but we still do not know how or to what extent.

How the future plays out in terms of the relative importance of these different types of drivers, and Australia's position in different types of drivers, will be crucial to the nation's competitiveness going forward.

Traditional or Basic Competitiveness Drivers

There are a number of drivers of competitiveness that have long been a focus of analysts and policy makers. These include the nation's factors of production, including land, labour, geographic location, resource endowments, capital, and access to suitable infrastructure within the country and between the country and the rest of the world. They also include the basic institutional structures that allow companies to operate and economic activity to be undertaken smoothly. These include rule of law, appropriate legal and regulatory frameworks, coherent economic policies, transparency and fairness in decision making, and related features.

At the national level, Australia does very well in several of these drivers. It has a large land mass, high quality labour force, extensive resource deposits, and reasonably good infrastructure. It gets high marks globally for its legal and institutional system, quality of economic policy, lack of corruption, transparency, and the basic business environment for companies. Australia also gets very high marks in areas involving openness, business flexibility, and ease of creating companies. Strengths in these areas now appear woven into the fabric of Australia's economy, and we should expect that they will be ongoing sources of advantage, at least until such time as other nations make the changes necessary to catch up. These drivers by themselves separate Australia from most of the world's economies.

On the other side of the spectrum, Australia's population is small, it is located far from many major markets and information sources, its infrastructure does not rank with the world's best, and some features of its policy regime, particularly with regard to tax and regulation, also lag behind those of several other economies. Thus, while Australia's position in traditional or basic drivers separates it from most of the world's economies, it does not guarantee Australia a leading position.

Advanced Competitiveness Drivers

Advanced competitiveness drivers are those that directly influence a nation's ability to compete in today's knowledge-innovation economy on a global basis. These include the nation's innovation system (especially the ability of the nation's individuals, organisations, and companies to create and leverage commercially valuable knowledge), highly educated knowledge workers, the sophistication and capabilities of its companies, the density of its supply chains, its level of integration with the global economy, the presence of advanced communication and transportation infrastructure, business competition that stimulates improvement, strong links between research organisations and businesses, a culture that promotes innovation and entrepreneurship, and an incentive structure that makes the country attractive for talented individuals and dynamic companies.

Again, Australia has a strong position in several of these drivers. Australia tends to rank highly in terms of education, the quality of business professionals, in having active competition, and in some features of the knowledge economy, but its innovation system does not measure up to the world's best, its business sophistication lags several economies in its own region, entrepreneurship is not on par with the global leaders, it is not as integrated with the global economy as many other nations, and its supply chains are not well developed. In addition, given its location, size of market, limited capital base, and the incentive structures faced by individuals and companies, Australia faces a greater danger that talented individuals and dynamic companies will leave. Thus, in terms of advanced competitiveness drivers, Australia has a good position, but not as good a position as the leaders globally and within the Asia-Pacific region.

New Age Competitiveness Drivers

There are a number of what we might call *new age* competitiveness drivers that increasingly come into play when we examine advanced economies in today's competitive environment. These drivers reflect new opportunities or concerns that are becoming more prominent in discussions about national and regional economies. These include the sustainability of an economy's industries and companies, resource constraints or self-sufficiency of an economy, the environment, the quality of living for mobile professionals, the presence or absence of world-class cities, and the presence or absence of innovative clusters of firms and industries.

Sustainability, resource constraints, and the environment figure prominently in today's economic debates, and nations are increasingly looking to sustainable solutions to development issues. Quality of living is becoming a key competitiveness driver in industries that are powered by mobile professionals that can pick and choose where to live. The presence of world-class cities is crucial because cities are sources of innovation, provide connectivity nationally and globally, and are centres of culture, arts, and other features that add to quality of living. The development of regional clusters of firms and industries has become a focal point for economic development programs all over the world. The interaction among firms and individuals found in regional clusters is becoming increasingly important to competing in the knowledge-innovation economy.

Australia does very well in several of these *new age* drivers of competitiveness. Australia is a leader in terms of its focus on sustainability, has resource endowments and land resources that make it far more self-sufficient than most nations, has a large land mass for its population, and has a high level of environmental consciousness. Australia is a world leader in terms of quality of living, making it an attractive location for mobile individuals. Australia has attractive cities, with high quality of living, but does not have leading cities that can be leveraged for advantage within the Asia-Pacific region or globally. Australia also does not have the depth and breadth of vibrant clusters of companies and industries that we find in many other countries, particularly advanced European nations.

The Future of Competitiveness

We project that more and more countries will create or obtain the basic conditions that allow them to enter the global economy in meaningful ways (i.e., as viable locations for business activities for international markets for at least some significant industries). We also project that most of today's developing countries will continue to compete on the basis of the traditional or basic drivers, using labour costs, resource endowments, and framework conditions of moderate quality to gain a position in international markets. However, we project that certain Asian developing countries, particularly China and India, but perhaps Malaysia and other Southeast Asian countries as well, will compete at two tiers, on basic drivers of competitiveness in some industries and activities, and more advanced drivers in other industries and activities.

With respect to advanced drivers of competitiveness, we project that these will become even more important to the economic success of advanced economies going forward. The main reasons will be a combination of advances in the developing countries just described and greater competition among nations to create advantages in advanced drivers through investments in education, research and development, branding, and efforts to bring companies and other organisations together through cluster development initiatives. The sophistication of firms will also become more important as firms from some nations develop the capabilities to leverage global sources of information and productive resources to enter international markets and firms from other nations do not.

Finally, while we project that *new age* drivers will become more important, we do not believe that they will be decisive in more than a handful of industries for the foreseeable future. In other words, these drivers will contribute more to competitiveness in the future than in the past, but advantages in these drivers are not likely to be sufficient to overcome disadvantages in basic and advanced drivers any time soon.

Understanding Australia's Future Competitiveness

So where does this analysis leave us in terms of understanding or projecting Australia's future competitiveness? Understanding global economic trends gives us a better picture of the world in which Australia, Australian companies, and individuals will operate. Understanding trends in competitiveness gives us a better picture of the sources of advantage and disadvantage that are likely to be most important in the future.

Understanding the global trends and trends in competitiveness also allows us to frame the ways in which Australia's competitiveness can be improved. If the relative importance of the different drivers of competitiveness remains the same, then one way for Australia to improve its competitiveness, overall and in individual industries, is to invest to improve its position versus relevant competitors in the important drivers. This could involve drivers in which Australia already has advantages, drivers in which it has disadvantages, or both. The crucial aspect is that efforts to improve should be directed at the drivers that are shown to be important for significant portions of Australia's economy.

Another way to improve Australia's overall competitiveness and productivity would be to evolve the economy (or allow the economy to evolve) towards industries in which Australia has advantages and away from industries in which Australia has disadvantages. This tends to happen naturally over time in market-oriented economies as higher returns attract capital and individuals into more competitive industries and lower returns cause capital and individuals to move on. This is more or less the approach that the Australian Treasury and Productivity Commission have been urging, one that allows market forces to push the economy to adjust to maximise its output by causing resources to be allocated to the most productive uses. Of course, this can create substantial adjustment costs for individual companies and people employed in industries that become less competitive over time. It can also be politically difficult since the industries of the past often have a political constituency, while the industries of the future often do not.

Another way in which Australia's competitiveness could improve is for industries and the global economy to evolve in ways that make Australia's strong points more important and its weak points less important. If, for example, *new age* drivers in which

Australia has advantages become more important, either in individual industries or in aggregate, then Australia's competitiveness and competitive position are likely to improve. While it might be beyond the capability of the Australian Government or Australian companies to influence the evolution of industries and the global economy in most industries, it might be possible in some, and it is within the capability of the Australian Government and companies to try to anticipate which drivers of competitiveness will be more important in the future and to make investments that build up Australia's position in these drivers.

Some Specific Scenarios for Australia's Economic and Business Future

Combining an understanding of global trends, trends in competitiveness, and Australia's current position when it comes to drivers of competitiveness allows us to generate several scenarios for Australia's future. Here we focus on four pairs of scenarios, focusing on Australia's development in the context of (1) the resource boom and Australia's resource position, (2) how Australia fits into the globalised, "flat" world economy in which knowledge and innovation are key to prosperity, (3) how Australia deals with the rise of the economies of the Asia-Pacific region, and (4) Australia's position with respect to *new age* competitiveness drivers. While each pair of scenarios are opposites, or are mutually exclusive, there is potential overlap across the pairs, with similar factors contributing to the positive scenarios across the different uncertainties and similar factors contributing to the negative scenarios across the different uncertainties.

The Resource Boom and Australia's Future

The first two scenarios take different views on how Australia's resource boom will influence its overall competitiveness and economic development.

FROM LUCKY COUNTRY TO COMPETITIVE COUNTRY   A positive scenario for the future of Australia as a resource-rich country is a scenario in which resource wealth gets reinvested into building a broader, competitive economy. In this scenario, the wealth generated from improving terms of trade and burgeoning markets for resources, particularly in developing Asia, is reinvested in ways that build upon some world-leading fundamentals, a strong education system, a relatively advanced innovation system, and a strong financial system. Investments are also made to improve infrastructure to levels on par with the world's leading nations, to develop stronger management systems, to foster business networks, and to facilitate the development of clusters of innovative companies.

In this scenario, resource companies form a vanguard and a bridgehead that allow the formation of international relationships that other Australian companies then leverage to internationalise and leverage Australian capabilities to wider markets. At the same time, significant portions of the resource revenues eventually get recycled into the capital markets, creating a deeper pool of angel investment, venture investment, and equity capital than has been the case to date. This in turn allows for increased opportunities for Australian start-up companies and entrepreneurs to obtain the capital they require without having to go offshore in order to get it.

We note that this scenario postulates a situation in which a substantial portion of the gains from the resource boom get recycled into the Australian economy through increased tax payments (either directly from the resource sector, or from the personal and corporate incomes that arise from the expansion of the resource sector) that get recycled through government investments, through returns to Australian-based shareholders that can then reinvest within the country, and through the resource companies themselves reinvesting in Australia.

In this scenario, the rewards to entrepreneurship in Australia and Australia's potential to build businesses both increase. At the same time, the wealth generated allows a shifting of the tax burden away from other forms of economic activity, which when combined with improved quality of living in Australia attracts larger numbers of capable individuals and reduces the incentives for talented Australians to emigrate. In this scenario, Australia builds a more diversified economy that is able to support a highly valued currency and high wages due to the investments made across the economy. Eventually, these investments allow Australian companies to penetrate growing Asian markets in a wide range of industries and make the Australian economy more resilient to commodity booms and busts.

ONE-LEGGED STOOL   A negative scenario for the future of Australia as a resource-rich country is one in which resource wealth is enough to drive up the Australian dollar, make other forms of economic activity uncompetitive, reduce incentives to develop other economic engines, and fund just enough of a social safety net so that enough people feel satisfied that more active development does not take place. In this scenario, Australia's resource wealth bids up the wages in low-skilled occupations, at least on a temporary basis, skewing incentives towards short-term paydays and away from more schooling and joining more knowledge-intensive industries.

In this scenario, the knowledge-intensive service sectors, such as the accounting and legal sectors, account for, distribute, and argue over existing wealth rather than working to create new sources of wealth. The proceeds from the resource boom in this scenario either go to shareholders outside of Australia, go toward short-term consumption, are reinvested in new projects outside of Australia, or go into bidding up real estate and other asset prices within Australia rather than being reinvested in ways that build new advantages, overcome bottlenecks, or enhance capabilities within Australia. This could happen either because there is no mechanism to obtain and redeploy some of the proceeds for the public good, or because companies and individuals choose not to do so.

As indicated, in this scenario investment in Australia might occur, but it is largely in the real estate sector or in existing resource businesses, pushing up the price of existing assets rather than creating new assets. Political battles ensue over how the wealth is to be divided, rather than over how it can be increased, expanded, and invested. The result is more rent seeking and less productive investment. Meanwhile, efforts to ensure equal outcomes create a tax system that drives many who do not have resource or real estate wealth to emigrate to seek opportunities in emerging Asian markets.

While the resource boom fuels growth in incomes, in this scenario it does not result in the sort of investment that builds a more diversified and innovative economy. The result is that the international portion of Australia's economy, with the exception of the resources sector, narrows significantly. In this scenario, domestically oriented

Australian companies are able to make reasonable livings at home, at least for a while, but face additional disadvantages in trying to go abroad, and see no reason to try to build the capabilities to internationalise. In this scenario, any resource bust or negative movement in commodity prices immediately translates into changes in domestic asset prices and substantial dislocation within the country. However, as the country has not improved its infrastructure, sharpened its skills, and built its international competitiveness in other sectors, the only thing that can be done is to wait for the next resource boom.

Australia's Future in the Flat World

The next two scenarios focus on how Australia fits into the globalised, flat world economy in which knowledge and innovation are key to prosperity.

AUSTRALIA AS FLATTENOR IN THE FLAT WORLD   A positive scenario for Australia in the globalised, flat world is for Australia to be what we call a *flattenor*. In this case, Australian companies and individuals generate ideas and knowledge that are commercially valuable and then leverage them into international markets. This would involve Australian companies understanding the needs of customers in global markets, developing the right products and services to meet these needs, and building the ability to market and sell remotely into key countries. This could result in substantial increases in exports of knowledge-intensive products and services as well as increased productivity in the domestic economy.

This in turn would involve Australian companies harnessing productive resources in Asia and elsewhere, using modern ICT to overcome the diseconomies of distance, and developing corporate systems and processes to manage complex international systems. It would require that Australia extend its advantages in some basic competitiveness drivers and overcome disadvantages in others, particularly involving infrastructure. It would involve Australia and Australian companies parlaying an advanced education system, sizable number of knowledge workers, and a favourable institutional environment into a more dynamic innovation system with close links between research organisations and companies, market-driven product and service development, and interaction among clusters of firms and industries.

In this scenario, because Australian entities are developing the knowledge and intellectual property that drives the economy, Australia controls its economic destiny, at least to the extent possible given the interdependence of economies around the world. The key is that in this scenario it is Australian entities that make the decisions about where to carry out different corporate activities, what to leave in Australia and what to place elsewhere, and it is Australian entities that reap the benefits and profits that are produced by the entire productive system that they put together and orchestrate. This puts Australia in an enviable position of being able to react to changes in the world economy from a position of strength.

AUSTRALIA AS FLATTENEE IN THE FLAT WORLD   The opposite scenario is one in which Australia is a *flattenee* in the globalised, flat world. In this scenario, Australia is unable to become an idea maker or knowledge maker, so is relegated to be an idea taker or knowledge taker. This could be due to an inability to understand global markets, a lack of the ability to generate commercially valuable knowledge, the failure to generate a sufficiently dynamic innovation system, or a lack of ability to leverage what advantages Australia has into global markets.

There could be many reasons for these failures or shortcomings. It could be that distance still matters and Australia is too far away to be plugged into global markets and sources of information and innovation, or that Australia does not overcome its infrastructure challenges to become better connected domestically and internationally. It could be that Australia does not develop the innovation system necessary to compete with the world's best due to a lack of connection between research organisations and companies, a mismatch between what the education system produces and the needs of companies, the absence of dynamic interaction among clusters of firms, or incentive structures that work against innovation and entrepreneurship.

In this scenario, the flat world still exists, but it is foreign companies that take advantage, commercially valuable knowledge is generated elsewhere, and easier communication and transportation allow this knowledge to be leveraged into Australia by foreign firms rather than the other way around. In this scenario, Australia's cities are not competitive enough to be generators of knowledge, but are sufficient to be conduits for foreign companies selling products and services into Australia. In this scenario, because the valuable ideas and knowledge are generated abroad, it is foreign entities that decide which business activities are located in Australia in many industries, and they are extremely careful in identifying the advantages and disadvantages of individual locations. In this scenario, Australia and Australian firms are on the periphery of globalisation, rather than at its core. Because it is foreign entities that generate the ideas and manage the systems, many key decisions that affect Australia's economic well-being are made outside the country, leaving Australia's economic destiny, at least in part, in the hands of others.

Australia's Future in the Asia-Pacific Region

The next two scenarios focus on how Australia deals with the rise of the economies of the Asia-Pacific region, in particular Australia's ability to benefit from the rise of the region and its ability to compete in knowledge and innovation-intensive industries and activity in the Asia-Pacific region.

RIDING TIGERS, DRAGONS, AND ELEPHANTS   A positive scenario with respect to Australia's interaction with the economies of the Asia-Pacific region is one in which Australia "rides tigers, dragons, and elephants."[3] In this scenario, resource demand from China, India, Japan, Korea, and ASEAN nations continues to grow, supporting substantial new investment in Australia, increasing volumes of resource exports, and relatively high resource prices. As these economies become more affluent, they become even more important markets for Australia's tourism and education industries, which grow dramatically based on Asian demand. At the same time, Australia uses the fact that it is a more advanced economy than most of those in the region, and that it is more closely linked to the region than North American or European economies, to sell an increasing range of knowledge-intensive products and services into Asian economies.

In this scenario, Australia and Australian companies are able to extend and utilise their knowledge advantages by leveraging free trade agreements with the region; through a better understanding of the markets and business practices of the region; through the development of extensive marketing, sales, and distribution systems in the region; and through national and company strategies that make penetrating Asian markets high priorities. Australia overcomes the issues of distance to some Asian markets by improving connectivity through ICT and better air and sea connections made possible by world-class infrastructure. Asian immigration and investment create closer economic ties with Australia, which are mirrored by deeper diplomatic relations. An Australian brand develops in the region whereby Australia is associated with high quality, strong capabilities, high standards of professionalism, an attractive environment, and excellent business practices.

In this scenario, Australian resource companies are able to outcompete resource companies operating in other countries due to proximity and advantages in transportation costs. Australian companies are able to outcompete Asian competitors in a variety of other industries by leveraging knowledge capabilities, an advanced innovation system, and better management and business practices than Asian competitors. At the same time, Australian companies are able to outcompete North American and European competitors in Asia due to proximity in terms of time zone, better information flows, and greater understanding of Asia-Pacific economies based on the fact that the Australian companies and Australia in general focus much more of their attention on the Asia-Pacific region than companies and governments from outside the region. This combination allows Australia to ride the tigers, dragons, and elephants better than economies from outside the region.

EATEN BY TIGERS, BURNED BY DRAGONS, TRAMPLED BY ELEPHANTS   A negative scenario for Australia when it comes to its interaction with rising Asia-Pacific economies is one in which it is "eaten by tigers, burned by dragons, trampled by elephants." In this scenario, Asian demand for resources moderates, or Asian countries are able to find or develop alternative sources of supply that allow them to bargain down the prices paid for Australian resources. As Asian economies become more affluent, they also become better at providing educational services and tourism amenities that make them tougher competitors for the Australian industries. At the same time, Asian economies become more competitive, and some are already considered more competitive than Australia, reducing the potential for Australian business, while North American and European firms also turn their attention to the region and outcompete Australia in knowledge-intensive products and services.

In this scenario, Asian economies catch up to Australia in knowledge-generating capability, take advantage of their proximity to Asian customers, and use the fact that several are already considered more competitive than Australia to sell into Asian markets. In this scenario, Australia and Australian companies do not overcome infrastructure disadvantages, do not leverage ICT to the extent necessary to overcome distance, do not develop the innovation system sufficiently to outcompete others, do not invest sufficiently to understand the region well enough to become major suppliers, and do not develop the capabilities to leverage productive resources around the region. In this scenario, Australia stays aloof from the region, politically and economically, and closes itself off from Asian investment and immigration. The Australian brand is reasonably well regarded, but not considered something special.

In this scenario, Australia falls behind several Asian economies in terms of competitiveness, and further behind those that are already ahead. As capabilities in the region increase, there is less and less that Australia is viewed as being able to offer.

In this case, intra-Asia-Pacific trade and investment continues to grow, but Australia is peripheral to this growth. As the other economies in the region become stronger, their companies emerge to compete in third markets as well as in Australia itself. Reinforced by investments that have enhanced the competitiveness in their home economies, these new competitors begin to outcompete Australian entities on their home turf. The tax and incentive systems in Asian economies start to exert a strong pull. In this context, Asia continues to represent opportunities, opportunities for talented Australians and dynamic Australian companies to relocate from Australia to Asia. The net result is that Australia is bypassed by developments in Asia.

Australia and the World

The final two scenarios refer to uncertainties with respect toward trends in the global economy as well as Australia's position with respect to *new age* competitiveness drivers.

THE WORLD TURNS TOWARD AUSTRALIA   With respect to Australia's interaction with the rest of the world, a positive scenario ("The World Turns to Australia" Scenario) starts with the positive features associated with the basic business and political environment in Australia. Then it layers in the fact that Australians are well-educated and the country has a reasonably strong academic base in the sciences and the professions. The advent of modern information and communication technology then makes it much easier for Australian companies with good ideas to access productive resources and markets all over the world. Australian companies, just like companies from other nations, find they can produce in China, do backroom operations in India, have call centres in the Philippines, and so on. The fact that Australia is in some ways better linked to these economies makes it easier for Australian firms to access the relevant resources than firms from other parts of the world. At the same time, the growth of the markets in the Asia-Pacific region means that Australia is not nearly as far away geographically, and in terms of time zone, as the large traditional markets.

In this scenario, these features get combined with a growing importance of sustainability, resource self-sufficiency, and quality of living to enhance Australia's competitiveness. Australia proves to be a more sustainable economy than most others, its self-sufficiency in the context of resource shortages elsewhere proves to be an enduring advantage, and Australia's unmatched quality of living causes talented Australians to stay and attracts mobile professionals from the rest of the region and the rest of the world. These developments enhance Australia's position in the knowledge-innovation economy and foster the emergence of strong Australian brands into international markets.

In this scenario, Australia invests sufficiently to overcome its disadvantages in basic and advanced drivers of competitiveness. In this regard, it makes changes sufficient to put it on track for the positive scenarios with respect to the resource boom, the flat world, and the rise of the Asia-Pacific region. It then is able to leverage advantages in *new age* drivers to generate even better economic performance than what it experienced in the 1990 to 2011 period. The result is that Australia's standard of living outpaces that of other economies around the world by an even wider margin than before. In this scenario, the world turns towards Australia, not only in that trends in the global economy play to Australia's strengths, but also in that Australia becomes a model for economic development in the post-GFC world.

THE WORLD TURNS AWAY FROM AUSTRALIA   The negative scenario in terms of Australia's interaction with the rest of the world ("The World Turns from Australia" Scenario) starts with Australia's geographic distance from markets, its dispersed population, its shortcomings in infrastructure, complex regulatory and tax systems, lack of integration with regional and global markets, and limited sophistication of firms and supply chains in the nation. Then it layers in assessments that question the resilience of Australia's economy, that indicate that the sorts of clusters that would embed companies into the local environment are not as well developed as they might be, and question its ability to hold leading edge companies, business activities, and individuals, rather than losing them to migration. In this scenario, although Australia tries to improve on these dimensions, others improve more, leaving Australia behind in key drivers of competitiveness.

In this scenario, greater connectivity results in the world being able to access Australian markets more easily than Australia accesses world markets. In this scenario, globalisation results in winner-takes-all markets in which those that generate the key ideas and knowledge capture all, or virtually all, of the value created. In this world, scale and scope efficiencies in generating commercially valuable ideas and knowledge mean that these are generated in North America, Europe, and Asia, not Australia. As a result, Australia becomes a knowledge taker (and therefore price taker), not a knowledge maker (and therefore not a price maker). A rising Asia is served not out of Australia, but out of other countries that focus increasing attention to the region, and use the business centres of Hong Kong and Singapore (centres that rate even higher than Australia in terms of openness and basic business environment and are tightly embedded into the Asian economies) to access the region.

In this scenario, the rise of Asia provides an inexorable attraction that pulls many of Australia's remaining highly qualified professionals and entrepreneurs away from Australia, the attractions of the country notwithstanding. There is evidence that already this is happening and that Australians and Australian companies are being drawn to Asia, particularly to Hong Kong and Singapore, where the business opportunities are perceived to be more significant and abundant. Hong Kong, for example, now has the second-largest number of Australians living outside of Australia and companies including Qantas have started off-shoring substantial parts of their business to Singapore. Anecdotal evidence suggests that Australians are increasingly populating the managerial and professional service ranks in Asia.

The result of this scenario, in which the world turns from Australia, is not economic collapse, but rather a gradual relative decline in which Australia retains a relatively good position in terms of aggregate wealth and overall living standards, but in which its relative position is gradually eroded as the nation becomes less and less relevant to the global economy.

The Scenarios in Perspective

While it is unlikely that any one of the scenarios will play out to its full extreme, the scenarios are useful in helping identify the opportunities and challenges that Australia will face in the coming years. As a result, they are useful tools for assessing Australia's economic and business future.

In our view, perhaps the most interesting feature of the scenarios, positive and negative, is that they are all plausible. Australia has a strong position in many drivers of competitiveness, a good policy base, and advantages in resources of many types. In addition, it has a history of being able to identify important issues, undertake independent reviews, and come up with reasoned analysis of the present situation and recommendations. When we take these features of Australia's economy, combine them with particular views of global trends and trends in competitiveness, and postulate that Australia can develop and execute the strategies appropriate to its circumstances, the positive scenarios are all plausible.

On the other hand, Australia lacks advantages in some drivers of competitiveness, competition is getting tougher, competitors are getting better, and resource advantages might only take the country so far. In addition, while Australia has a history of identifying and reviewing important issues, it has less of a history of successfully implementing the recommendations of these reviews, and still has issues associated with developing and implementing strategies at federal, state, and local levels at the same time. When we take these features of Australia's economy, combine them with slightly different views of global trends and trends in competitiveness, and postulate that Australia will have difficulty in developing and executing the appropriate strategies, the negative scenarios are all plausible.

What this means is that in terms of Australia's competitiveness and development potential, it is all to play for. It means that the choices that Australia makes will have an enormous impact on its economic future. In fact, the analysis suggests that Australia has the potential to influence its economic future to a greater extent than most other countries, including those that are less advanced, are less advantaged, or are hamstrung by debt positions that limit their flexibility.

This is a strongly positive message, but it is a message that places great responsibility on individuals, companies, business organisations, politicians, political parties, and government agencies in Australia to put aside differences when necessary to work for the public good. The reason is that the analysis suggests that the determinants of Australia's future prosperity will not be found so much in its stars as in itself.

Notes

1. This phrase comes from Yves L. Doz, José Santos, and Peter Williamson, *From Global to Metanational: How Companies Win in the Knowledge Economy* (Boston: Harvard Business School Press, 2001).
2. This phrase comes from Thomas L. Friedman, *The World Is Flat: A Brief History of the Twenty-first Century* (New York: Farrar, Straus and Giroux, 2005).
3. The "Asian Tigers" was the name given to four rapidly developing Asian economies in the 1980s, Hong Kong, Singapore, South Korea, and Taiwan. China is often referred to as a "rising dragon." India is often referred to as "the elephant," particularly when being compared to China.

CHAPTER 9

Implications for Australia

There are several implications that come out of the analysis in the earlier chapters and the larger project upon which it is based. Some come directly from trends in the global economy that go well beyond Australia alone. Others are specific to Australia and cut across the economy as a whole. Then there are implications for individual drivers of competitiveness in the Australian context. The list of implications included here is not exhaustive. Many implications have been identified by others, and several have been addressed in greater detail elsewhere. We hope that bringing them together in one place adds to the discussion and debate over Australia's economic future.

Global Implications

There are a number of global implications of the work reported in earlier chapters concerning the importance of competitiveness, competing in the knowledge economy, understanding the systemic nature of competitiveness, and the roles that different actors can play in improving competitiveness.

Competitiveness Is More Important than Ever Before

The challenges created by the Global Financial Crisis, the emergence of new competitors, the increasing ability of companies to place individual corporate activities in different locations, and increasing interconnections around the world are combining to make the competitiveness of nations and regions more important than ever before. Companies are under increasing pressure to perform while resources, particularly financial resources, are in shorter supply. Global markets are growing slower than they had been and slower than most expected. New competitors promise to drive down prices and drive up competition in a range of industries and activities. Increasing access to new productive locations will allow companies to play locations off against each other to an unprecedented extent. All of this will make the competitiveness of nations and regions, overall, in individual industries, and in individual corporate activities, more important than before.

Competitiveness in the Knowledge-Innovation Economy Is Vital

For advanced economies, competing in the knowledge-innovation economy will be more important than before. The alternative will be competing with developing nations that have vast populations, are eager to enter global markets, are improving in infrastructure, and will be guided by multilateral development agencies and some of the world's leading companies towards the improvements they need to make to succeed. In addition, the fragmentation of production chains means that they only have to be able to compete in one or two activities (such as assembly manufacturing or handling telephone calls) to enter global markets; they no longer have to be able to support entire production chains. Among today's developing nations, several are already looking to compete in the knowledge-innovation economy themselves, forcing the more advanced economies to move higher and higher up the ladder in order not to get caught. The result is one where increasingly the value of new ideas and knowledge will be captured by those that can generate the ideas and leverage them through global production systems and global markets.

Competitiveness Is Systemic

As indicated in Chapter 3, in the modern world economy there are five levels of drivers that influence a nation's competitiveness and the competitiveness of its industries and companies. These are the meta or supranational level (how the nation fits into the global economy), the macro or national level (conditions that are national in scope), the meso or cluster level (the ecosystems that surround individual industries), the micro or industry level (the firms that produce products or services of similar form and function), and the firm level. Nations will succeed in industries when they have sufficient favourable conditions across all five levels of drivers. In other words, no single level can create competitiveness, but any single level can thwart or kill competitiveness. Thus, competitiveness must be viewed as systemic in nature, and advantages at one level do not necessarily overcome or mitigate disadvantages at other levels.

Competitiveness Is Everyone's Job

What this means is that competitiveness is everyone's job. There is a tendency in some countries, including Australia, for the private sector to point to the public sector to solve competitiveness problems, for the public sector to point to the private sector, for management to point to labour, and for labour to point to management. The systemic nature of competitiveness means that government officials, managements, labour, those working in supporting institutions, and others need to point to themselves. Competitiveness is everyone's job. All of the major actors must pull together if the nation is to improve its competitiveness. One of the problems in fostering greater competitiveness in Australia is the frequent inability of different actors to put aside short-term posturing for the long-term benefit of the country. Until this happens, Australia will not reach its potential.

Australian Implications

There are some implications that cut across the analysis of the Australian scene that need to be understood in order to move forward.

Australia's Performance Has Been Strong

There is no doubt that Australia's overall economic performance has been strong in recent years. Australia has performed much better than the vast majority of OECD nations, enjoys one of the world's highest standards of living, and probably its best quality of life. The overall policy regime has been praised internationally and has contributed to a high-growth, low-debt situation that should be the envy of many other nations. One result, reflected in our business competitiveness survey, is a general satisfaction with most drivers of competitiveness in the Australian context. Even those that have a more negative outlook, such as those that focus on the difficulties of the manufacturing sector or at traditional measures of productivity, probably overstate Australia's problems given that the pressures on manufacturing will probably result in some resources being shifted to higher productivity activities in the future, large investments in utilities and mining being made today will show up in productivity gains tomorrow, and fixing prices and exchange rates at pre-boom levels to measure productivity more or less misses the point because no company today will invest assuming pre-boom prices and exchange rates.

Avoiding Complacency and the Wrong Concerns

We notice an odd mix of complacency and concern that exists in Australia. In some quarters, it appears that Australia's strong performance has been used implicitly or explicitly as a reason to slow or ignore needed investments and reforms. Why undertake politically difficult programs, one might ask, when the need is not so apparent and while the recent good performance can hide deficiencies? On the other hand, some of the concerns registered are over the loss of industries that have been in decline for some time, in some cases are legacies of a protectionist past, and are more likely to be drains on Australia's wealth than contributors over the longer term. Similarly, claims that every change in government policy is going to end Australia's prosperity and send investors scurrying for the exit lack credibility. The trouble is that these particular brands of complacency and concern move the discussion and debate away from what Australia needs to do to build a strong high-value economy for the future.

Understanding the Future Scenarios Is Crucial

In order to properly identify and frame the concerns that Australia should have going forward it is useful to address the scenarios developed in Chapter 8. Although Australia might not wind up following any particular scenario in all its detail, it is not hard to understand what Australia will need to do to maximise its chances of achieving the positive scenarios and minimise its chances of experiencing the negative scenarios. Australia needs to map out the programs, policies, and strategies that give it the best chance of moving from the lucky country to the competitive country; of riding the tigers, dragons, and elephants; of becoming a *flattenor* rather than *flattenee* in the globalised, quasi-flat world; and of having the world turn towards Australia rather than turning away. In order to do so, it will need to deal with a range of issues that cut across the economy, many, but certainly not all, of which have been raised earlier.

The Asian Century Does Not Necessarily Mean the Australasian Century

The rise of Asia-Pacific economies will provide Australia a unique opportunity to serve burgeoning markets that are much closer than the traditional American and European markets in terms of geography and time zone.[1] Australia's proximity, the fact that it has a more advanced economy than many in the Asia-Pacific region, and the fact that there are a large number of Australians that know the region should mean that Australia and Australian companies can be major players providing knowledge-intensive goods and services to the region to a much greater extent than is the case today. However, such a future is not pre-ordained. Companies from other parts of the world are focusing on Asia. Several Asian economies are as advanced if not more advanced than Australia. A number of them have easier business environments and incentive structures more aligned with economic growth than Australia, and are embedded geographically and culturally into the region in a way that Australia can never match. The opportunities arising from Asian development will only be realised in Australia if individuals, companies, labour, and governments at all levels in Australia create the conditions that will allow these opportunities to become opportunities that take root in Australia as opposed to passing it by.

Modern ICT Is a Two-Edged Sword

Similarly, modern information and communication technology (ICT) is creating huge opportunities for Australia and Australian companies to use the technologies to better understand international markets, market and sell globally, set up and manage international production and distribution systems, develop the *weightless* economy, and dramatically reduce the disadvantage of moderate economic size and distance from many major markets. However, the same technologies that can be used to leverage global business from an Australian base can be used to leverage foreign skills and capabilities into Australian markets in competition with Australian entities. This is already being seen in online retail and in many other sectors. The upshot is that Australia must have the skill base, the policy regime, the knowledge of technologies and markets, and the right environment for firms in Australia to generate the ideas, products, and services that penetrate international markets if it is to be a winner in an ICT-powered world.

Australia Can Act from Strength

Australia's economic performance has been strong. Its government debt and overall tax levels are low. It has a generally sound policy framework. It has good institutions and capable people. Australia has excellent analysts, commissions, and organisations that provide independent, expert reviews of policy and strategy issues of concern to the country as a whole. Australians tend to get on well with each other, at least outside the political or workplace relations context. All of these are great strengths. As all Australians know, the way to succeed on the sporting field is not to gain an advantage and then sit back, it is to gain an advantage, extend that advantage, overcome weak points, and press the advantage home. In that sense, building economies is no different. Australia has the ability to act from a position of strength, a much better position than many other countries that have to improve competitiveness as a matter of national economic survival.

Australia and the Drivers of Competitiveness

It is also useful to organise the implications for Australia through the Five Level Competitiveness Framework (FLCF)™ described earlier. This allows us to be systemic and not to leave out important drivers. In a nutshell, Australia has had significant disadvantages in meta or supranational drivers of competitiveness due to distance from markets, the fact that it has not been a member of significant free trade zones, the fact that its agricultural exports have been limited by protection elsewhere, and the fact that foreign companies tend to treat Australia as being at the periphery of their operations rather than at or near the centre. However, the rise of Asian economies and modern ICT have the potential to reverse some of these disadvantages. Australia has had significant advantages in macro or national-level drivers involving natural resources, macroeconomics, several aspects of government policy, government and social institutions, quality of life, and political stability, but disadvantages in terms of attitudes toward business success, and potential disadvantages in terms of tax and regulatory systems, and the potential for divided politics to make the political situation a liability rather than an asset.

At the meso or cluster level, Australia has had advantages in terms of education and training and infrastructure (the latter compared to developing and middle-income competitors), and disadvantages versus world leaders in some aspects of infrastructure, costs, density of supply chains, and efforts to promote clusters of successful firms and industries. At the micro or industry level, Australia has some advantages in terms of the strength of industry associations and professional bodies, as well as active competition across most of the economy, but has disadvantages in terms of inter-firm co-operation to penetrate international markets and the ability to generate and leverage leading firms that can dramatically improve the competitiveness of entire industries. At the firm level, Australia has capable managers and some internationally successful companies, but far fewer successful international companies than many smaller nations, managers and directors that tend to be insular, and business people that appear to overrate their own capabilities as well as the capabilities of their firms.

Further analysis, also organised around the Five Level Competitiveness Framework (FLCF)™, allows us to draw more detailed implications for Australia going forward, including implications for drivers not explored previously in this book due to space considerations. We note that several of the implications have been raised by others and many of the issues are well-known. What we hope to bring is some fresh perspectives based on the research performed for the present project as well as our experience inside and outside Australia.

Firm-Level Drivers

Nations will not succeed economically unless they have firms that are efficient and effective. This requires capable people, the right strategies, and the ability to operate in the domestic and international environments. It is the firms that must take the resources that are available to them and create the products and services that capture markets and support employment. Australia has many capable firms, but relatively few world-class firms with an international presence. Australia had eight companies in the top 500 in the Fortune Global 500 list in 2012 (based on revenues). These were BHP Billiton (108), Wesfarmers (171), Woolworths (175), Commonwealth Bank of Australia (227), Westpac Banking (229), National Australia Bank (254), Australia & New Zealand Banking Group (291), and Telstra (438).[2] All of these except BHP Billiton had the vast majority of their sales and operations in Australia.

Australia does not have firms like A.P. Møller-Maersk, ISS, Nokia, Royal Dutch Shell, ING Group, Schlumberger, Lyondell-Basell Industries, Phillips, Heineken, Volvo, Ericsson, Electrolux, Glencore, Nestlé, Novartis, UBS, Credit Suisse, ABB, Roche, Adecco, Xstrata, Holcim, Noble Group, Jardine Matheson, Hutchison Whampoa, Hon Hai, Quanta, Wistron, or dozens of other world-leading firms found in similar sized or smaller economies. Australia is going to have to develop more strong internationally oriented firms if it is to continue to prosper in a world of tougher competition and difficult markets.

FIRMS NEED TO TAKE RESPONSIBILITY FOR COMPETITIVENESS   At the firm level, one of the more interesting results of the competitiveness survey was that respondents in all of the industries examined in detail indicated that they believed that several government-related drivers of competitiveness were more important than the strategies of Australian companies in influencing the competitiveness of Australian industries. In our discussions with business people in Australia, it was striking that when the topic of competitiveness came up, the focus was immediately on what government was doing or was not doing that was helping or hurting Australia's competitiveness. Only after prompting did the discussion turn to firms and firm strategies. Thus, the first implication for firm-level drivers is that more Australian companies need to view themselves as an integral part of the competitiveness discussion and they need to explore ways in which their own activities, inside the firm, interacting with other firms, working with business groups and industry associations, and interacting with government, affect the country's competitiveness. Companies cannot leave important matters like workforce development, learning about markets and technologies, competitor intelligence, and developing strategies to succeed in domestic and international markets to others.

AUSTRALIAN MANAGERS OVERRATE THEIR CAPABILITIES AND THOSE OF THEIR COMPANIES   Australian managers tend to rate themselves and their companies relatively highly when it comes to their knowledge and capabilities. However, Australia trails the world leaders and several Asia-Pacific economies in international comparison of company and managerial capabilities and experience. The survey results suggest that many in Australia might not recognise that they are behind on these dimensions. Australian managers and companies in general will need a greater knowledge of international markets, international productive resources, and the tools that can be used to reach and manage these markets and resources, particularly in Asia, but in the rest of the world as well. They also need a better understanding of how modern developments in technologies and markets make it easier to go international today than ever before. Overrating managerial and company capabilities could result in less urgency to fill gaps that need to be filled.

A NEED TO GET OUT MORE   Another implication is that Australian companies and their managers need to get out more. While only a minority of Australian businesses will become exporters and an even smaller number will invest overseas, many more will face international competition. Understanding the opportunities and challenges can only be done by getting out into the markets, seeing what customers want, seeing what competitors are doing, checking on the inputs and sources of supply in their industry elsewhere, and so on. Only in this way will it be possible to make informed decisions about whether internationalisation makes sense for the individual company. We find a dichotomy among Australian managers and professionals. Some are among the world's most well-travelled and internationally knowledgeable, and others are among the world's least well-travelled and internationally knowledgeable. We note that some Australian companies, like ANZ, have hired senior managers with extensive international experience, particularly in Asia, and are recruiting people with Asian language capabilities for all levels in the organisation. More Australian companies need to follow suit.

BECOME THE FLATTENOR, NOT THE FLATTENEE   While there are some Australian companies that have developed ideas in Australia and then leveraged global resources to penetrate international markets, the number is still very small. There is no reason that more Australian companies cannot do what companies from elsewhere are doing. Today, more and more companies are *born global*, with an international mindset and operations from day one. However, this pattern is still rare in Australia. Today companies do not generally become international leaders by leveraging the capabilities and resources of a single nation. Australian companies need to follow this trend like companies from other economies.

FIND DIRECTORS WITH THE RIGHT EXPERIENCE   Australian companies should also find directors with the right experience to guide the companies into the future. Australia's largest companies have boards that include international heavyweights, but very few Australian companies have directors that live abroad at present or that have extensive international experience, especially Asian experience. While we do not know the numbers, we are reasonably sure that few Australian companies have directors that have first-hand knowledge of the way that cloud computing and social media will reshape markets around the world. The trouble here is that it can be difficult to identify and attract directors that have the right experience, are willing to travel frequently to Australia, and are willing to invest to learn enough about Australia to understand the local context in which the companies operate. One potential solution could be "director sharing," in which two or three non-competing companies jointly search for directors suitable for all of them and then separately appoint the same individuals. This could provide better incentive for the candidates to come to Australia and invest in learning about Australia than a single directorship.

IMPROVE DOMESTIC PRODUCTIVITY   Improving productivity is always an important objective for firms operating domestically or internationally. In terms of numbers of firms, Australia is dominated by small and medium-sized firms that operate domestically. One way to improve productivity throughout the economy is for these companies to improve their productivity in domestic operations. There are many sources of information for small and medium-sized enterprises (SMEs) in Australia as to how they can develop better business plans, access supporting services and other resources, manage their businesses better, and improve their productivity in general. While perhaps not turning directly into export sales or success in international markets, improved capabilities can lead to improved productivity that will help Australia as it helps the companies involved. Improving competitiveness in Australia means improving productivity across the board in companies that employ the bulk of the workforce and that help set the context that helps or hinders export or internationally oriented companies.

Micro or Industry-Level Drivers

Industry-level competition can be a spur to innovation and improvement, while industry-level co-operation can allow firms to pool resources and jointly overcome challenges. Leading firms in an industry can sometimes provide direction and impetus for an entire industry. Australia tends to have active competition in industries, but not much in the way of co-operation that leads to international success. Although Australia has leading firms that have strong positions internationally, they are relatively few and far between, leaving the country without leading firms that can spearhead international activities in most industries.

WELCOME COMPETITION AS A SPUR FOR IMPROVEMENT   There are several implications that arise at the industry level in Australia as well. There is active competition in many sectors in Australia, but others in which local oligopolies prevail or situations in which limited competition exists. Companies, of course, will often try to limit competition in order to reduce the pressure on prices and improve profits. Here government has an important role in ensuring that competition exists and persists in industries. We would also suggest that companies should not shy away from competition, but rather use competition to learn, as a spur to innovation, and to improve. In many countries, we find that tough competition at home builds skills and capabilities that can be used abroad. Australian companies should seek out tough competitors, figure out how to compete with them, and determine in which markets the capabilities they develop can be deployed. Similarly, in our view business groups and industry associations should not attempt to obtain protection or to limit competition, but rather to provide information and knowledge that can help companies up their game.

SEEK OPPORTUNITIES FOR CO-OPERATION   While tough local competition is often a hallmark of competitive industries in competitive countries, there is also scope for co-operation as well. This is particularly true for SMEs that might be able to co-operate to overcome common disadvantages in terms of infrastructure, place marketing, ability to obtain information (particularly about foreign markets), and penetrating foreign markets. Co-operation in these areas, while retaining competition in end markets, occurs in the wine industry and other industries in Australia, but not so often. Companies, industry associations, and business groups need to seek out opportunities for co-operation to enhance the competitiveness of groups of firms and industries. We note that a domestic market focus, inter-firm rivalries, and suspicions tend to make fostering competition in Australian industries very difficult. In our view, companies hugely overestimate what they have to lose and hugely underestimate what they have to gain.

Join Forces to Obtain Information   Australian companies, particularly SMEs, can join forces to obtain industry-specific information, particularly information on foreign markets, international competitors, new technologies, and cutting edge business practices on a cost-effective basis. Such shared information can allow multiple companies to up their game without diminishing competition on other dimensions.

Join Forces to Brand and Market Where Appropriate   In some cases, like the tourism industry and the wine industry, we see Australian companies co-operating to jointly brand and market the Australian industry. Depending on the sector, joint branding can take on a form as complex as sophisticated place-based marketing programs, from which all benefit, to something as simple as a website that allows for potential customers to find promotional material and web links to several companies on a non-discriminatory basis. Such joint activity can again be a very cost-effective tool for SMEs.

LEVERAGE LEADING FIRMS   Australia has lead firms that drive competitiveness in some industries, such as the resources sector, but not in most others. While Australia is a good environment for starting firms, it appears not to be as good an environment for growing firms into international leaders with firm-level advantages, world-class management, and a capital base that allows them to grow and prosper.

Create Conditions That Allow Leading Firms to Emerge   While government usually plays a small direct role in creating lead firms in Australia, providing a supportive environment, facilitating the internationalisation of medium-sized firms, and ensuring that domestic capital markets are deep enough to support lead firms can be crucial to their development. Australia needs a specific investigation into the challenges associated with growing firms in the country, and the incentives that dynamic firms have to leave as opposed to stay in Australia. It needs a strategy that maps out ways to provide the skills, capabilities, knowledge, information, and capital necessary for dynamic small or medium-sized firms to become leading firms.

Leverage Relations with Leading Firms into World Markets   From the standpoint of SMEs, and even larger firms, particularly those that wish to internationalise, we find that entering the supply chain of the leading companies that do exist can be a good way of being *carried abroad*. Serving leading companies at home can create relationships that allow for the creation of vibrant, international businesses. Australian engineering and construction companies have used relationships with large Australian-headquartered resource firms to push into international markets. SMEs should consider the extent to which their relationships with customers can be leveraged into international markets. Serving leading companies at home that already have international activities and require international standards at home can be one way of building capabilities to go abroad.

ASSOCIATIONS   AND   PROFESSIONAL   BODIES   SHOULD   FOCUS   ON   IMPROVING COMPETITIVENESS   Industry-level associations and professional bodies often act as lobbyists on short-term issues, but they can play an important role in improving competitiveness as well. They can link Australian-based businesses and professionals to those in other countries. Professional associations in Australia have played this role for years. Some, like CPA Australia, have extensive international networks that connect Australia to dozens of countries around the world.

Make Improving Competitiveness a Primary Goal   Industry associations and institutions should view improving Australia's competitiveness in their industries as a primary goal. This entails obtaining knowledge about the industry or profession globally, benchmarking Australia's capabilities with those of leading competitor or comparator countries, helping members identify industry best practice, and organising co-operative activities that can enhance company and industry competitiveness.

Make Competitiveness a Focus of Interaction with Others   Industry associations and professional bodies often can act as interlocutors with government and the education sector. They often provide continuing education and training. They promote and in some cases enforce high standards in their industries. In many cases, these activities are carried out with a domestic focus, rather than an international scope. As a result, the focus is often on incremental improvement for members rather than the discontinuous improvement possible through a focus on competitiveness, along with the assessment of the capabilities and systems in competing or comparator countries that a focus on competitiveness entails.

AVOID THE TEMPTATION TO DISTORT MARKETS   The scope for sector targeting, government support policies, and government incentives for particular industries in Australia is limited given the overall philosophy toward economic development that is apparently shared by both major political parties and the majority of the general public. Of course, Australia does invest in industry-specific infrastructure, education, and R&D. We have no argument with Australia's approach, but suggest that what is done should be framed in terms of public goods that are focused on Australia's future rather than private goods that are focused on its past.

Meso or Cluster-Level Drivers

As indicated earlier, there is a wide range of meso or cluster-level drivers that have an important influence on competitiveness in terms of inputs and supply, customers and demand, related industries, and the clustering process itself. Australia has some weaknesses at this level that should be addressed going forward.

LEVERAGE GEOGRAPHIC LOCATION   Australia's geographic location has shaped its past and present, and will shape its future. Historically the location was a disadvantage in most industries, possibly with the exception of some food industries in which a Southern Hemisphere location was countercyclical with producers in the Northern Hemisphere. Today, the shift in economic weight towards Asia, and Australia's proximity to Asia in terms of distance and time zone, can make location an advantage rather than a disadvantage.

Leverage Proximity to Asia   In more recent years, location near Asia has benefitted the education, tourism, and resource sectors. It has also made Australia a good location for technical support centres and software and IT centres for the Asia-Pacific region. We expect that as Asia grows in importance that Australia's geographic location will become less of a disadvantage and more of an advantage. Modern information and communication technology also will continue to reduce the importance of distance, allowing Australia to grow its digital content, software, and professional service activities. We should also remember that Asia can be leveraged as a source of inputs and as a production location, not just a market.

Build 24-Hour-a-Day Business   Modern technologies combined with location also give Australia the potential to be the Asia-Pacific centre for 24-hour a day operation in knowledge-intensive activities of international companies. There are already companies that work on projects 8 hours in the Americas, 8 hours in Europe, and 8 hours in Australia, or in which Australian professionals provide overnight firepower for projects based in the Americas or Europe. There is vast potential for Australia to leverage its technical and professional capabilities, English language capabilities, and geographic location in terms of time zones for research and development, architecture, design, software, engineering, legal services, consulting, and accounting, among others.

MANAGE RESOURCE ENDOWMENTS FOR THE NATION'S BENEFIT   Managing Australia's resource endowments will continue to be a major challenge. The challenge is to manage the resources so that the nation achieves the maximum benefit, the appropriate levels of investment to develop the sectors are attracted, Australia continues to be the home of strong resource companies, environmental concerns are handled appropriately, and the industry develops in a manner that is economically, strategically, financially, environmentally, socially, and politically sustainable.

Write Contingent Contracts and Tax Rules   Large resource projects are governed by contractual agreements, many of which have been ratified by state or territorial parliaments. In such cases, it should be possible to write contingent contracts to cover situations, such as the huge swings found in resource booms and busts, that can only be imagined today. Contingent contracts are contracts in which the terms change with changing circumstances, but in ways agreed upon in advance. For example, royalty or tax rates can change in pre-determined ways with changing revenues. The key feature is that the terms are negotiated and agreed up front rather than being subject to *ex post* attempts at renegotiation. The idea would be to allow all parties to benefit from unexpected windfalls, and share in the pain of unexpected downturns, but more importantly, to create a situation in which there is no uncertainty over whether a contract signed at a particular point in time will be honoured or not, or whether royalties and taxes will change in unanticipated ways with changes in markets. Putting into place such contracts, as well as sliding scales for taxes on other resources depending on price and volume levels, could build reasonable solutions into the process before the booms or busts occur. There will never be certainty in the resources sector. The best we can hope for is that arrangements are put in place that are fair and that the rules do not change in unexpected ways in the middle of the game.

Budget a Portion of Expected Resource Tax Revenues   It strikes us as inappropriate for governments to budget the full projected tax and royalty revenues from the resource sector for current expenditures. The revenues are just too volatile. By October 2012, the Australian Government was already forced to rewrite its 2012–2013 budget due to lower than expected revenues. A sounder approach would be to budget only a portion of projected revenues for current expenditure. Excess revenues banked in years in which resource revenues equal or exceed projections could be spent in years in which revenues fall significantly below projections. This mechanism could be an automatic stabiliser for an economy subject to volatile resource price movements, rather than an automatic destabiliser that compounds reduced resource revenues with reduced government expenditures.

We believe that a sound approach over time is to rely on only a portion of projected resource tax revenues for current spending, or to put some of the revenues into an endowment with only a percentage accessible for normal current budget expenditures in a given year. Other proceeds could either go to a fund that would be used to fund needed long-term infrastructure investments, some of which could be accelerated or delayed depending on economic conditions, or in the case of extreme windfalls be invested overseas to mitigate potential swings in exchange rates. In any case, budgeting to spend the full proceeds of resource taxes that are inherently more volatile than most other sources of income is not a wise approach.

Raise the Discourse on Resources   Finally, with respect to resource management, we note that given the large stakes involved, the discussions and debates can get very heated. Ultimately, governments at the federal, state, and local levels; local and foreign resource companies; and labour will all have to converge on a *modus vivendi* in order for the sector to deliver the most to Australia. Quite frankly, the slanging matches between government officials, corporate managers, and labour leaders we have seen in recent years do not help anyone. We would hope that the discourse over the resource sector would take on a more reasoned tone and that the Australian public would demand more from all of the concerned parties.

MEET AUSTRALIA'S INFRASTRUCTURE CHALLENGES   Given Australia's geographic location, the size of its land mass, and the dispersion of its population, Australia faces substantial infrastructure challenges. Australia's transportation and communication infrastructure does not rank with the world's best, and key airports and ports have reached or will reach capacity in the not-too-distant future. It is claimed that Australia has underinvested in urban infrastructure, resulting in overreliance on the automobile and inefficient city structures. Uncertainty has kept private investment from figuring more prominently in infrastructure investment.

Reverse Urban Sprawl   Australia's cities suffer from too much sprawl. While existing city plans increasingly emphasise infill development more than adding new land to the urban system, this does not go far enough. Instead, Australia should consider keeping the same city footprint as today for leading cities, or in some cases reducing the footprint. This would need to be coupled with increased high-rise construction, investments in mass transit, and investment in cultural and service amenities in nodes within the cities. It would also involve decisions not to provide infrastructure to areas that would simply expand urban sprawl. The idea would be to reduce the reliance on the automobile; create attractive, 24-hour-a-day city centres; provide housing for empty nesters who would value easy access to amenities and healthcare; and create vibrant cities that are far more energy efficient and sustainable than they are today. Such cities are also more likely to develop the concentrated central business districts (CBDs) that appear to be necessary to develop high value, high interaction services that can link with the rest of the country and rest of the world.

Do What Is Necessary to Attract Private Capital   Australia needs to bring more private sector capital into the infrastructure sector. This issue is being addressed by the Infrastructure Finance Working Group, and we support its recommendations, which include having clear infrastructure priorities, using user-pays principles to fund projects, government co-funding, monetising existing assets where possible, and mitigating refinancing risks.[3] We would go further. Given its vast distances and dispersed population, there will always be some infrastructure that will be unsuitable for private sector investment in Australia. Since government funds are always going to be limited, we suggest that an analysis be done of which infrastructure sectors are most amenable to private investment, to set up the legal framework and contractual system necessary to attract private sector investment into these sectors, and to ensure that governments hold up their end of the bargain. Then an approach that is consistent with the analysis should be implemented. Private solutions might not be optimal in some cases, but if private investment can free up government funds for other projects that would not go forward otherwise, then the nation benefits.

Make the Tough Decisions   Australia needs to think through what infrastructure is cost-effective to provide and what infrastructure is not cost-effective to provide. Australia has many relatively remote communities that naturally wish to be as fully served by infrastructure investment as possible. However, careful consideration should be made before providing infrastructure to remote areas that will be expensive and will serve far fewer people than similar levels of investment elsewhere. The full cost of building and maintaining infrastructure to and within remote areas should be made transparent so that difficult public choices can be made with full information.

Let's Get On with It   It is time for the enormous amount of good work that has been done to understand Australia's infrastructure needs to be put to use and for programs to be funded and implemented. Our own priority list would be, in this order, (1) communication infrastructure that allows for world-class broadband connectivity in major cities and suburban regions around the country and good access elsewhere (the NBN should go a long way toward meeting this goal), (2) urban transportation infrastructure that ensures that Australia's major cities can function as efficiently as leading cities around the world, (3) air and sea ports that improve international connectivity and reduce capacity constraints, and (4) transportation infrastructure that allows Australia's leading cities to interact with each other and with their surrounding regions. As we have stated several times before, if Australia is not ahead in infrastructure, it is behind.

WORKFORCE-RELATED DRIVERS   Workforce-related drivers are among the most important for Australia going forward. The economy will only go as far as people in Australia can take it. Australia has a strong workforce and elements of its workforce development system are world-class. However, a more comprehensive strategy that explicitly links workforce development programs with the needs of business and that examines the incentive structures faced by participants, or non-participants, in the workforce is needed.

Build a National Workforce Framework   The first implication is that workforce planning must take place in the overall context of the needs of the economy and society.

A detailed framework for the workforce needs to be developed at the national, state, and local levels. The newly created Australian Workforce and Productivity Agency is working on a National Workforce Development Strategy. This is expected to follow on from the 2010 Strategy that recommended a fundamental overhaul of the way that Australia approaches and supports workforce development, but appears not to have had much follow through. The terms of reference for the new Strategy suggests that the right issues are being addressed, including migration, skill needs and gaps, workforce participation by older and female workers, sustainability, an Asia-capable workforce, and others. These are the right issues, and this in and of itself is promising, but to be useful the strategy should be comprehensive, have a long time horizon, and be flexible enough to allow for adjustment along the way.

Adopt Results of Education Reviews   With respect to schooling, Australia gets high marks for participation in education and on some measures of education achievement. In order to build upon this base, Australia needs to ensure that sufficient funding is available. We believe that the recommendations made by the recent Review of Funding for Schooling should be implemented, in particular the recommendations that public subsidies for schooling be reward-based, that funding be linked to costs and outcomes, and that the focus should be on delivering the best education for each student. ICT skills should be introduced earlier in the curriculum.

In order to make Australian students more ready for the "Asian century," a greater emphasis should be placed on Asian studies and Asian languages (particularly Indonesian and Putonghua, or Mandarin Chinese). Australia should consider a "reverse Colombo Plan" in which Australian students are sent to study in Asian nations to learn more about them and build closer connections with Asian nations. We also support adopting the recommendations from the Bradley Review of Australian Higher Education, in particular the call for a renewed focus on quality and relevance in teaching and research, the need to better prepare university graduates for entry to a global workforce, and the need to widen the international student base.

Learn from International Experience   Australia's education system has been successful in educating Australian students and in attracting students from abroad. However, it is possible to learn from other systems. Finland and Singapore have both been successful with almost opposite approaches to primary education from each other. The United States has long had a four-year university system. Hong Kong, which had a three-year system, is switching to a four-year system after extensive research concluded that the extra year would promote broader thinking, more interdisciplinary capabilities, and improved lateral thinking among students. While there are many in Australia's education establishment familiar with international experiences, we suggest that these are worth assessing.

Develop Alternatives to the University Track   Australia also might consider expanding the sandwich programs in place in some institutions to enable closer collaboration between universities and business, and to train more students under an apprenticeship type model that more closely matches the learning and development of the student with the specific needs of industry. Not everyone is suited to university study, and not all skills necessary for Australia's future prosperity are taught at universities. The vocational and trades programs offered by Australia's Technical and Further

Education (TAFE) institutes and other similar providers should remain an important part of Australia's education and training framework. Leading exponents of the apprenticeship model globally are Switzerland, Germany, and the Netherlands, three countries that are on par with or better than Australia when it comes to ratings of the workforce. These models are certainly worth investigating.

Make Lifelong Learning and Increased Participation Priorities Lifelong learning and training need to be more important parts of Australia's workforce development strategy. An aging population, decline of some industries, and evolving needs of the economy mean that older workers will be needed to step into jobs in Australia, and they will have to be able to do those jobs. The Grattan Institute has estimated that increasing workforce participation on the part of older workers and female workers could be a major positive step for the Australian economy.[4]

Improve Transparency in the Workforce Development System The costs and benefits of workforce development should be made more transparent and measureable to inform the debate as to where and how resources are best committed. The My School initiative that has been enabled by the Australian Curriculum, Assessment and Reporting Authority Act 2008 (ACARA), which in 2010 began publishing on its website nationally comparable data on all Australian schools, is an example of how to make information more transparent and accountable.

Business Must Step Up on Education and Training Businesses cannot stand on the sidelines when it comes to workforce development. Workforce planning will be extremely important for businesses as well as government. Business needs to enhance its own training and education offerings to help meet its own needs. Unfortunately, anecdotal evidence suggests that some large firms that used to engage in extensive staff training are actually doing less, instead relying on the market to provide job-ready candidates. If sufficient talent and skills cannot be found at home, then businesses will have to seek these abroad. Businesses also must be prepared to employ older workers and to be more flexible in its employment arrangements for female workers in order to fill the positions that need to be filled.

Business Needs to Engage with Government on Workforce Issues The business sector must communicate to government what skills are needed for business to succeed and what skills are found to be in short supply. This must be done early enough to impact on policymaking, noting that the benefits of changes will take years to flow through to positively impact in most cases. Several professional and industry groups in Australia are active in this regard. These groups and others should continue to work with the business and political communities to articulate the needs of businesses in the economy and to promote constructive solutions to workforce issues. The case needs to be clearly made to government that excellent training and education institutions and a high quality of living are necessary, but not sufficient, to make Australia more competitive. Business also should continue to provide information that informs the public discussions of immigration, tax laws, workplace relations, and other workforce issues.

Address the Incentives to Emigrate and Leverage Émigrés Australia has attracted many highly qualified individuals over the years and the net migration balance is positive.

However, many highly qualified Australians have emigrated as well. We suggest that Australia needs to understand who emigrates, why, and what incentives they faced to go as opposed to stay. Anecdotal evidence from discussions with dozens of Australian émigrés indicates that a combination of job opportunities, tax rates, and an ability to live in more vibrant locations have been the major reasons for leaving. Australia needs to examine the reasons in order to determine whether a shift in incentives within the nation could change matters. On the other hand, Australian émigrés can provide linkages to key economies in Asia and elsewhere. The same is true of students who studied in Australia and then returned home or went elsewhere to build their careers. It strikes us that this network is not leveraged nearly as much as it could be for business leads, directors, and other contacts.

Reform Counterproductive Workplace Relations   Finally, Australia's confrontational workplace relations system needs to be addressed. Australia's finely balanced political system and the histories of the leading political parties tend to promote confrontational workforce relations. Management and labour both know that they are at most three years away from having a government that is predisposed to be supportive of their interests. The result can well be a focus on delaying and confronting and hoping to swing an election rather than on reaching reasoned compromise.

For its part, management and ownership must understand that companies cannot exist without labour and that when companies experience a windfall, workers expect a share. For its part, labour must understand that wages cannot rise faster than productivity for long without killing the companies and industries involved, and that prosperity in some industries does not necessarily mean prosperity in others. For its part, the Australian Government has to acknowledge that it is the government of all Australia, not just the most fervent supporters of a political party. It is disappointing to view the description of the Fair Work Act of 2009 and the workforce relations system it ushered in on the Government's workforce website to find a description that focuses almost exclusively on the rights of labour with virtually no mention of the obligations of labour or the rights of others.[5] Of course, the opposite was undoubtedly the case at times in the past. The irony is that the short-term jockeying for position probably leaves both sides worse off than a situation in which management and labour could work out a *modus vivendi*. Unfortunately, that day seems far off.

FINANCE-RELATED DRIVERS   The ability of a nation's financial sector to support the start-up and growth of companies is crucial to the nation's economic well-being. Australia is relatively well situated when it comes to financial drivers. The banking sector is strong. Australia has relatively large equity, derivative, foreign exchange, and fund management markets when compared to the size of the economy. There are challenges in terms of venture capital and financing for small and medium-sized businesses, but that is true in most countries. Australia also attracts substantial foreign investment. Foreign-owned assets represent a much higher percentage of capital stock than the OECD average, foreign investors account for roughly 40 percent of holdings of companies listed on the ASX, and approximately 35 foreign banks are active in the country.

Ensuring Sufficient Competition and Local Flavour in Banking   Australia's four largest banks, Australia and New Zealand Banking Group (ANZ), Commonwealth Bank of

Australia (CBA), National Australia Bank (NAB), and Westpac Banking Corporation (WBC) account for around 80 percent of Australian banking assets and over 70 percent of loans to non-financial corporations.[6] The rough balance among the big four ensures that there is active competition in the sector. In addition, 12 local and regional banks and at least 35 foreign banks are active in the country.

There are a few challenges associated with this structure. One is to ensure that there is sufficient competition to provide funds and services at competitive rates. Another is to ensure that there are incentives to seek out new businesses. Still another is to ensure that local and regional markets, including those far from the main business and financial centres, are served. This is one place where the regional and local banks can come in. While the bulk of the business of regional and local banks in Australia is for consumers, several of these banks also have active commercial lending businesses. The overall structure of the banking sector appears to serve the country well, and we see no particular reason it should be changed.

Continue Venture Capital Programs Australia has limited venture capital and private equity available for industry. According to the Australian Venture Capital and Private Equity Industry Association, venture capital investment in Australia was AUD 121 million in 2011, and private equity investment was AUD 3.5 billion. Roughly half of the AUD 3.6 billion total in that year was foreign.[7] The Australian Government provides some venture capital through its Innovation Investment Fund and works with private sector fund managers through the Early Stage Venture Capital Limited Partnerships program. Australia also provides favourable tax treatment to qualifying domestic and foreign venture capital companies. While to a certain extent this approach creates distortions by favouring one type of investment, the amounts involved are relatively small and there is general acceptance of the view that venture capital is under-provided by the market in most countries. Thus, Australia's range of policies seems appropriate for the country's situation.

No Apparent Need for a Small Business Administration or SME Bank There have been calls by some for Australia to consider a government loan guarantee system for small and medium-sized enterprises modelled on the United States' Small Business Administration or a government bank to lend to SMEs as exists in Canada. The rationale is that SMEs have difficulty accessing bank capital at reasonable costs, that the guarantees reduce the cost of funding for the SMEs, and that the programs can pay for themselves. Our view is that while such vehicles can always be considered, there is no apparent need to institute such vehicles in Australia at this time. Such schemes would create new bureaucracies, would result in many companies focusing on applications and bureaucracy rather than their business, and could create moral hazards in lending because government could be left to pay the bill. The combination of four large national banks, each of which has the scale to self-insure their small business loan portfolio, and regional banks, which presumably have good contacts in local communities and with SME clients, should be a good combination to serve these markets, and are probably best situated to assess the credit risk of SME customers.

One reason that SMEs often find it hard to get loans and that they pay higher rates than large companies is that they are riskier customers with much higher default rates than large companies. The market should price this risk into their loans. We would rethink this position if it could be shown that SMEs could not get loans at rates that were priced in a reasonable view of their risk profile because of a gap in the market (for example, if it became clear that the large banks were ignoring the SME market and it were becoming apparent that entry to serve the market to fill the gap was too difficult) or if banks and other finance providers were shown to systemically pull finance from SMEs in times of crisis, forcing even good firms to the wall in the process. However, this does not explain why many borrowers and potential borrowers consider the conditions attached to loans as onerous and in some cases a bigger obstacle than the cost of finance. We would encourage lenders to work with SMEs to develop conditions that protect the lender, but are not onerous on SME borrowers.

LEVERAGING CLUSTERS AND BUSINESS ECOSYSTEMS   Firms and industries do not exist in a vacuum. Instead, they are embedded in larger clusters of industries or business ecosystems that include firms, their competitors, supplier industries, customer industries, and supporting institutions. Increasingly, when it comes to international competition, it is not so much firm versus firm as cluster versus cluster or ecosystem versus ecosystem. Thus, it is in every company's interest to understand its own cluster or ecosystem, to understand those of competitors, and to develop strategies to leverage advantages and overcome disadvantages in one's own cluster or ecosystem.

Leverage, Create, or Find Competitive Supply Chains   A firm's supply chain can be a source of advantage if it provides needed inputs superior to those of other supply chains in terms of quantity, quality, or cost. A nation is benefitted if it has strong supply chains that can support its downstream industries. In Australia, competitive supply chains have developed around the mining sector, in the agriculture and food sectors, in software, in the wine industry, in creative industries, in marine industries, and in others. In these industries, companies in Australia can draw upon world-class suppliers who themselves are knowledgeable about international markets, trends, and competition.

Overall, however, Australia is rated behind most OECD nations, and several economies in the Asia-Pacific region, in terms of supply chain development. This is due in part to the size of the economy and to the fact that supply chains in Australia have difficulty expanding into international markets to achieve scale and scope. Australian companies need to make an assessment of the supply chains that are available to them, whether they are or can be made to be world-class, whether supply chains in other locations are better, and what impact such analysis should have on sourcing and location decisions. Today in some industries we see supply chains spanning the world, or vast regions. In other industries, supply chains can be leveraged only if they are local. Australian companies in general will have to be more aggressive in developing local supply chains and in leveraging supply chains elsewhere if they are to succeed.

Leverage or Build Strong Clusters   Clusters of interlinked firms and industries are a simple fact of life in most economies. Numerous examples of clusters exist in virtually any economy, and there are numerous examples of clusters that dominate or are prominent in industries around the world. Clusters involve supply chains, customers, competitors, and supporting institutions as well. Again, it is important for Australian companies to assess the state of their own "cluster" or their business ecosystem, compare it to that in competing locations, determine whether building stronger linkages in a local cluster or ecosystem can create advantages, or determine that the firm needs to seek linkages in other locations.

Expand the Activities of Enterprise Connect   Enterprise Connect provides a wide range of services to small and medium-sized companies, including business reviews, workshops, advisory services, researcher placement, technical and market information, and related services. In order to be eligible to use Enterprise Connect, a firm must be operating in manufacturing or manufacturing-related services, resources technology, defence, clean technology, creative industries, remote Australia, or tourism. To us it makes little sense to limit eligibility in this way. Other industries can contribute to Australia's economy, too. We suggest that Enterprise Connect's activities be extended to any industry that can reasonably be expected to be able to add to Australia's export base or the overall productivity performance of the country. We also suggest that its networking activities be emphasised as it might be easier to leverage networks of SMEs to improve economic performance than to create larger firms.

Macro or National-level Drivers

Australia has a strong position in many macro or national-level drivers of competitiveness. Its macroeconomic performance has been strong. Its overall policy approach has been successful. Its institutions are strong, and the country gets high marks for social stability and quality of life. There are some features in the tax and regulatory system, as well as in the contentious approach that is often taken to issues that should be addressed going forward.

MACROECONOMIC CONDITIONS   Australia's macroeconomic performance has been strong in recent years. Growth has been strong compared to other advanced economies, unemployment has been relatively low, workforce participation has been high, and income inequality has been on par with other developed economies. Interest rates have been high, and the currency has appreciated compared to many other countries, and while these have affected some industries, they have not stifled the economy. Productivity growth, as it is typically measured, has been slow in recent years, but measures of productivity that fix prices and exchange rates at pre-resource boom levels do not provide a reasonable picture of what has been going on in the economy. Perhaps the most important implications regarding macroeconomic conditions are to ensure that complacency does not set in and that the concerns that are raised are the right ones.

Avoid Complacency, Creeping and Otherwise   "Avoid complacency" is obvious advice, but there does appear in Australia to be a tendency to expect that good times will go on longer than they might. For example, while demand for resources from China and other Asian nations might have resulted in a step change from the previous situation, the resources sector is subject to cycles and volatility. In October 2012, for example, Government rewrote parts of its budget due to shortfalls in expected resource tax revenues due to a fall-off in commodity prices and volumes. It also appears that Australia's strong economic performance has slowed the impetus for reform in several dimensions and has allowed politically difficult decisions to be put off. This "creeping complacency" is perhaps more of a danger to Australia's economy today than too much self-satisfaction.

Raise the Right Concerns   Concerns have been raised about the future of Australia's manufacturing sector and other industries that have been affected by an appreciating currency and rising local costs. These are valid concerns; however, they are often voiced in terms of the potential loss of specific industries rather than how Australia can evolve to deal with the pressures and make adjustments. In this regard, the Prime Ministerial Task Force on Manufacturing has done a great service by taking a detailed look at the circumstances surrounding the manufacturing sector and how Australia needs to develop a smarter manufacturing sector for the future.[8] The future-oriented approach, and raising concerns about Australia's ability to adjust and develop higher value-added industries and activities, is to us the right set of concerns to raise. We would prefer a focus on what Australia can gain by embracing modern ICT, leveraging international production systems, and commercialising its ideas and innovations than on what it might lose in traditional industries whose competitiveness is unlikely to improve significantly any time soon.

Adjust, Adjust, Adjust   Companies and industries can discuss the macroeconomy, and can try to influence economic policy, but at the end of the day they must take the environment as they see it and adjust accordingly. Understanding how successful Australian companies are dealing with macroeconomic conditions, how leading foreign companies from high-cost locations have prospered, how to improve efficiency in existing corporate activities, and how to develop strategies that use branding and superior intellectual property to provide insulation against short-term price pressure will be crucial to Australian companies and industries going forward. In any case, companies and industries need to anticipate future developments to the extent possible and develop the flexibility to adjust to changing circumstances. Westfarmers is an example of a company that has focused on continuing adjustment and renewal in the domestic market. We would like to see more Australian companies doing so in international markets.

GOVERNMENT POLICIES   A wide range of government policies influence the competitiveness of Australia's companies and industries. The overall policy regime in Australia has contributed to the country's resilience. However, there are issues associated with the complexity of multi-tiered government and the politicisation of various aspects of economic policy that are causes for concern.

Continued Prudence in Fiscal and Monetary Policy   Australia's fiscal and monetary policies have been prudent and conservative, leaving the country in an enviable position with respect to government finances and with the flexibility to act in the face of global economic and financial crises. We note that CPA Australia, other business groups, and several economists have criticised the Australian Government for attempting to return to surplus in the 2012–2013 budget, claiming that the world economy is still in flux and a return to surplus would hurt the economy. We also note that these commentators agree that Australia should be fiscally prudent. Australia's commitment to fiscal prudence is admirable when compared to the situation in the United States and European Union, among other places in the world.

Continued Market-Orientation   Market-oriented trade, exchange, and competition policies have worked well for Australia in recent years. Australia has prospered without extensive industrial policies, significant industrial targeting, or introducing major market distortions. It has not tried to intervene to control the exchange rate, and it is committed to free trade in most sectors. We see no reason to change direction in these areas.

Continued Openness in Investment Policies   Despite a few high-profile cases in which potential foreign investments into Australia have been rejected, Australia has generally been open to foreign investments. There are sensitivities around foreign investments in the resources sector and concerning agricultural land, and these are understandable as these types of investments are sensitive in many countries. We do note that the concerns voiced over Japanese investments decades ago gradually receded. There are concerns about investments from China, and these are understandable. Chinese investors are relatively new on the scene, many are linked to or controlled by the Chinese Government and might have different motives from other investors, and many are learning how to operate in foreign countries. With respect to these investors, it makes sense for Australia to proceed on a step-by-step, case-by-case basis until there is more familiarity and understanding on both sides.

Emphasis on Skills, Capabilities, Information, and Infrastructure   Skills, capabilities, information provision, and infrastructure should be major focal points of government policy toward the economy. For the most part, these are taken up elsewhere in this chapter. We do note here the important role that government plays in gathering and disseminating information on foreign markets, foreign rules and regulations, and foreign business practices.

A Focus on Demand-Driven Investments   One common theme that comes through in business response to government investments in education, training, science, and technology is a disconnect between the investments that are made and the needs of business. The Prime Minister's Taskforce on Manufacturing echoed this view in their final report. This, in turn, has been criticised by research organisations as not recognising the importance of basic research in society and the economy. In a sense both parties are correct. Basic research is important, but government funding of research in general is usually sold to the public on the basis of potential economic benefits, or by using examples of research projects that have generated commercially valuable technologies. The issue may be one of failing to be explicit on the goals of the research funding.

Be Explicit on Goals   The solution here is to be explicit. Specific portions of the government research budget should be allocated for basic research that would be evaluated by peer review by panels of Australian and international experts. On the other hand, specific portions of research budgets should be allocated for research that is supposed to generate commercial outcomes. This research should be evaluated by business people, financiers, and through analysis of actual commercial contributions realised. The trouble in the existing system is that ambiguity in terms of intent means that basic research is not sufficiently respected and research in general is often not relevant to the needs of the economy. Australia suffers on both counts as a result.

Consider the Best Vehicles for Research Programs   A side note is that while there are many successful examples of university research resulting in commercially valuable technologies in Australia, the first two priorities of university personnel tend to be on academic publications and teaching, with commercially oriented research a distant third. This raises the question of whether commercially directed research is best housed in universities, university-related research institutes, independent research institutes, or companies. Australia has several types of research organisations. The appropriate division of labour is a question that should be revisited from time to time as priorities and the nature of research undertaken changes.

Do we Have All the Best Ideas? If the goal, or one goal, of government-funded research is to generate commercially valuable research for exploitation in Australia, we should ask if Australia is necessarily the best place for this work to be carried out. Leading companies often have research and development in multiple locations and seek to learn from anywhere in the world in which relevant research is done. The idea is that no one place is likely to generate all the interesting ideas or all the complementary technologies that might go into a new product or service. Such companies are also spending an increasing amount of time and effort on scanning developments around the world to find technology they can learn from, buy, or incorporate into their activities. Other countries, like Denmark, actually have government-funded research facilities in other countries in order to tap into pockets of world-class research. Australia should consider how much of government funding should go to onshore research in Australia, offshore research in other parts of the world, and to technology-scanning on a global basis.

A Focus on Cluster-Based Development Policies As mentioned earlier, cluster development initiatives have become an important, if not dominant, means of developing regional economies and groups of small and medium-sized firms around the world. In Australia, most such initiatives have had a limited time horizon and have had limited resources, and too little local control. Not surprisingly, there has been limited high-profile success, and the whole field has gotten a bad name in some policy quarters in Australia. We note that there has been much progress over the last two decades on cluster development initiatives, and there is a wealth of experience that can be leveraged into the Australian context. If the United States, Germany, France, Sweden, Singapore, Finland, Denmark, Brazil, the United Kingdom, and numerous other countries are home to examples of successful cluster strategies, we really have to ask whether the world turns that differently in Australia.

- **Recognise the Importance of Regional Clusters.** When the concepts are defined and Australian business people are asked whether their firms are part of a regional cluster, the vast majority say no, even when there is objective evidence that the industry in which they participate is dominated by small geographic areas and there is significant inter-firm interaction that benefits the industry. This seems to be the result of Australian business people being used to thinking in terms of companies and industries, but taking the interaction among industries for granted. It also may reflect a tendency to think of the economy more in national terms than regional or local terms.
- **Introduce Cluster Development Initiatives to the Policy Mix.** We suggest that Australia formally introduce cluster development programs into its economic policy mix. We note that such programs have many elements in common with

business support programs already available through Enterprise Connect for qualifying companies. Cluster development strategies work to improve the generalised business environment, provide information on business and economic trends as well as on specific markets, provide seminars and advice to improve business management, facilitate interaction with educational and research organisations, foster business networking and inter-firm collaboration, and in some cases provide business services to firms in the cluster. Here we note that the additional pieces of the puzzle often involve cluster identification, the establishment of collaborative mechanisms, and bringing together groups of interrelated companies, local government officials, and representatives from supporting institutions.

Cluster Initiatives Are Not Picking Winners and Are Not That Expensive. The best cluster initiatives focus on specific market failures involving impacted information, managerial myopia, provision of public goods, and co-ordination failures. Cluster initiatives often involve providing the sorts of information, management training, infrastructure, and links between business and the education sector that government tries to do anyway. Using clusters as a unit of analysis and action often makes this process more efficient and effective. Successful cluster initiatives also involve overcoming co-ordination failures in environments in which firms are not used to co-operating with each other. Globally, many cluster initiatives are catalytic in nature, requiring only limited government funding.

The Steps Are Well-Known. Typical steps in cluster development programs include determination of the overall goals and the geographic scope of the initiatives, initiation of the cluster development process by leaders from the public and private sectors, identification of clusters and location-specific attributes in the economy, prioritisation of efforts by cluster, elaboration of the relevant public and private support entities, obtaining information relevant to development of the cluster, generation of strategies to improve the cluster, investment in the skills and capabilities necessary to build the cluster, investment in the relevant public goods, co-ordination of public and private activities to enhance competitiveness, and institutionalisation of mechanisms that have proven to work.

Cluster Initiatives Have Several Similarities with Services Provided by Enterprise Connect. Many of the services provided by Enterprise Connect are similar to those provided in cluster development programs in other countries. Groups of companies are eligible to apply for support from Enterprise Connect, and the organisation operates all over the country. What this process does not do is help identify groups of firms and industries that could benefit from co-operation, joint identification and solution of problems, and facilitating linkages within supply chains and clusters. Adding these functions and organising the groups of firms to be able to take advantage of the Enterprise Connect services would be a very useful next step.

Improving the Tax System   Australia has a low tax take as a percent of GDP compared to most OECD nations due in part to low levels of government debt and therefore low government interest payments. The tax take on the other hand is much higher than in many other Asia-Pacific economies. The top rate of personal income tax is comparatively high, as is the rate of corporate tax. Many inefficient taxes remain on the books despite several recommendations that they be abolished. The complexity of the tax system is a drawback. There are several implications for Australia's tax system that come out of this work.

- **Benchmark against Asia-Pacific Economies.** There is a tendency to benchmark Australia against other OECD countries, particularly medium-sized economies, when it comes to tax. Unfortunately, for many industries and corporate activities these countries are neither major markets nor competitors. Thus, the benchmarking with other OECD countries is interesting, but not particularly useful, except perhaps versus the United States, which repeatedly comes up as a market and competitor for Australian industries. On the other hand, when one looks at Australia's major competitors and markets in the Asia-Pacific region, we see that the tax take and tax rates are much lower. This is important in that individuals and corporations are increasingly comparing taxes in Australia to taxes in these economies in order to decide where to locate. And when Hong Kong, Singapore, and other Asian economies are put into the mix, Australia's tax system is just not competitive. Again, decisions about tax levels and systems involve social choices. These choices should be made with a full understanding of their implications for competitiveness and the costs of middle class welfare to Australia.

- **Implement the Main Findings of the Henry Tax Review.** Government's response to the Henry Review of Australia's tax system has been underwhelming at best. Of the 138 recommendations, very few were adopted in full or part. In addition, the base and rate for the Goods and Services Tax (GST) was excluded from the terms of reference and so were not addressed. We suggest that the main findings in terms of shifting the burden more towards a smaller set of relatively efficient taxes, abolishing inefficient taxes, and streamlining the tax system should be implemented as soon as practicable. Expansion of the GST base and adjusting its rate should be put on the table, as well as any other adjustments that potentially serve the purpose of reducing the compliance costs, streamlining the system, and improving Australia's competitiveness, particularly in comparison with Australia's emerging markets and competitors in the Asia-Pacific region. We would suggest that the payroll tax be a prime candidate for abolition.

- **Review the Funding Model for State Government.** One reason that Australia's tax system is complex is that there is a mismatch between the expenditures that state governments need to make and the tax revenue they are able to raise. The result is that states often have to plead with the Federal Government to obtain the funds they need, are forced to resort to local taxes that are not that efficient, and generally add to the complexity faced by Australian taxpayers. This system creates challenges in terms of federal-state government relations and opens state and local funding to intergovernmental politics.

- **Reassess Where the Tax Burden Falls.** Compared to other OECD nations, Australia's tax burden falls disproportionately on high-income individuals, corporations, and resources. This would seem to be ideal for a progressive nation. Or rather it would be ideal if Australia were the only country in the world.

However, it is not, and the high-income individuals, including senior managers, leading professionals, and business owners and corporations, might well consider moving to other locations, particularly places like Hong Kong and Singapore, which have much lower personal and corporate tax rates. Tax rates and the distribution of tax burdens are social choices, but Australia does not exist in a vacuum, and so it must assess the impact of tax rate differences on mobile professionals and companies. Australia should take the competitiveness implications of different tax options into account when making its choices.

Improve the Regulatory Environment Much of the discussion about regulation in Australia is not about the content of regulation, but rather about the multiple levels of regulators, differences among the states in regulations, and high compliance costs due to complexity. The regulatory burden falls disproportionately on small and medium-sized companies that are the least-equipped to handle the burden, and that are relied upon as sources of employment, dynamism, and growth.

- **Benchmark against Relevant Comparators, Competitors.** As with other drivers, Australia tends to compare itself to other OECD nations when it comes to regulation. As indicated earlier, this is not necessarily the right comparison. Increasingly, international companies, as well as Australian companies and individuals, are choosing to locate in Australia or elsewhere depending on the comparison with specific economies, including the United States, Hong Kong, Singapore, and other Asia-Pacific economies. Thus, the primary comparisons that should be made are not necessarily the ones that are usually made. We note that this does not mean watering down Australia's regulatory environment, but rather taking additional economies into account and understanding the competitiveness implications of Australia's regulatory system to inform Australia's choices concerning regulation.
- **Simplify and Unify State-Level Regulations.** Much of the discussion about the regulatory system in Australia is not so much on the actual substance of the regulations, but on the complexity of a system with multiple overlapping jurisdictions and significant differences among the states. This creates a substantial compliance burden that again might have nothing to do with the substance of the regulation. Australia should work to simplify the system by clarifying jurisdiction and by unifying state-level regulations where possible.
- **Calculate and Reduce the Costs Imposed on SMEs.** Many countries around the world have programs to support SMEs. In virtually every case we have investigated, reducing the regulatory and reporting burden that SMEs face would be more beneficial than any support policy or program. In many countries, rules and regulations are set with large companies in mind and/or after consultation with large companies, or associations dominated by large firms, even though the vast majority of firms, and in many cases the vast majority of GDP, comes from SMEs. The regulatory burden for full compliance by SMEs should be assessed on an ongoing basis and explicit commitments made to reduce the time, effort, and expense required for compliance. Australia is one of the easiest places in the world to set up a business. It should become among the most efficient and least costly in terms of regulatory compliance.

- **Use the Productivity Commission's Work.** Australia's Productivity Commission has done extensive work on the regulatory system in Australia, the compliance burden for companies and employees, and the potential for streamlining the regulatory process. In a wider sense, Australia needs the Productivity Commission to continue to work on Australia's regulatory system. However, it appears that many of the recommendations of the Commission have yet to be implemented. To us, the existence of an organisation like the Productivity Commission is a distinct competitive advantage for Australia. We believe its analysis should be brought into policy more often than is the case today.

IMPROVING THE IMPACT OF INSTITUTIONS AND SOCIETY   A nation's institutions and the nature of civil society provide an important context for its economy. The extent to which the attitudes, goals, and norms of a society support economic and social development is highly influential on the economy and society that ultimately develops. Australia has strong institutions and a well-functioning society. These provide important underpinnings that can be leveraged for potential advantage. If anything, ways should be found of leveraging these into further business opportunities.

Leverage High-Quality Institutions   Australia gets high marks for its legal, governmental, educational, and research institutions. These are viewed as highly capable and professional when compared to other OECD nations and other nations in the Asia-Pacific region. Australia's legal system is fair and professional. In discussions with business people in Australia, we do receive anecdotal evidence that legal processes can become drawn out and expensive, and that perhaps too much leeway is given to frivolous law suits. Education and research organisations are also considered of high quality. The issue here is whether they are fully aligned with providing what business and the economy need. In any case, Australia's institutions are strong selling points for companies coming into Australia and provide benefits that Australian companies can draw upon.

Avoid the Superficial Assessments When it Comes to Institutions   A particularly superficial line of reasoning we have seen in Australia is that many Asian economies have legal, regulatory, and other institutions that are different and in many ways weaker than those in Australia, that this difference makes it more difficult to penetrate Asian markets, and therefore the strength of Australia's institutions is not a competitive advantage. Many Asian economies do have different business practices and weaker systems of governance than in Australia. And this means that Australian companies will have to learn how to operate in these systems if they are to succeed in the region. However, this does not mean that Australia's systems need to be weakened in order to compete. Strong institutions benefit Australia's economies in many ways. Economies in Asia are growing despite weaker systems, not because of weaker systems. Australian firms are increasingly selling to Asia based on reliability and high standards, and the trend toward more discriminating consumer and industrial markets in the region will make such strategies more promising in the future.

Leverage Stability and Quality of Life   Australia is known for political stability, social stability, and having a high quality of life. These, of course, are all pluses for the development of the economy. We expect that as value creation in more and more industries is carried out by mobile professionals developing commercially valuable ideas and innovations, quality of life will become more important as a competitive weapon. Australia should be identifying which industries tend to be driven by mobile professionals and are not location-sensitive (funds management falls into this category as well as creative industries and *weightless economy* industries, such as digital content, advertising copy, contract research, and others). We would expect these industries could be drawn to Australia to a greater extent if the right environment and incentive structures were present.

Does It Have to Be "Us versus Them"?   It appears that much of the discussion in Australia today over the direction of the economy, and the direction of the country in general, is framed in us-versus-them terms. In the economy we have a resources sector that has grown rapidly in recent years in ways that have put pressure on other parts of the economy. The result is discussion on what to do about it, when sometimes a boom is a boom and we just have to adjust. Resource rents have given rise to arguments about how to share the proceeds, with ownership, management, labour, and government all in for a piece of the action. Then, of course, we have Australia's robust political environment in which contention and opposition are the order of the day. At times, it must appear to outsiders that Australia is a nation made up of different groups of people, surrounded by vast stretches of water, united by sport, and divided by almost everything else. We do wonder if the tone of social discourse makes it difficult for different groups to work together and find common cause in building the nation. This is symptomatic of a fundamentally insular and inward-oriented society worried about dividing up the pie, rather than an outward-oriented society with different groups joining forces to improve Australia's competitive position in the world. We would suggest that Australia has much to gain by focusing on *us-and-us* rather than *us-and-them*.

Let's Pretend We Have Stability and a High Quality of Life   As indicated above, Australia is a leader in terms of political stability, social stability, and quality of life. A visitor landing in Australia, reading local newspapers, and watching local TV, however, would be hard pressed to reach that conclusion. Low standards of political discourse, where *ad hominem* attacks seem more common than reasoned policy discussion; bickering among various groups claiming they are not getting a fair share of Australia's riches, again often in less than totally civilised tones; and vocal interest groups contending against each other seem to be the order of the day. While robust debate is healthy, and self-congratulation is not particularly useful, recognising that Australia has many advantages and focusing on leveraging those advantages, rather than on tearing others down, would be a good start.

Improve Attitudes toward Business   Attitudes of the community provide the context for policy and strategy decisions within any country. Australia is no different in this regard. The extent to which the community supports business, entrepreneurship, and innovation will influence the incentives that companies and individuals face, which in turn will influence Australia's competitiveness. Business sometimes gets a bad name in Australia. There is a tendency to think of business as cold, faceless, and in some ways in opposition to individuals. Some business people are viewed as greedy and working against Australia's interest. The Australian business community needs to work to improve its image. Business's role in creating employment, building the economy, providing needed goods and services, and supporting community initiatives should be highlighted. Business and businesses will receive more support from the community if the community believes it is getting support from business and businesses.

Improve Attitudes toward Innovation and Entrepreneurship   While Australians tend to be supportive of innovation and entrepreneurship in the abstract, they often seem less supportive of concrete examples of innovation and entrepreneurship. The nation lacks a culture of innovation and entrepreneurship that would make innovators and entrepreneurs heroes in the national context. Too often, the tall-poppy syndrome comes into play to knock down successful innovators and entrepreneurs. Innovators and entrepreneurs should be celebrated as adding to employment, the tax base, and national development. This should be done in the education system, by political leaders, by the business community, and hopefully by the business press to a greater extent than is the case today.

Enhancing the Contribution of the Media   Australia has an active and free press, and that is the way it should be. However, we find much of the coverage of business, the economy, and issues related to competitiveness in mainstream media relatively superficial. From time to time we do see efforts in the mainstream media (more in the print media for obvious reasons) to go beyond whether interest rates are up or down, the stock market is up or down, or resource prices are up or down, but in general we see relatively little coverage that would provide the average citizen with sufficient information to figure out why, what it means for the Australian economy, and what options companies and governments might have to do something about it. Like it or not, the media are the main source of information and education on the economy for the bulk of the population. The number of major economic issues that Australia faces is actually not that great. There is no particular reason that Australians should not be better informed about them. We also note the tendency to focus on creating confrontation on the part of the media when it comes to business and economic stories, again as in many other places, and would hope that the Australian media could move beyond that to a greater extent than has been the case.

Meta or Supranational-Level Drivers

The main implications for meta or supranational-level drivers of competitiveness in Australia have to do with access to regional markets, the impact of foreign government actions, and the potential to leverage the presence of foreign firms in Australia. Again, we can argue that Australia is potentially moving from a situation in which meta or supranational drivers have been a disadvantage to a situation in which they might be less of a disadvantage or even an advantage.

ACCESS TO GLOBAL MARKETS   Australia has historically been disadvantaged when it comes to access to international markets. Australia has long called for an end to agricultural protectionism and to foreign subsidies for the agricultural sector. As one of the world's most efficient agricultural producers, Australia would benefit substantially from free trade in agricultural goods. As an advanced service economy, Australia would also benefit from more open trade in services. As a nation with an advanced research capacity and infrastructure, and one that affords others protection of their intellectual property (IP), it would also benefit from expanded international protection of IP. As a nation that is at or near the forefront in several aspects of environmental protection and environmental consciousness, Australia would also benefit from a greater recognition of environmental standards in international trade rules and duty-free access for environmental products and services.

All of these items have been on the agenda for the Doha Round of the World Trade Organization (WTO) negotiations, and all have been stymied by the inability of developing and developed countries to reach a grand agreement. Australia is one of the few nations that would benefit from all of these agenda items moving forward and thus has substantial amounts to gain through a successful conclusion of the Doha Round that encompasses all of these dimensions, and a substantial amount to lose, at least in terms of lost opportunity, by the lack of a positive conclusion to the Doha Round. The Australian Government continues to push on all of these dimensions, as it should, and has moved on a number of bilateral and regional arrangements in the absence of a global agreement, as it also should. Unfortunately, we are unlikely to see substantial global trade progress any time soon.

ACCESS TO REGIONAL MARKETS   The Australian Government has been actively pushing to provide greater access to the markets of the Asia-Pacific region for Australian companies and industries. Much progress has been made, and more is likely to follow. However, access from a trade and investment standpoint is just the starting point for truly accessing regional markets.

Continue with Regional Free Trade Agreements   Historically, Australia has preferred to emphasise multilateral trade agreements rather than bilateral agreements. The main reason is that since it is not part of a natural economic grouping, except with New Zealand, Australia has had more to potentially gain through multilateral agreements than through bilateral ones. However, given that the WTO process has slowed to a crawl, bilateral and regional agreements (through the Transpacific Partnership initiative, for example) seem to be the only path open for trade liberalisation at the moment.

Australia should continue to pursue trade liberalisation with leading trade partners for several reasons. The obvious reason is that better access to growing markets could be a substantial benefit to Australian companies and industries. Another is that Australia is already relatively open and therefore does not have to give up too much in the quest for freer trade. Another is that the existence of a free trade agreement will tend to focus the minds of Australian business people on the relevant markets. One major impact of the North America Free Trade Agreement was a dramatic increase in cross-border shopping, even though the agreement did not change the personal allowance for such shopping at all. The fact that there was a free trade agreement simply caused more people to do exactly what they could have done all along.

Expand the Australian Government Presence   Mere access, however, will not be sufficient for most Australian companies to succeed in the Asia-Pacific region. There will be needs for consular support and the types of information provision and access to key officials and counterparties that only formal government representation can provide. Thus, we agree with assessments that Australia should significantly expand its consular presence and trade offices in China, India, and Southeast Asia to support the growth of trade and investment to and from those places.

Improve Understanding of Markets   The Asia-Pacific region will only become more accessible to Australian companies and industries when they have sufficient under-standing of markets, business practices, social norms, economic systems, and sources of further information upon which to build business plans and strategies. This has been stated in the *Australia in the Asian Century* White Paper[9] and has been stated by analysts and business leaders. Governments, analysts, academics, the press, and others all have an important role to play in making the region more accessible. Again, as we stated before, even if all of these actors make Asia-Pacific markets and pro-duction systems more accessible, it will be for naught if Australian companies and industries do not take up the challenges, build their own capabilities, and make their own investments.

ACTIONS OF FOREIGN GOVERNMENTS   Australian governments and companies need to understand the actions of foreign governments and the potential opportunities and threats they entail. This is particularly true in the Asia-Pacific region, where political systems, legal and regulatory systems, the role of government in the economy, cultural norms, and business practices can be vastly different from those in Australia. Australian companies need to understand the ins and outs of these foreign systems if they are to prosper in the region.

China Represents a Multifaceted Puzzle   China and its government actions represent a particular puzzle for foreign governments and foreign firms. The run-up to the lead-ership transition that started in October 2012 has shown that China's leadership is not monolithic, but rather is made up of people with different interests and a variety of alliances that will shape decision making for the next decade. Most foreign govern-ments and companies have little idea what the recent leadership change in China will mean for the economy as a whole and for foreign business in particular. It could represent a continuation of a tougher environment for foreign companies or greater openness. Which direction China goes, and the details of that direction, will have enormous implications for its economy and the economies of the Asia-Pacific region.

China's 12th Five Year Program, which will run from 2011 to 2015, provides numerous potential obstacles and opportunities for foreign companies. On the one hand, the Program calls for an increased reliance on indigenous innovation. This is viewed as a threat by many foreign companies, as in practice it has meant favouritism for Chinese companies in government procurement, direct subsidies for research and development in favoured industries, and forcing foreign companies to transfer intel-lectual property to Chinese partners in order to be able to sell into the country. On the other hand, the same Five Year Program has energy efficiency targets that can only be met by using a combination of local and foreign technology, calls specifically for foreign developers to be attracted to help build new cities and city centres, and encourages foreign investment in the rapidly growing healthcare industry to an unprecedented extent. The same Program calls for a rapid expansion of consumption, which will create larger markets for consumer goods, and outward investment by Chinese companies, which has the potential to create competitive and political challenges.

Both the leadership transition and China's 12th Five Year Program will result in a range of obstacles and opportunities for foreign companies. The better that the Australian Government and Australian companies understand these obstacles and opportunities, the better off they will be.

India Is Another Conundrum   Government action in India represents another conundrum. India began a reform program in the early 1990s which included deregulation, privatisation, trade liberalisation, greater openness to foreign investment, and tax reform. However, the pace of reform has slowed. In recent years, it has been one step forward and one step backward, with examples like the retail sector in which new rules allowing greater foreign participation were announced and then rescinded. In addition, labour markets and agricultural support programs remain unreformed. While reforms have not been reversed with changes in government since the early 1990s, there is still a sense that reform is fragile and a return to a more controlled economy could be only one election away.

Operating in India is complicated by the fact that Indian states are very powerful and state governments are controlled by different political parties with very different outlooks toward business and toward foreign companies. The result is a patchwork in which one cannot be sure that national government policy will be effectively implemented at the local level. Combined with red tape and corruption that hinder local and foreign companies, these features make India a definite challenge and a difficult place to do business. Again, a detailed understanding of the government decision-making process and political dynamics at the national, state, and local levels is crucial for business success.

ASEAN Is Trying to Find Its Way   The Association of Southeast Asian Nations (ASEAN) has announced an extensive program of trade reforms and regional initiatives that could make it much easier for firms of all types to operate seamlessly across the ASEAN economies. The trouble is that ASEAN nations have made such announcements before, but have not followed through. The history of ASEAN trade agreements has been that major countries have demanded continued protection for their own favoured sectors, others have responded, and by the time everyone is done, vast areas of the economy remain outside the liberalising measures.

The ASEAN 2015 Program is much more ambitious in terms not only of freer trade, but harmonisation of standards, mutual recognition, and a variety of other features designed to bring the ASEAN economies closer together. However, momentum appears to be slowing, more and more of the agreement is being pushed into the future, and there appears to be less urgency in major ASEAN economies, such as Indonesia, which is focused on its domestic situation. Meanwhile, Singapore and Brunei continue to be solid and predictable from a government standpoint. Greater political stability in Indonesia has been accompanied by solid growth. Thailand continues to do reasonably well despite its political tensions. The Philippines has been doing better economically since the Aquino Government made taking on corruption a major emphasis. Vietnam is opening and reforming its economy, though in fits and starts. Malaysia has become more open to greater Australian participation in regional forums. Cambodia and Laos are starting to become more interesting as they start to open. Most recently, Myanmar has started to open up to the rest of the world after decades of isolation.

With more than 500 million people, ASEAN represents a vibrant, growing, but diverse and complicated set of markets that Australia cannot ignore. ASEAN countries are some of Australia's nearest neighbours, have potentially complementary resources, and should be good markets for Australian expertise and companies. They are crucial to Australia from a geopolitical standpoint as well as from an economic standpoint. Again, figuring out their directions, individually and collectively, will be key to maximising the potential of Australian business in the region.

Understand the Moves of Other Governments   Actions of governments in the United States, Europe, Latin America, and Africa have the potential to influence the competitiveness of firms from those countries as well as their openness as markets. All of this is known by the Australian Government and by Australia's large, international companies. However, all of this is not known by the vast majority of Australian firms, including many that will wish to go international eventually. The Australian Government is already a major source of information on these nations for Australian business. The policies of the United States and Western Europe with respect to stimulus programs, interest rates, quantitative easing, government bailouts, and other subsidies, as well as trade and investment policies, affect the rest of the world. Though of lesser importance, policies in the rest of North America, Latin America, Eastern Europe, Africa, the Middle East, and the rest of Asia will also influence the prospects for Australian industries.

An Asian Century?, Yes But . . .   While much has been written and postulated about the potential for Asia to dominate the 21st century (including in the *Australia in the Asian Century* White Paper), we note that the expectation is that Asian economies will account for 35 percent of global GDP by 2030, not 100 percent or even 50 percent. Thus, while the bulk of economic growth may take place in Asia, other markets will still be as important. These should not be forgotten in the rush to adjust to the rise of Asia.

Another issue arises with respect to the difference between Australia's direct trade flows and its positions when it comes to international negotiations over trade, investment, intellectual property, and other matters. While the bulk of Australia's trade is with Asia, and the portion is set to grow significantly, this does not necessarily mean that Australia should throw its lot in with other Asia-Pacific economies when it comes to international negotiations. To date, the rules of international economic engagement that do exist have been written for the most part by the large Western economies, with others left to go along or not as they see fit. Thus, the "rules" tend to reflect the interests of Western and Western-like economies.

While 2012 witnessed some back and forth between former prime ministers Paul Keating and John Howard over whether Australia's ties to the United States have hurt it or helped it in its political and economic relations with Asia, to us there is little doubt that a rules-based system of international economic relations based on "Western" tenets, even though some of the rules or lack of rules have hurt Australia in the past, is likely to be far better for Australia than any alternative. To put it in another way, in our view, Australia is more likely to benefit in a world in which rules of international economic engagement are set in Geneva, Washington, and Brussels, rather than in Beijing, Mumbai, and Jakarta. Thus, Australia needs to throw its weight behind negotiating positions that will benefit the country in the long run as well as the short run.

Assess and Act Where Appropriate   Part of understanding the actions of foreign governments is to understand how these actions influence the competitiveness of firms from their nations, whether or not the activities are consistent with international agreements, and whether or not they are consistent with Australian laws. This in turn provides a better backdrop for decisions that have to be made about foreign investments, trade and investment promotion activities, and whether to take action in response to actions of foreign governments.

LEVERAGE FOREIGN COMPANIES   Foreign companies are prominent if not dominant in many industries in Australia. Foreign companies have brought needed investment, have fostered the development of world-class industries in the country, have created jobs for a large portion of the nation's workforce, and have been major customers of many local Australian businesses.

Understand What Foreign Companies Do and Don't Do in Australia   The presence of foreign companies in Australia has, in our view, been an enormous positive. However, the strategies of foreign companies and the activities that they perform in Australia have not generated some of the benefits that they could potentially generate. As described earlier, foreign multinationals tend to serve the Australian market from their Australian bases and little else. They tend not to put knowledge-intensive activities for regional or global markets into the country, and their Australian operations are not well-integrated into their global networks. While foreign companies source inputs, goods, and services from Australian firms for their Australian operations, few have incorporated Australian firms into regional or global supply chains or operations. Australia needs to develop a detailed understanding of what multinationals do in the country, what they do not, and why. Such knowledge can then be used to make improvements to attract more high-value activities of multinationals and to market Australia's positive attributes more effectively.

Learn from the Foreign Multinationals   There are several implications of the facts that there are few Australian world-class companies and that major multinationals tend not to incorporate Australian companies into their global operations. One is that Australian companies in relevant industries should assess the potential for supplying foreign multinationals not just for Australia, but for the region and the world. Australian companies should investigate the potential for foreign multinationals to incorporate the local company's goods or services into the multinationals' global offerings. Australian companies should use contacts with the multinationals to try to learn how to sell into global markets.

Local and federal government agencies and education and training providers should seek out the views of the multinationals on the types of skills and capabilities that will be needed from the education and training system to staff Australian companies capable of going international. Government agencies such as Austrade should take a page out of the playbook of Invest 2000, the investment promotion program developed around the 2000 Sydney Olympics. This program started by researching the strategies of major multinationals, understanding how Australia could fit into these strategies, and then tried to "sell" what the companies were mostly likely to buy, rather than what local governments might want to sell. In this regard, selling Australia as a knowledge-intensive node in regional or 24-hour a day operations could be a fruitful direction. In any case, Australia and Australian companies are not leveraging the presence of foreign multinationals in the country to nearly the extent that they should.

Conclusions

Trends in the global economy are making the competitiveness of nations and regions in individual activities and industries a more important determinant of prosperity than ever before. There has been a great deal of discussion and debate about Australia's economy and its future competitiveness. A great deal of good work has been done. Even so, we believe that further perspectives can usefully add to the discussion and debate. In order to add some of these perspectives, we have undertaken a detailed assessment of Australia's competitiveness by investigating the nation's overall economic performance, compiling international perspectives on Australia's competitiveness, surveying across Australia's business community to determine which drivers of competitiveness are important to individual Australian industries and how Australia performs in those drivers, identifying and assessing key issues that cut across the economy, and then trying to pull the various threads together.

In recent years, Australia has clearly outperformed most other OECD countries in terms of growth and in its ability to generate a high standard of living for its residents. GDP growth has been relatively high, unemployment low, workforce participation up, and inflation manageable. Questions have rightly been raised about Australia's productivity performance, but part of Australia's apparent poor performance is due to how productivity growth is measured and with large investments that will generate higher levels of output in the future. While other economies in the Asia-Pacific region have been growing faster than Australia, and in some cases have been showing faster productivity growth, Australia's per capita income and other measures of standard of living have been well beyond those of most of its regional neighbours.

International assessments of Australia's competitiveness for the most part tell a similar story, regardless of whether the focus is on aggregate competitiveness, ease of doing business, state of the knowledge economy, economic freedom, city competitiveness, or measures of transparency and corporate governance. The story is one of a country that is in the upper echelon of nations, but not on par with the world's best, and is in many cases a strong performer that is well ahead of most Asia-Pacific economies, but behind the leaders in the region. A review of the international assessments shows that the league tables of the aggregate indices are interesting, but far more useful is the detailed information that the various sources supply. This information allows us to break down the assessments to their components and use these to generate a picture of what Australia does well and not so well.

In broad terms, Australia does well in assessments of quality of life, political and social stability, institutions, ease of starting businesses, education, and some measures of capabilities. On the other hand, it does not compare well in terms of links to the global economy, infrastructure, complexity of taxes and regulations, brain drain, supply chains and industry clusters, business sophistication, tendency of companies and corporate activities to leave the nation, city competitiveness, and some dimensions of costs. On these drivers, it tends to lag behind the global leaders, as well as a limited number of economies in the Asia-Pacific region. What is also interesting is that Australia tends to do well in what we might call *threshold drivers*. That means that once a certain level is achieved in terms of quality of life, social stability, political stability, and so on, industries are not helped that much by making them incrementally better. In addition, these are features that set the context for industries and companies, and this is important, but they are not direct inputs into most industries. The drivers in which Australia does not do so well, on the other hand, are ones in which more generally is better and that represent direct inputs into a wide range of industries.

A wide-ranging survey of business people in Australia allowed us to assess the importance to competitiveness and Australia's position relative to key competitors in 76 different drivers of competitiveness in all of Australia's major industries. We were able to show that the small and medium-sized OECD countries that are usually compared to Australia tend not to be relevant competitors nor significant markets for Australia's industries. Thus, while the traditional comparisons are useful in a general sense, when it comes to thinking about the real world of specific industries, competitors, and markets, they are not. Instead, it is large economies, like the United States, the United Kingdom, and China, that repeatedly appear as competitors, along with a range of other Asia-Pacific economies, like Hong Kong, Singapore, India, New Zealand, Japan, and others.

The industry-level results show that the relative importance and Australia's performance for a given driver of competitiveness may differ significantly from industry to industry. The survey responses, particularly in terms of Australia's performance across drivers in a given industry, can often be mapped to actual industry outcomes. Australia tends to have clear, highly competitive outcomes in industries in which it has a preponderance of favourable drivers of competitiveness. The industry level results highlight the importance of exchange rates, staff costs, staff capabilities, and various aspects of government policy in influencing competitiveness. They highlight Australia's strong position in quality of life, social stability, political stability, capabilities, institutions, and related variables. They also reflect a view that Australia has advantages, at least mild advantages, in most of the drivers of competitiveness in most industries. However, they also reflect views that Australia is less competitive or uncompetitive in a significant number of industries when it comes to some government policies, taxes, costs, market size, and others.

The international assessments and survey results highlight several areas that were investigated further, including workforce issues, infrastructure, resource management, economic policies, regulation, taxation, Australia's position in the knowledge economy, Australia's integration with the rest of the Asia-Pacific region, and the competitiveness of Australia's cities.

The Australian workforce was generally found to be capable and education and training institutions strong, but the workforce is in danger of being mismatched with the needs of the economy; efforts should be made to increase workforce participation, education and training need to be better focused, and alternatives to universities should be strengthened. Infrastructure investments need to be increased, priorities set and carried through, more private funding needs to be attracted, and infrastructure investments should be depoliticised to the extent possible. Resource management needs to take into account the booms and busts inherent in the sector, use contingent contracts so that low probability events are planned for so the rules are not changed in the middle of the game, ensure that relevant stakeholder interests are taken into account, and mitigate the uncertainty inherent in resource tax revenues by having a buffer that could be banked in good years and dispersed in bad years.

Economic policies were generally found to be sound, but tax and regulatory policies suffer from complexity, inefficiency, and the lack of co-ordination among multiple jurisdictions. The result is a higher burden on individuals and businesses than is necessary. We also note that the tax system appears to place much of the burden on individuals and companies that are most able to leave for other locations. A balance between revenue needs, fairness, and competition with other jurisdictions for talent and dynamic companies needs to be reached.

Australia's position in the knowledge economy was found to be good, but not great. Its trade with the Asia-Pacific region tends to involve exports of resources, education, and tourism, and imports in most manufacturers, including knowledge-intensive manufacturers. In looking at the trade profile, one could conclude that the other Asia-Pacific economies were the advanced economies and Australia the laggard rather than the other way around. Australia's knowledge of Asian economies is good compared to the rest of the world, but not as good as in Asia, and Australia actually is behind at least some economies in the region on most measures of competitiveness. Finally, Australia's cities are not on par with global leaders or leaders in the Asia-Pacific region. This limits the cities' ability to leverage Australia's good points into the global economy.

The analyses from the international assessments, the business competitiveness survey, and selected areas that cut across the economy have been used to generate a series of positive and negative scenarios for Australia's future. Australia can go from being the lucky economy to the competitive economy with a diversified knowledge and innovation base, or can become a one-legged stool reliant on resources; it can ride the tigers, dragons, and elephants in the Asia-Pacific region, or get eaten, burned, and trampled by them; it can become the flattenor in the quasi-flat world controlling its own destiny, or the flattenee with its destiny controlled by others; it can leverage its strong points and global trends to have the world turn toward Australia, or it can fail to do so and have the world turn away from Australia.

The scenarios, in turn, help provide a basis for a series of implications as to how Australia might maximise the chances of achieving the positive scenarios and minimising the chances of experiencing the negative scenarios. Many of the implications and suggestions found in this chapter are not new. In fact, there has been a great deal of good work done on several of these issues, and reasonable recommendations have been made in many areas. However, in many cases the work that has been done has either been ignored, or needed action delayed. We would suggest that it is important for Australia to move ahead in these areas while it is still in a position of strength and it has the flexibility to make needed investments. After all, that position may not last forever.

This work has tried to dive into the details of Australia's competitiveness and to come up with suggestions to improve competitiveness going forward. But there is an overarching feature that has arisen again and again in the course of our work. That is, that in order to move ahead, Australia and various groups within the country need to develop a shared goal of improving competitiveness, a shared vision of how to do it, and the ability to work together to make and execute the necessary strategies. This will require that politicians of all persuasions, company owners, managers, labour, and civil society find ways of coming together. No single group can create competitiveness; any single group can kill competitiveness. Only when the various groups find ways to come together can Australia go from being the lucky country to being the competitive country. Only then can Australia ride the tigers, dragons, and elephants rather than being eaten, burned, or trampled. Only then can Australia be a flattenor in the quasi-flat world rather than the flattenee. And only then will the world turn toward Australia rather than away from Australia.

Australia is a land of opportunity and a country whose future is more in its own hands than most. Australia has choices. Its future competitiveness and prosperity depend on the extent to which it makes these choices wisely.

Notes

1. See Commonwealth of Australia, *Australia in the Asian Century*, 2012.
2. "The Global 500," *Fortune*, 23 July 2012.
3. Infrastructure Finance Working Group, *Infrastructure Finance and Funding Reform*, April 2012.
4. John Daley, Cassie McGannon, and Leah Ginnivan, *Game-changers: Economic reform priorities for Australia*, Grattan Institute, Melbourne, 2012.
5. Workplace Australia, *Australia's New Workplace Relations System*, January 2010.
6. Australian Trade Commission, *The Austrian Banking Industry*, May 2011.
7. Australian Venture Capital and Private Equity Industry Association, *Annual Report*, 2011.
8. Task Force on Manufacturing, *Smarter Manufacturing for a Smarter Australia*, August 2012.
9. Commonwealth of Australia, *Australia in the Asian Century*, 2012.

Index